Shojo Beat

love☆com

Story & Art by
Aya Nakahara

love ★ com

contents 14

The Story So Far. . .

Risa and Ôtani are their class's lopsided comedy duo...and they've become a couple! Ôtani has been accepted into a teachers' college, while Risa, on her friend Nobu's advice, decides to study fashion and become a stylist. Their friend Suzuki, however, fails his entrance exam and is on the verge of having his girlfriend Chiharu stolen. But with Risa and the others rooting for him, Suzuki salvages his pride and wins back Chiharu. ♥ Out of the blue, Risa's grandfather returns home from abroad. He doesn't approve of Risa's height-challenged boyfriend and comes up with a plan to separate the two. Beautiful Hitomi, a mysterious woman with a big rack, suddenly appears before an unsuspecting Ôtani...

♥ To really get all the details, check out *Lovely Complex* volumes 1—13, available at bookstores everywhere!!

Shojo Beat

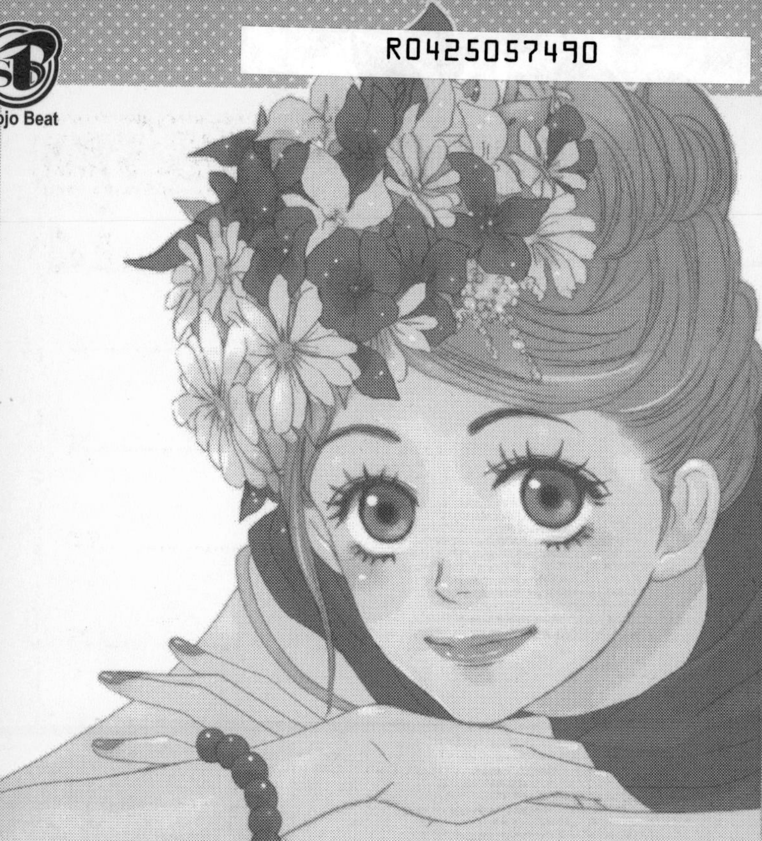

Lovely★Complex
love★com

14

Story & Art by
Aya Nakahara

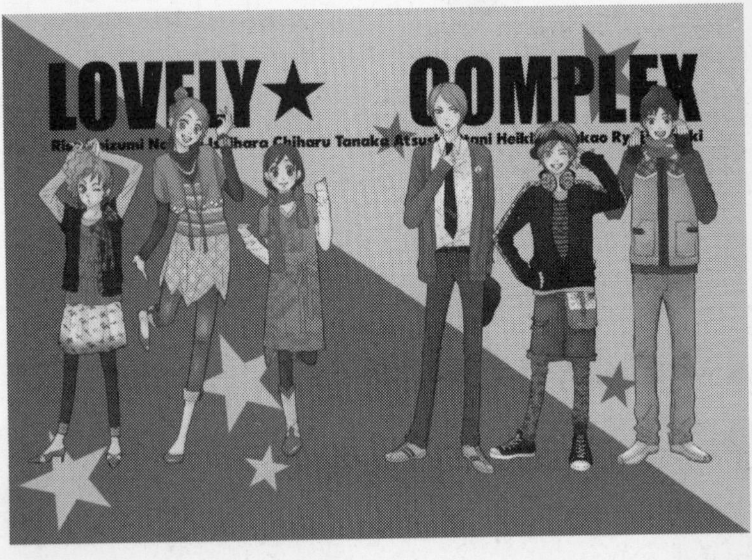
LOVELY★COMPLEX
Chiharu Tanaka

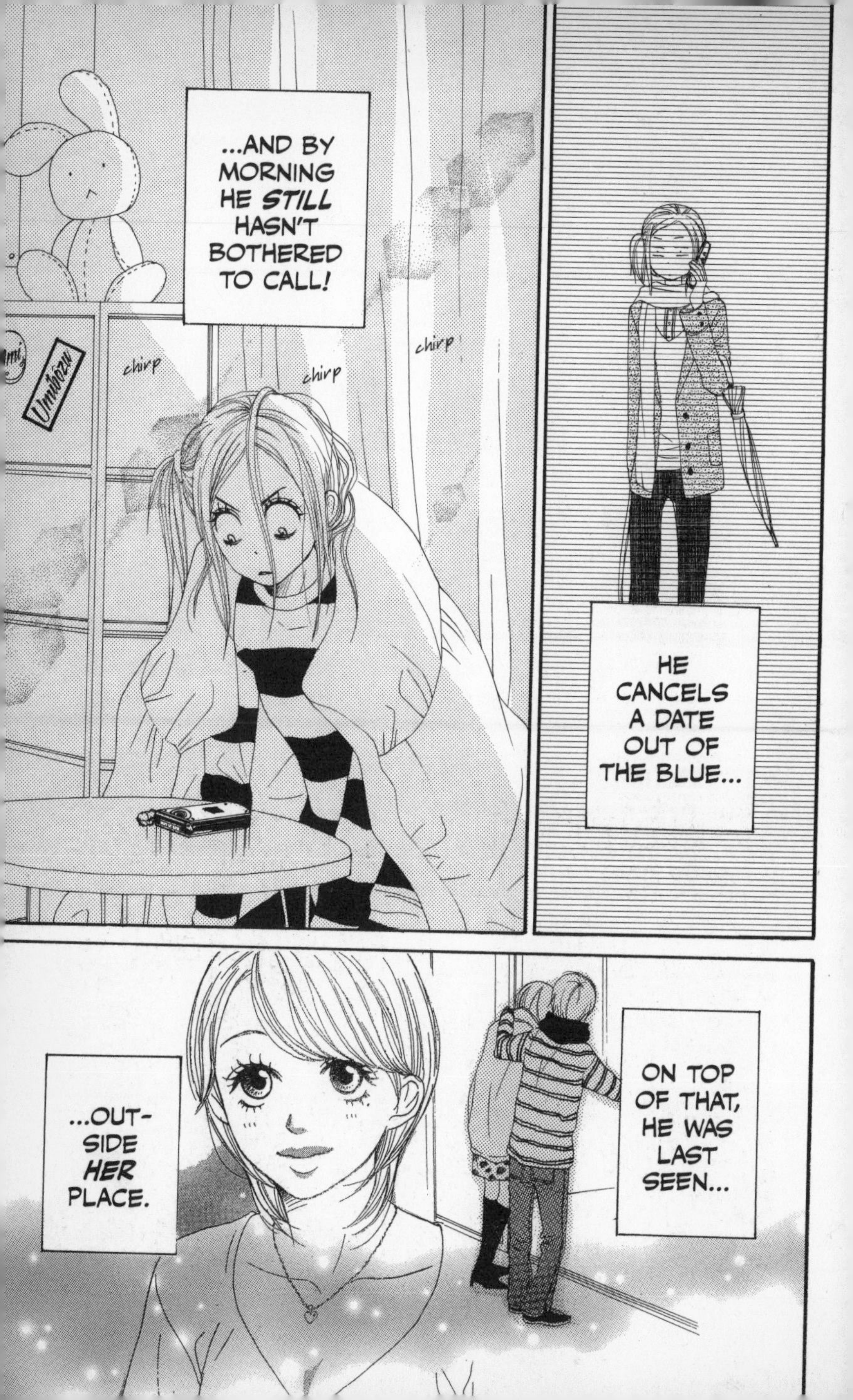
HE CANCELS A DATE OUT OF THE BLUE...
...AND BY MORNING HE STILL HASN'T BOTHERED TO CALL!
chirp
chirp
chirp
Umibozu
ON TOP OF THAT, HE WAS LAST SEEN...
...OUT-SIDE HER PLACE.

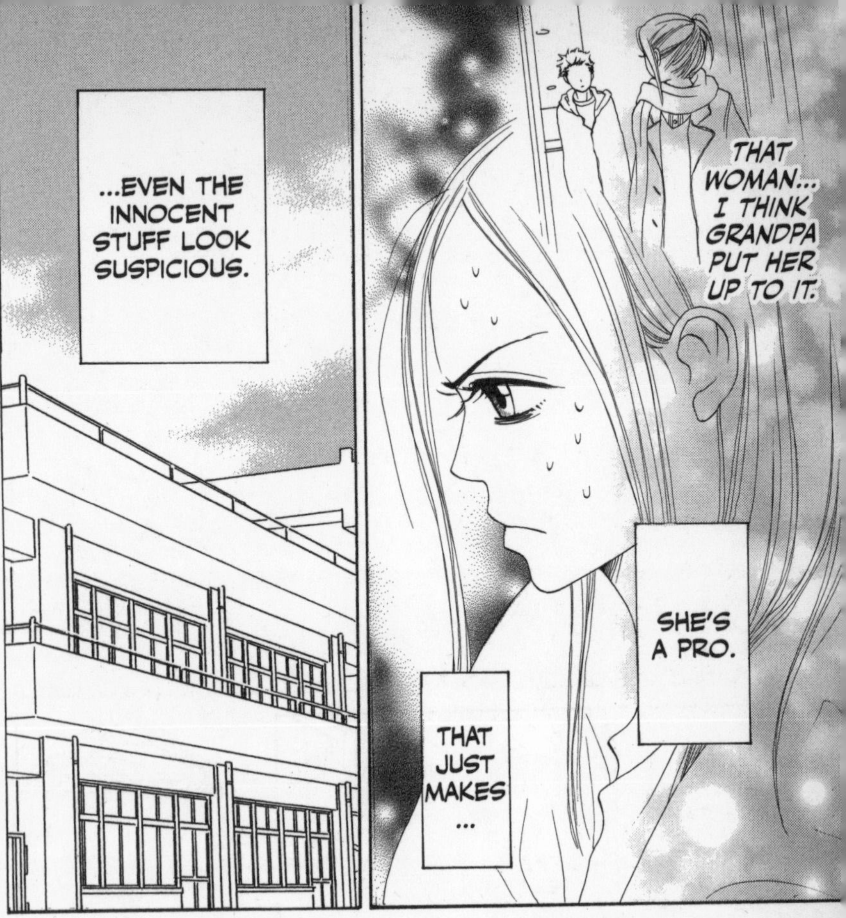
THAT WOMAN... I THINK GRANDPA PUT HER UP TO IT.
SHE'S A PRO.
THAT JUST MAKES ...
...EVEN THE INNOCENT STUFF LOOK SUSPICIOUS.

CHAPTER 52

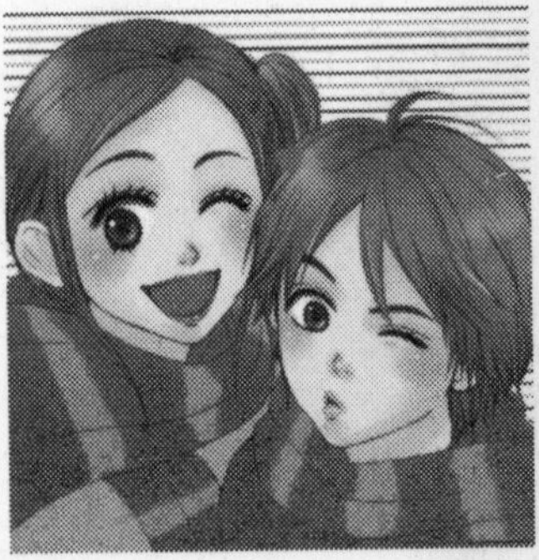

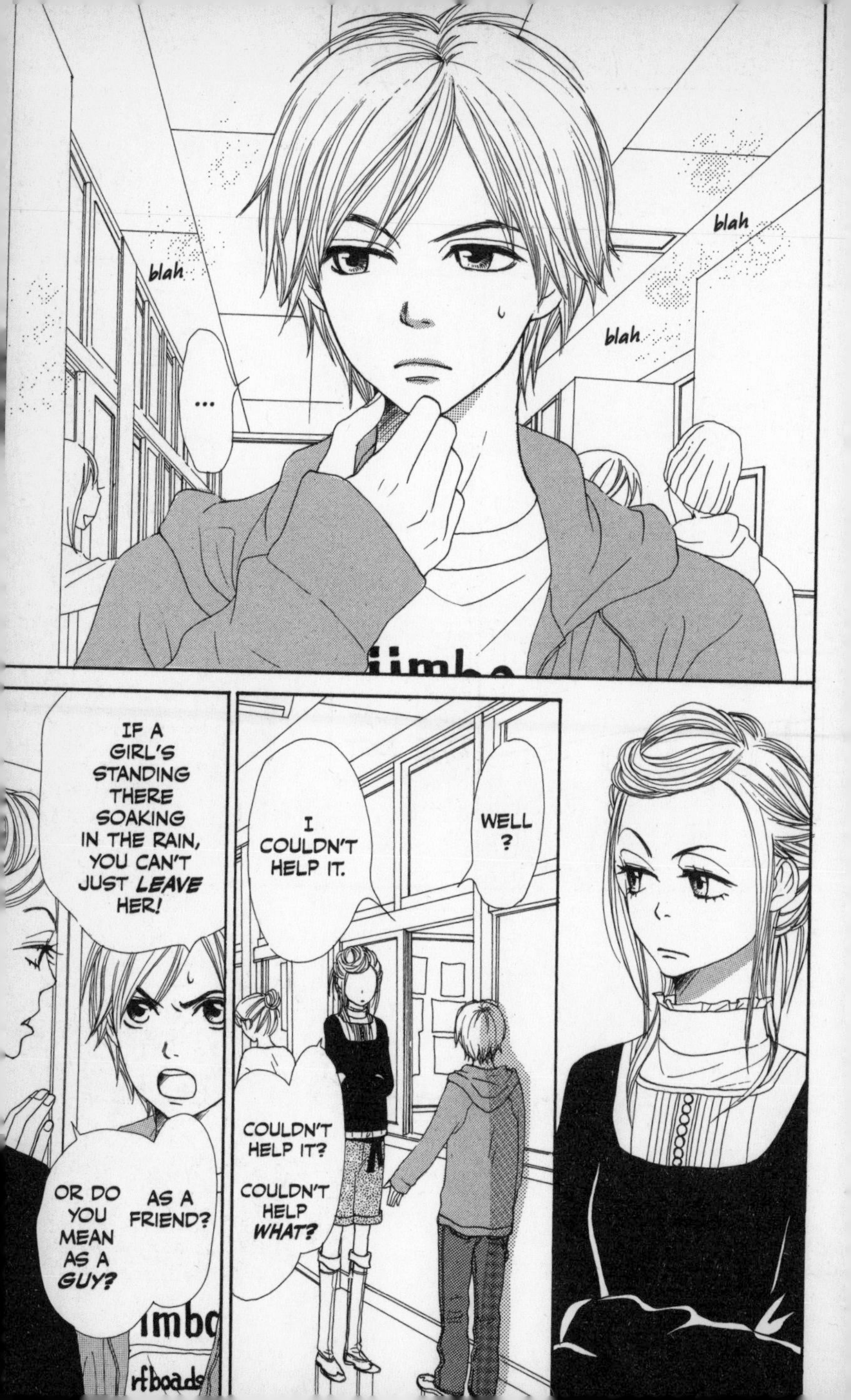

blah
blah
blah
...
WELL?
I COULDN'T HELP IT.
COULDN'T HELP IT?
COULDN'T HELP WHAT?
IF A GIRL'S STANDING THERE SOAKING IN THE RAIN, YOU CAN'T JUST LEAVE HER!
AS A FRIEND?
OR DO YOU MEAN AS A GUY?

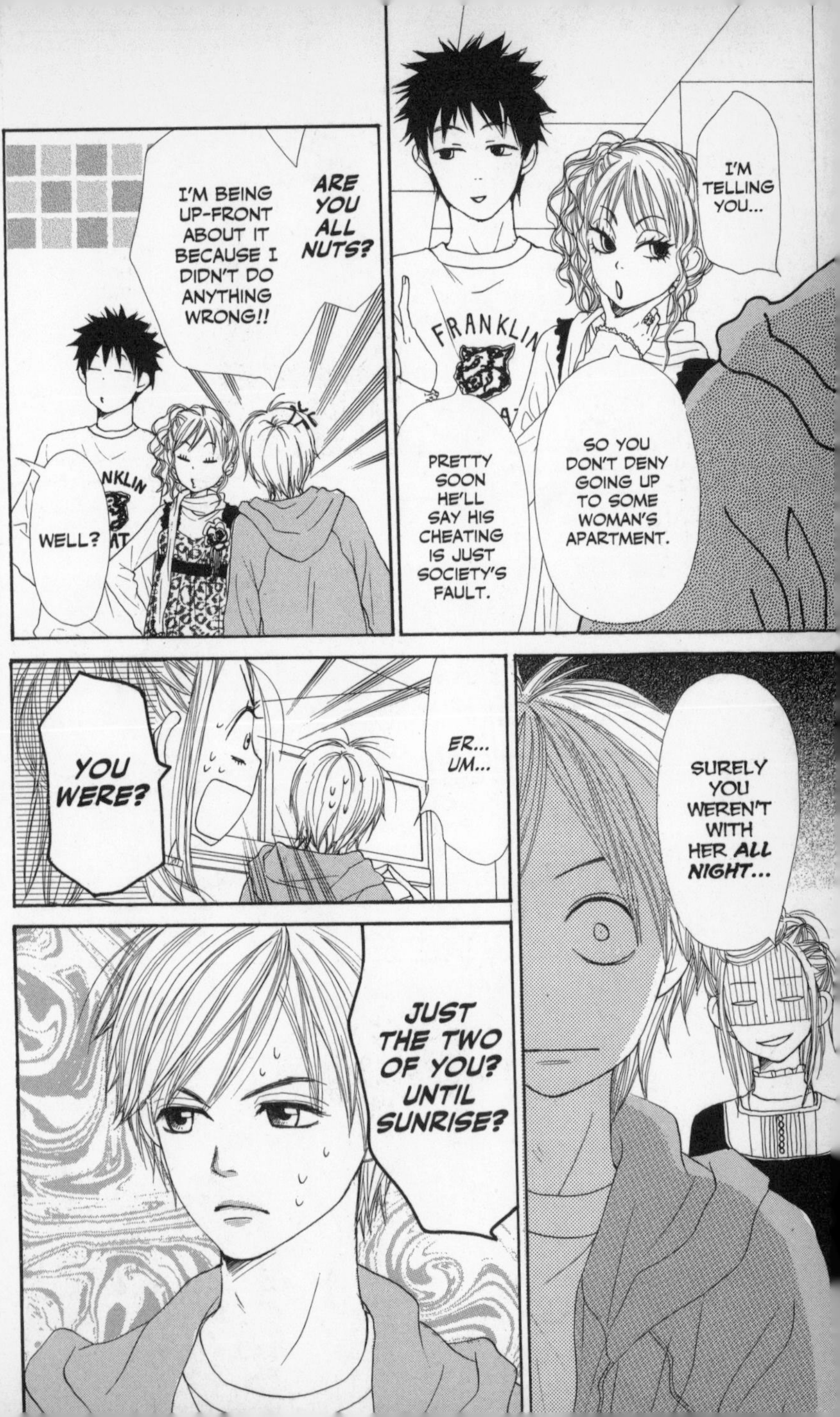
I'M TELLING YOU...
SO YOU DON'T DENY GOING UP TO SOME WOMAN'S APARTMENT.
PRETTY SOON HE'LL SAY HIS CHEATING IS JUST SOCIETY'S FAULT.
ARE YOU ALL NUTS?
I'M BEING UP-FRONT ABOUT IT BECAUSE I DIDN'T DO ANYTHING WRONG!!
WELL?
SURELY YOU WEREN'T WITH HER ALL NIGHT...
ER... UM...
YOU WERE?
JUST THE TWO OF YOU? UNTIL SUNRISE?

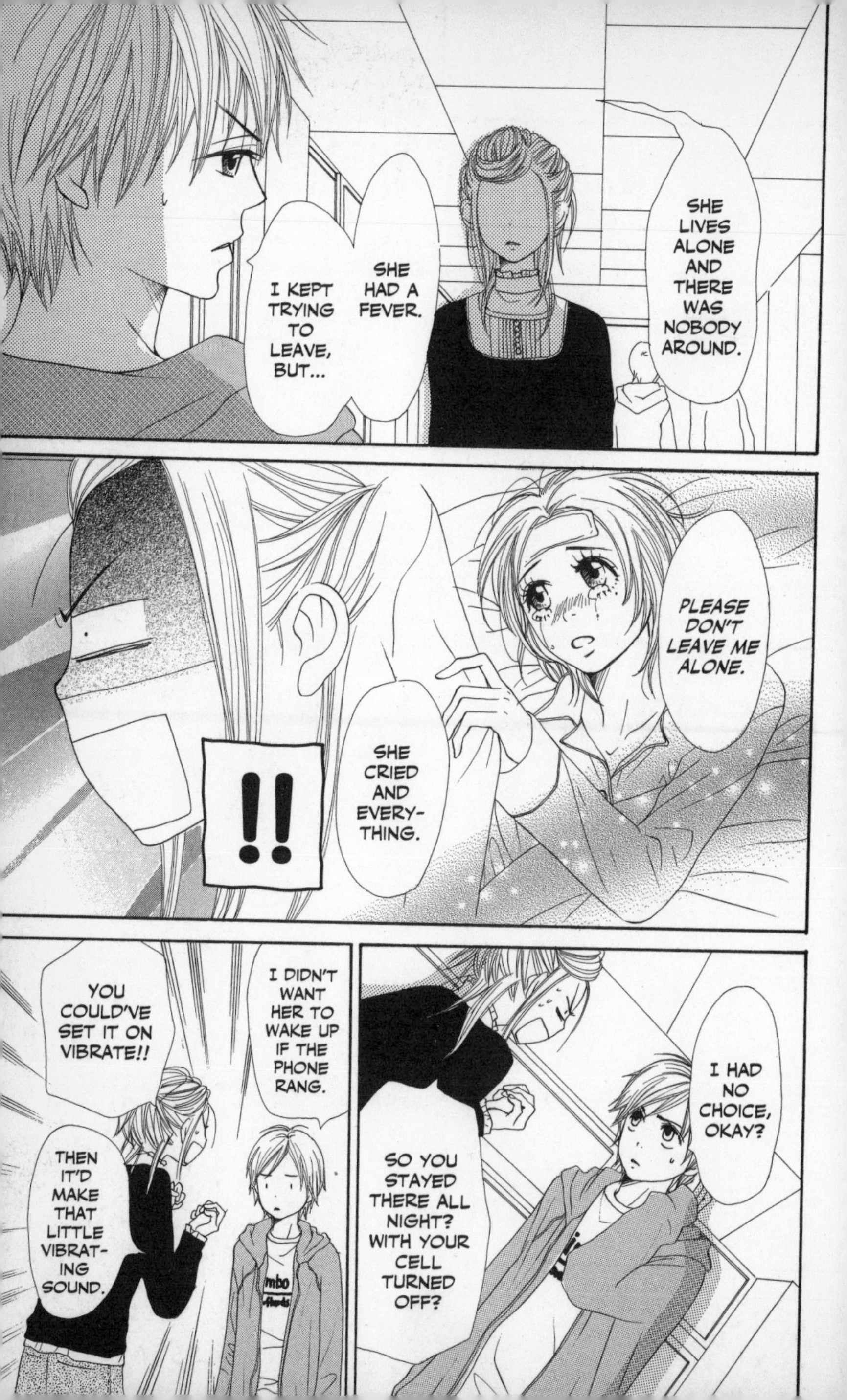
SHE LIVES ALONE AND THERE WAS NOBODY AROUND.
SHE HAD A FEVER.
I KEPT TRYING TO LEAVE, BUT...
PLEASE DON'T LEAVE ME ALONE.
SHE CRIED AND EVERYTHING.
!!
I HAD NO CHOICE, OKAY?
SO YOU STAYED THERE ALL NIGHT? WITH YOUR CELL TURNED OFF?
I DIDN'T WANT HER TO WAKE UP IF THE PHONE RANG.
YOU COULD'VE SET IT ON VIBRATE!!
THEN IT'D MAKE THAT LITTLE VIBRATING SOUND.

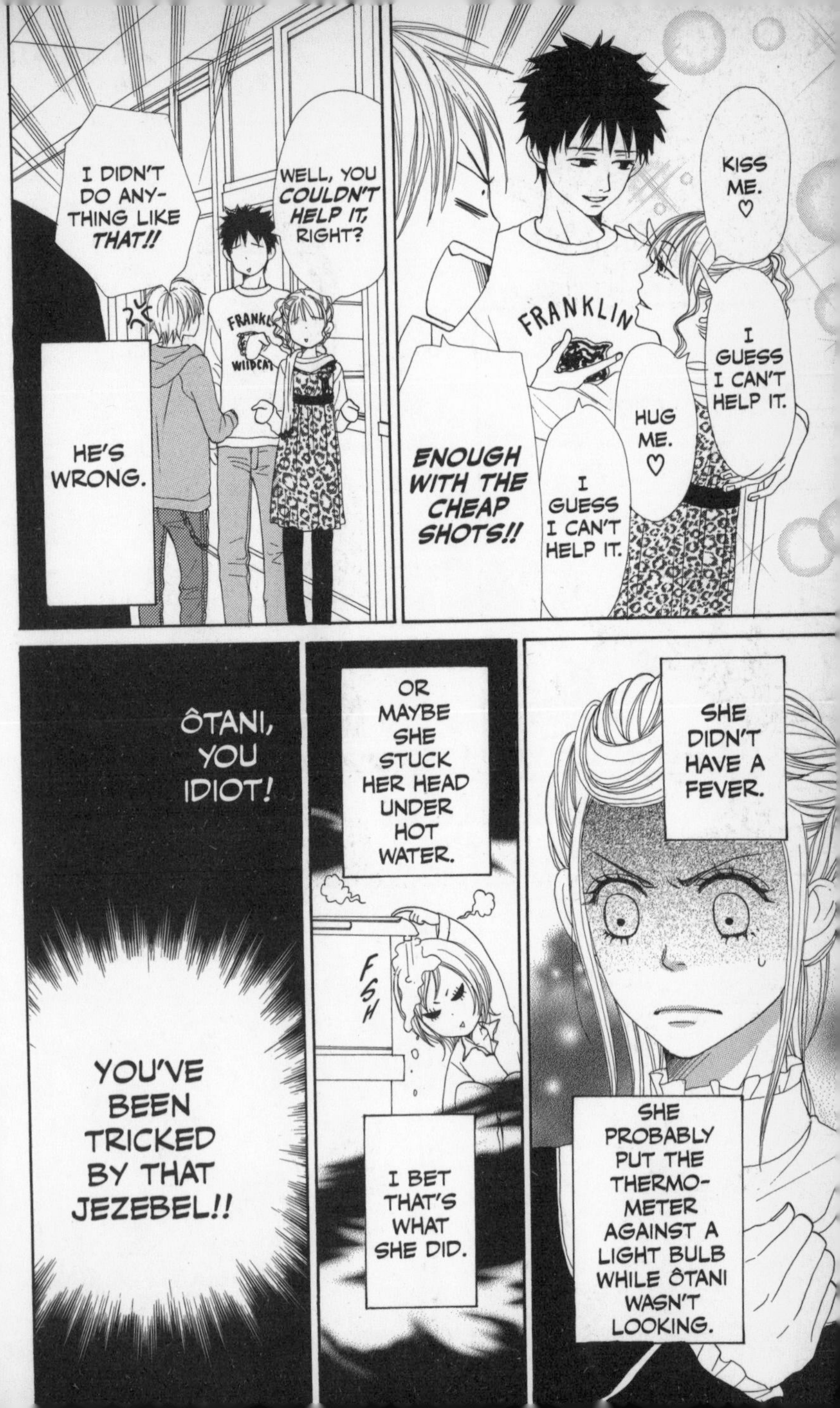
KISS ME. ♡
I GUESS I CAN'T HELP IT.
FRANKLIN
HUG ME. ♡
I GUESS I CAN'T HELP IT.
ENOUGH WITH THE CHEAP SHOTS!!
WELL, YOU COULDN'T HELP IT, RIGHT?
I DIDN'T DO ANYTHING LIKE THAT!!
HE'S WRONG.
SHE DIDN'T HAVE A FEVER.
SHE PROBABLY PUT THE THERMOMETER AGAINST A LIGHT BULB WHILE ÔTANI WASN'T LOOKING.
OR MAYBE SHE STUCK HER HEAD UNDER HOT WATER.
FSH
I BET THAT'S WHAT SHE DID.
ÔTANI, YOU IDIOT!
YOU'VE BEEN TRICKED BY THAT JEZEBEL!!

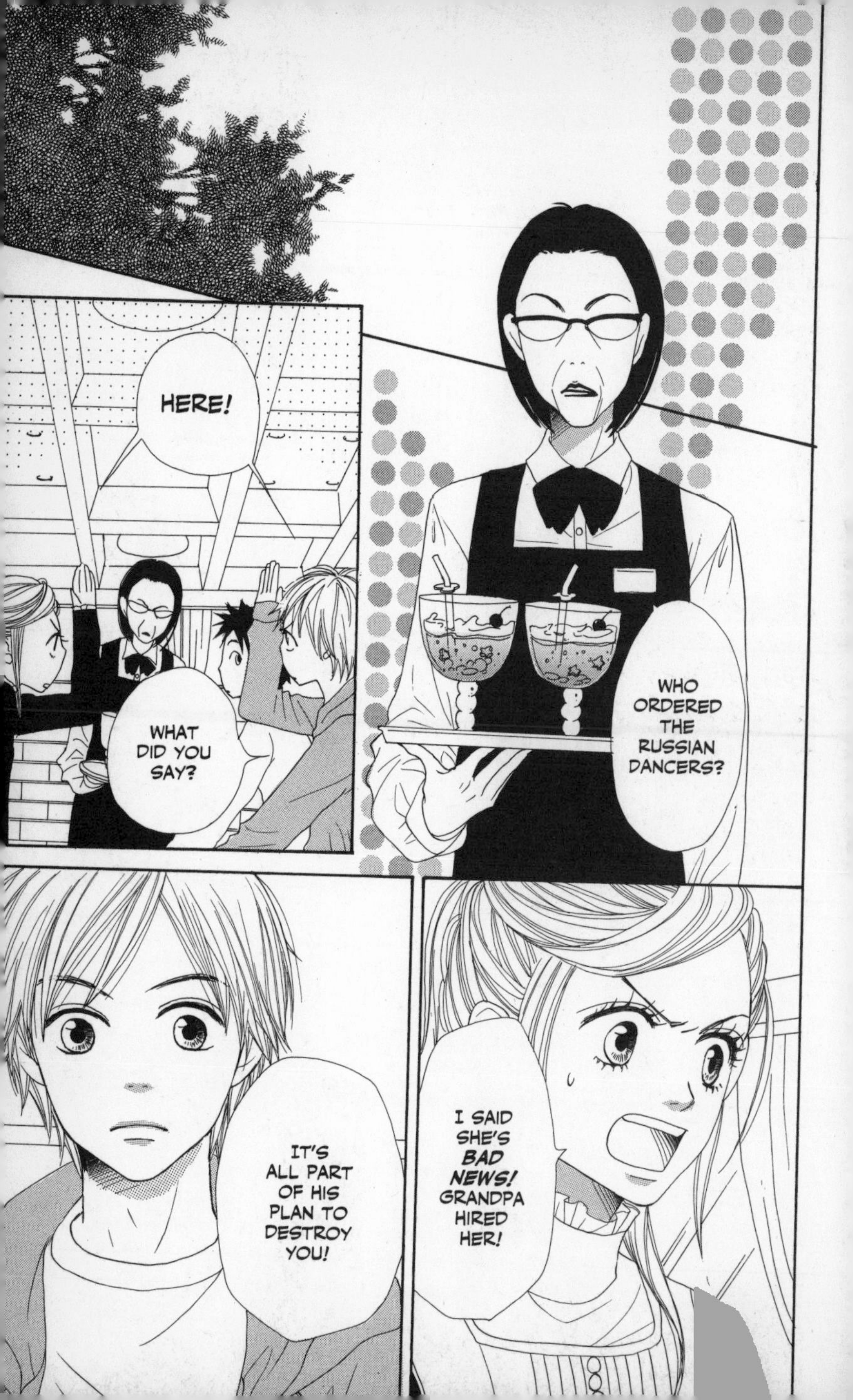
WHO ORDERED THE RUSSIAN DANCERS?
HERE!
WHAT DID YOU SAY?
I SAID SHE'S *BAD NEWS!* GRANDPA HIRED HER!
IT'S ALL PART OF HIS PLAN TO DESTROY YOU!

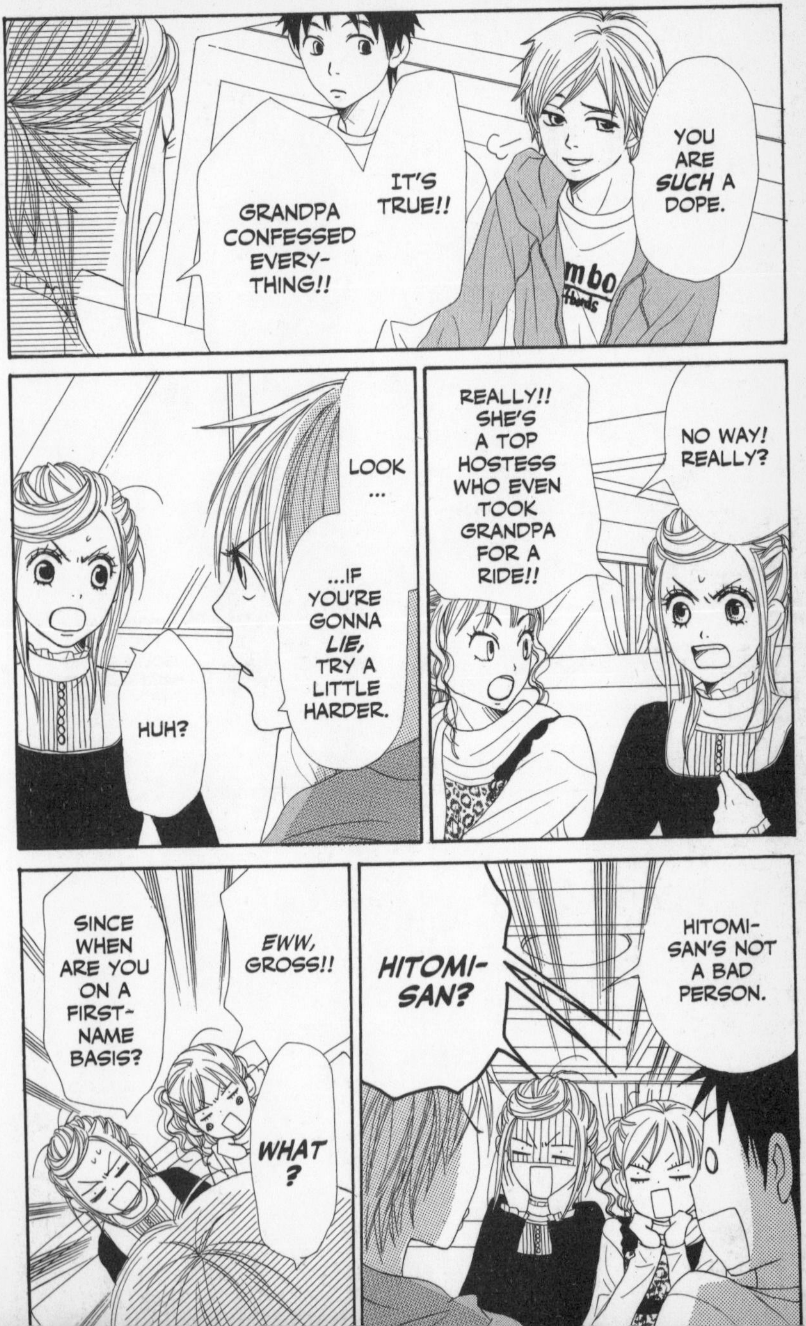
YOU ARE *SUCH* A DOPE.
IT'S TRUE!!
GRANDPA CONFESSED EVERY-THING!!
NO WAY! REALLY?
REALLY!! SHE'S A TOP HOSTESS WHO EVEN TOOK GRANDPA FOR A RIDE!!
LOOK ...
...IF YOU'RE GONNA *LIE,* TRY A LITTLE HARDER.
HUH?
HITOMI-SAN'S NOT A BAD PERSON.
HITOMI-SAN?
EWW, GROSS!!
SINCE WHEN ARE YOU ON A FIRST-NAME BASIS?
WHAT?

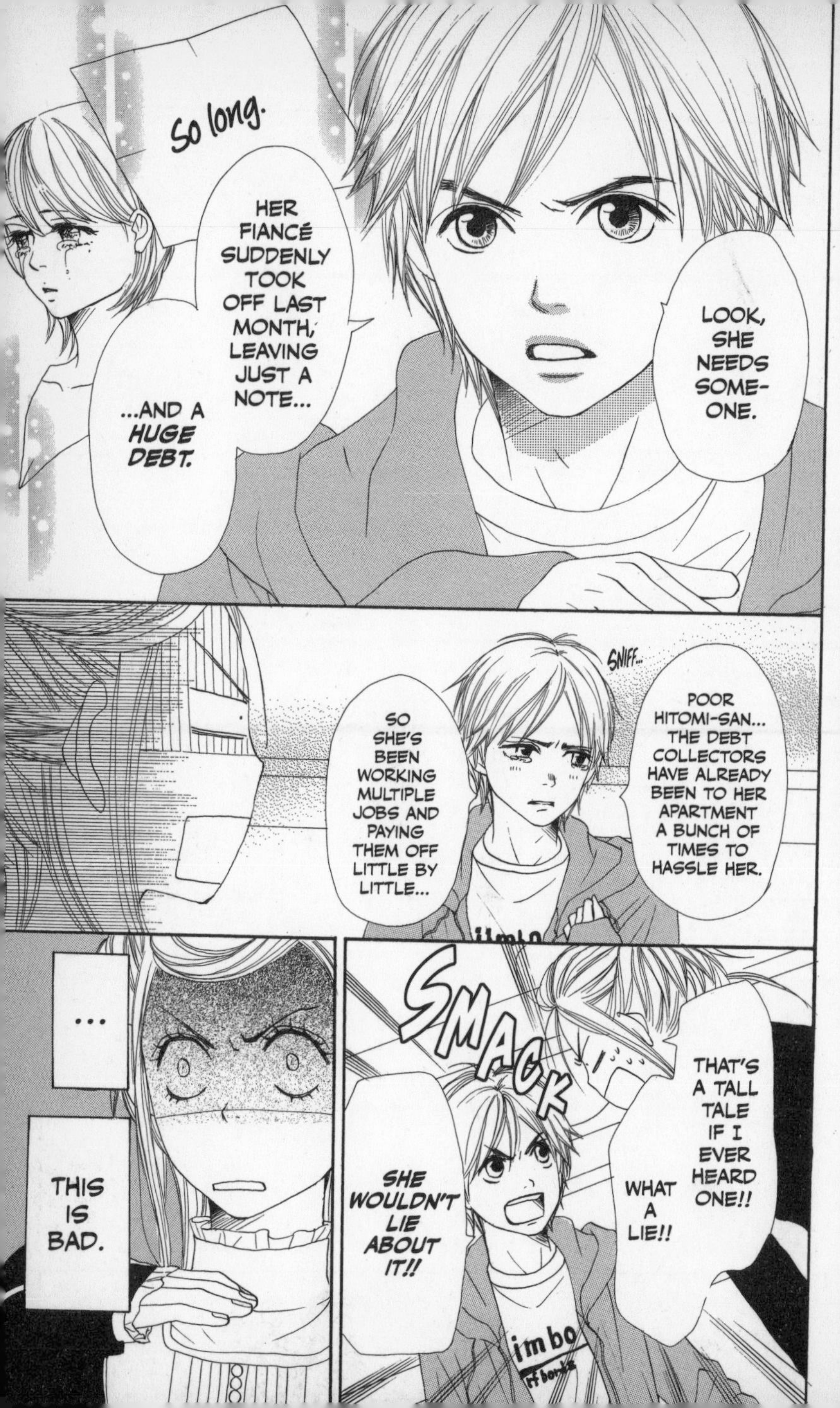
LOOK, SHE NEEDS SOME-ONE.
HER FIANCÉ SUDDENLY TOOK OFF LAST MONTH, LEAVING JUST A NOTE...
So long.
...AND A *HUGE* DEBT.
SNIFF...
POOR HITOMI-SAN... THE DEBT COLLECTORS HAVE ALREADY BEEN TO HER APARTMENT A BUNCH OF TIMES TO HASSLE HER.
SO SHE'S BEEN WORKING MULTIPLE JOBS AND PAYING THEM OFF LITTLE BY LITTLE...
SMACK
THAT'S A TALL TALE IF I EVER HEARD ONE!!
WHAT A LIE!!
SHE WOULDN'T LIE ABOUT IT!!
...
THIS IS BAD.

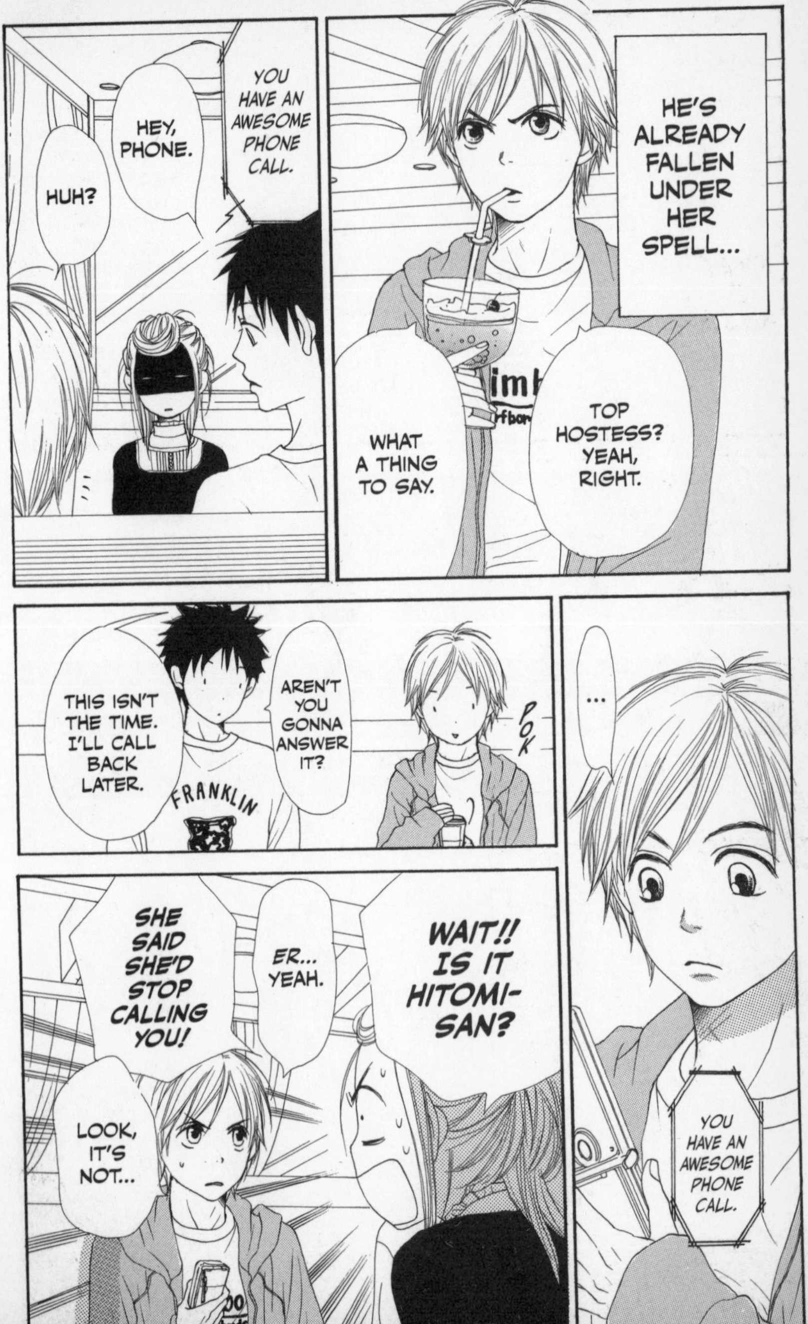
HE'S ALREADY FALLEN UNDER HER SPELL...
TOP HOSTESS? YEAH, RIGHT.
WHAT A THING TO SAY.
YOU HAVE AN AWESOME PHONE CALL.
HEY, PHONE.
HUH?
...
YOU HAVE AN AWESOME PHONE CALL.
AREN'T YOU GONNA ANSWER IT?
POK
THIS ISN'T THE TIME. I'LL CALL BACK LATER.
FRANKLIN
WAIT!! IS IT HITOMI-SAN?
ER... YEAH.
SHE SAID SHE'D STOP CALLING YOU!
LOOK, IT'S NOT...

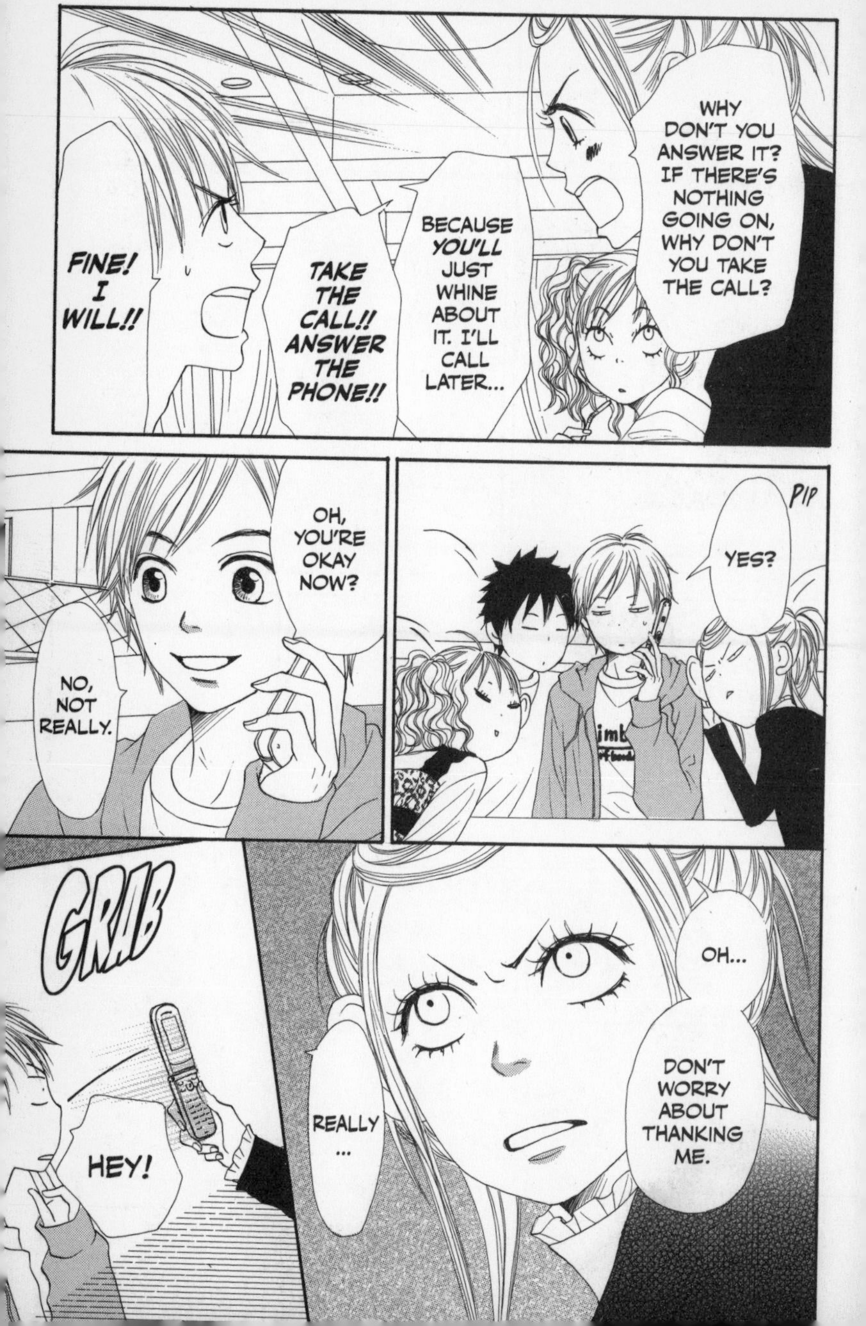
WHY DON'T YOU ANSWER IT? IF THERE'S NOTHING GOING ON, WHY DON'T YOU TAKE THE CALL?
BECAUSE *YOU'LL* JUST WHINE ABOUT IT. I'LL CALL LATER...
TAKE THE CALL!! ANSWER THE PHONE!!
FINE! I WILL!!
PIP
YES?
OH, YOU'RE OKAY NOW?
NO, NOT REALLY.
OH...
DON'T WORRY ABOUT THANKING ME.
REALLY...
GRAB
HEY!

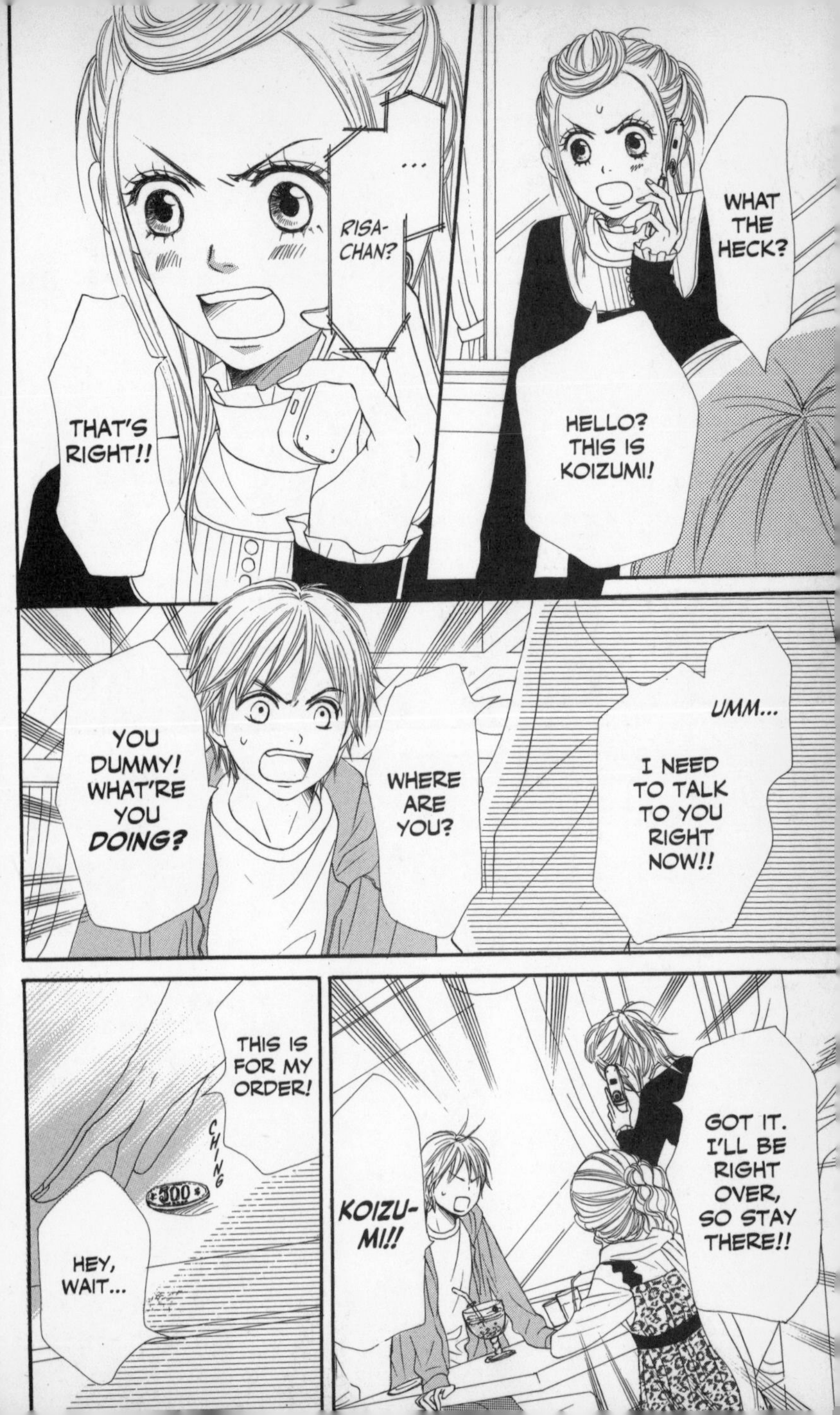
WHAT THE HECK?
HELLO? THIS IS KOIZUMI!
...
RISA-CHAN?
THAT'S RIGHT!!
UMM...
I NEED TO TALK TO YOU RIGHT NOW!!
WHERE ARE YOU?
YOU DUMMY! WHAT'RE YOU DOING?
GOT IT. I'LL BE RIGHT OVER, SO STAY THERE!!
KOIZU-MI!!
THIS IS FOR MY ORDER!
CHING
500
HEY, WAIT...

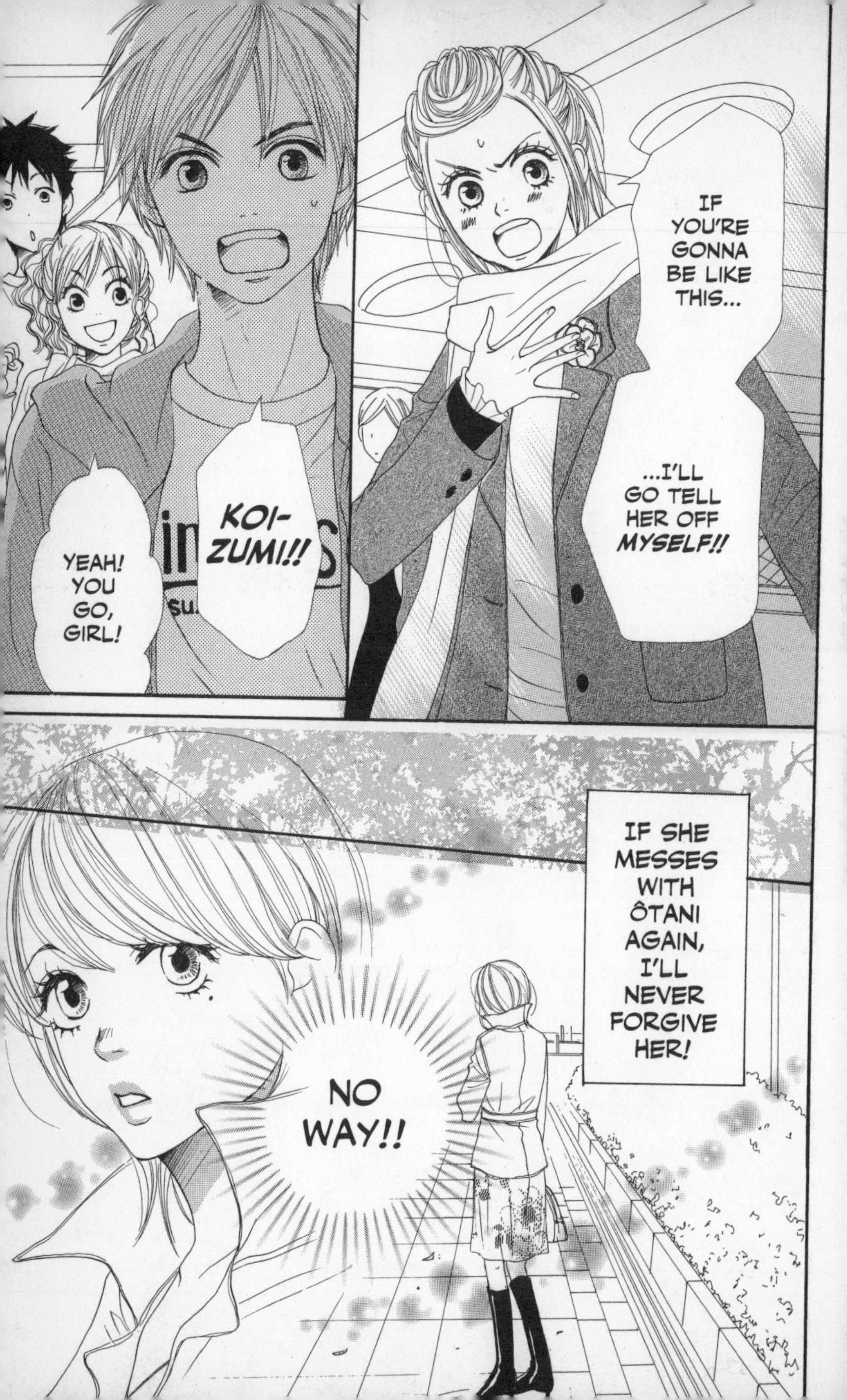
IF YOU'RE GONNA BE LIKE THIS...
...I'LL GO TELL HER OFF MYSELF!!
KOI-ZUMI!!
YEAH! YOU GO, GIRL!
IF SHE MESSES WITH ÔTANI AGAIN, I'LL NEVER FORGIVE HER!
NO WAY!!

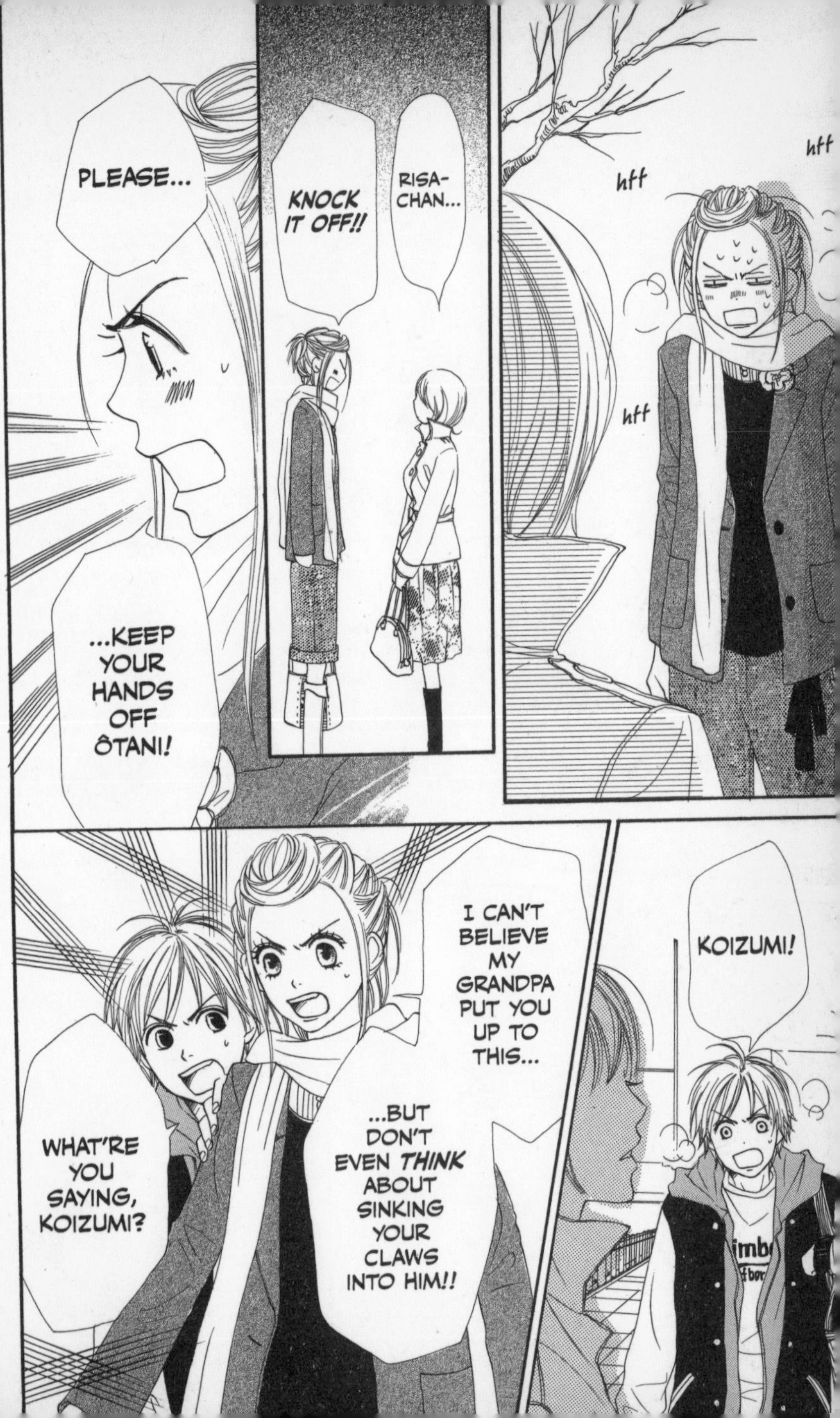
hff
hff
hff
RISA-CHAN...
KNOCK IT OFF!!
PLEASE...
...KEEP YOUR HANDS OFF ÔTANI!
KOIZUMI!
I CAN'T BELIEVE MY GRANDPA PUT YOU UP TO THIS...
...BUT DON'T EVEN *THINK* ABOUT SINKING YOUR CLAWS INTO HIM!!
WHAT'RE YOU SAYING, KOIZUMI?

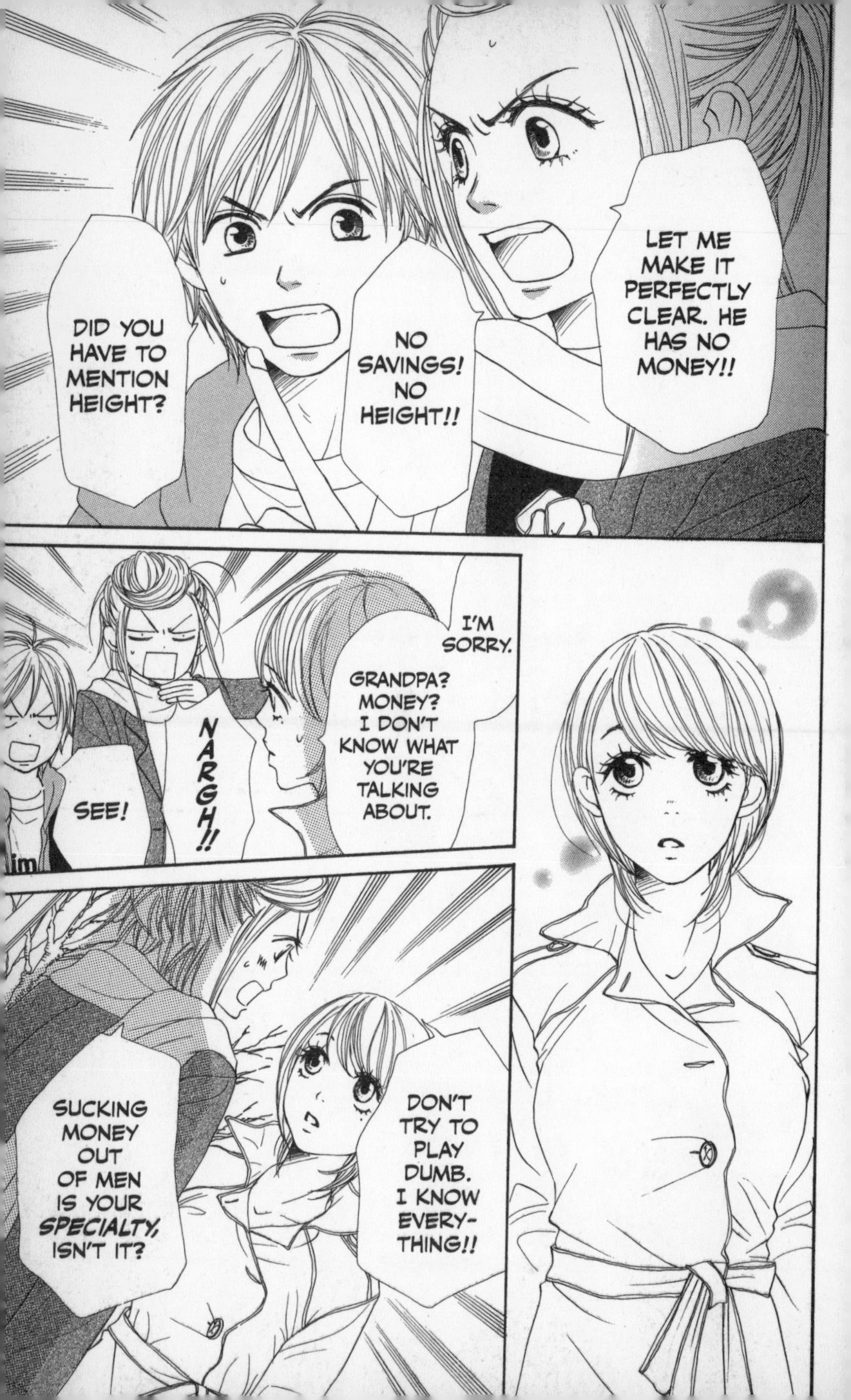
LET ME MAKE IT PERFECTLY CLEAR. HE HAS NO MONEY!!
NO SAVINGS! NO HEIGHT!!
DID YOU HAVE TO MENTION HEIGHT?
I'M SORRY.
GRANDPA? MONEY? I DON'T KNOW WHAT YOU'RE TALKING ABOUT.
NARGH!!
SEE!
DON'T TRY TO PLAY DUMB. I KNOW EVERY-THING!!
SUCKING MONEY OUT OF MEN IS YOUR *SPECIALTY*, ISN'T IT?

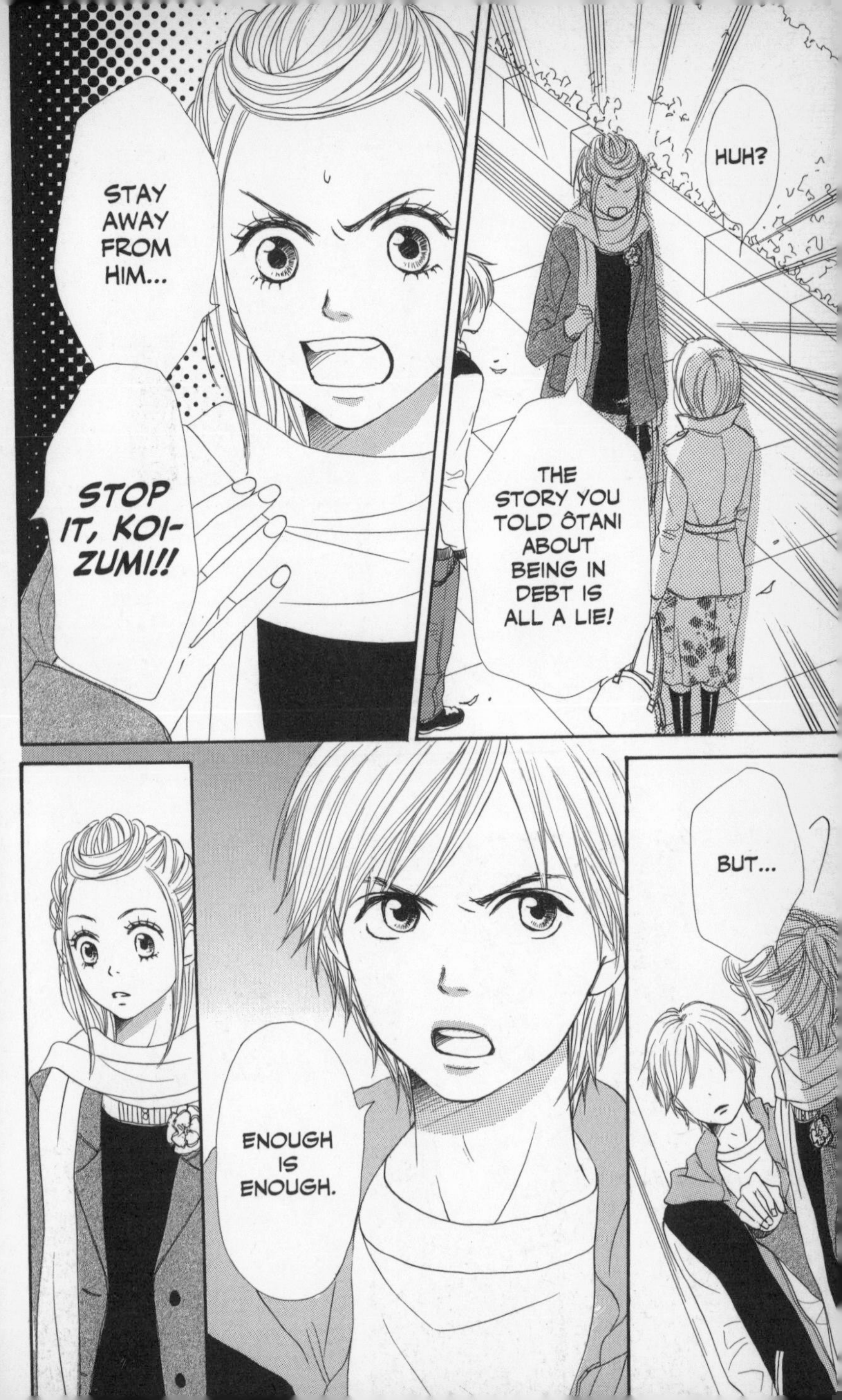
HUH?
THE STORY YOU TOLD ÔTANI ABOUT BEING IN DEBT IS ALL A LIE!
STAY AWAY FROM HIM...
STOP IT, KOI-ZUMI!!
BUT...
ENOUGH IS ENOUGH.

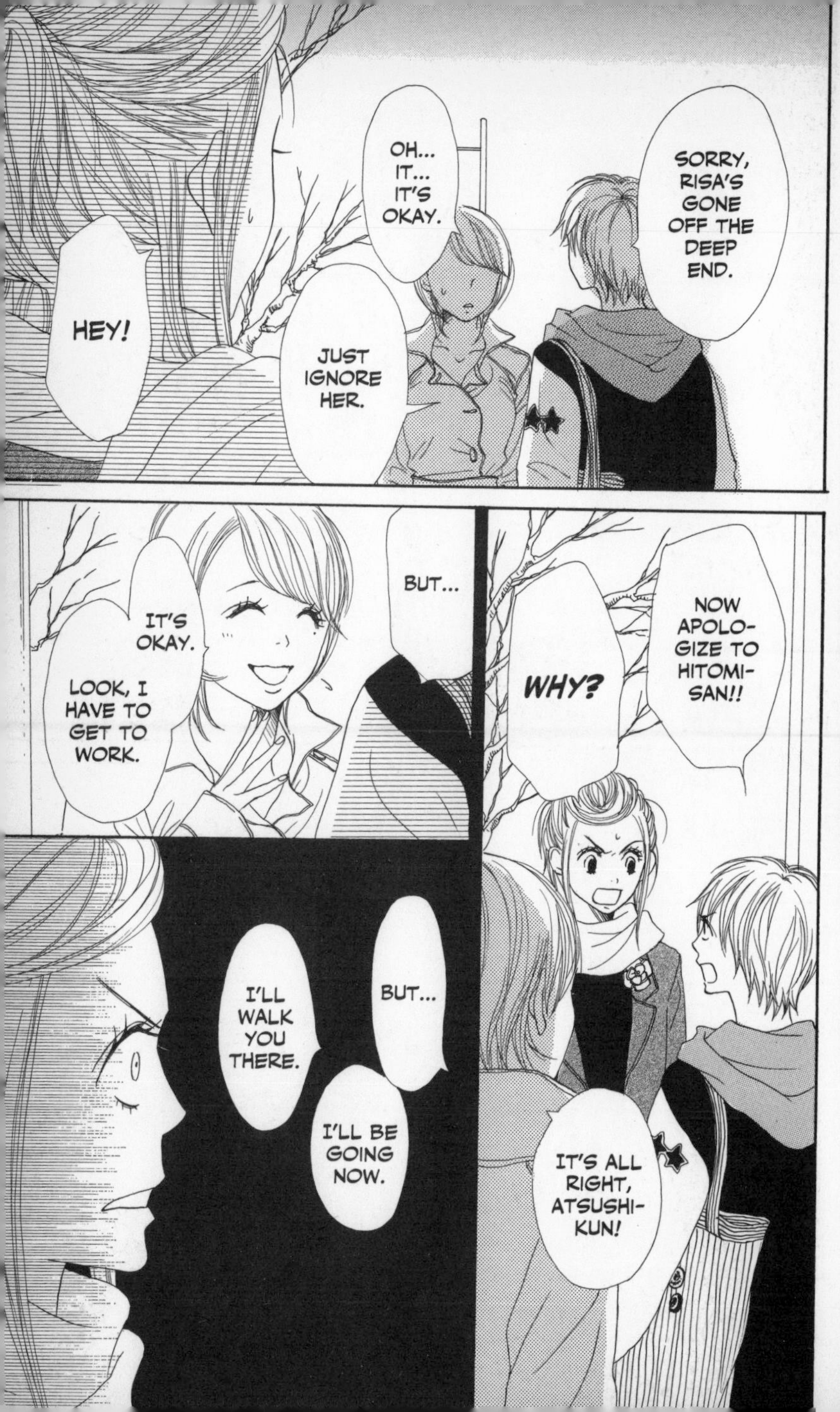
SORRY, RISA'S GONE OFF THE DEEP END.
OH... IT... IT'S OKAY.
JUST IGNORE HER.
HEY!
NOW APOLOGIZE TO HITOMI-SAN!!
WHY?
IT'S ALL RIGHT, ATSUSHI-KUN!
BUT...
IT'S OKAY.
LOOK, I HAVE TO GET TO WORK.
BUT...
I'LL WALK YOU THERE.
I'LL BE GOING NOW.

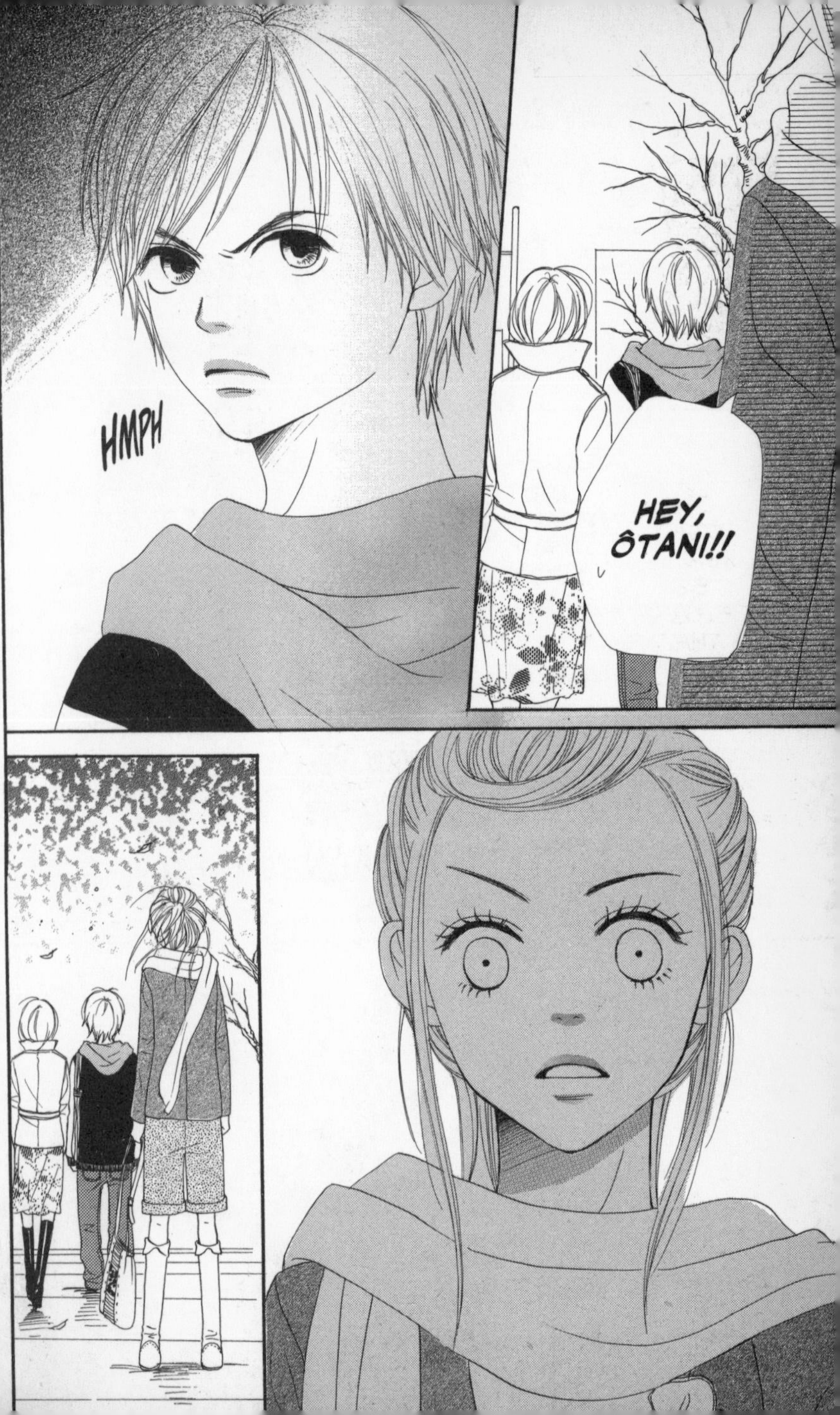
HEY, ÔTANI!!
HMPH

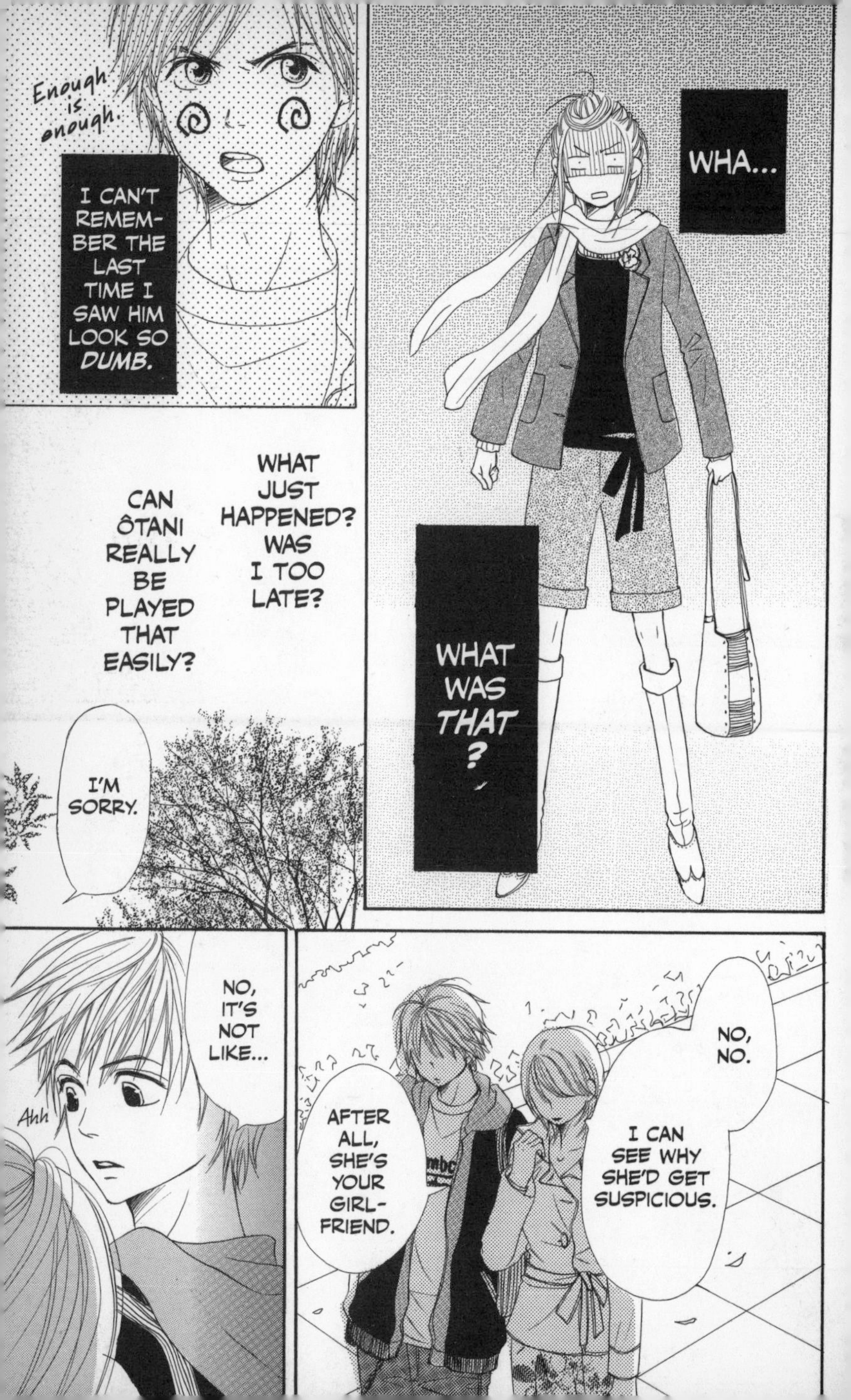
WHA...
WHAT WAS THAT?
Enough is enough.
I CAN'T REMEMBER THE LAST TIME I SAW HIM LOOK SO DUMB.
WHAT JUST HAPPENED? WAS I TOO LATE?
CAN ÔTANI REALLY BE PLAYED THAT EASILY?
I'M SORRY.
NO, NO.
I CAN SEE WHY SHE'D GET SUSPICIOUS.
AFTER ALL, SHE'S YOUR GIRLFRIEND.
NO, IT'S NOT LIKE...
Ahh

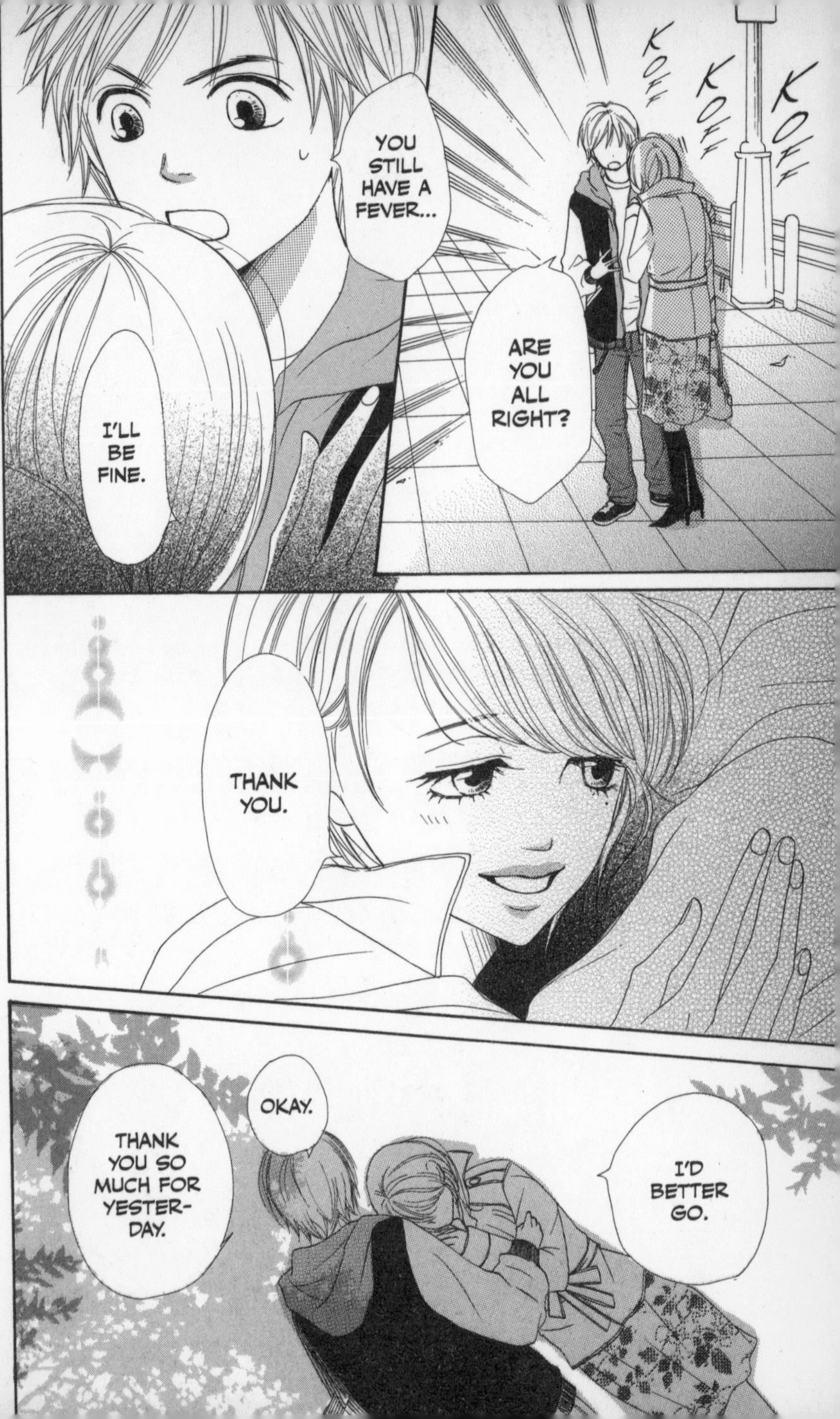
KOFF
KOFF
KOFF
ARE YOU ALL RIGHT?
YOU STILL HAVE A FEVER...
I'LL BE FINE.
THANK YOU.
I'D BETTER GO.
OKAY.
THANK YOU SO MUCH FOR YESTER-DAY.

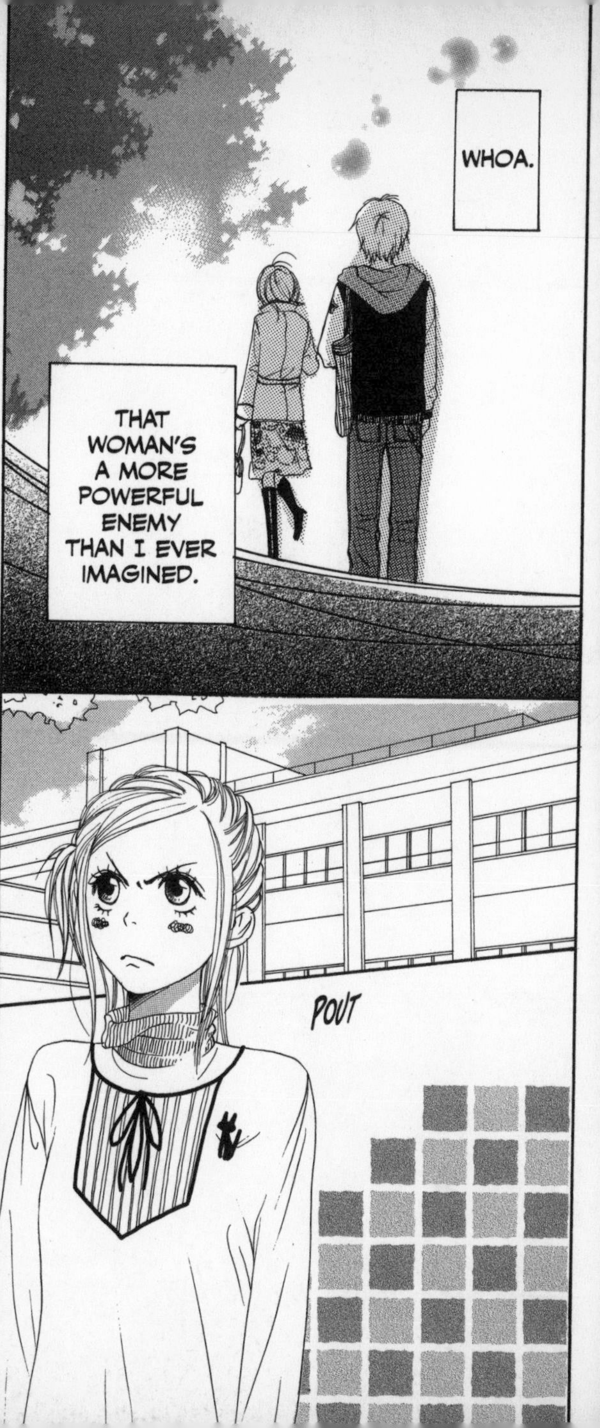
WHOA.
THAT WOMAN'S A MORE POWERFUL ENEMY THAN I EVER IMAGINED.
POUT

1

Hello!
It's me, Nakahara.
We're up to volume 14.
Thank you very much...
How is everyone?
Love ★ Com: The Movie is finally out.
Have you all seen it?
It's pretty cute.
That's the word on the street, so please go see it.
It's the cutest movie in Japan. Really.
I totally approve of it.
And I'm not just saying it because I'm the creator.
I'm saying it as a filmgoer. I bought advance tickets.
And even the tickets were cute!
Imagine that!! Yes!!
Next we'll scrutinize Love ★ Com: The Movie to determine the source of its incredible cuteness.

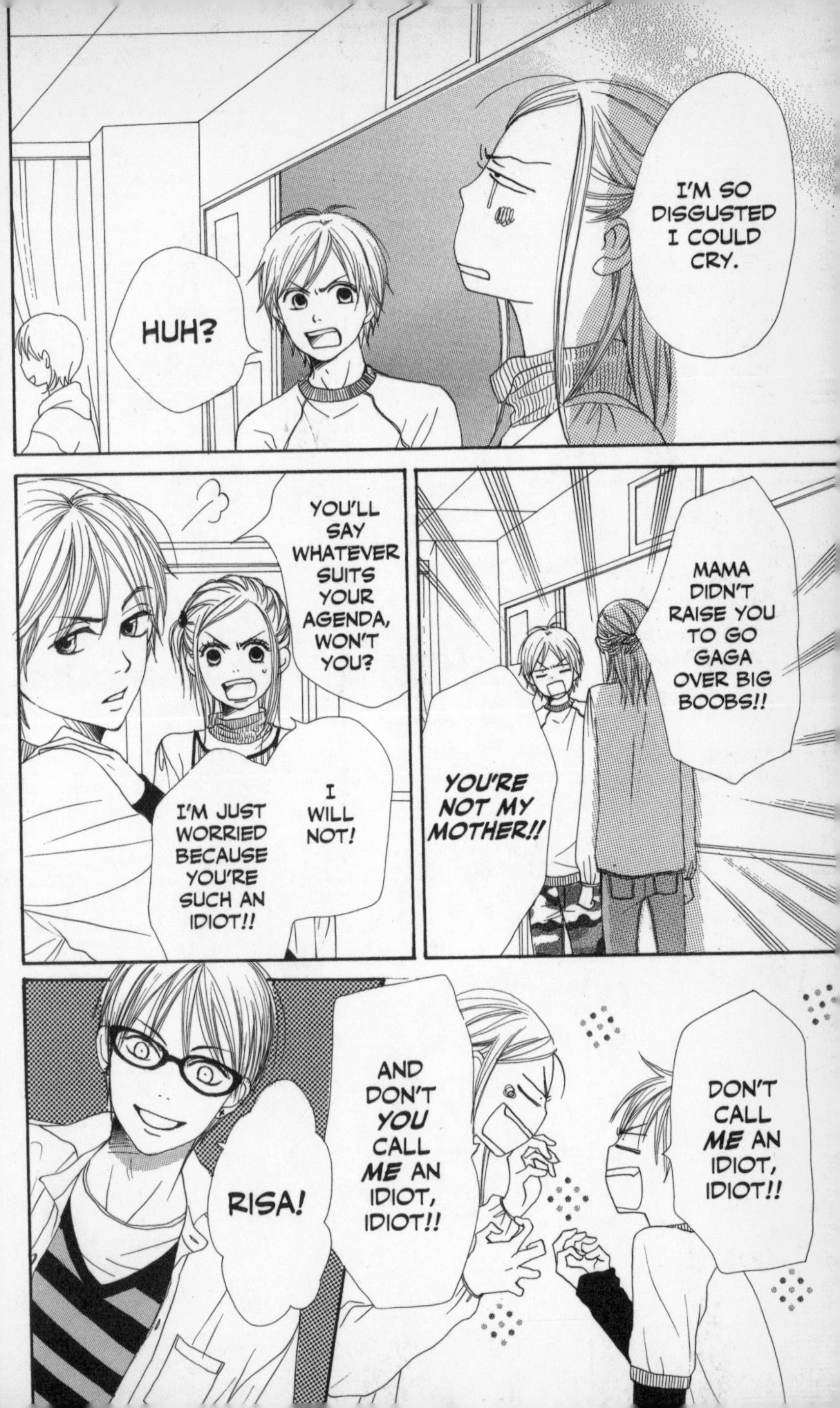
I'M SO DISGUSTED I COULD CRY.
HUH?
MAMA DIDN'T RAISE YOU TO GO GAGA OVER BIG BOOBS!!
YOU'RE NOT MY MOTHER!!
YOU'LL SAY WHATEVER SUITS YOUR AGENDA, WON'T YOU?
I WILL NOT!
I'M JUST WORRIED BECAUSE YOU'RE SUCH AN IDIOT!!
DON'T CALL ME AN IDIOT, IDIOT!!
AND DON'T YOU CALL ME AN IDIOT, IDIOT!!
RISA!

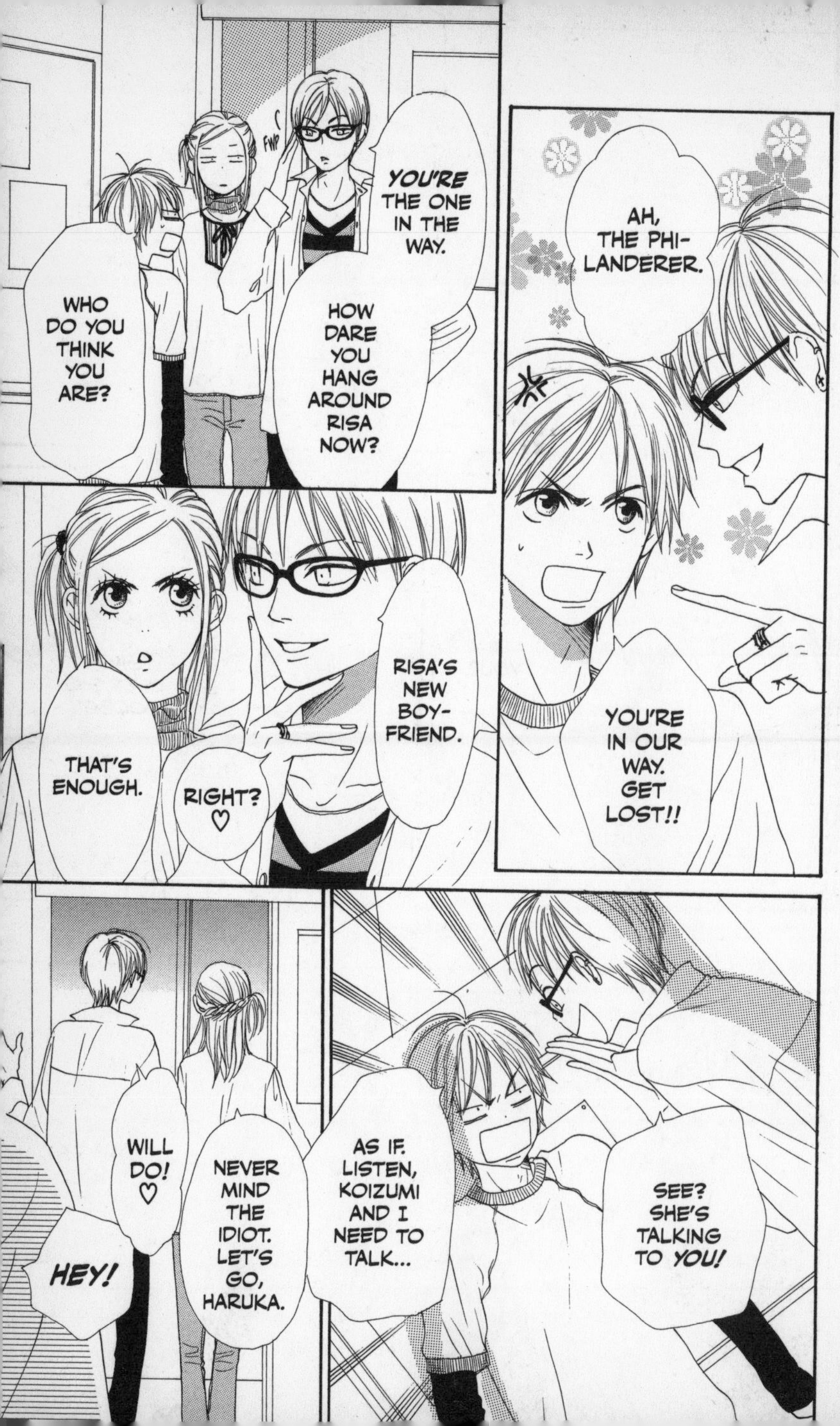
AH, THE PHI-LANDERER.
YOU'RE IN OUR WAY. GET LOST!!
YOU'RE THE ONE IN THE WAY.
FWP
HOW DARE YOU HANG AROUND RISA NOW?
WHO DO YOU THINK YOU ARE?
RISA'S NEW BOY-FRIEND.
RIGHT? ♡
THAT'S ENOUGH.
SEE? SHE'S TALKING TO *YOU!*
AS IF. LISTEN, KOIZUMI AND I NEED TO TALK...
NEVER MIND THE IDIOT. LET'S GO, HARUKA.
WILL DO! ♡
HEY!

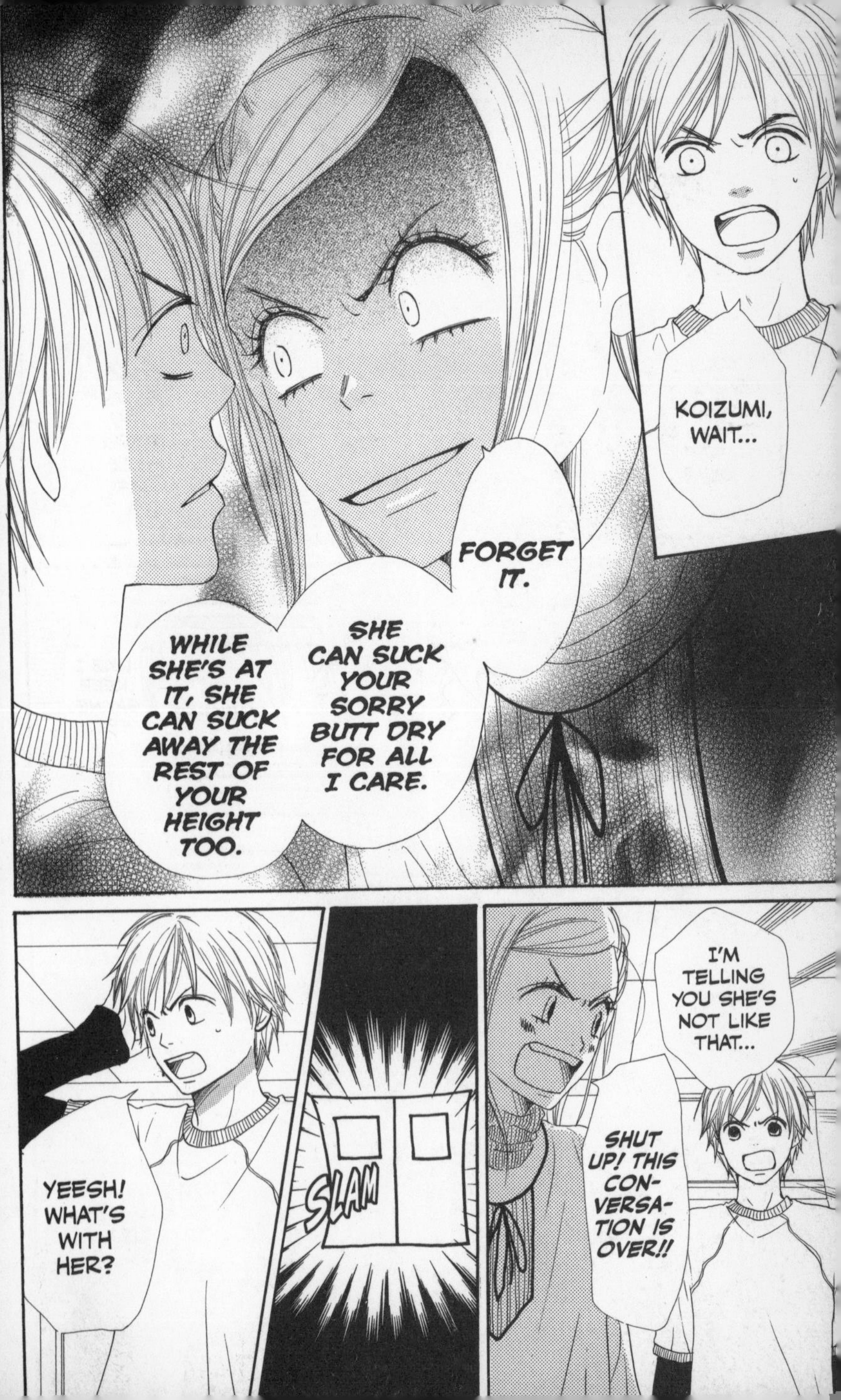
KOIZUMI, WAIT...
FORGET IT.
SHE CAN SUCK YOUR SORRY BUTT DRY FOR ALL I CARE.
WHILE SHE'S AT IT, SHE CAN SUCK AWAY THE REST OF YOUR HEIGHT TOO.
I'M TELLING YOU SHE'S NOT LIKE THAT...
SHUT UP! THIS CONVERSATION IS OVER!!
SLAM
YEESH! WHAT'S WITH HER?

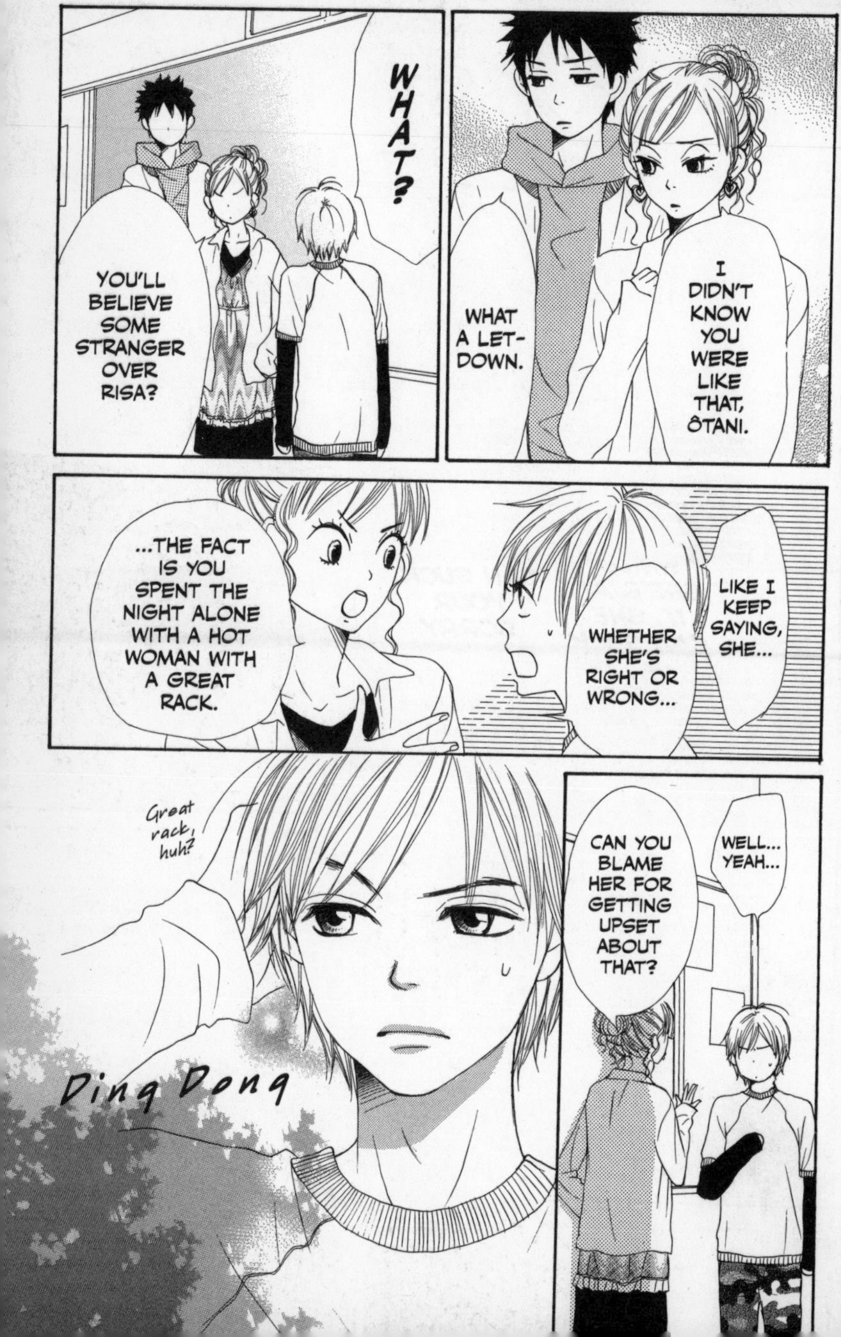
I DIDN'T KNOW YOU WERE LIKE THAT, ŌTANI.
WHAT A LET-DOWN.
WHAT?
YOU'LL BELIEVE SOME STRANGER OVER RISA?
LIKE I KEEP SAYING, SHE...
WHETHER SHE'S RIGHT OR WRONG...
...THE FACT IS YOU SPENT THE NIGHT ALONE WITH A HOT WOMAN WITH A GREAT RACK.
WELL... YEAH...
CAN YOU BLAME HER FOR GETTING UPSET ABOUT THAT?
Great rack, huh?
Ding Dong

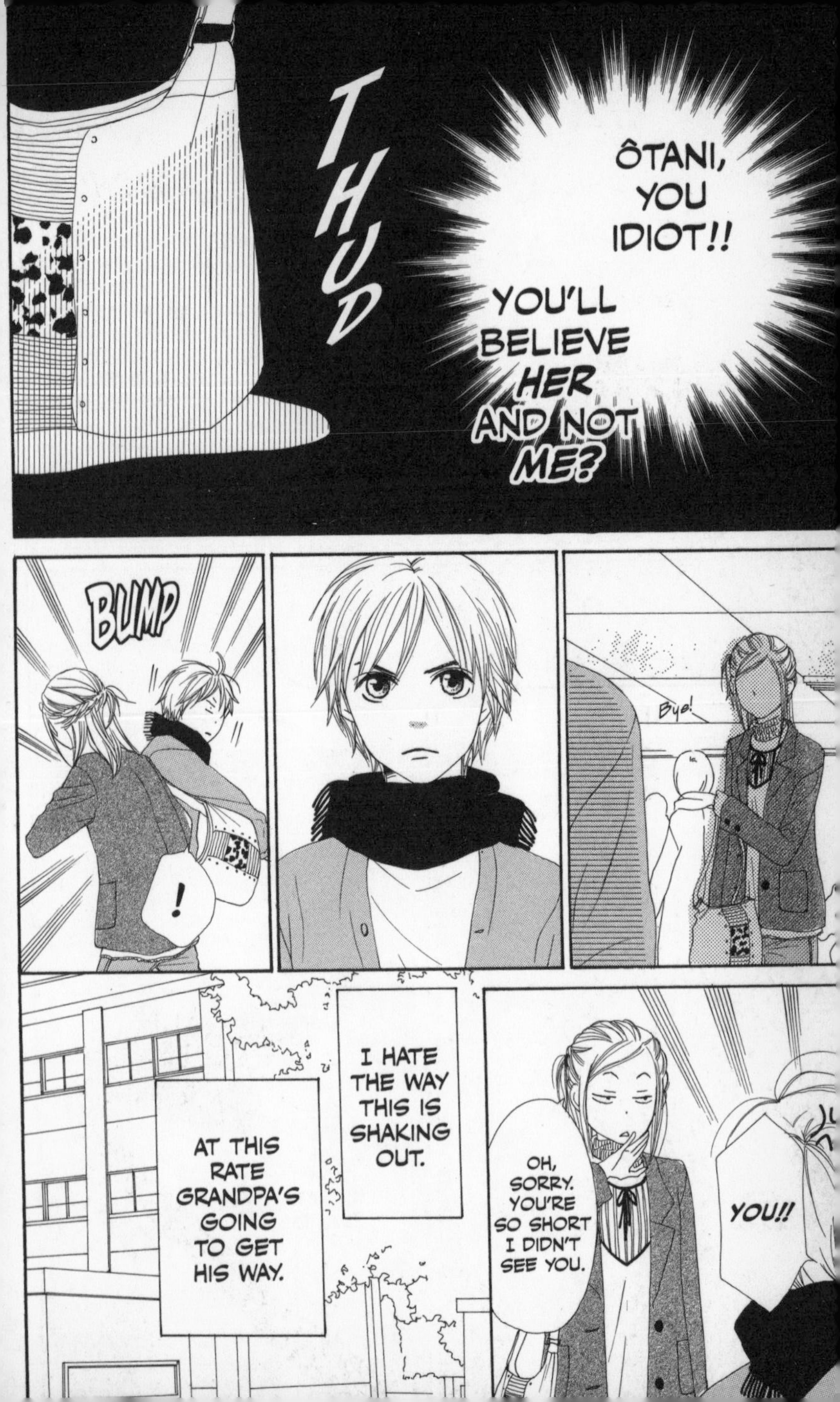
ÔTANI, YOU IDIOT!!
YOU'LL BELIEVE *HER* AND NOT *ME*?
THUD
Bye!
BUMP
!
YOU!!
OH, SORRY. YOU'RE SO SHORT I DIDN'T SEE YOU.
I HATE THE WAY THIS IS SHAKING OUT.
AT THIS RATE GRANDPA'S GOING TO GET HIS WAY.

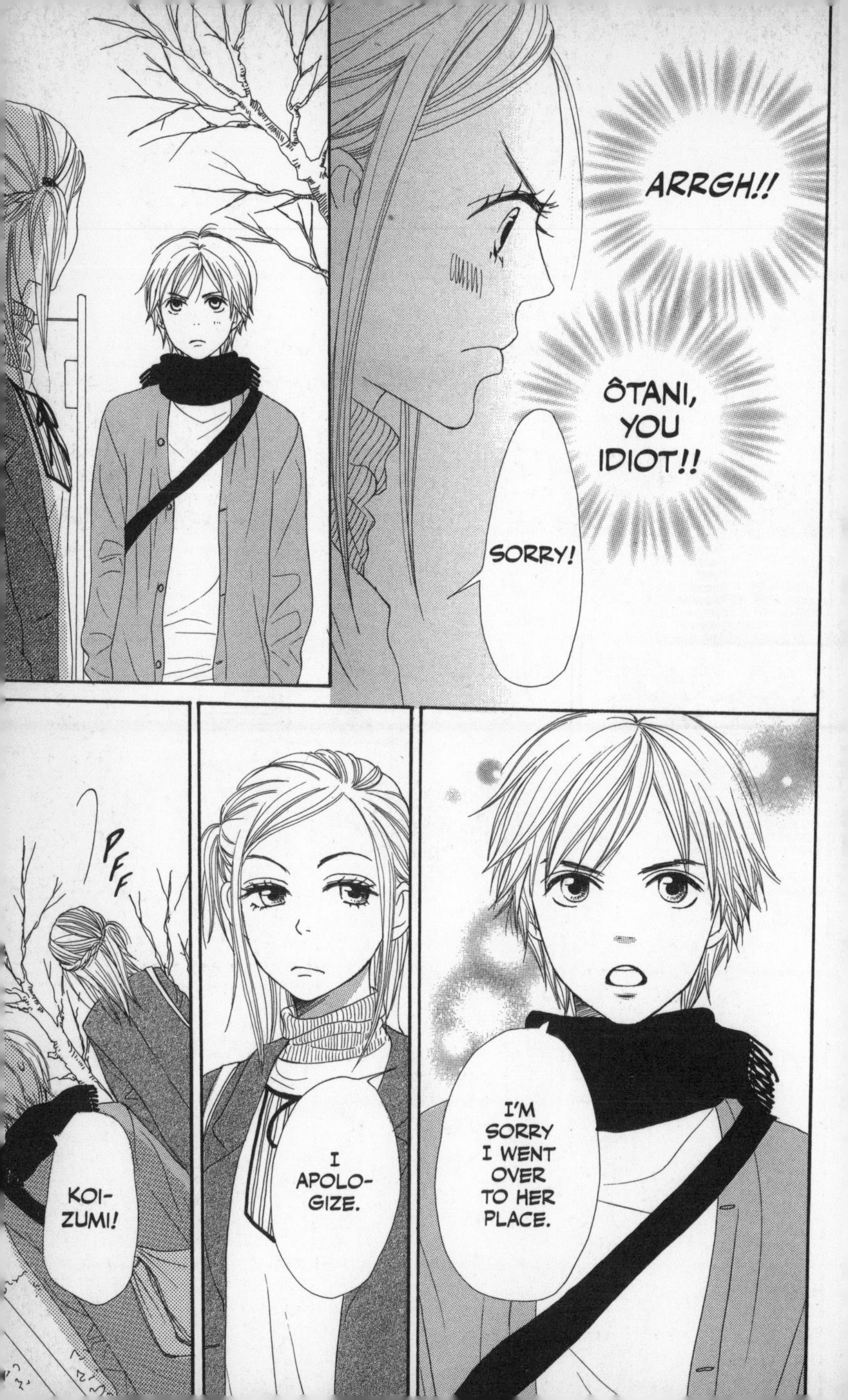
ARRGH!!
ÔTANI, YOU IDIOT!!
SORRY!
I'M SORRY I WENT OVER TO HER PLACE.
I APOLO-GIZE.
PFF
KOI-ZUMI!

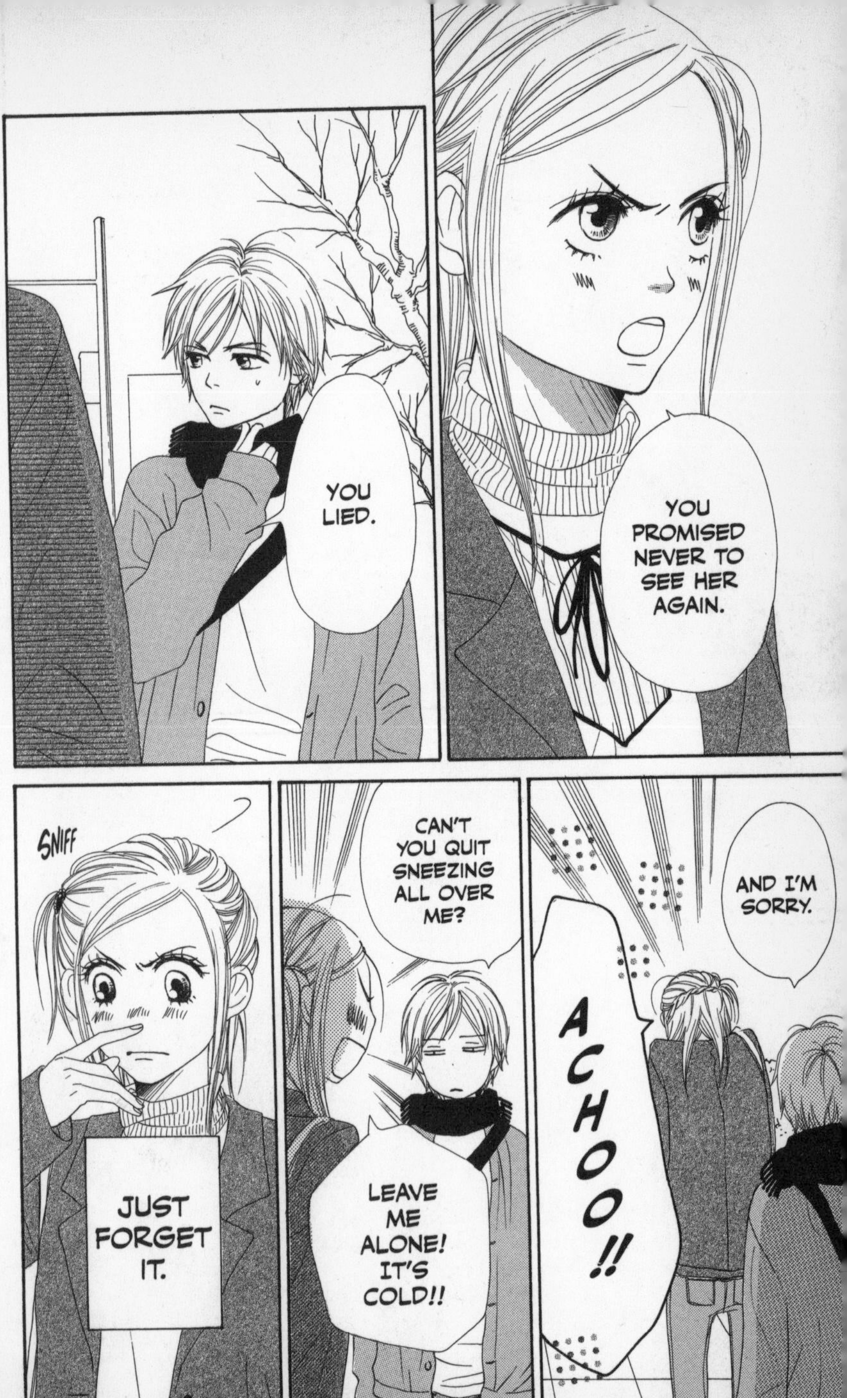
YOU PROMISED NEVER TO SEE HER AGAIN.
YOU LIED.
AND I'M SORRY.
ACHOO!!
CAN'T YOU QUIT SNEEZING ALL OVER ME?
LEAVE ME ALONE! IT'S COLD!!
SNIFF
JUST FORGET IT.

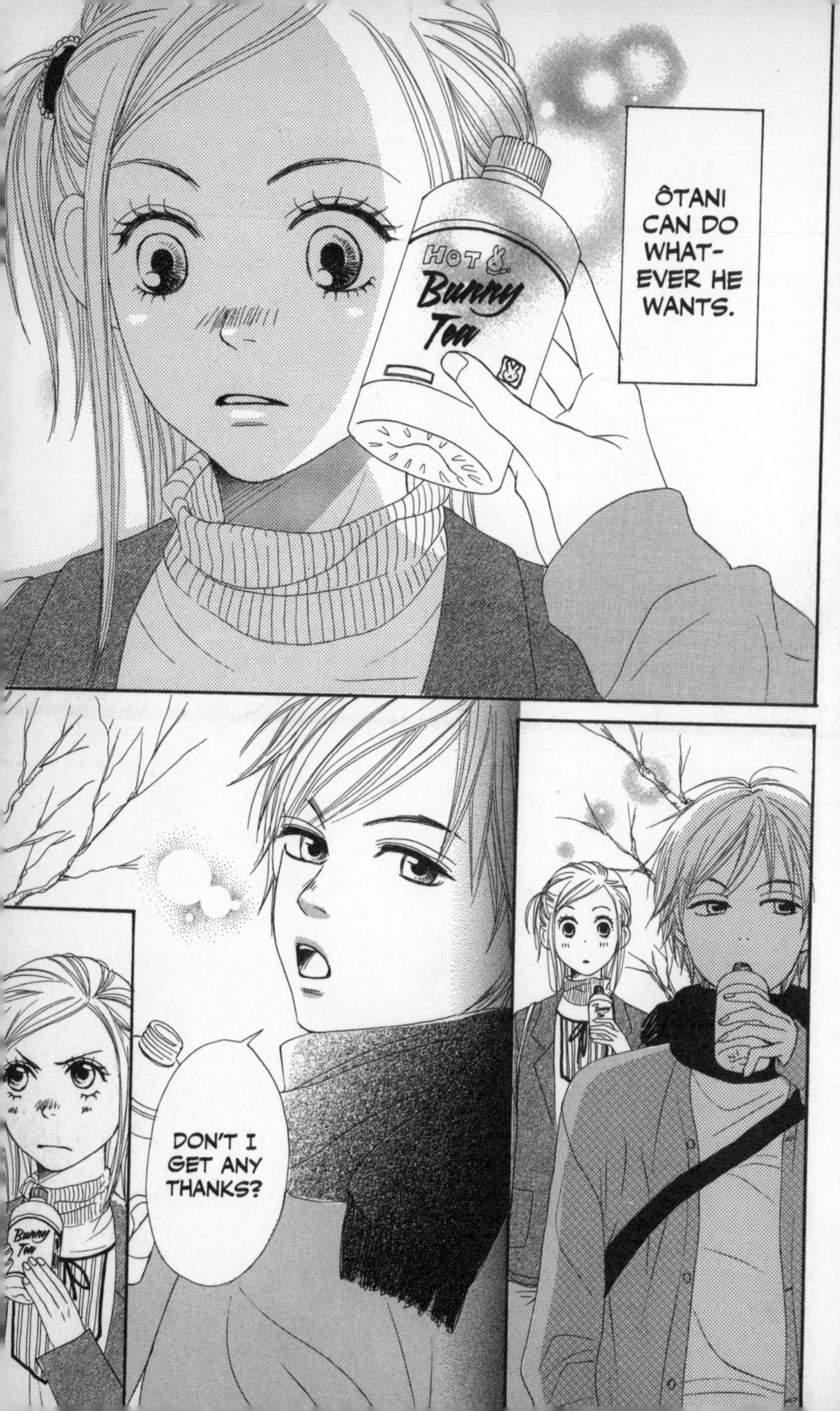
ÔTANI CAN DO WHAT-EVER HE WANTS.
HOT & Bunny Tea
DON'T I GET ANY THANKS?

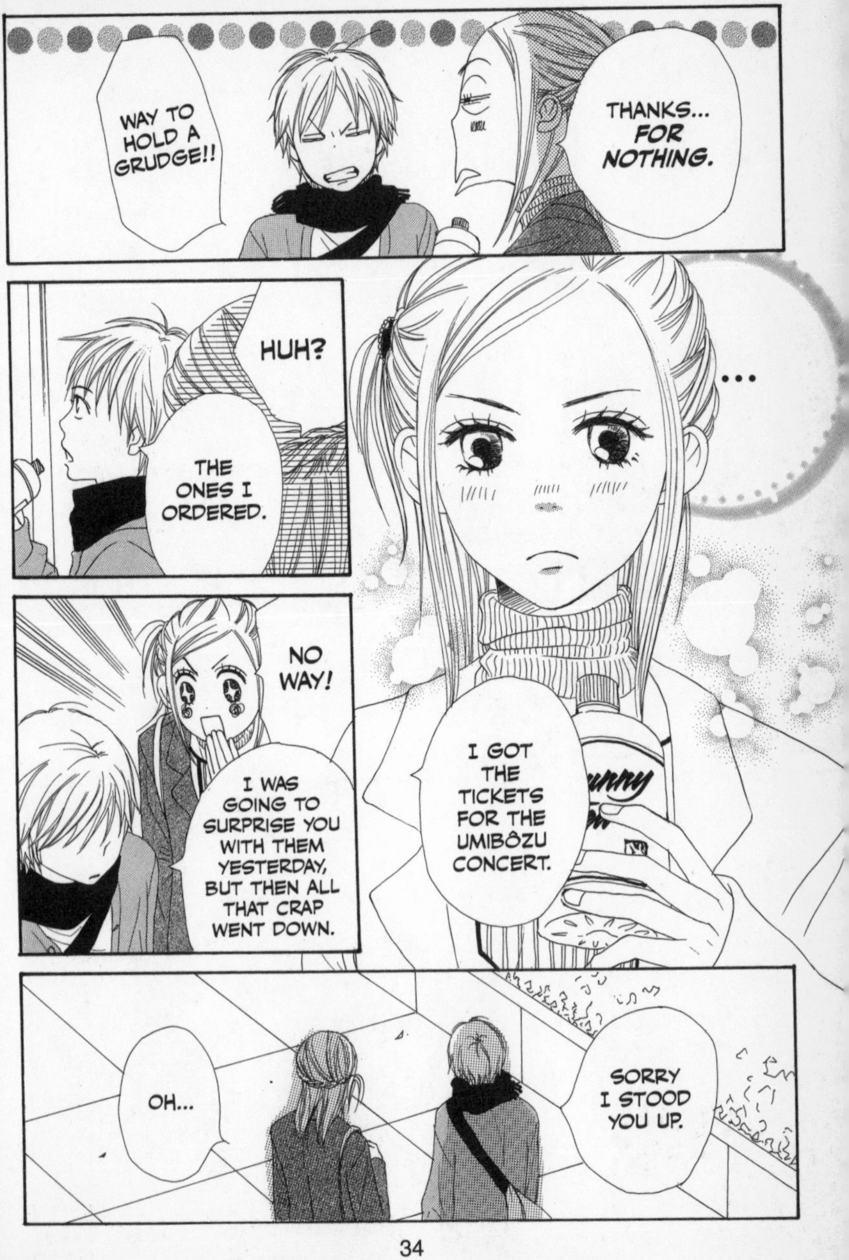
THANKS... *FOR NOTHING.*
WAY TO HOLD A GRUDGE!!
...
I GOT THE TICKETS FOR THE UMIBÔZU CONCERT.
HUH?
THE ONES I ORDERED.
NO WAY!
I WAS GOING TO SURPRISE YOU WITH THEM YESTERDAY, BUT THEN ALL THAT CRAP WENT DOWN.
SORRY I STOOD YOU UP.
OH...

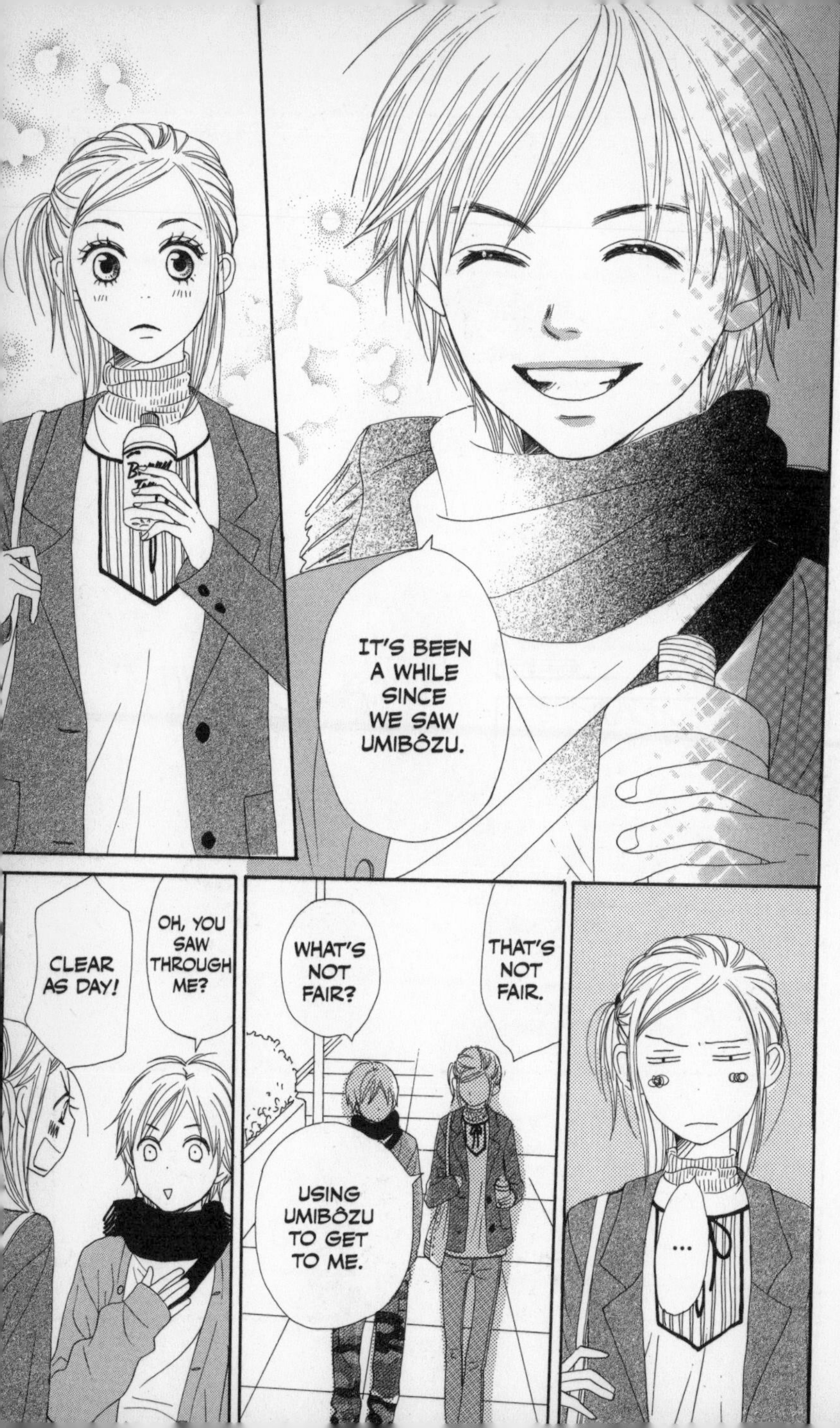

IT'S BEEN A WHILE SINCE WE SAW UMIBÔZU.
...
THAT'S NOT FAIR.
WHAT'S NOT FAIR?
USING UMIBÔZU TO GET TO ME.
OH, YOU SAW THROUGH ME?
CLEAR AS DAY!

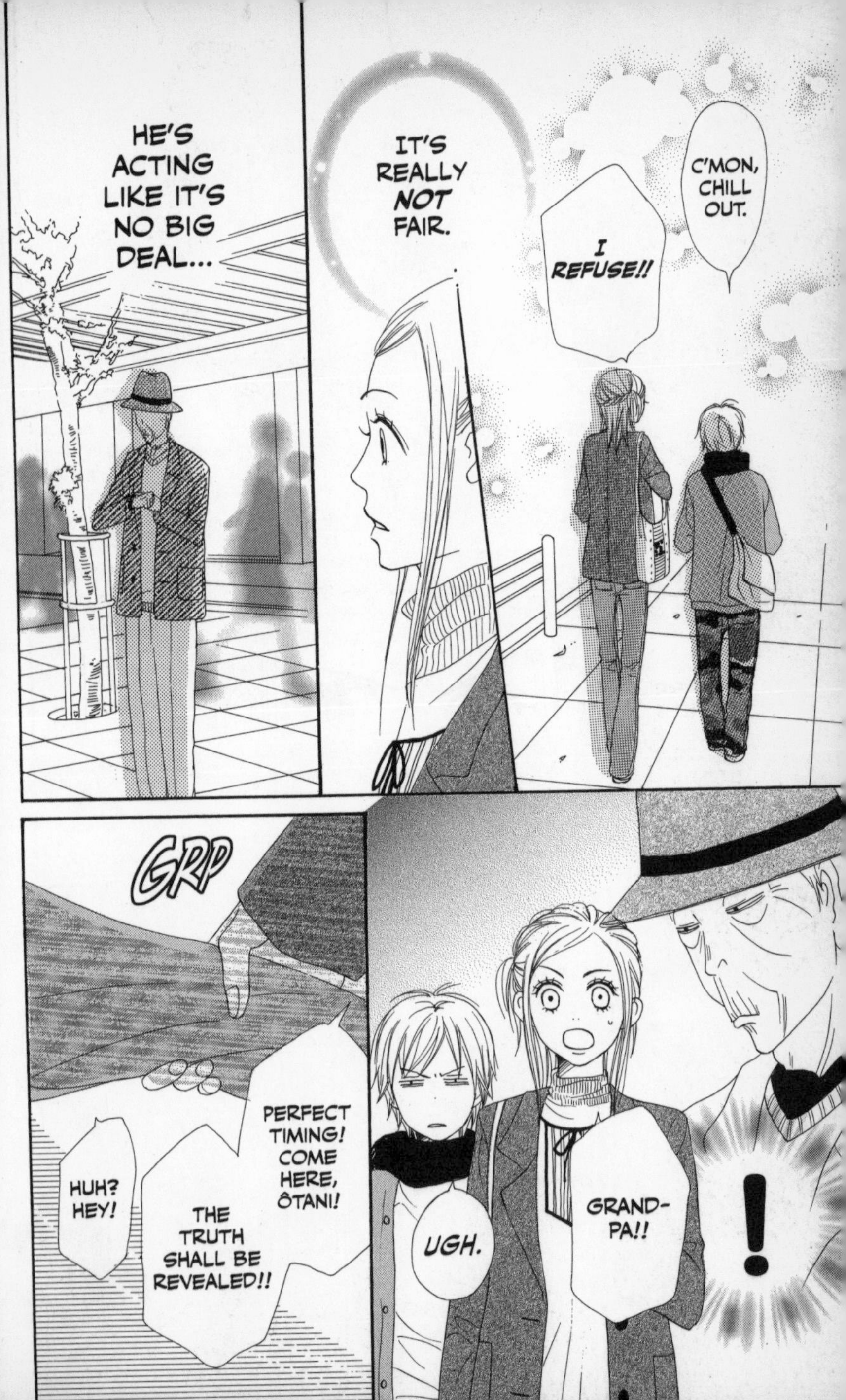
C'MON, CHILL OUT.
I REFUSE!!
IT'S REALLY NOT FAIR.
HE'S ACTING LIKE IT'S NO BIG DEAL...
!
GRAND-PA!!
UGH.
GRP
PERFECT TIMING! COME HERE, ÔTANI!
THE TRUTH SHALL BE REVEALED!!
HUH? HEY!

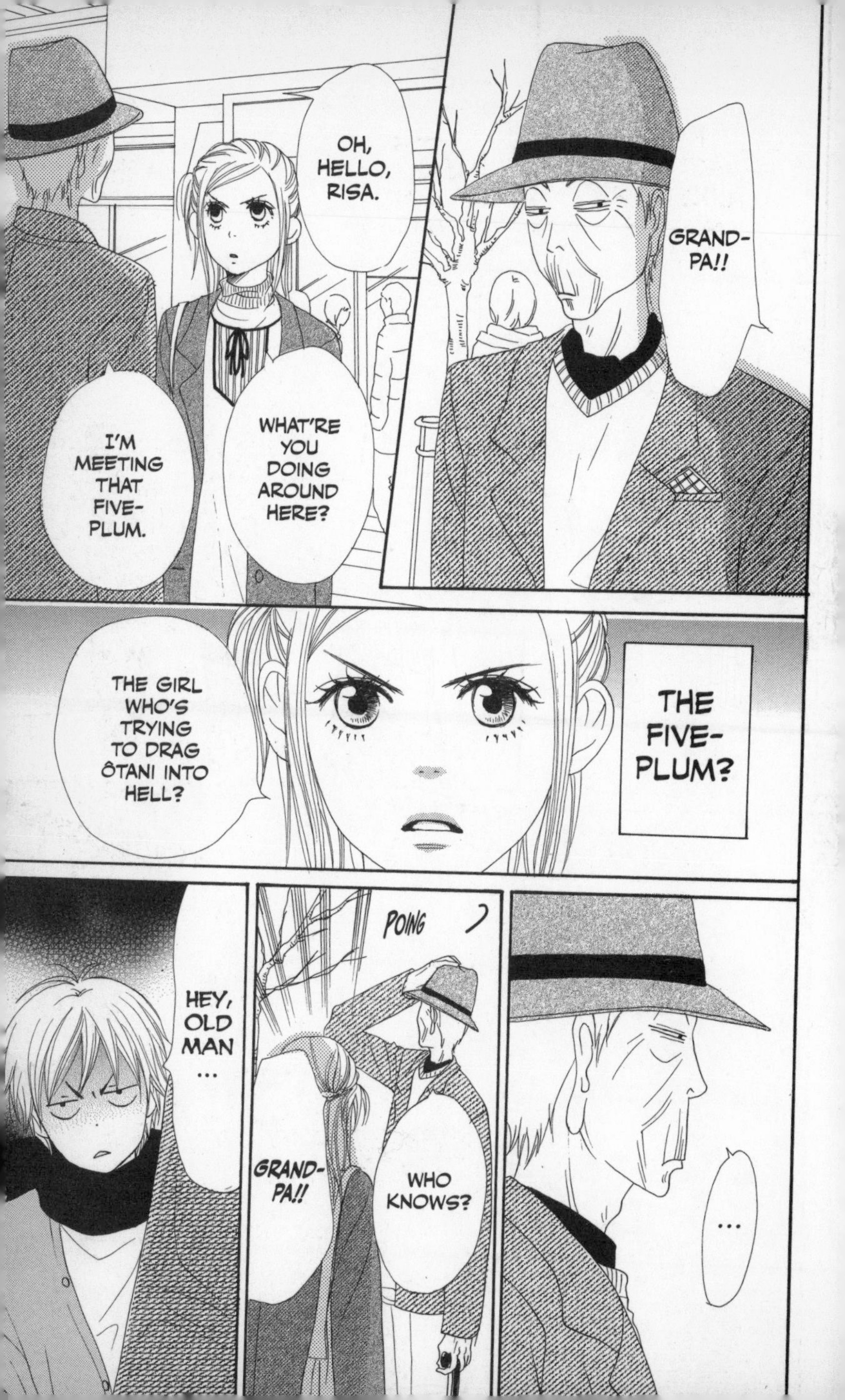
GRAND-PA!!
OH, HELLO, RISA.
WHAT'RE YOU DOING AROUND HERE?
I'M MEETING THAT FIVE-PLUM.
THE FIVE-PLUM?
THE GIRL WHO'S TRYING TO DRAG ÔTANI INTO HELL?
...
POING
WHO KNOWS?
GRAND-PA!!
HEY, OLD MAN ...

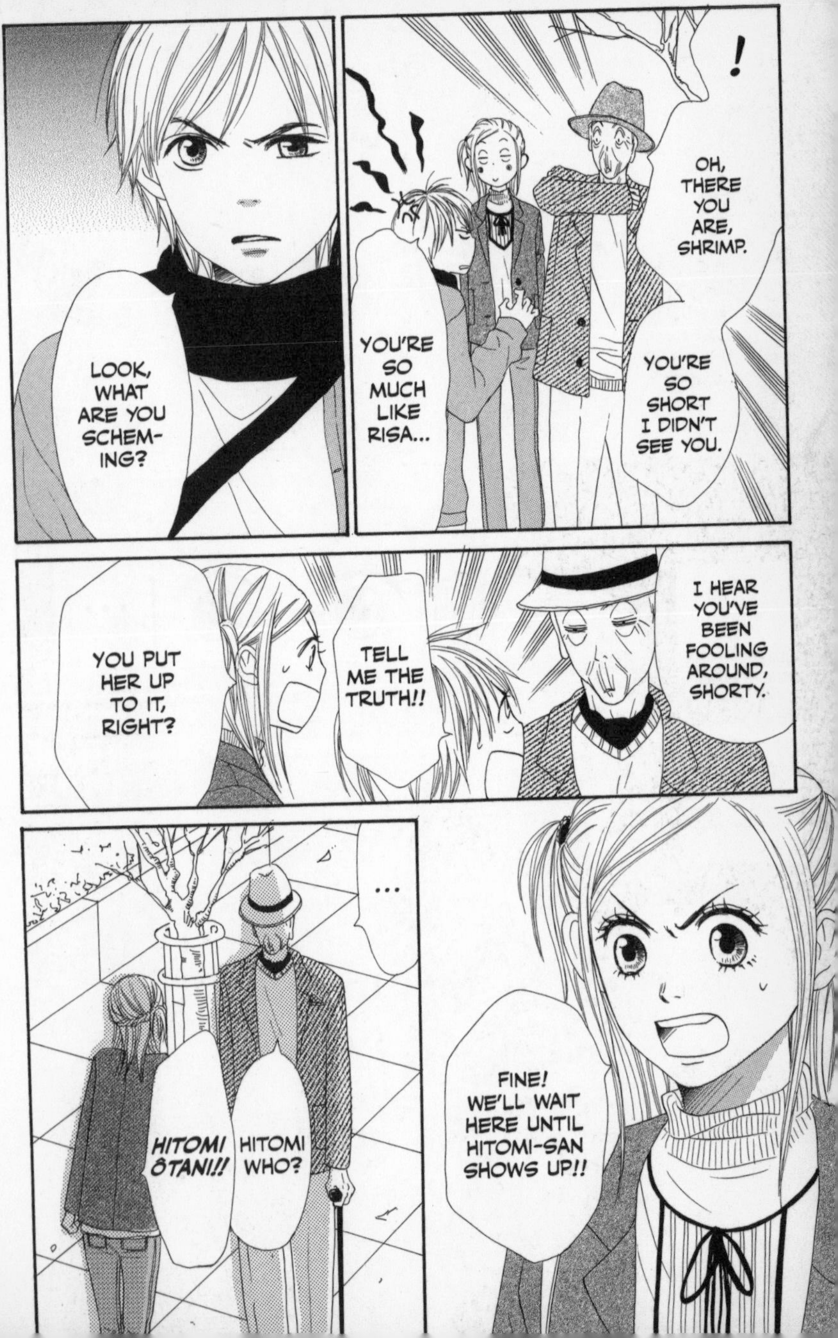
!
OH, THERE YOU ARE, SHRIMP.
YOU'RE SO SHORT I DIDN'T SEE YOU.
YOU'RE SO MUCH LIKE RISA...
LOOK, WHAT ARE YOU SCHEM-ING?
I HEAR YOU'VE BEEN FOOLING AROUND, SHORTY.
TELL ME THE TRUTH!!
YOU PUT HER UP TO IT, RIGHT?
FINE! WE'LL WAIT HERE UNTIL HITOMI-SAN SHOWS UP!!
...
HITOMI WHO?
HITOMI ŌTANI!!

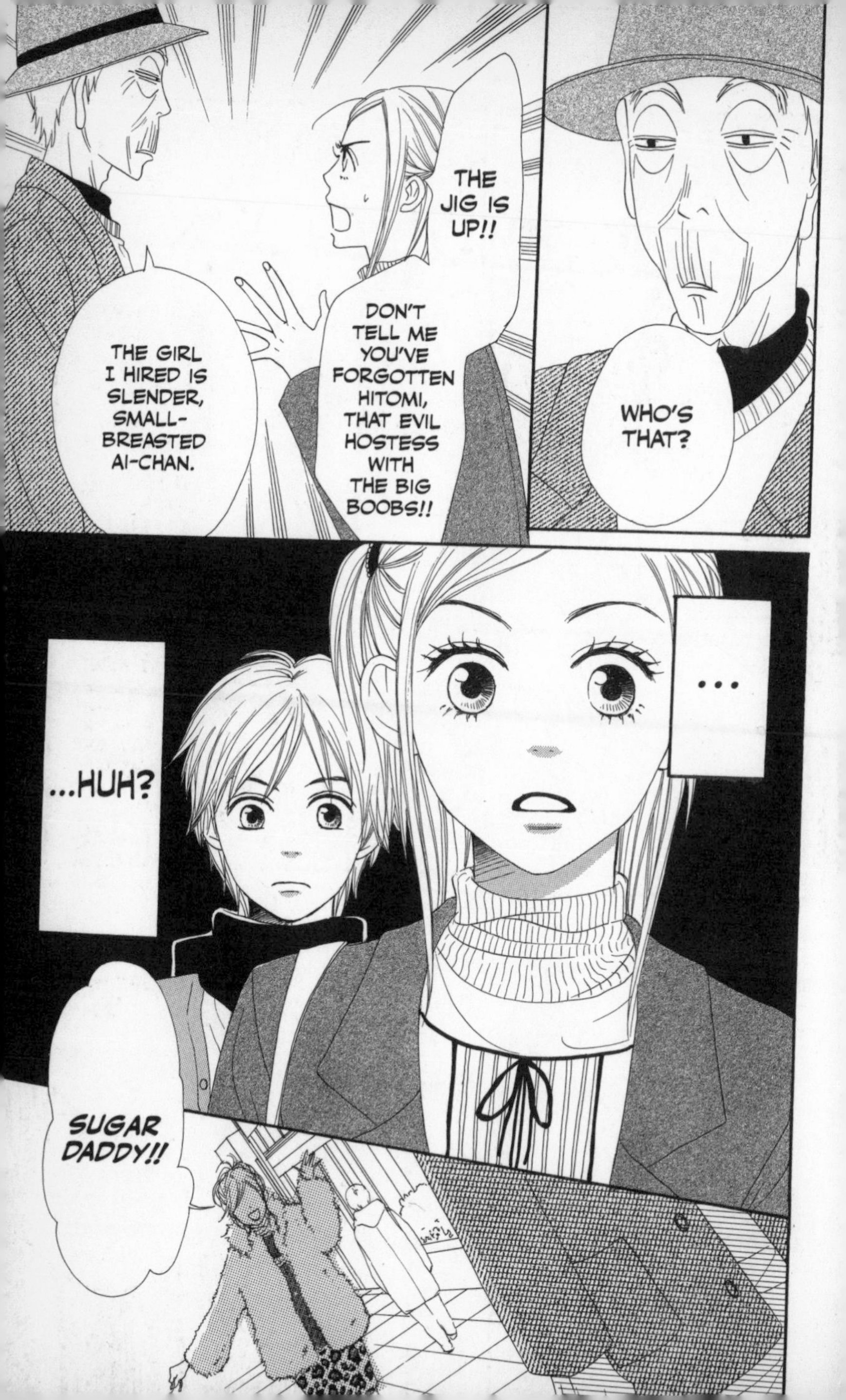
WHO'S THAT?
THE JIG IS UP!!
DON'T TELL ME YOU'VE FORGOTTEN HITOMI, THAT EVIL HOSTESS WITH THE BIG BOOBS!!
THE GIRL I HIRED IS SLENDER, SMALL-BREASTED AI-CHAN.
...
...HUH?
SUGAR DADDY!!

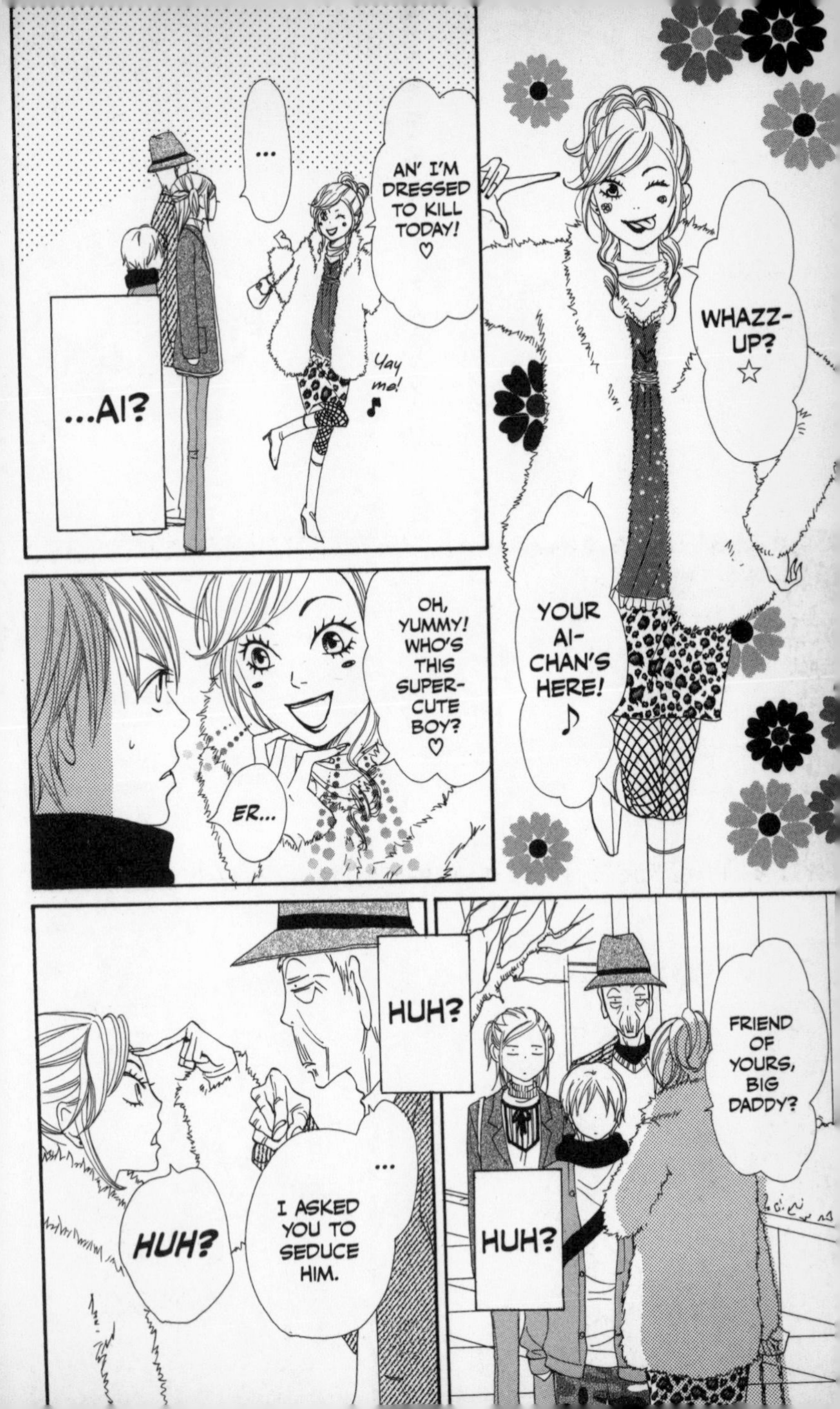
WHAZZ-UP? ☆
YOUR AI-CHAN'S HERE! ♪
AN' I'M DRESSED TO KILL TODAY! ♡
Yay me! ♪
...
...AI?
OH, YUMMY! WHO'S THIS SUPER-CUTE BOY? ♡
ER...
FRIEND OF YOURS, BIG DADDY?
HUH?
HUH?
...
I ASKED YOU TO SEDUCE HIM.
HUH?

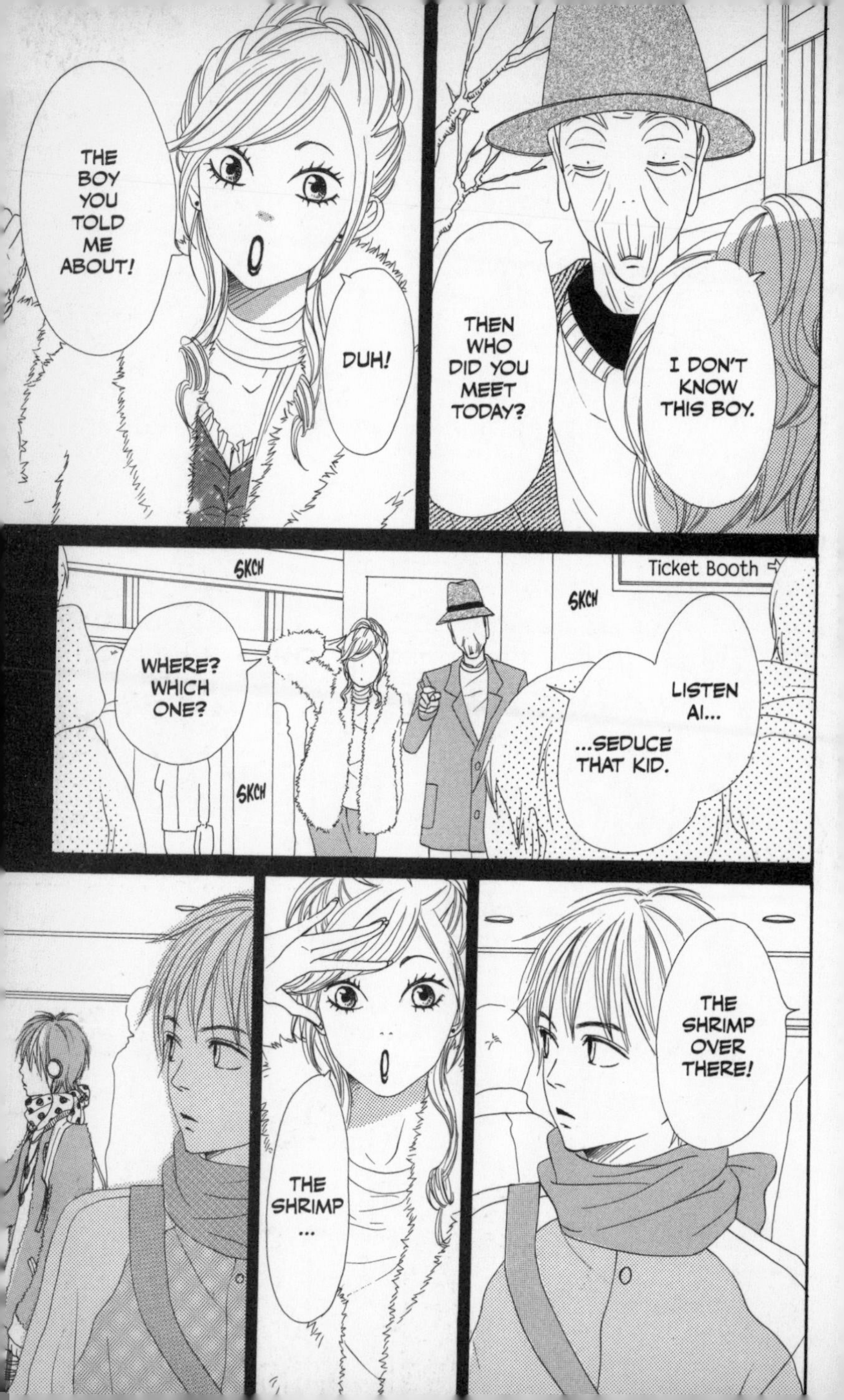
I DON'T KNOW THIS BOY.
THEN WHO DID YOU MEET TODAY?
DUH!
THE BOY YOU TOLD ME ABOUT!
Ticket Booth
SKCH
LISTEN AI...
...SEDUCE THAT KID.
SKCH
WHERE? WHICH ONE?
SKCH
THE SHRIMP OVER THERE!
THE SHRIMP ...

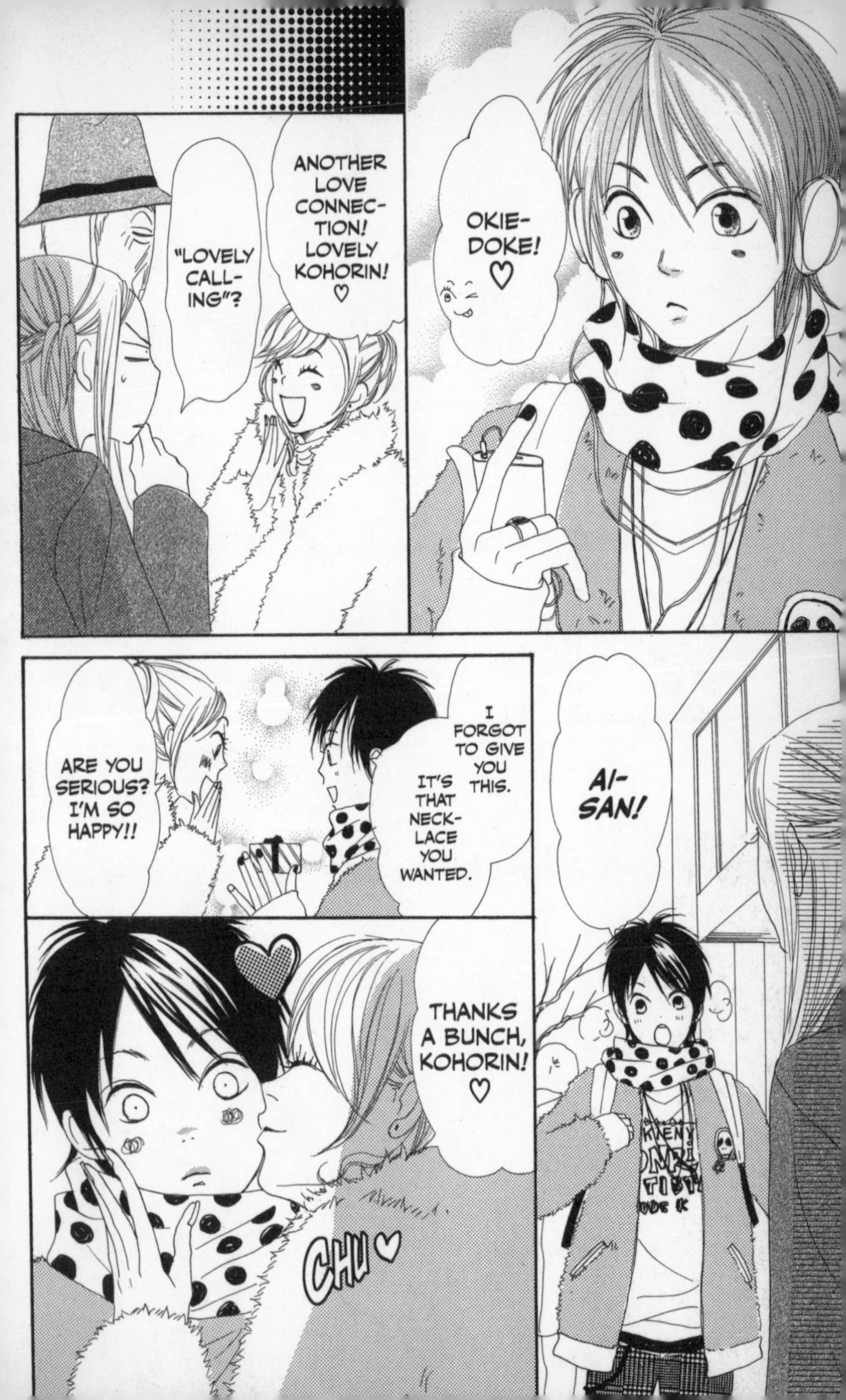
OKIE-DOKE! ♡
ANOTHER LOVE CONNECTION! LOVELY KOHORIN! ♡
"LOVELY CALLING"?
AI-SAN!
I FORGOT TO GIVE YOU THIS.
IT'S THAT NECKLACE YOU WANTED.
ARE YOU SERIOUS? I'M SO HAPPY!!
THANKS A BUNCH, KOHORIN! ♡
CHU ♡

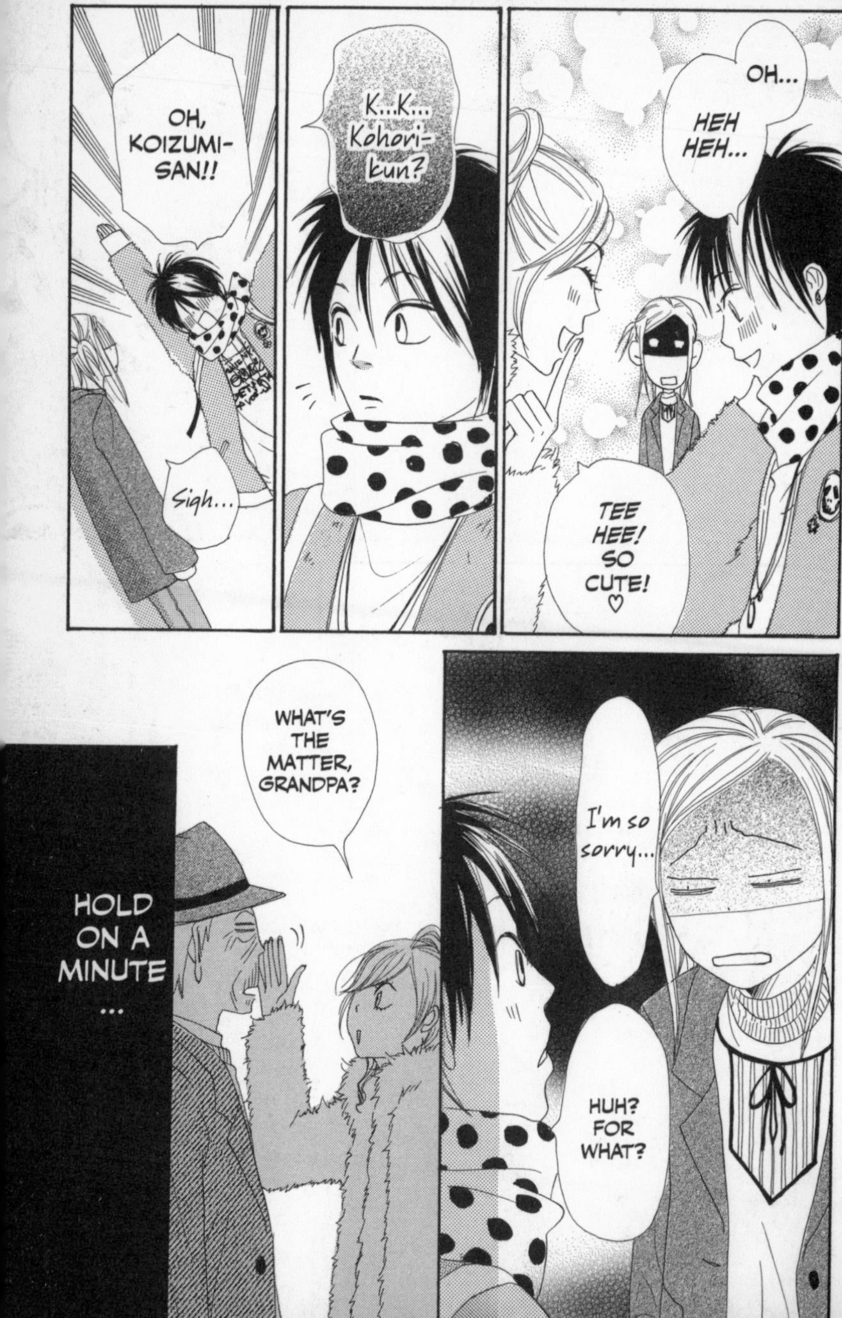
OH...
HEH HEH...
TEE HEE! SO CUTE! ♡
K...K... Kohori-kun?
OH, KOIZUMI-SAN!!
Sigh...
I'm so sorry...
HUH? FOR WHAT?
WHAT'S THE MATTER, GRANDPA?
HOLD ON A MINUTE ...

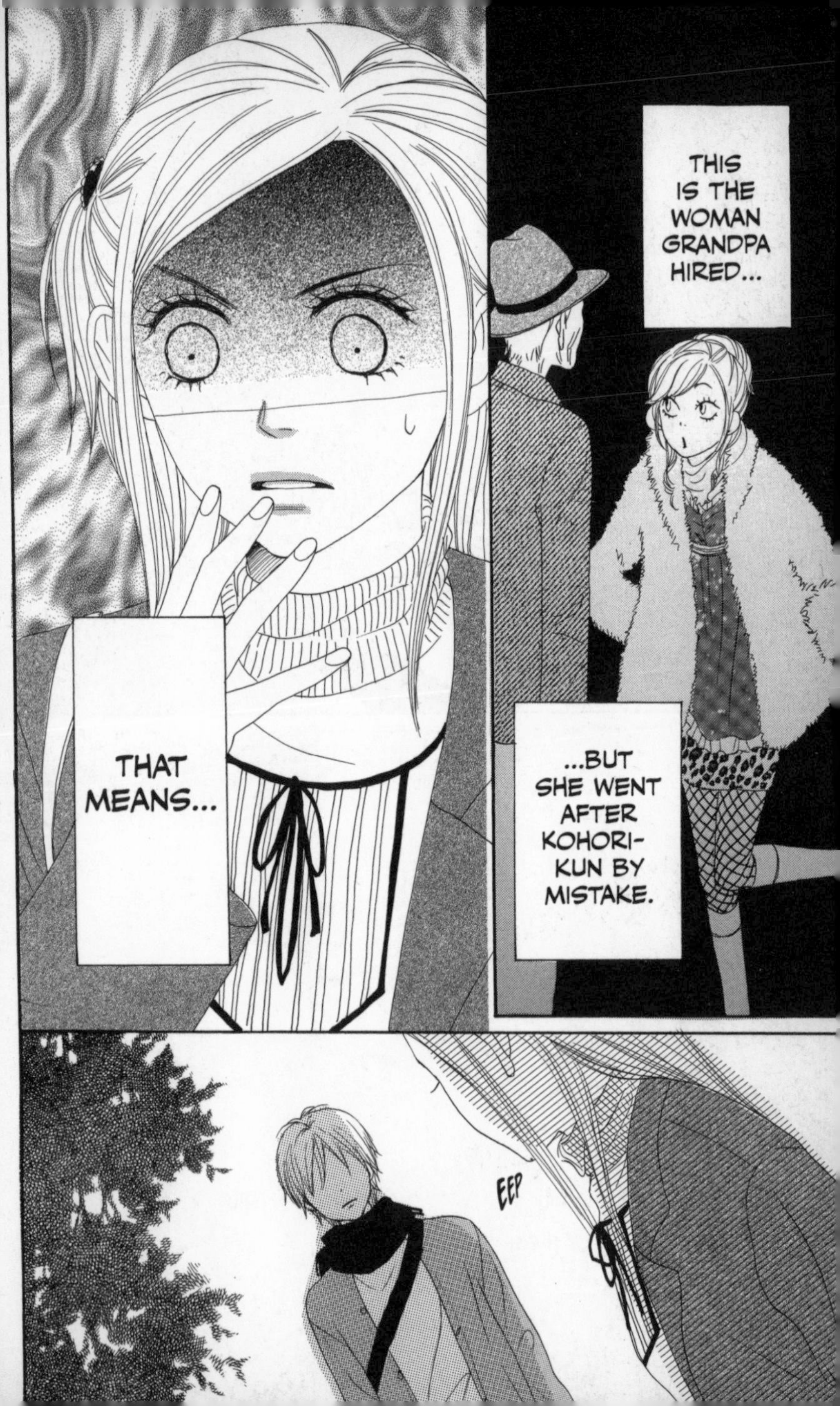
THIS IS THE WOMAN GRANDPA HIRED...
...BUT SHE WENT AFTER KOHORI-KUN BY MISTAKE.
THAT MEANS...
EEP

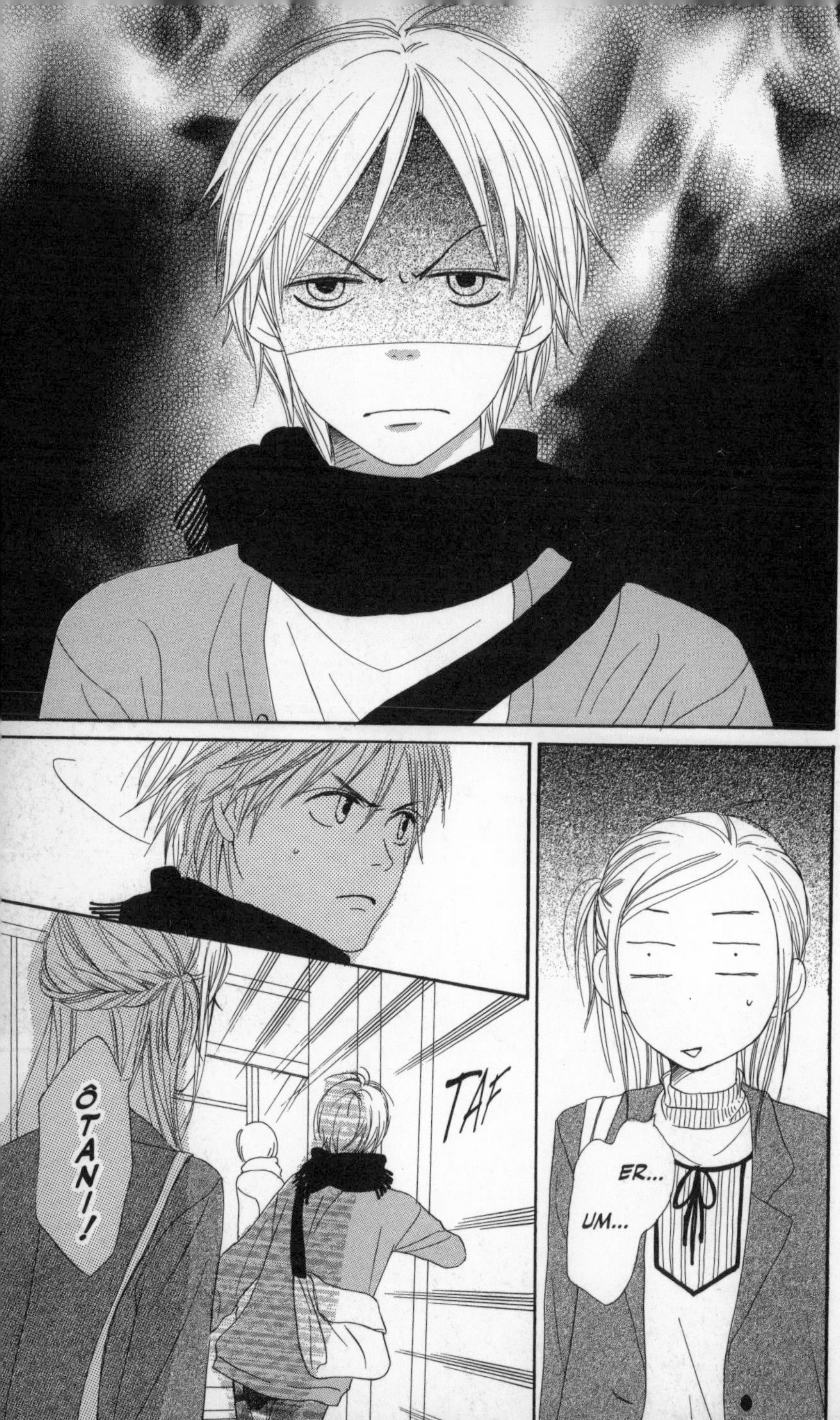
ER...
UM...
TAF
ÔTANI!

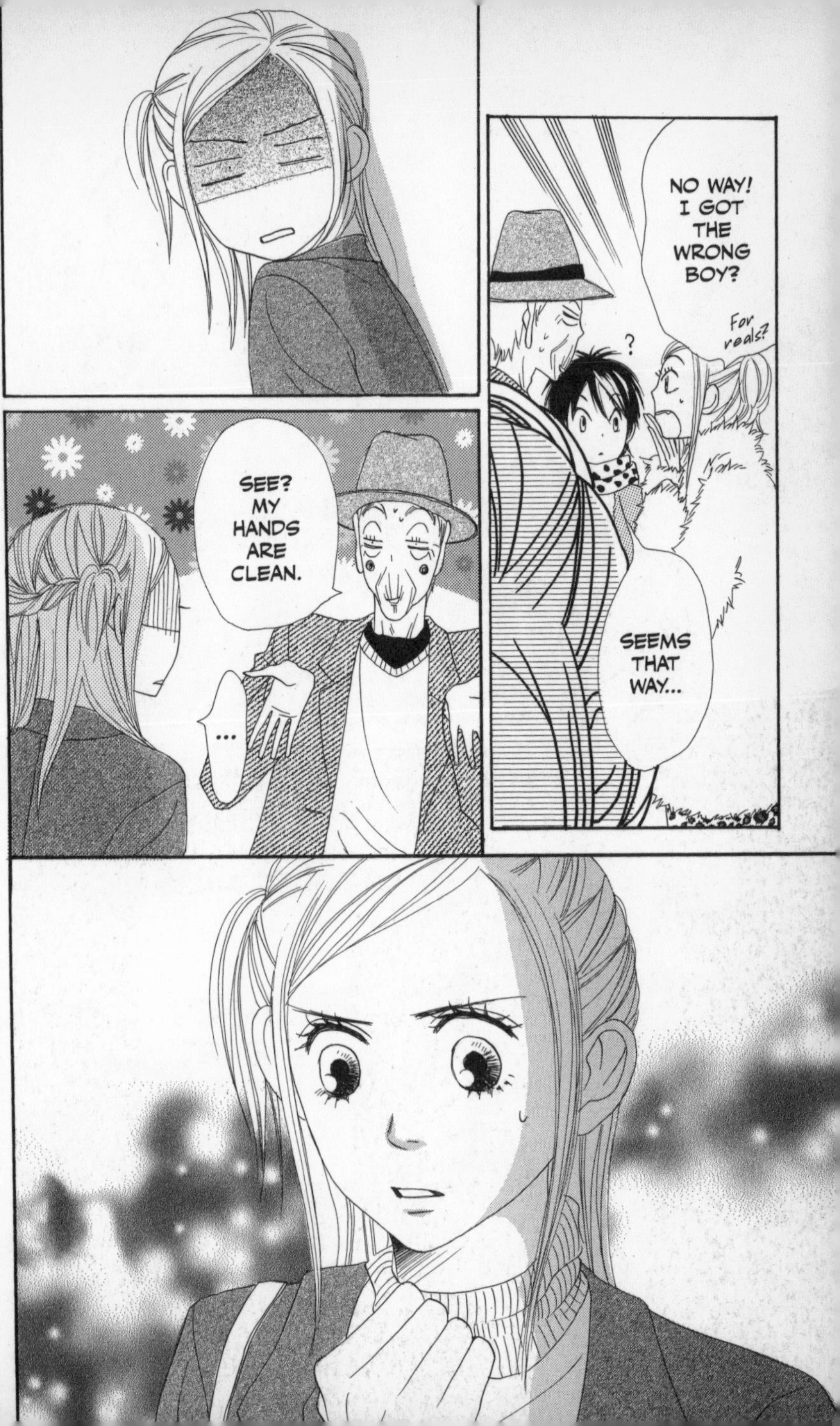
NO WAY! I GOT THE WRONG BOY?
For reals?
?
SEEMS THAT WAY...
SEE? MY HANDS ARE CLEAN.
...

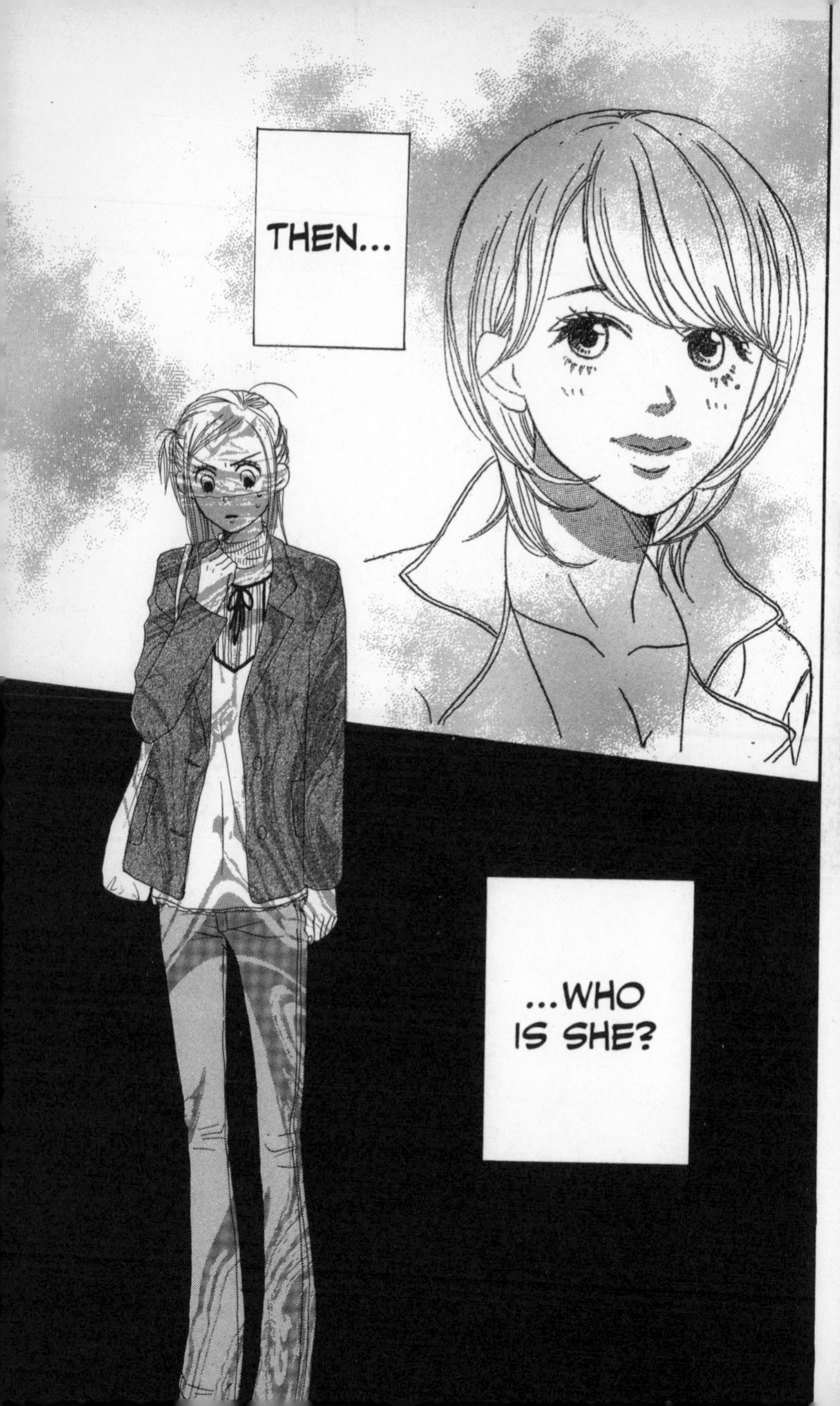
THEN...
...WHO IS SHE?

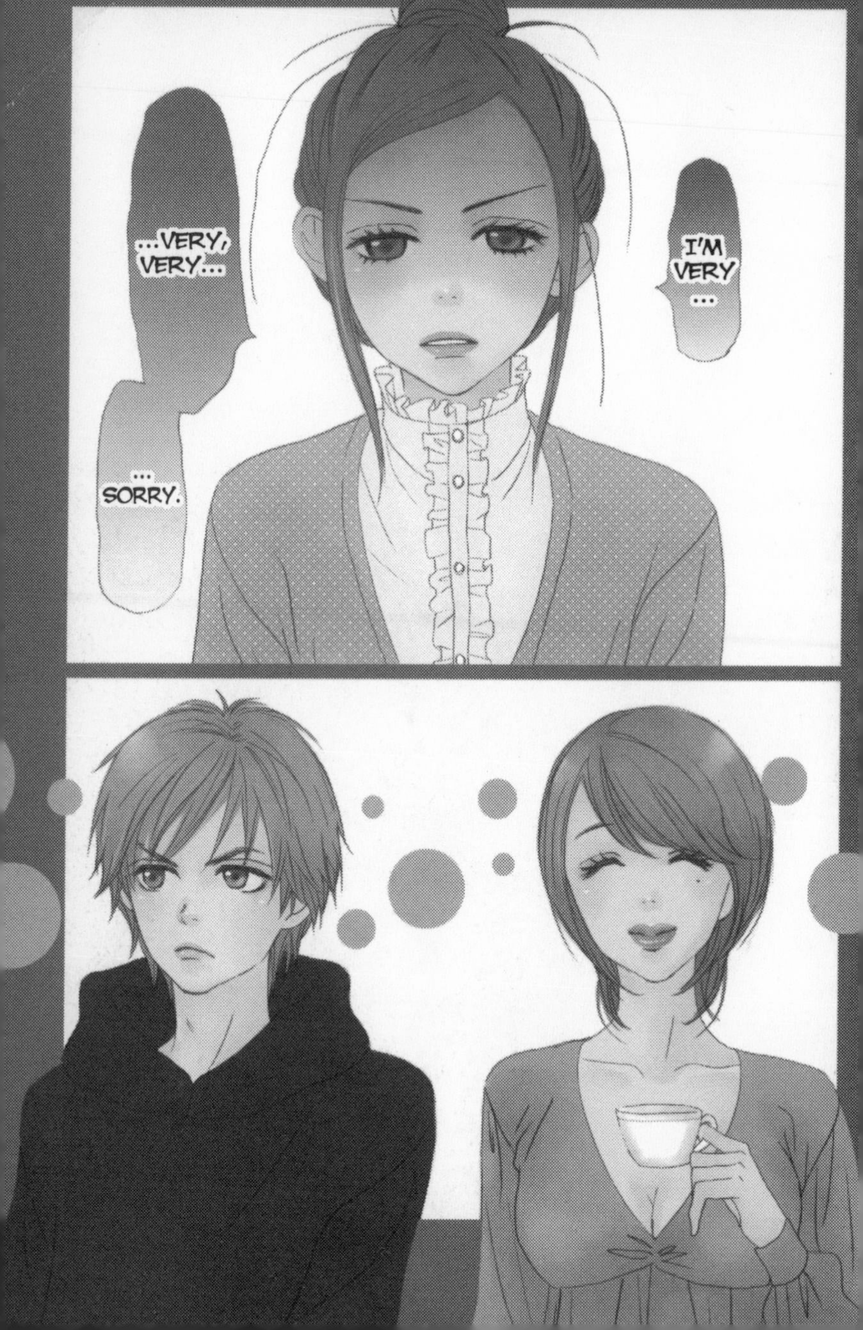
I'M VERY ...
...VERY, VERY...
... SORRY.

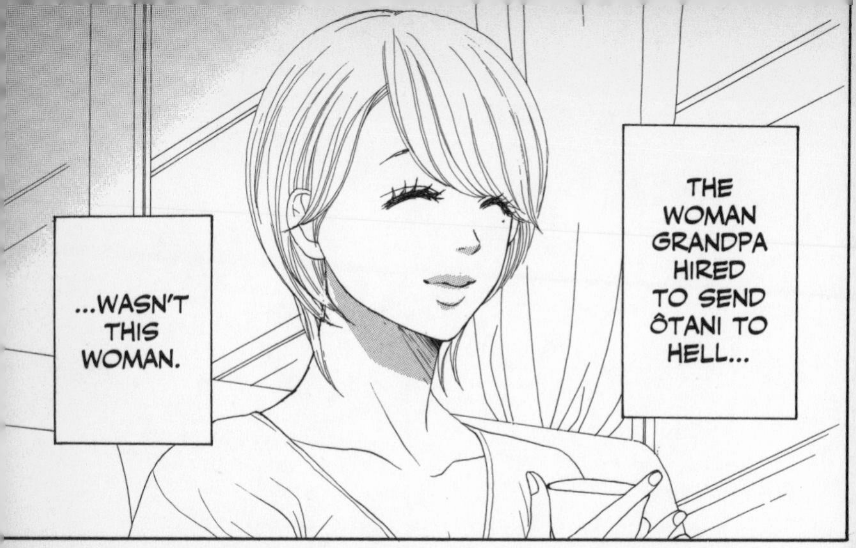
THE WOMAN GRANDPA HIRED TO SEND ŌTANI TO HELL...
...WASN'T THIS WOMAN.
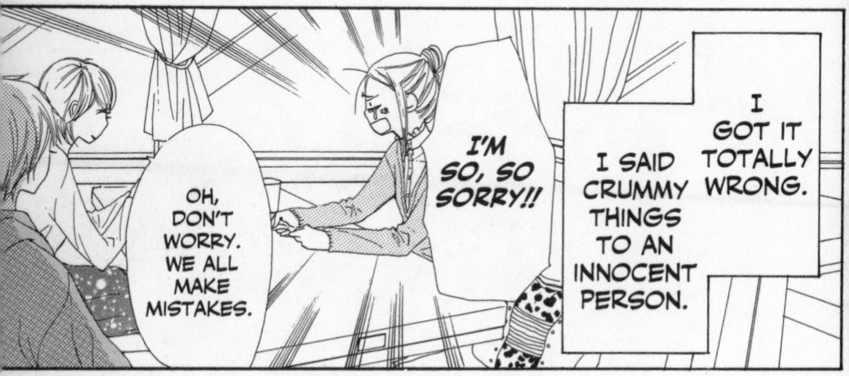
I GOT IT TOTALLY WRONG.
I SAID CRUMMY THINGS TO AN INNOCENT PERSON.
I'M SO, SO SORRY!!
OH, DON'T WORRY. WE ALL MAKE MISTAKES.

CHAPTER 53

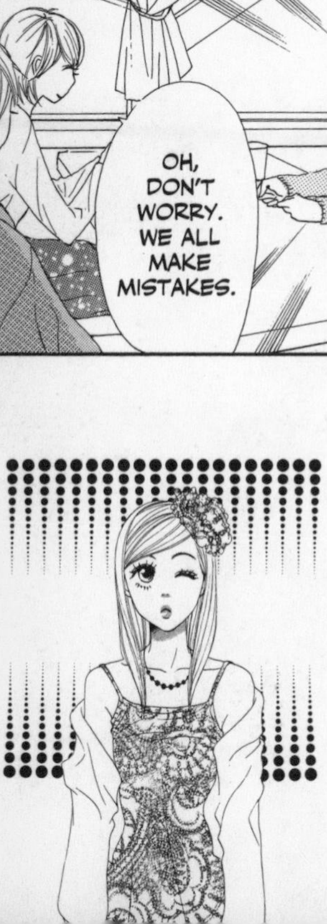

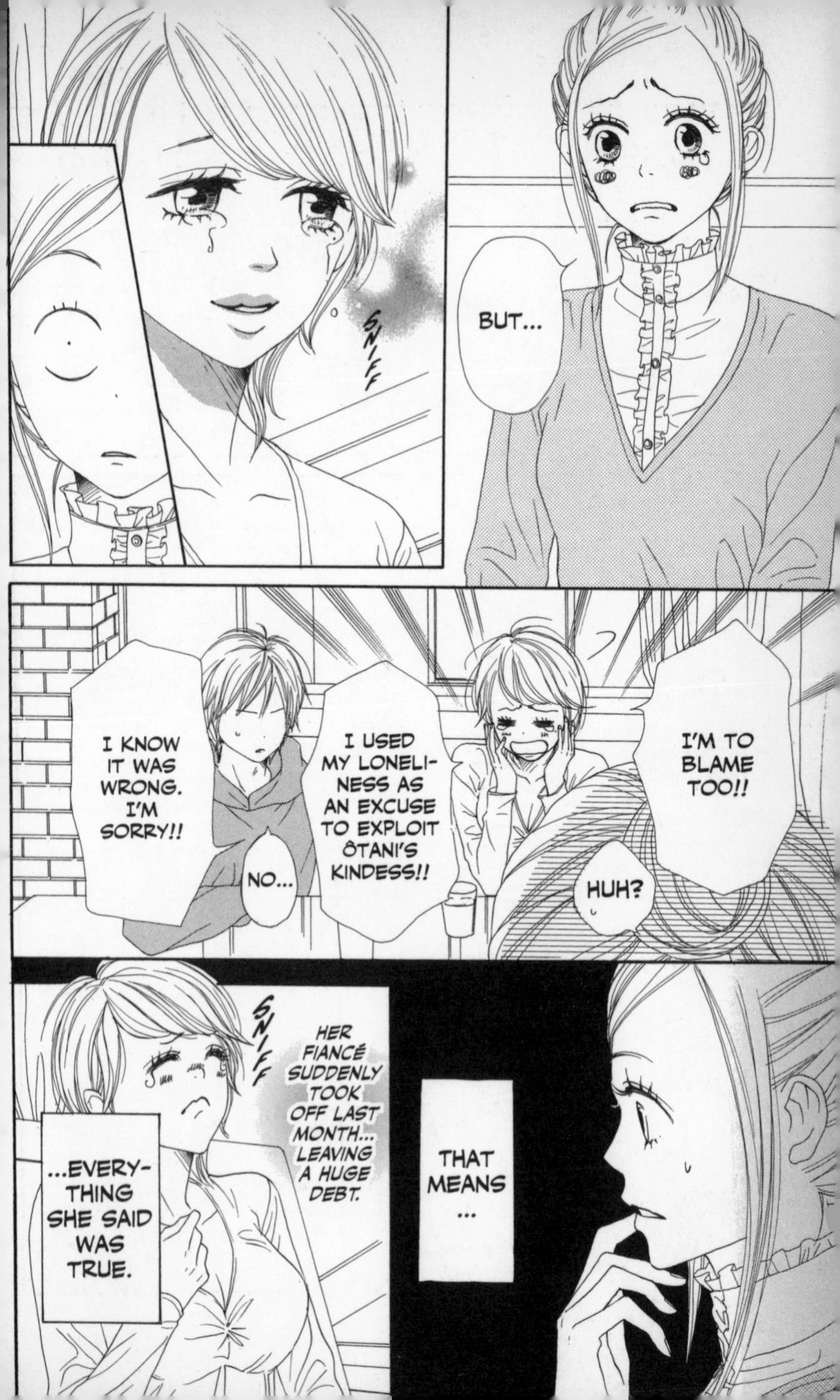

BUT...
SNIFF
I'M TO BLAME TOO!!
HUH?
I USED MY LONELINESS AS AN EXCUSE TO EXPLOIT ŌTANI'S KINDESS!!
NO...
I KNOW IT WAS WRONG. I'M SORRY!!
THAT MEANS ...
SNIFF
HER FIANCÉ SUDDENLY TOOK OFF LAST MONTH... LEAVING A HUGE DEBT.
...EVERYTHING SHE SAID WAS TRUE.

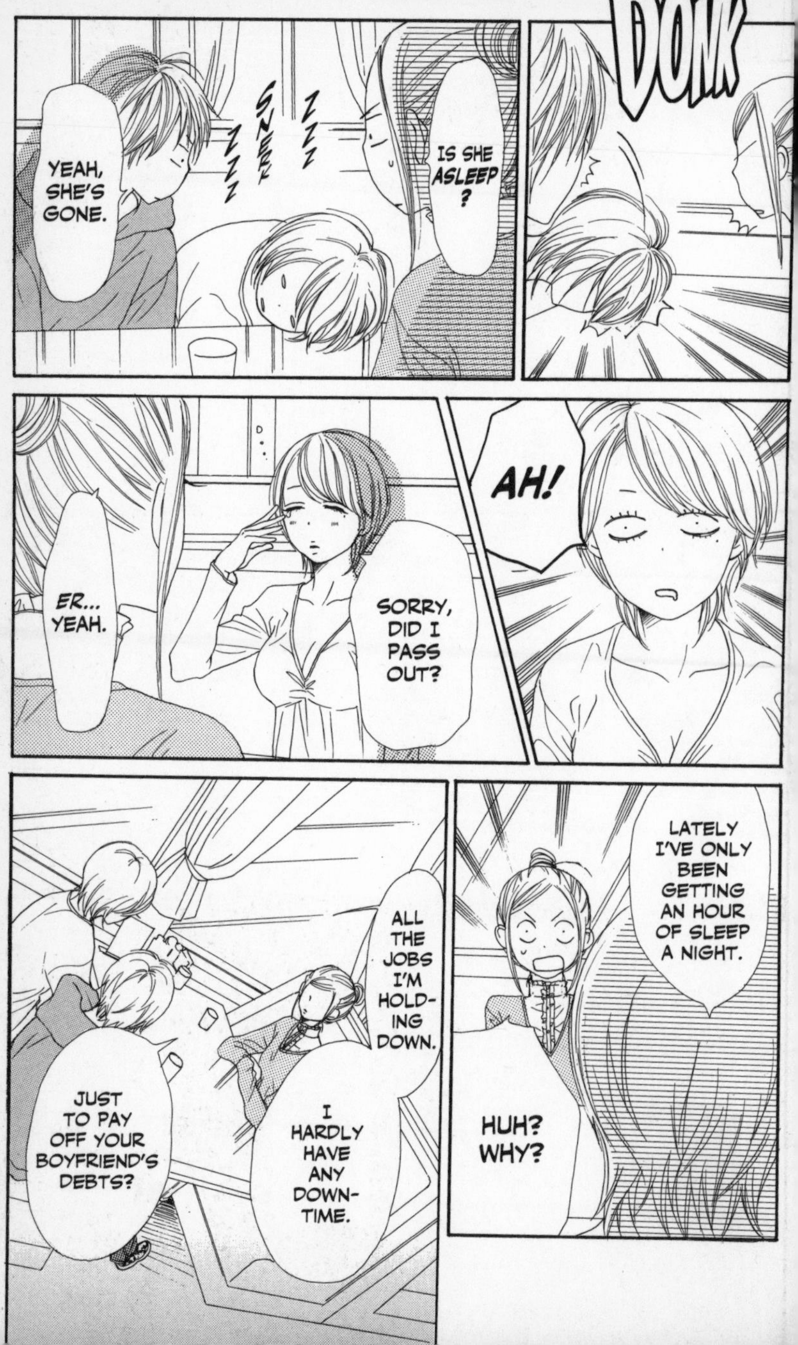
DONK
IS SHE ASLEEP?
ZZZ
SNERK
ZZZ
YEAH, SHE'S GONE.
AH!
SORRY, DID I PASS OUT?
ER... YEAH.
LATELY I'VE ONLY BEEN GETTING AN HOUR OF SLEEP A NIGHT.
HUH? WHY?
ALL THE JOBS I'M HOLDING DOWN.
I HARDLY HAVE ANY DOWNTIME.
JUST TO PAY OFF YOUR BOYFRIEND'S DEBTS?

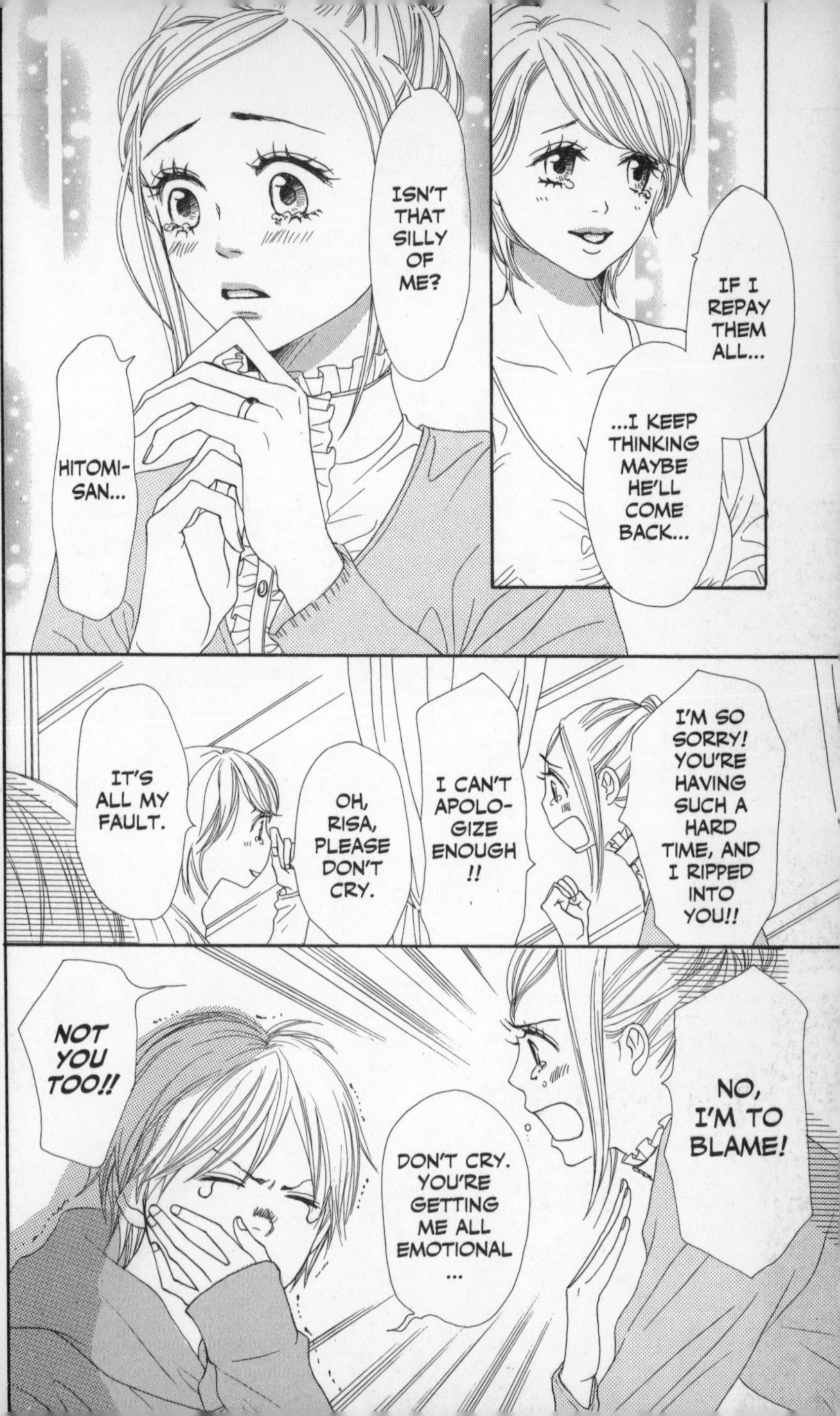
IF I REPAY THEM ALL...
...I KEEP THINKING MAYBE HE'LL COME BACK...
ISN'T THAT SILLY OF ME?
HITOMI-SAN...
I'M SO SORRY! YOU'RE HAVING SUCH A HARD TIME, AND I RIPPED INTO YOU!!
I CAN'T APOLOGIZE ENOUGH!!
OH, RISA, PLEASE DON'T CRY.
IT'S ALL MY FAULT.
NO, I'M TO BLAME!
DON'T CRY. YOU'RE GETTING ME ALL EMOTIONAL...
NOT YOU TOO!!

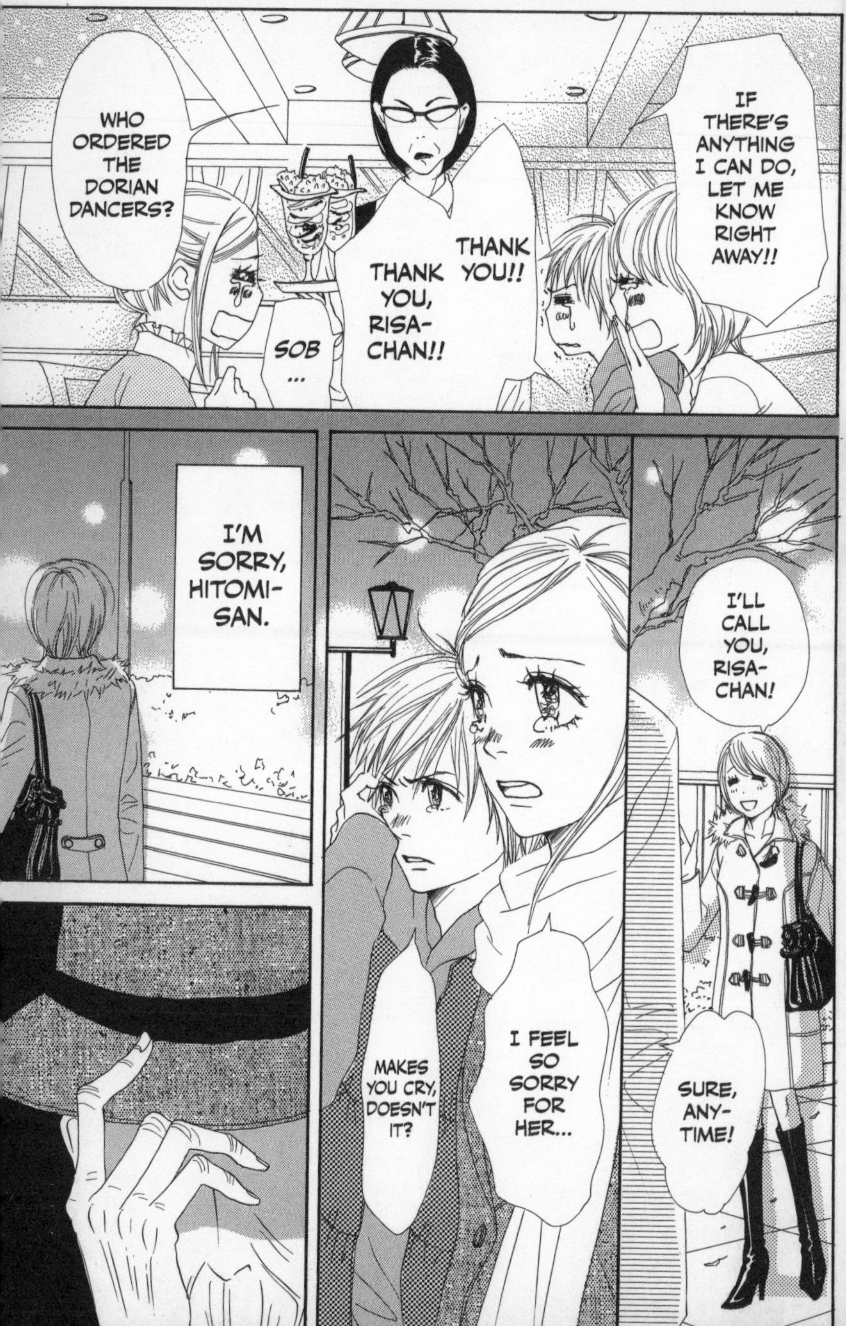
IF THERE'S ANYTHING I CAN DO, LET ME KNOW RIGHT AWAY!!
THANK YOU!!
THANK YOU, RISA-CHAN!!
SOB ...
WHO ORDERED THE DORIAN DANCERS?
I'LL CALL YOU, RISA-CHAN!
SURE, ANY-TIME!
I FEEL SO SORRY FOR HER...
MAKES YOU CRY, DOESN'T IT?
I'M SORRY, HITOMI-SAN.

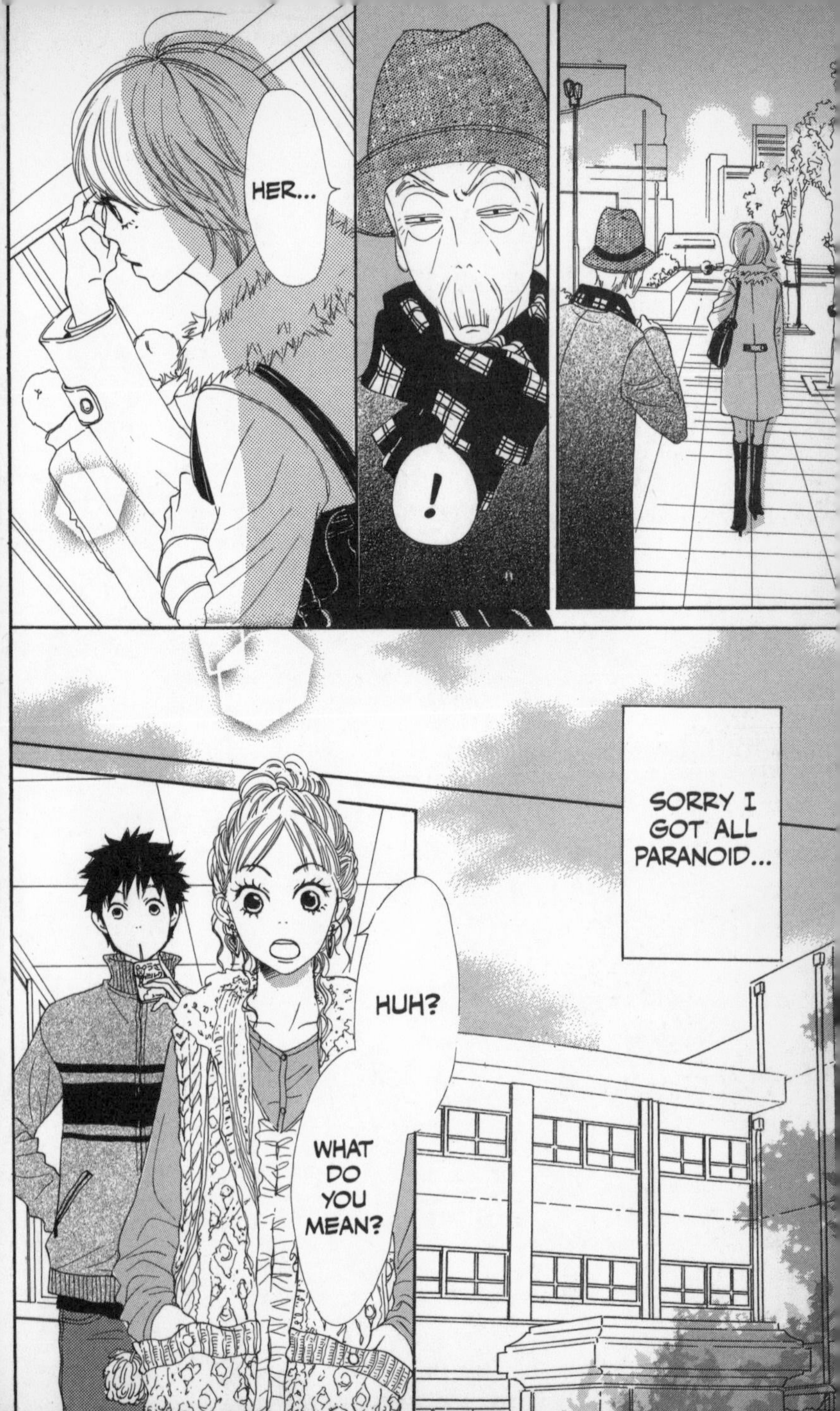
!
HER...
SORRY I GOT ALL PARANOID...
HUH?
WHAT DO YOU MEAN?

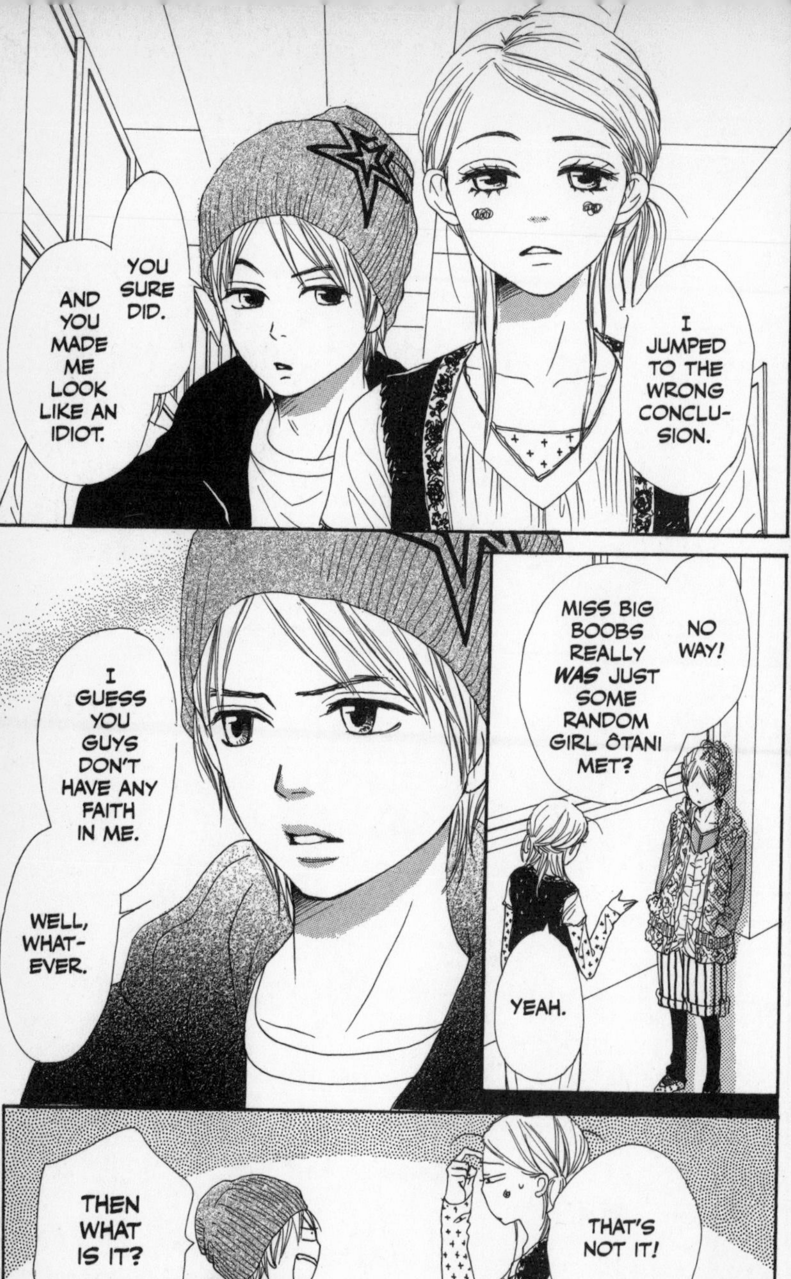
I JUMPED TO THE WRONG CONCLUSION.
YOU SURE DID.
AND YOU MADE ME LOOK LIKE AN IDIOT.
NO WAY!
MISS BIG BOOBS REALLY *WAS* JUST SOME RANDOM GIRL ÔTANI MET?
YEAH.
I GUESS YOU GUYS DON'T HAVE ANY FAITH IN ME.
WELL, WHATEVER.
THAT'S NOT IT!
THEN WHAT IS IT?

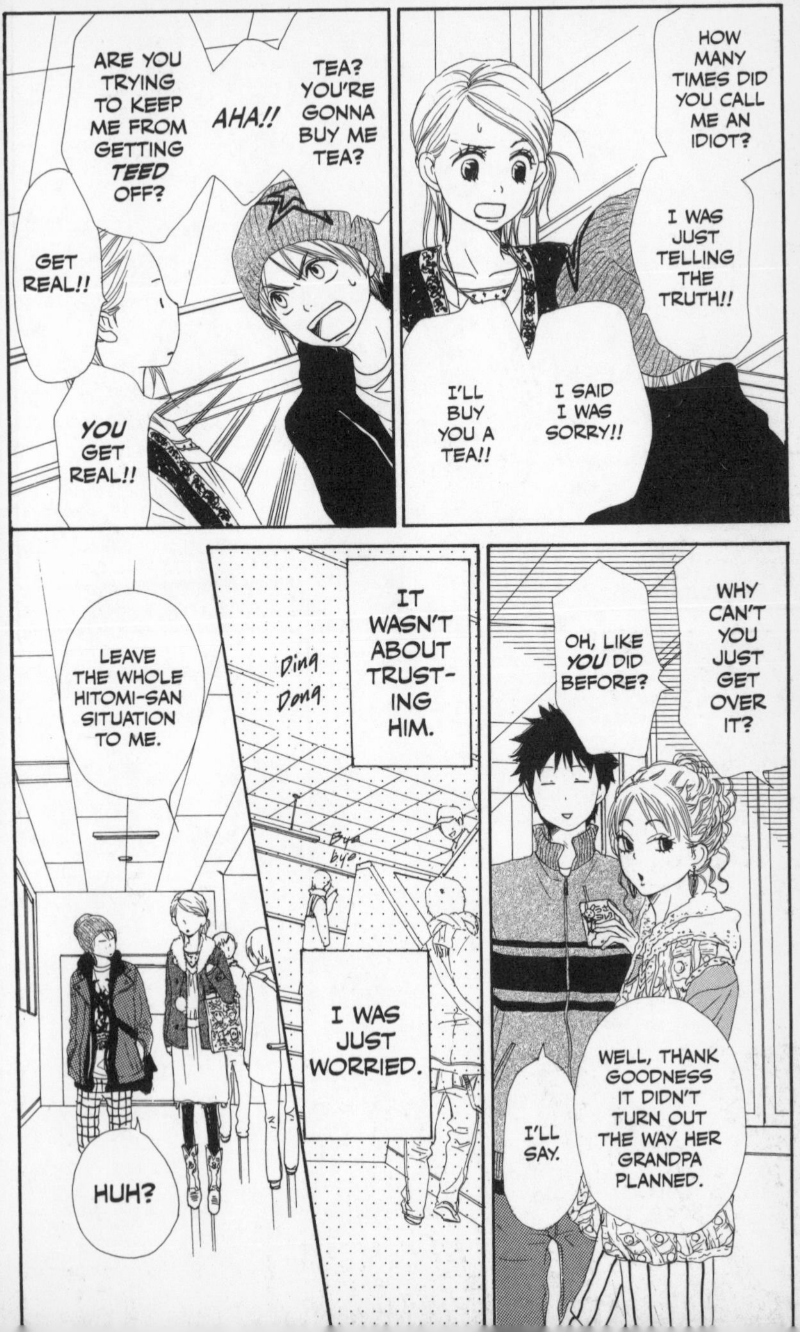
HOW MANY TIMES DID YOU CALL ME AN IDIOT?
I WAS JUST TELLING THE TRUTH!!
I SAID I WAS SORRY!!
I'LL BUY YOU A TEA!!
TEA? YOU'RE GONNA BUY ME TEA?
AHA!!
ARE YOU TRYING TO KEEP ME FROM GETTING *TEED* OFF?
GET REAL!!
YOU GET REAL!!
WHY CAN'T YOU JUST GET OVER IT?
OH, LIKE *YOU* DID BEFORE?
WELL, THANK GOODNESS IT DIDN'T TURN OUT THE WAY HER GRANDPA PLANNED.
I'LL SAY.
IT WASN'T ABOUT TRUSTING HIM.
Ding Dong
Bye bye
I WAS JUST WORRIED.
LEAVE THE WHOLE HITOMI-SAN SITUATION TO ME.
HUH?

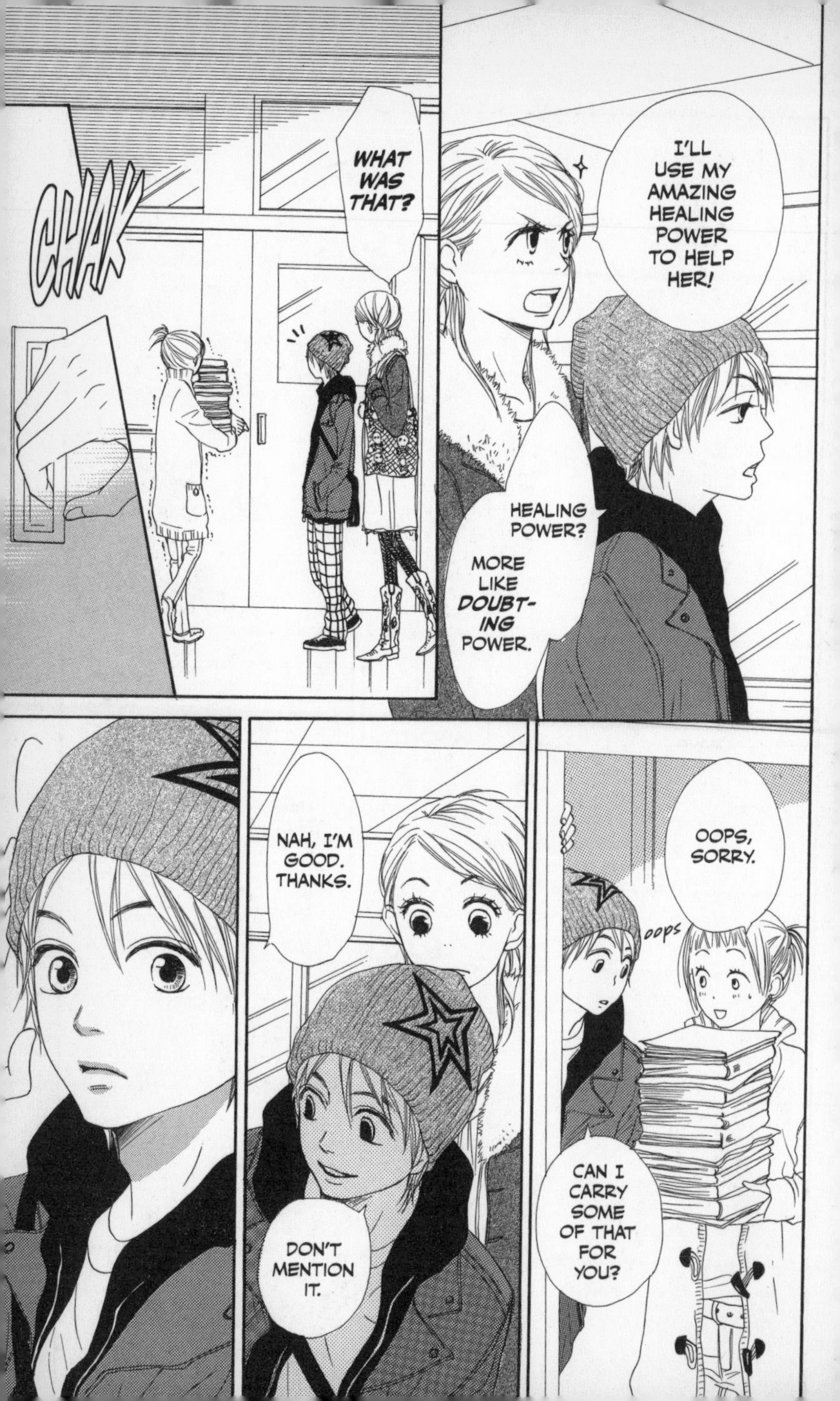
I'LL USE MY AMAZING HEALING POWER TO HELP HER!
HEALING POWER?
MORE LIKE *DOUBTING* POWER.
WHAT WAS THAT?
CHAK
OOPS, SORRY.
oops
CAN I CARRY SOME OF THAT FOR YOU?
NAH, I'M GOOD. THANKS.
DON'T MENTION IT.

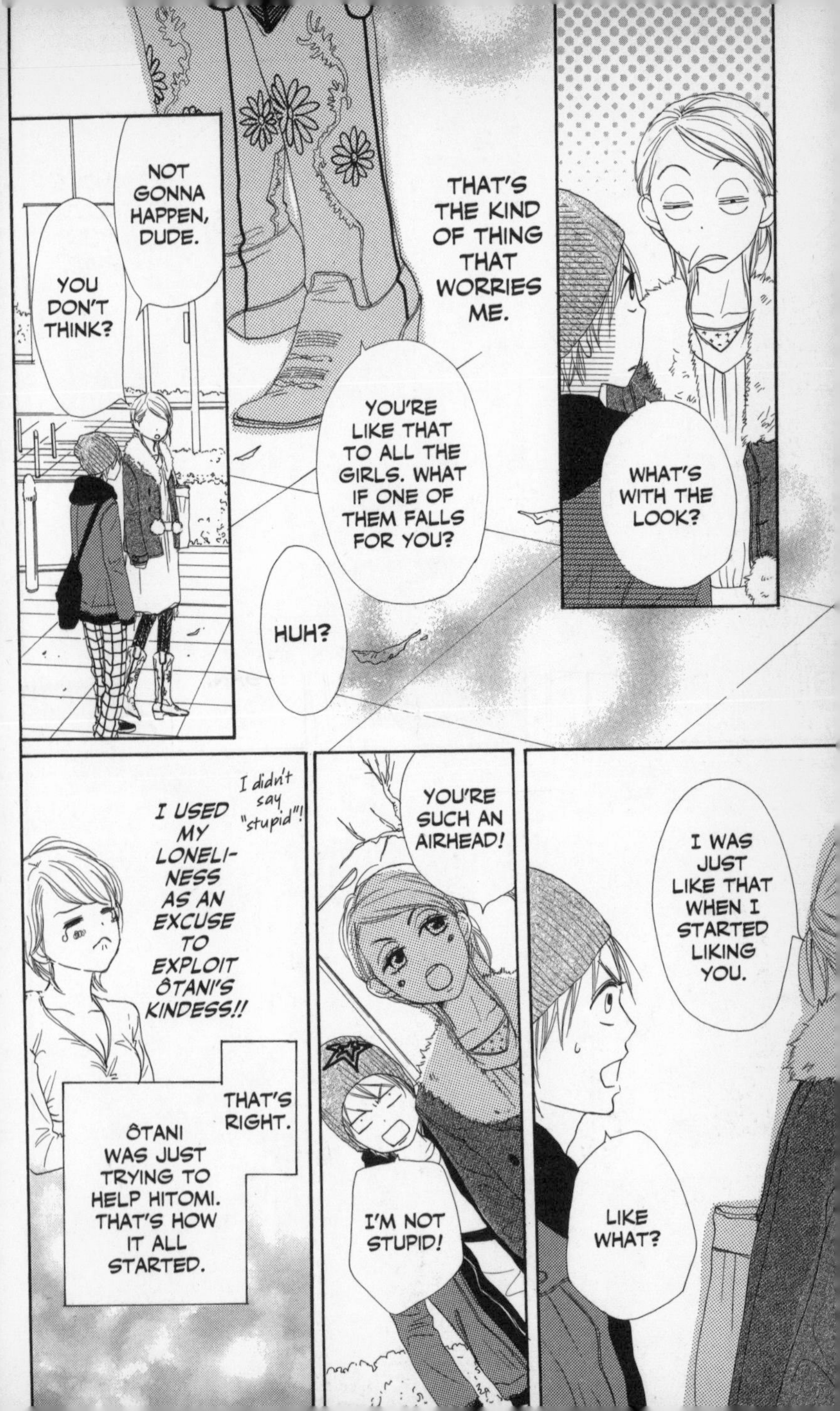
WHAT'S WITH THE LOOK?
THAT'S THE KIND OF THING THAT WORRIES ME.
YOU'RE LIKE THAT TO ALL THE GIRLS. WHAT IF ONE OF THEM FALLS FOR YOU?
HUH?
NOT GONNA HAPPEN, DUDE.
YOU DON'T THINK?
I WAS JUST LIKE THAT WHEN I STARTED LIKING YOU.
LIKE WHAT?
YOU'RE SUCH AN AIRHEAD!
I'M NOT STUPID!
I didn't say "stupid"!
I USED MY LONELI-NESS AS AN EXCUSE TO EXPLOIT ŌTANI'S KINDESS!!
THAT'S RIGHT.
ŌTANI WAS JUST TRYING TO HELP HITOMI. THAT'S HOW IT ALL STARTED.

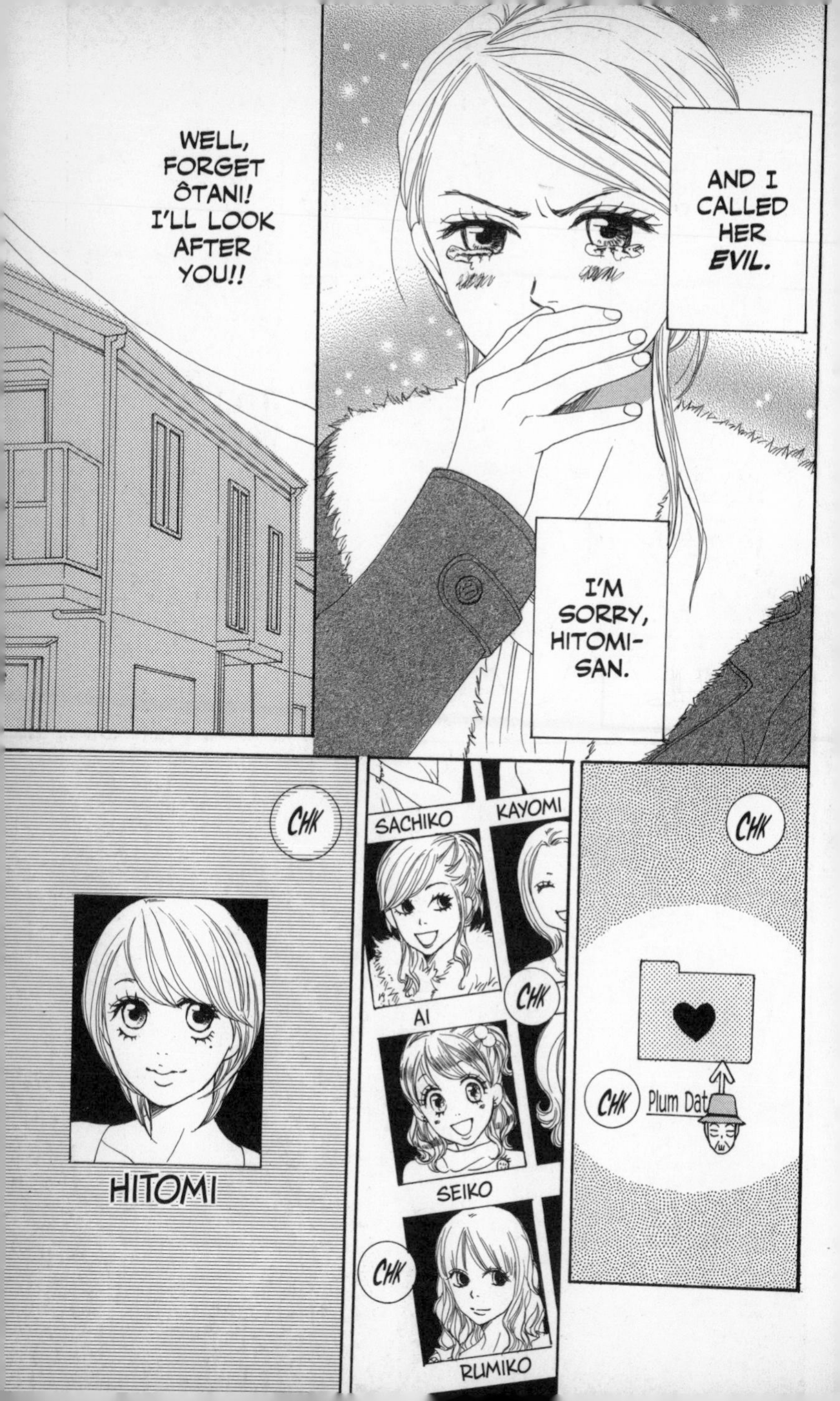
AND I CALLED HER EVIL.
I'M SORRY, HITOMI-SAN.
WELL, FORGET ÔTANI! I'LL LOOK AFTER YOU!!
CHK
CHK
Plum Dat
CHK
KAYOMI
SACHIKO
CHK
AI
SEIKO
CHK
RUMIKO
CHK
HITOMI

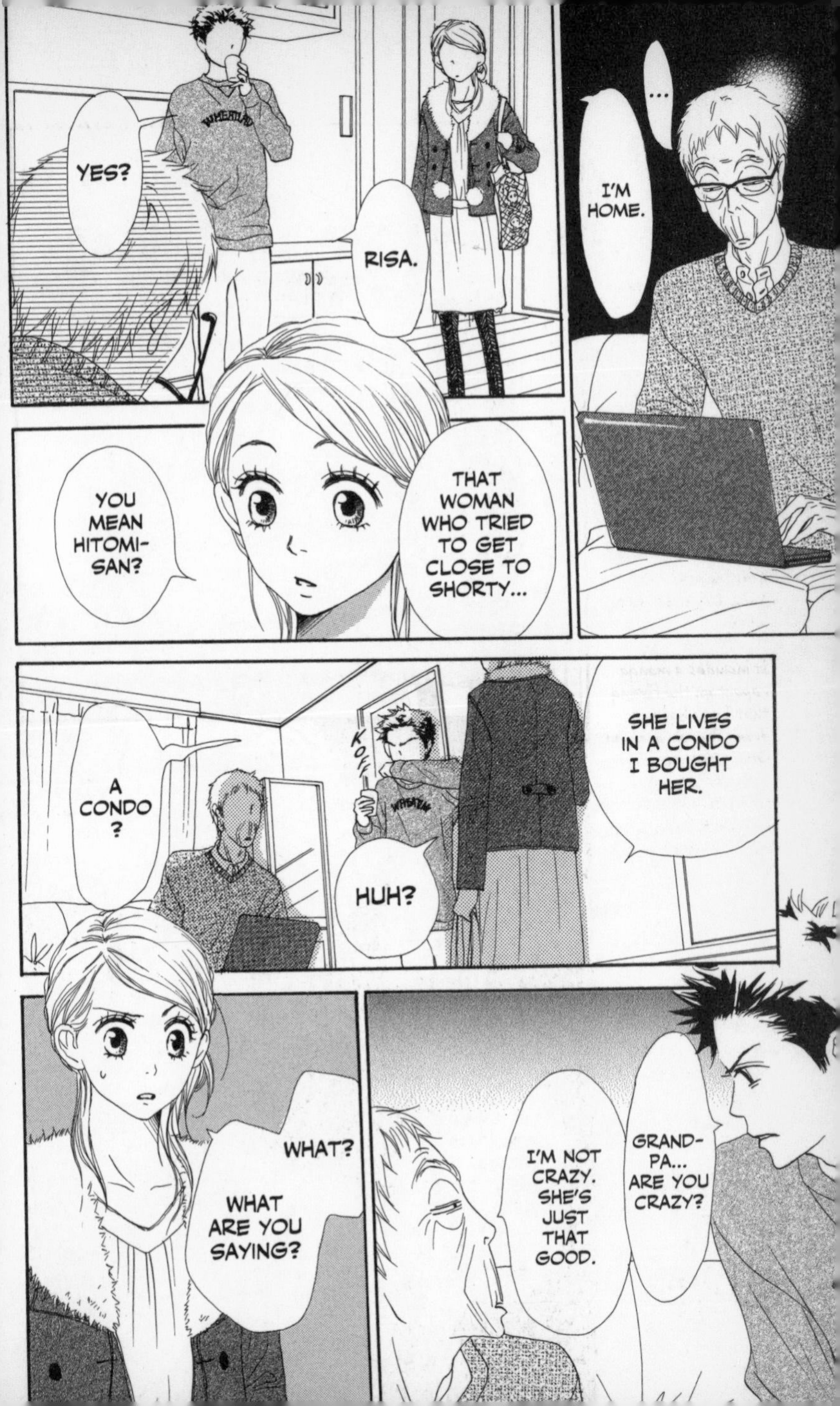
...
I'M HOME.
RISA.
YES?
THAT WOMAN WHO TRIED TO GET CLOSE TO SHORTY...
YOU MEAN HITOMI-SAN?
SHE LIVES IN A CONDO I BOUGHT HER.
KOFF
HUH?
A CONDO?
GRAND-PA... ARE YOU CRAZY?
I'M NOT CRAZY. SHE'S JUST THAT GOOD.
WHAT?
WHAT ARE YOU SAYING?

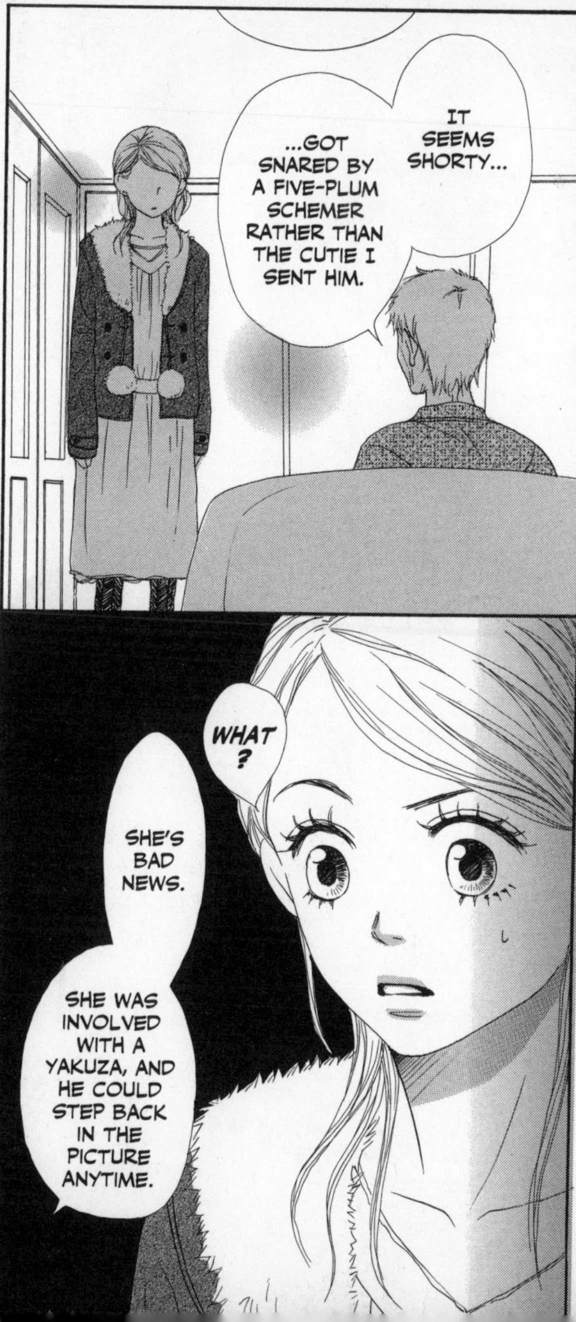
IT SEEMS SHORTY...
...GOT SNARED BY A FIVE-PLUM SCHEMER RATHER THAN THE CUTIE I SENT HIM.
WHAT?
SHE'S BAD NEWS.
SHE WAS INVOLVED WITH A YAKUZA, AND HE COULD STEP BACK IN THE PICTURE ANYTIME.

②

Sorry! Sorry!

I'm sorry the manga has such sorry-looking people compared to the movie stars. Heh...Please don't hold it against me.

A lot of tie-in merchandise is coming out in conjunction with the opening of the movie. The "Making of Love★Com" book is really cute, so please take a look.

It includes a manga report on the filming that I was happy to draw. There's even an illustration gallery. I requested that they use more photos instead of my drawings, but I was overruled.

stretch

I mean, the photos are so much cuter than my drawings.

Kyu

Kyu

Run away!

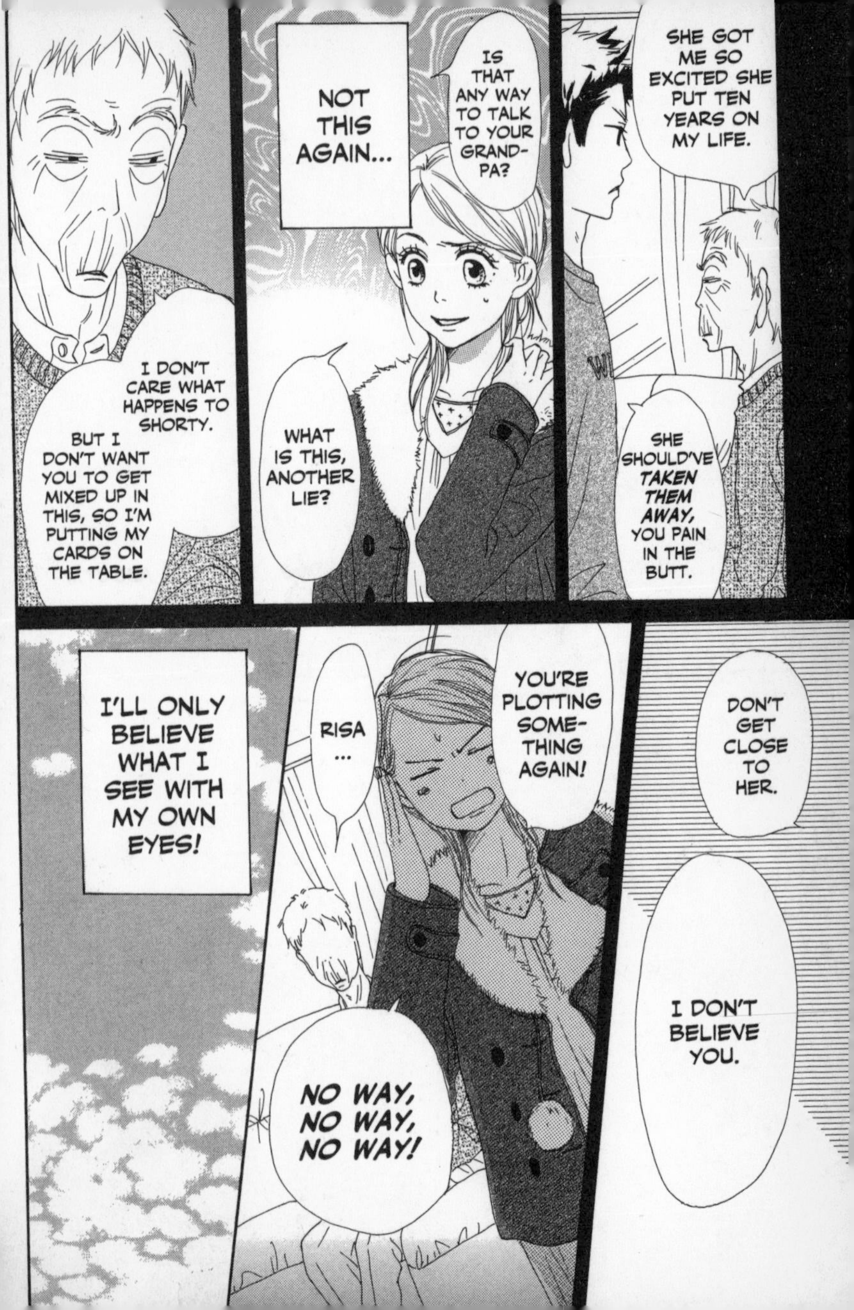
SHE GOT ME SO EXCITED SHE PUT TEN YEARS ON MY LIFE.
SHE SHOULD'VE *TAKEN THEM AWAY,* YOU PAIN IN THE BUTT.
IS THAT ANY WAY TO TALK TO YOUR GRAND-PA?
NOT THIS AGAIN...
WHAT IS THIS, ANOTHER LIE?
I DON'T CARE WHAT HAPPENS TO SHORTY.
BUT I DON'T WANT YOU TO GET MIXED UP IN THIS, SO I'M PUTTING MY CARDS ON THE TABLE.
DON'T GET CLOSE TO HER.
I DON'T BELIEVE YOU.
YOU'RE PLOTTING SOME-THING AGAIN!
RISA ...
NO WAY, NO WAY, NO WAY!
I'LL ONLY BELIEVE WHAT I SEE WITH MY OWN EYES!

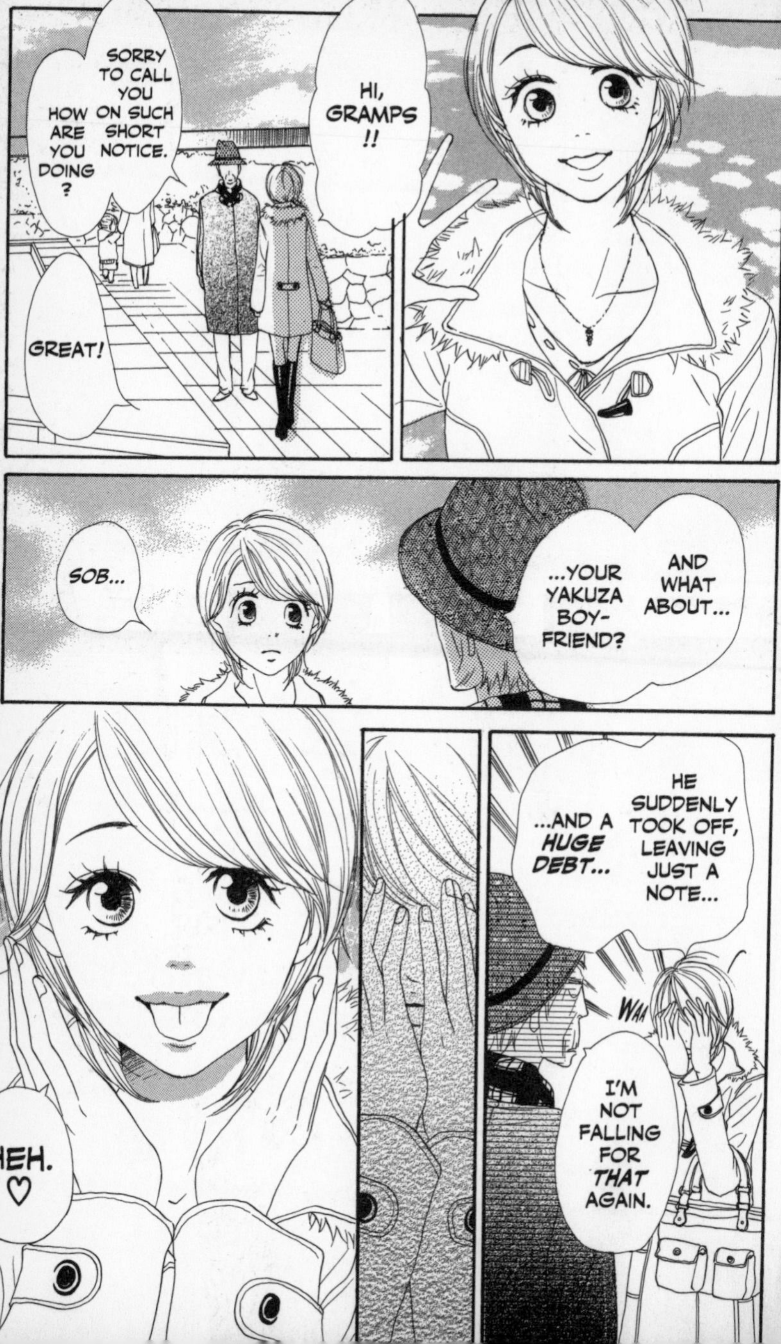
HI, GRAMPS!!
SORRY TO CALL YOU ON SUCH SHORT NOTICE.
HOW ARE YOU DOING?
GREAT!
AND WHAT ABOUT...
...YOUR YAKUZA BOYFRIEND?
SOB...
HE SUDDENLY TOOK OFF, LEAVING JUST A NOTE...
...AND A *HUGE DEBT*...
WAA
I'M NOT FALLING FOR *THAT* AGAIN.
HEH. ♡

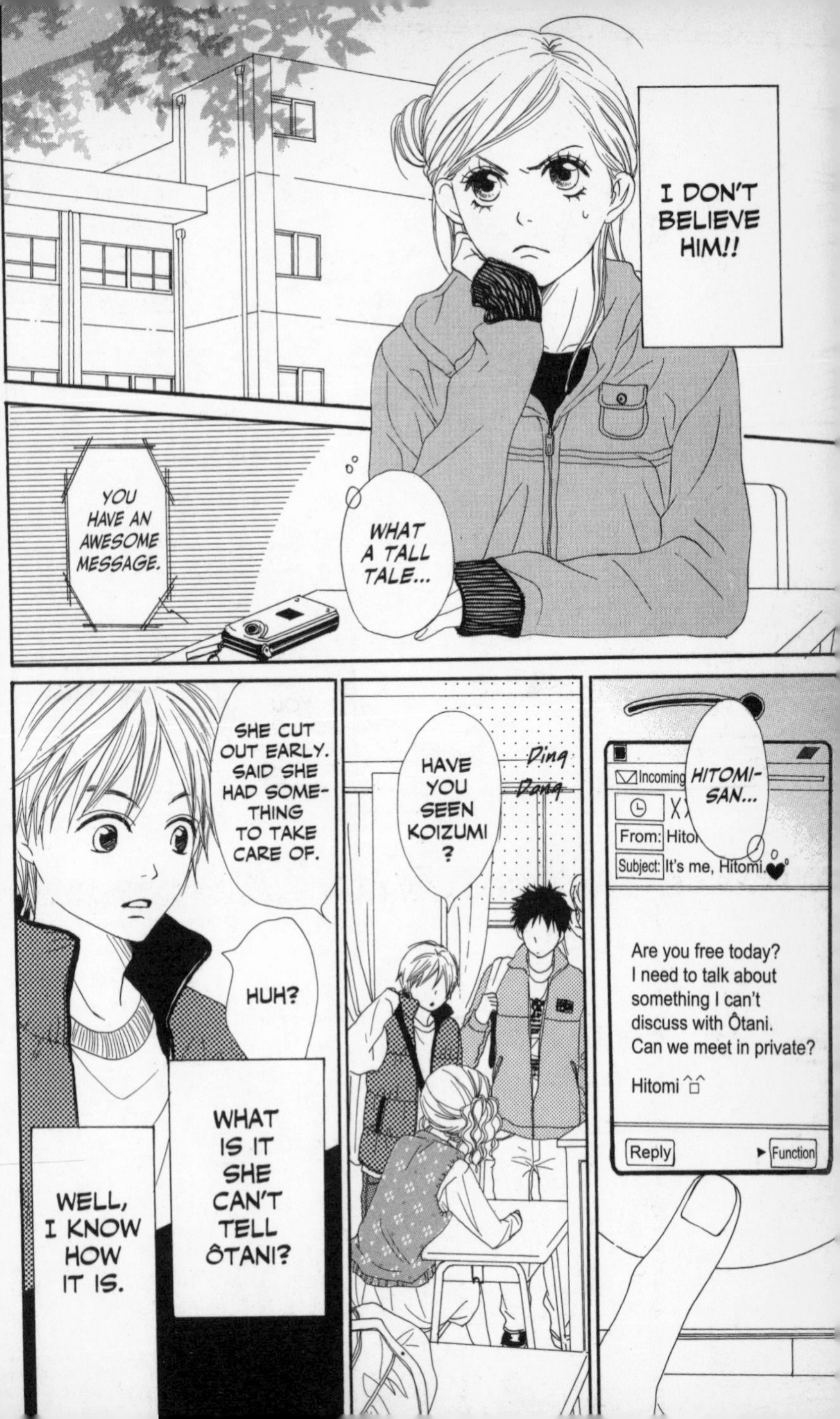
I DON'T BELIEVE HIM!!
WHAT A TALL TALE...
YOU HAVE AN AWESOME MESSAGE.
Incoming
From: Hitom
Subject: It's me, Hitomi.
Are you free today? I need to talk about something I can't discuss with Ôtani. Can we meet in private?
Hitomi
Reply
Function
HITOMI-SAN...
Ding Dong
HAVE YOU SEEN KOIZUMI?
SHE CUT OUT EARLY. SAID SHE HAD SOME-THING TO TAKE CARE OF.
HUH?
WHAT IS IT SHE CAN'T TELL ÔTANI?
WELL, I KNOW HOW IT IS.

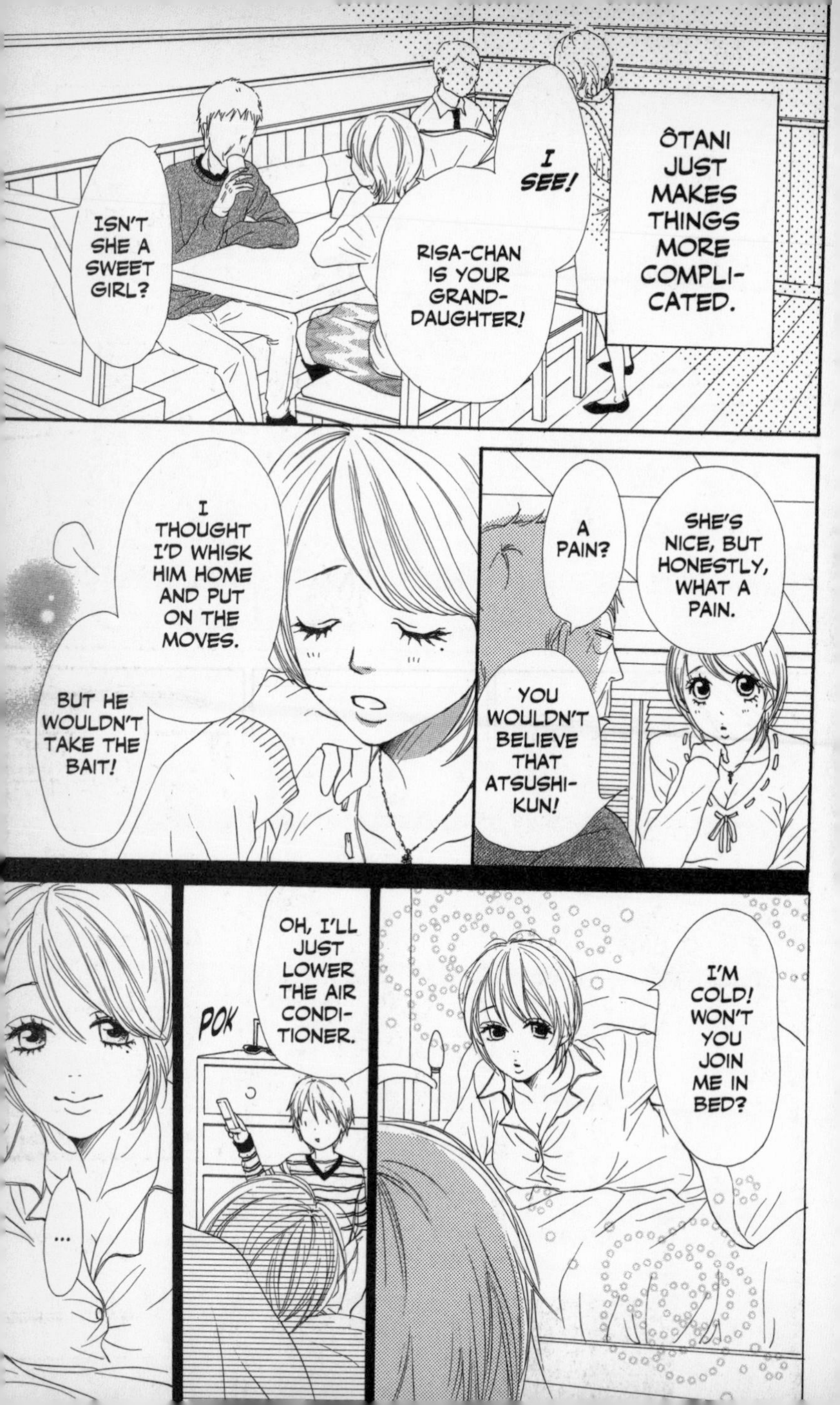
ÔTANI JUST MAKES THINGS MORE COMPLICATED.
I SEE!
RISA-CHAN IS YOUR GRANDDAUGHTER!
ISN'T SHE A SWEET GIRL?
SHE'S NICE, BUT HONESTLY, WHAT A PAIN.
A PAIN?
YOU WOULDN'T BELIEVE THAT ATSUSHI-KUN!
I THOUGHT I'D WHISK HIM HOME AND PUT ON THE MOVES.
BUT HE WOULDN'T TAKE THE BAIT!
I'M COLD! WON'T YOU JOIN ME IN BED?
POK
OH, I'LL JUST LOWER THE AIR CONDITIONER.
...

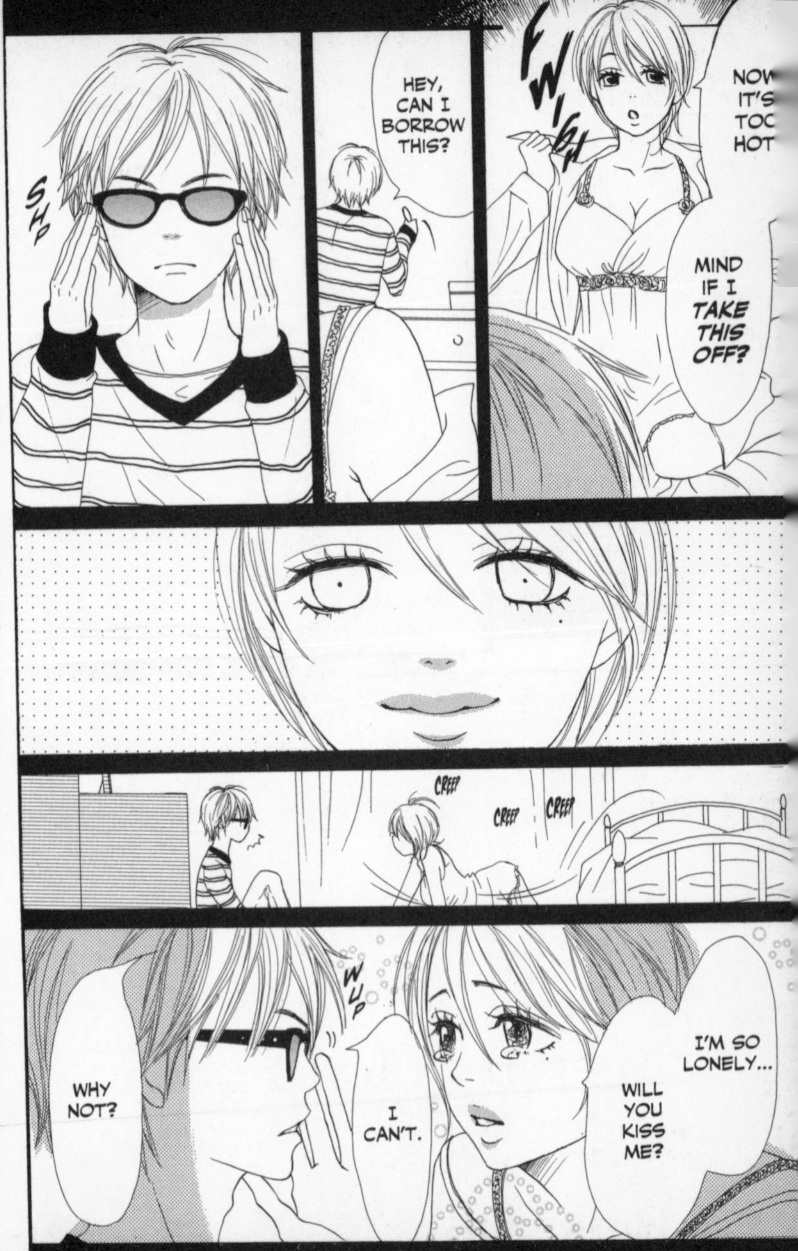
FWISH
NOW IT'S TOO HOT
MIND IF I TAKE THIS OFF?
HEY, CAN I BORROW THIS?
SHP
CREEP
CREEP
CREEP
I'M SO LONELY...
WILL YOU KISS ME?
WUP
I CAN'T.
WHY NOT?

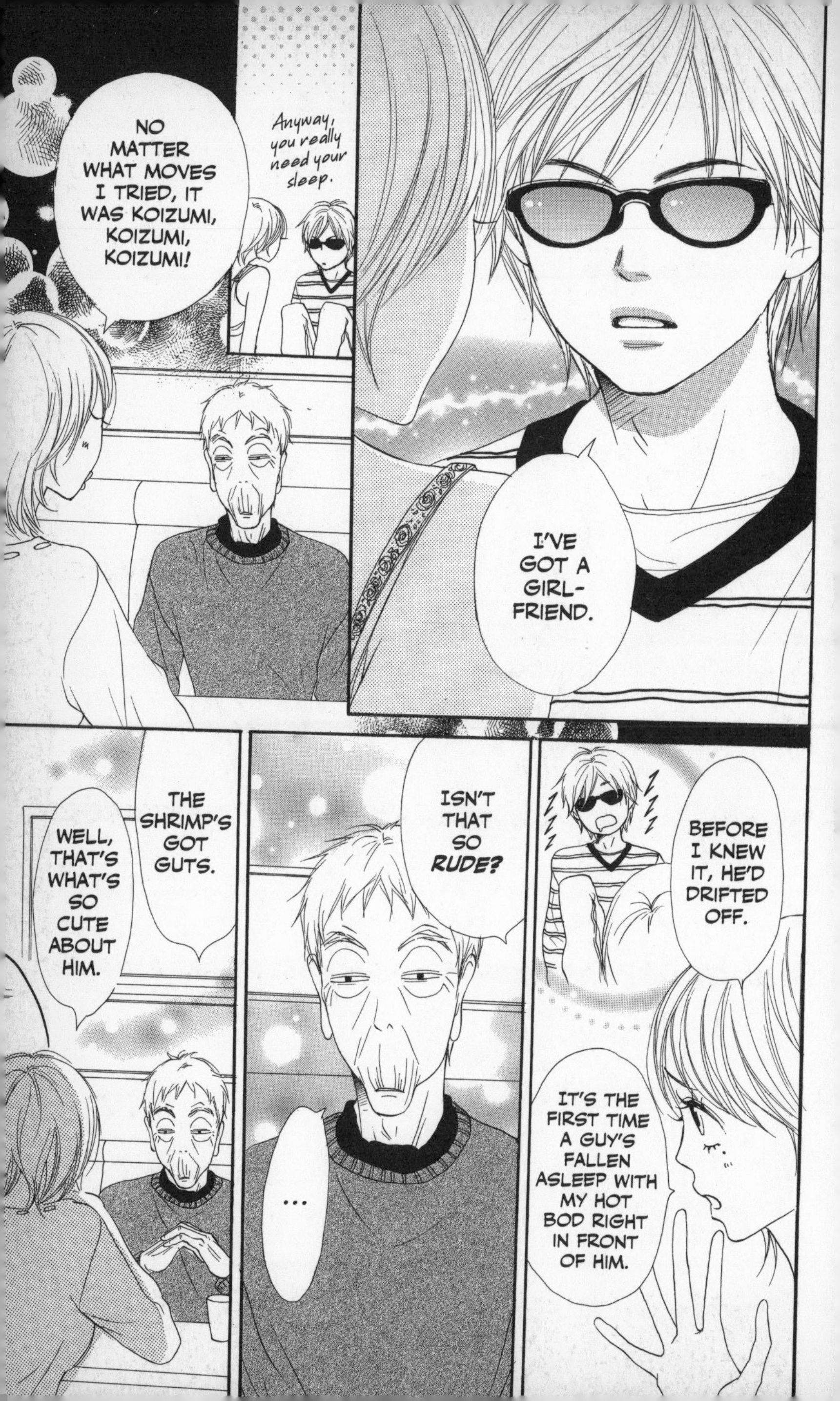
I'VE GOT A GIRL-FRIEND.
Anyway, you really need your sleep.
NO MATTER WHAT MOVES I TRIED, IT WAS KOIZUMI, KOIZUMI, KOIZUMI!
BEFORE I KNEW IT, HE'D DRIFTED OFF.
IT'S THE FIRST TIME A GUY'S FALLEN ASLEEP WITH MY HOT BOD RIGHT IN FRONT OF HIM.
ISN'T THAT SO *RUDE?*
...
THE SHRIMP'S GOT GUTS.
WELL, THAT'S WHAT'S SO CUTE ABOUT HIM.

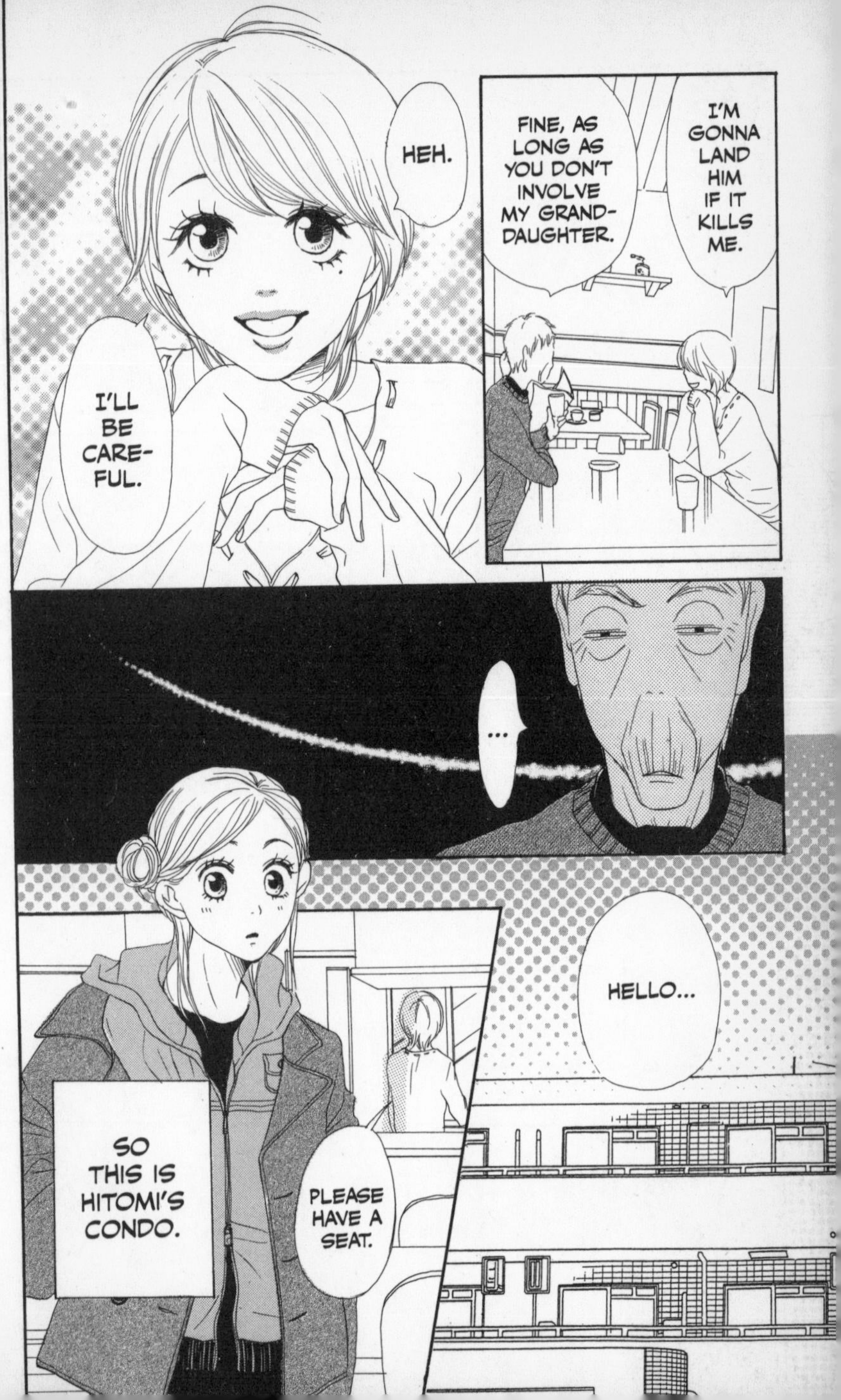
I'M GONNA LAND HIM IF IT KILLS ME.
FINE, AS LONG AS YOU DON'T INVOLVE MY GRAND-DAUGHTER.
HEH.
I'LL BE CARE-FUL.
...
HELLO...
PLEASE HAVE A SEAT.
SO THIS IS HITOMI'S CONDO.

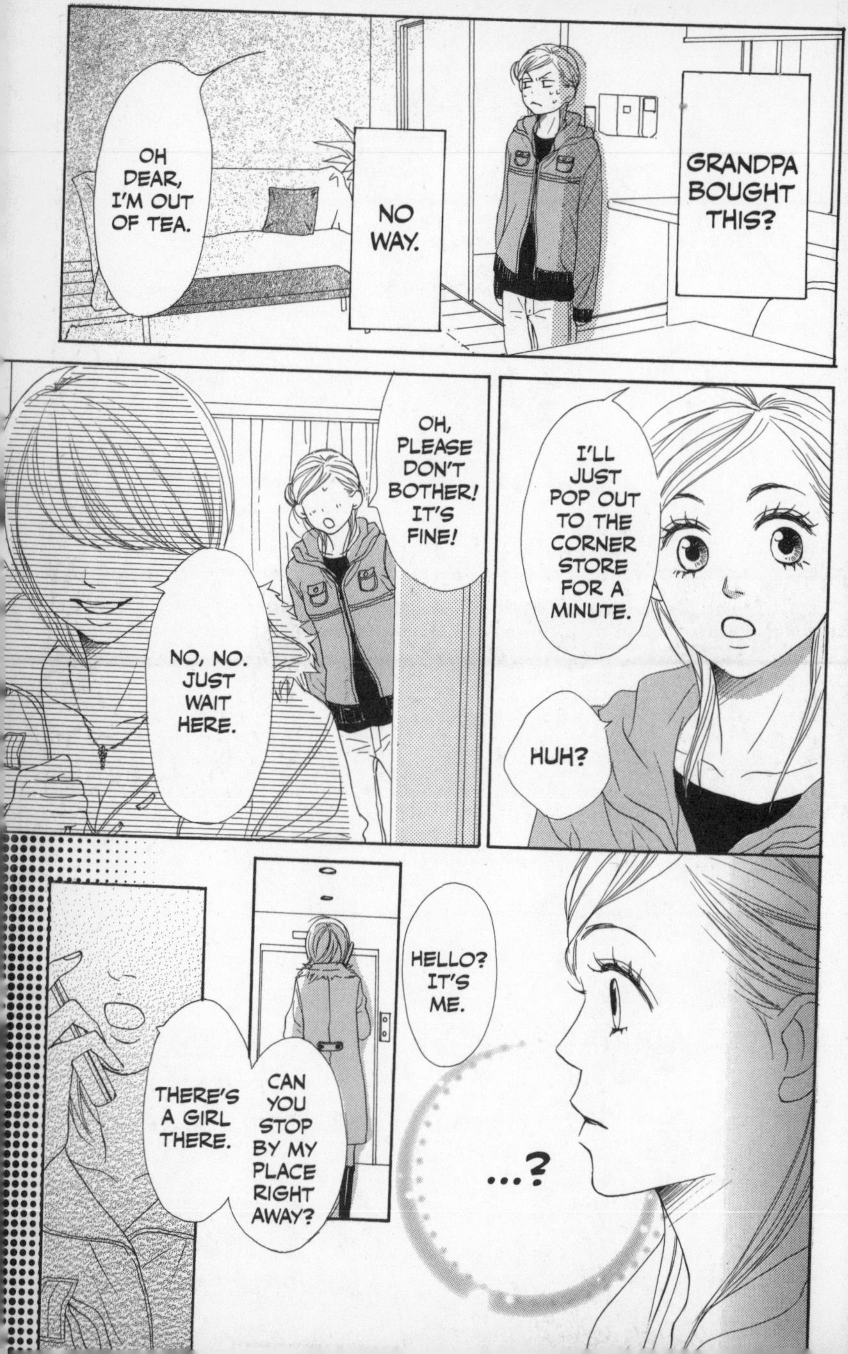
GRANDPA BOUGHT THIS?
NO WAY.
OH DEAR, I'M OUT OF TEA.
I'LL JUST POP OUT TO THE CORNER STORE FOR A MINUTE.
HUH?
OH, PLEASE DON'T BOTHER! IT'S FINE!
NO, NO. JUST WAIT HERE.
...?
HELLO? IT'S ME.
CAN YOU STOP BY MY PLACE RIGHT AWAY?
THERE'S A GIRL THERE.

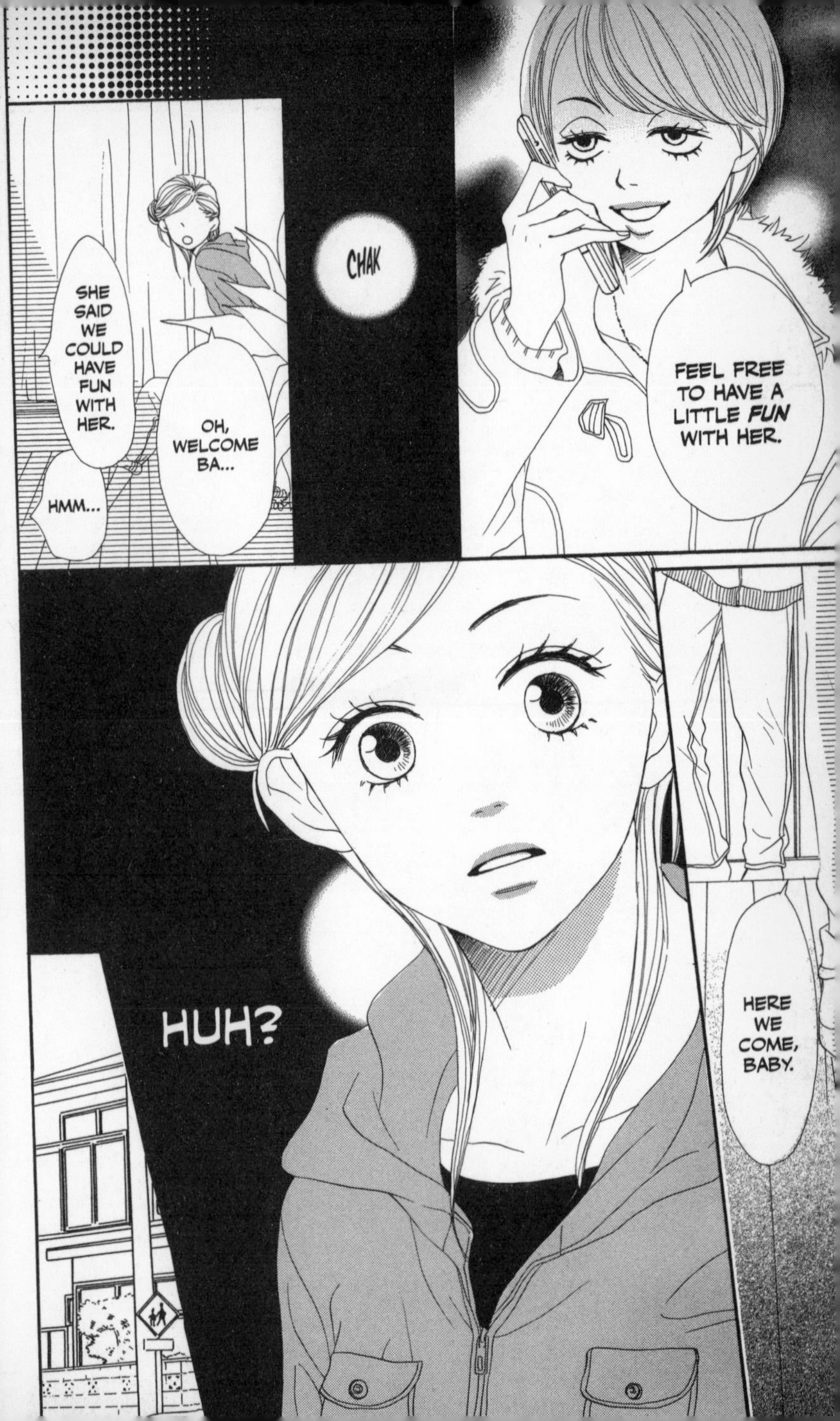
FEEL FREE TO HAVE A LITTLE *FUN* WITH HER.
CHAK
OH, WELCOME BA...
SHE SAID WE COULD HAVE FUN WITH HER.
HMM...
HERE WE COME, BABY.
HUH?

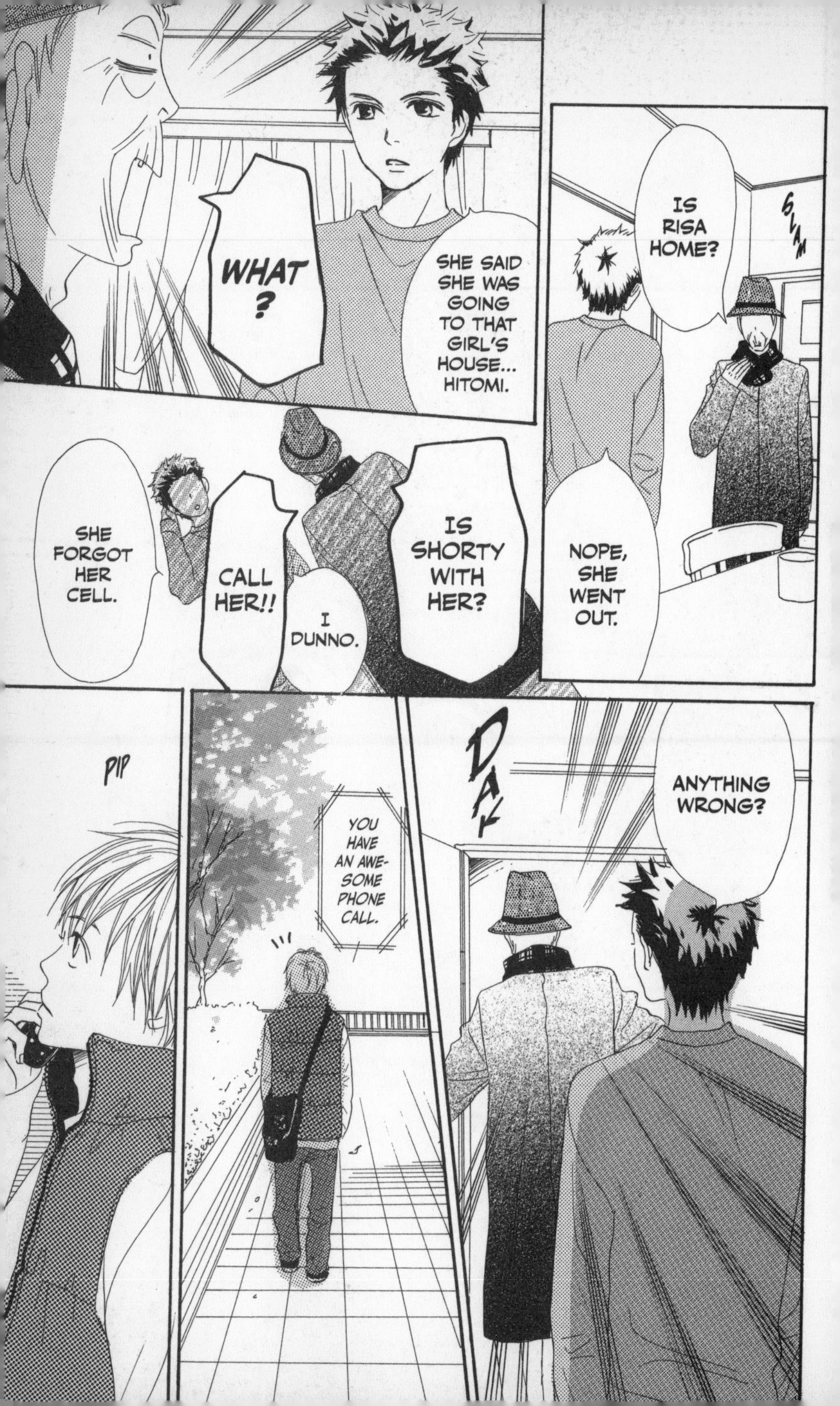
SLAM
IS RISA HOME?
NOPE, SHE WENT OUT.
SHE SAID SHE WAS GOING TO THAT GIRL'S HOUSE... HITOMI.
WHAT ?
IS SHORTY WITH HER?
I DUNNO.
CALL HER!!
SHE FORGOT HER CELL.
DAK
ANYTHING WRONG?
YOU HAVE AN AWE-SOME PHONE CALL.
PIP

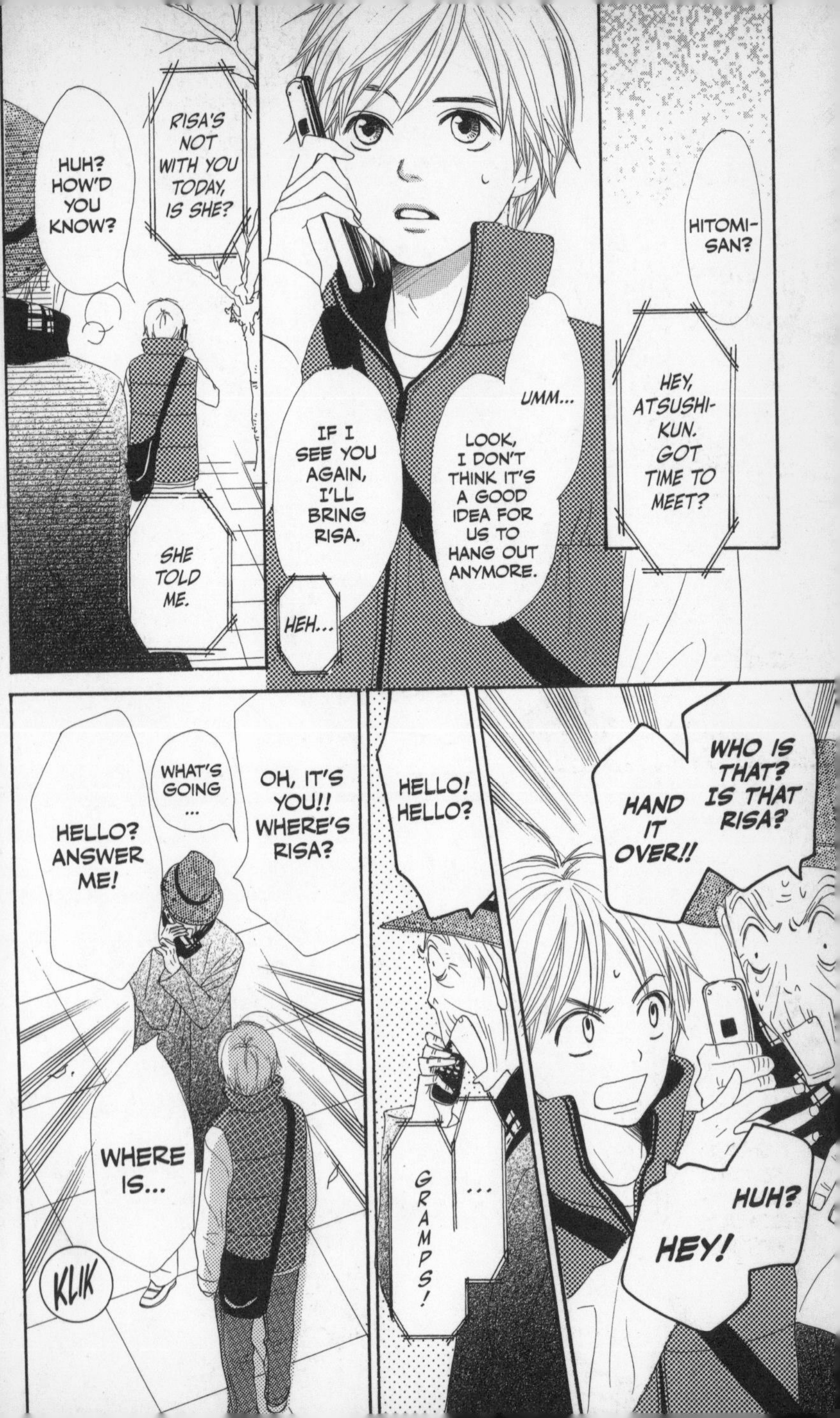
HITOMI-SAN?
HEY, ATSUSHI-KUN. GOT TIME TO MEET?
UMM...
LOOK, I DON'T THINK IT'S A GOOD IDEA FOR US TO HANG OUT ANYMORE.
IF I SEE YOU AGAIN, I'LL BRING RISA.
HEH...
RISA'S NOT WITH YOU TODAY, IS SHE?
HUH? HOW'D YOU KNOW?
SHE TOLD ME.
WHO IS THAT? IS THAT RISA?
HAND IT OVER!!
HUH?
HEY!
HELLO! HELLO?
...
GRAMPS!
OH, IT'S YOU!! WHERE'S RISA?
WHAT'S GOING ...
HELLO? ANSWER ME!
WHERE IS...
KLIK

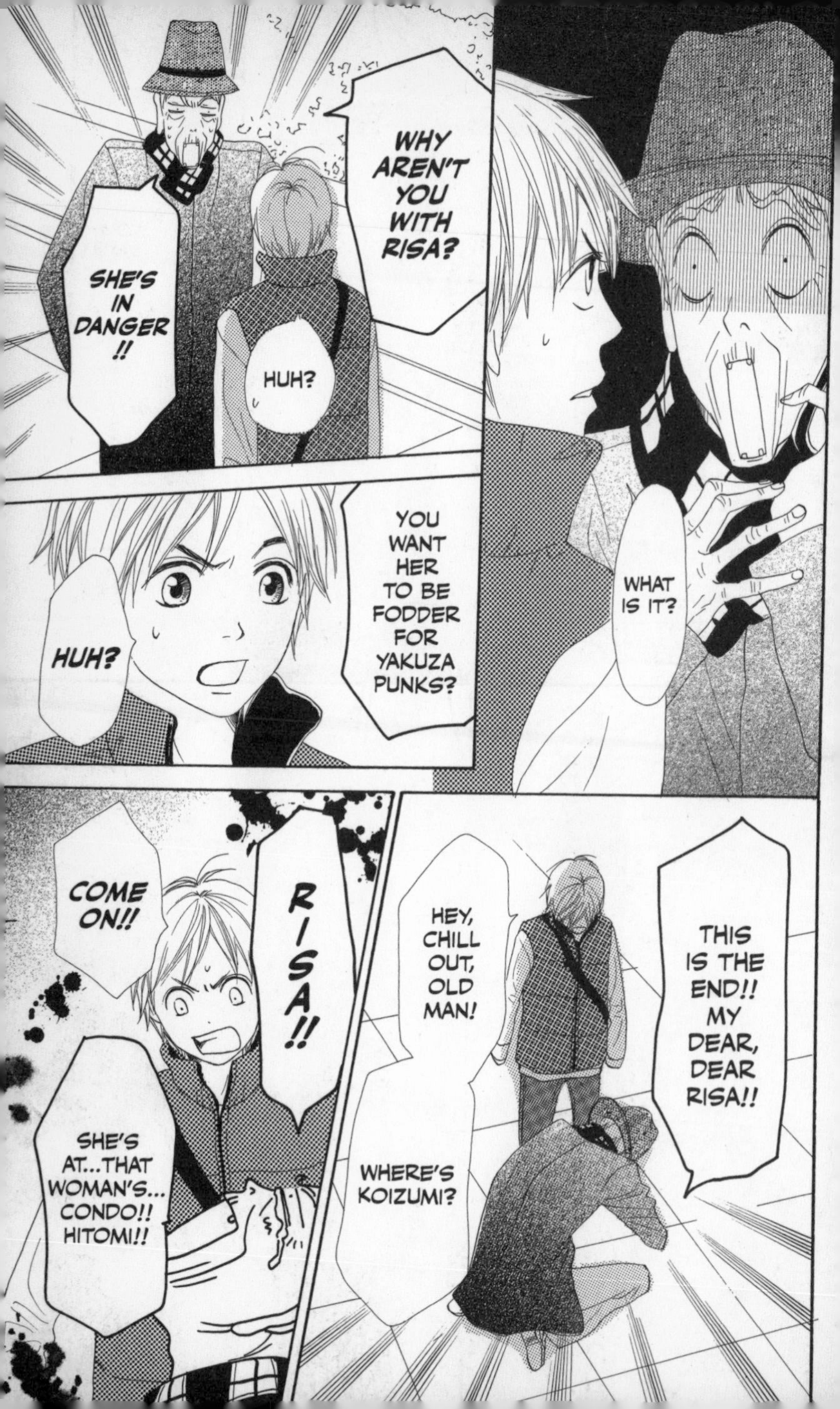
WHAT IS IT?
WHY AREN'T YOU WITH RISA?
SHE'S IN DANGER!!
HUH?
YOU WANT HER TO BE FODDER FOR YAKUZA PUNKS?
HUH?
THIS IS THE END!! MY DEAR, DEAR RISA!!
HEY, CHILL OUT, OLD MAN!
WHERE'S KOIZUMI?
RISA!!
COME ON!!
SHE'S AT...THAT WOMAN'S... CONDO!! HITOMI!!

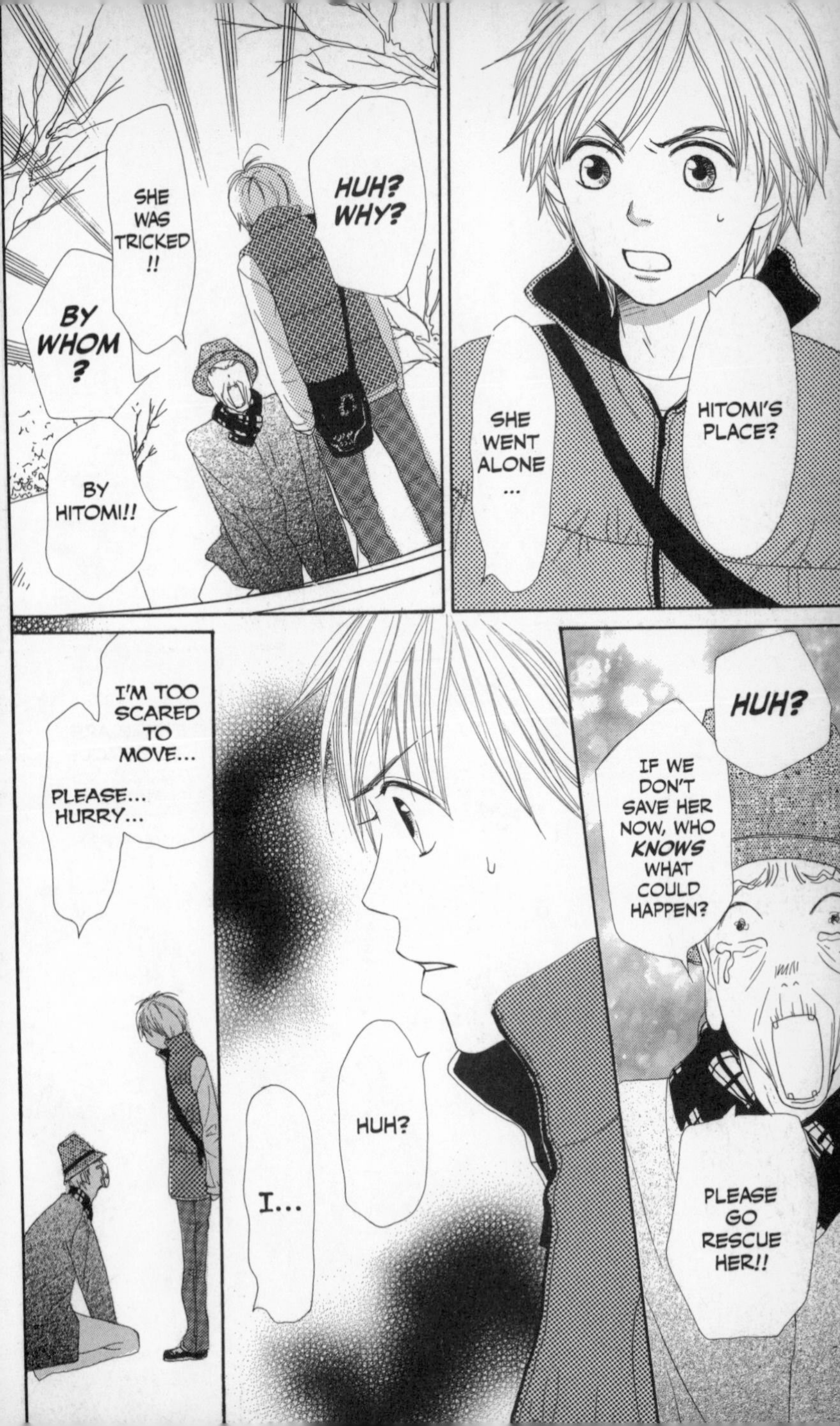
HITOMI'S PLACE?
SHE WENT ALONE ...
HUH? WHY?
SHE WAS TRICKED !!
BY WHOM ?
BY HITOMI!!
HUH?
IF WE DON'T SAVE HER NOW, WHO KNOWS WHAT COULD HAPPEN?
PLEASE GO RESCUE HER!!
HUH?
I...
I'M TOO SCARED TO MOVE...
PLEASE... HURRY...

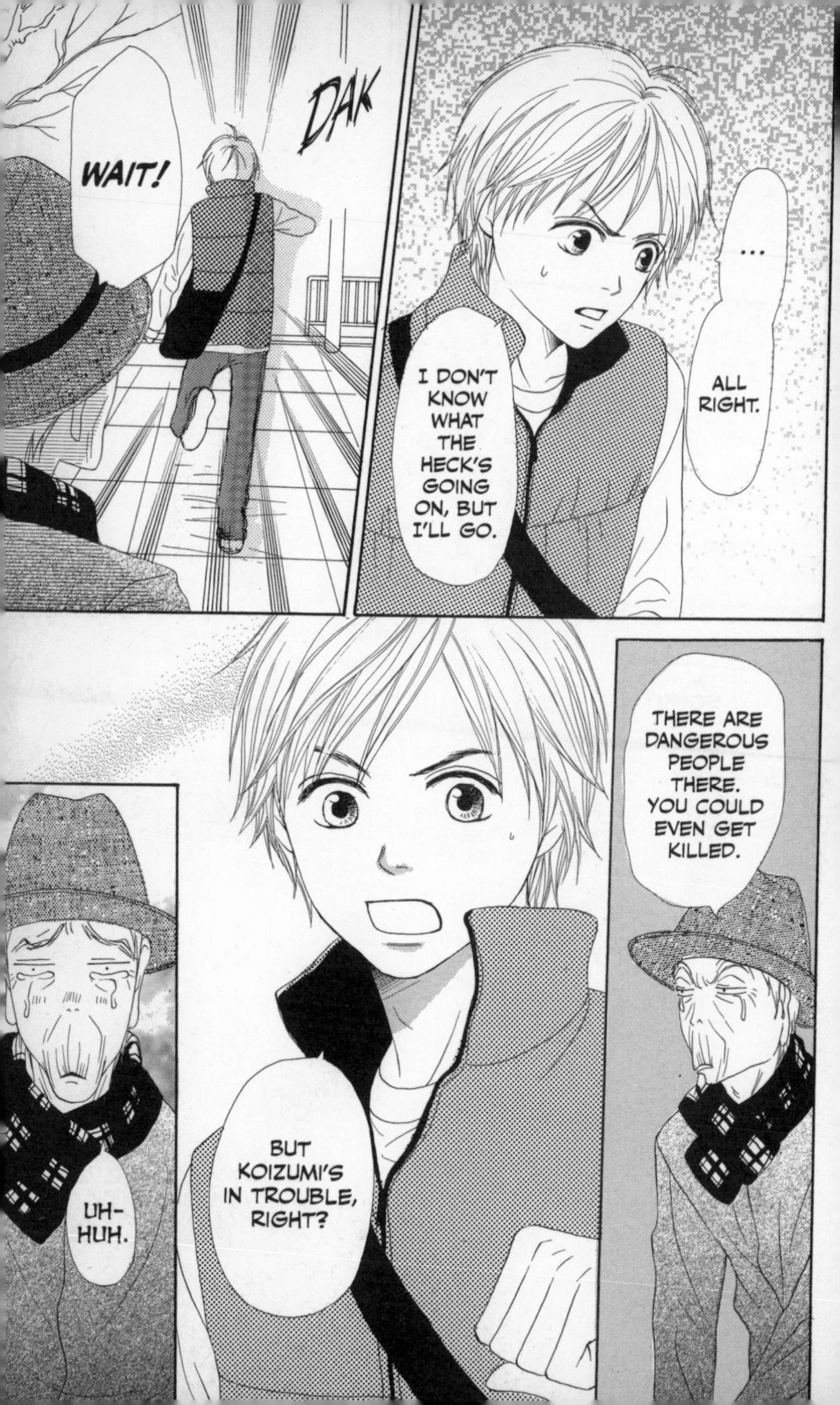
...
ALL RIGHT.
I DON'T KNOW WHAT THE HECK'S GOING ON, BUT I'LL GO.
DAK
WAIT!
THERE ARE DANGEROUS PEOPLE THERE. YOU COULD EVEN GET KILLED.
BUT KOIZUMI'S IN TROUBLE, RIGHT?
UH-HUH.

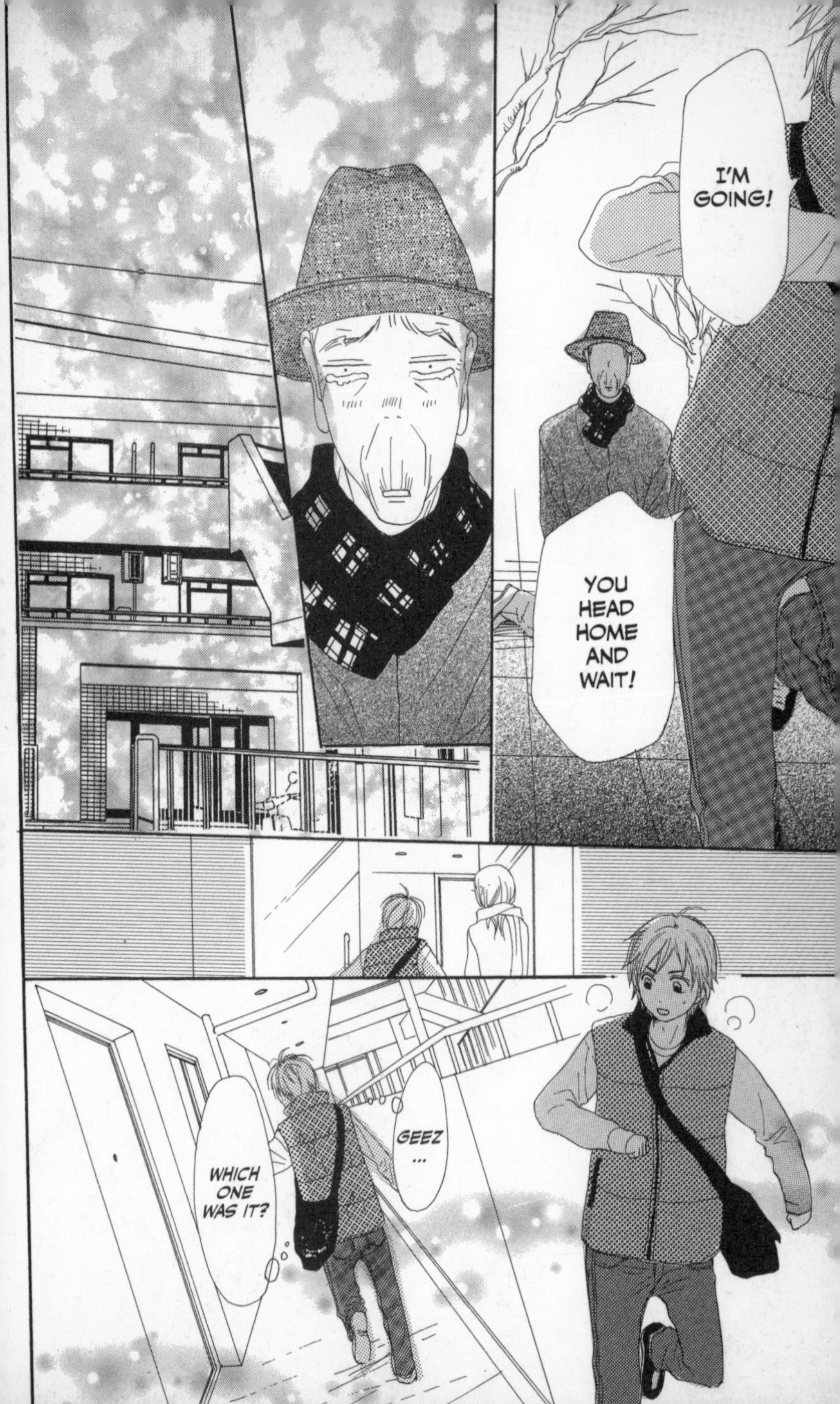
I'M GOING!
YOU HEAD HOME AND WAIT!
GEEZ ...
WHICH ONE WAS IT?

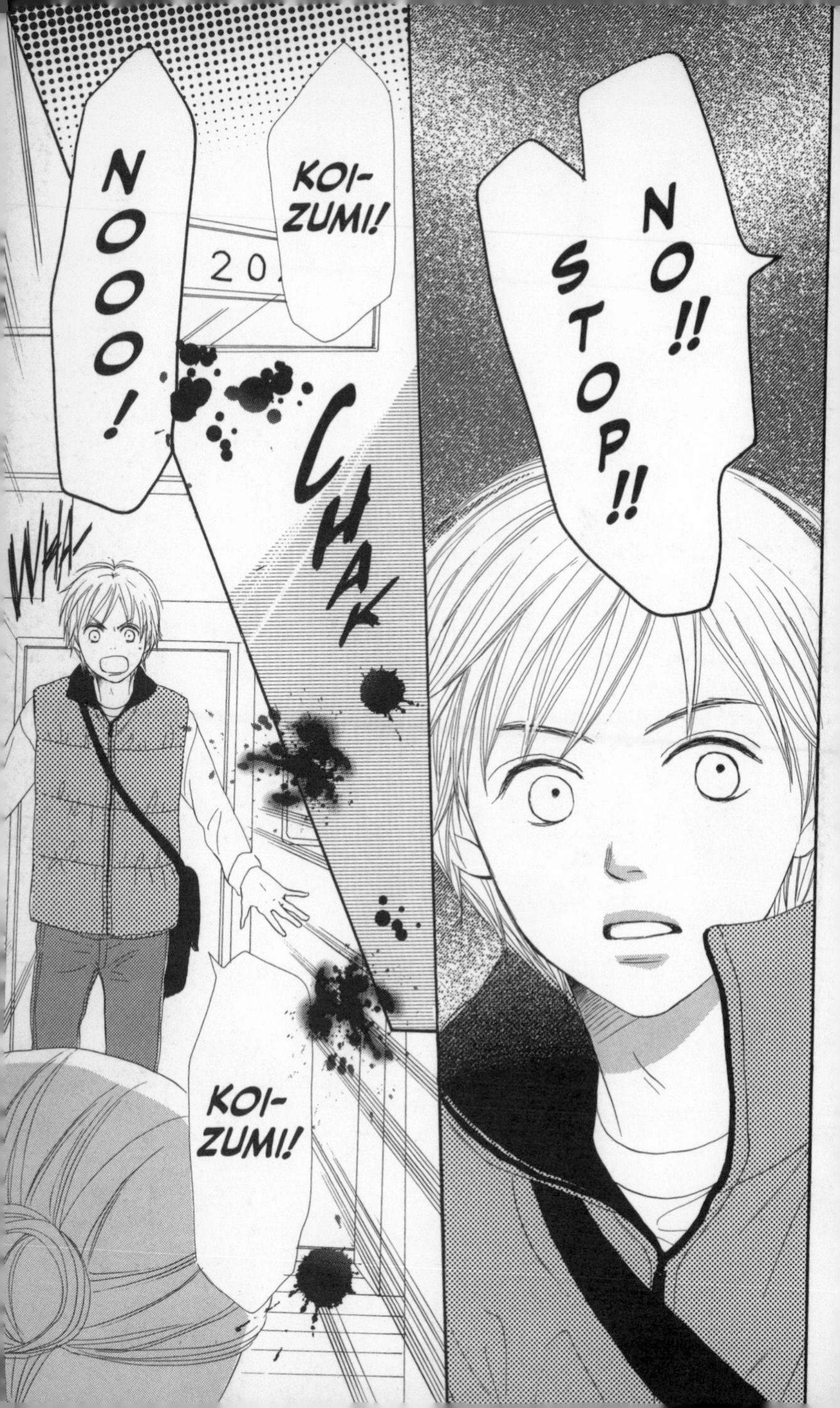
NO!! STOP!!
KOI-ZUMI!
NOOOO!
CHAK
WHA-
KOI-ZUMI!

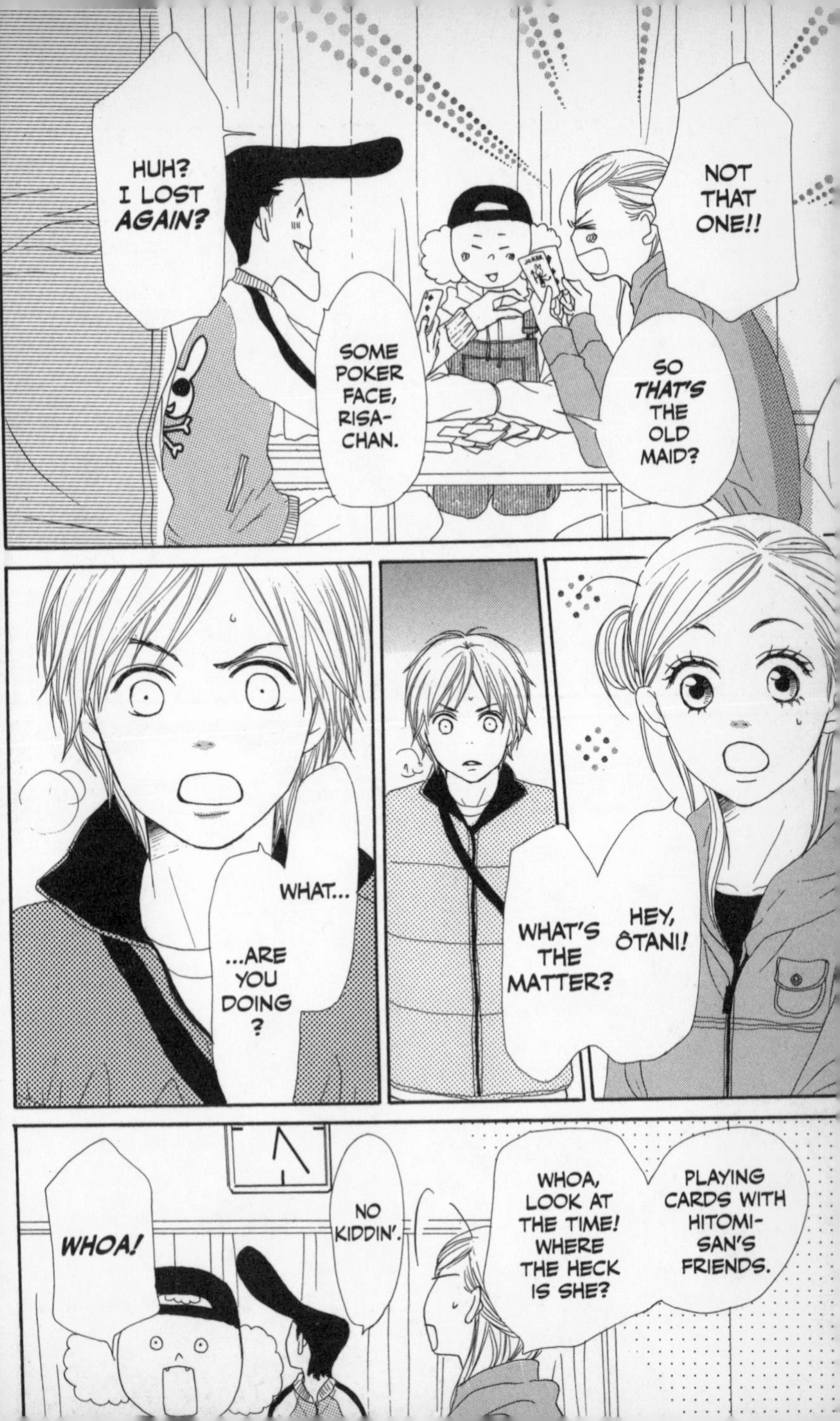
NOT THAT ONE!!
SO *THAT'S* THE OLD MAID?
SOME POKER FACE, RISA-CHAN.
HUH? I LOST *AGAIN?*
HEY, ŌTANI!
WHAT'S THE MATTER?
WHAT...
...ARE YOU DOING?
PLAYING CARDS WITH HITOMI-SAN'S FRIENDS.
WHOA, LOOK AT THE TIME! WHERE THE HECK IS SHE?
NO KIDDIN'.
WHOA!

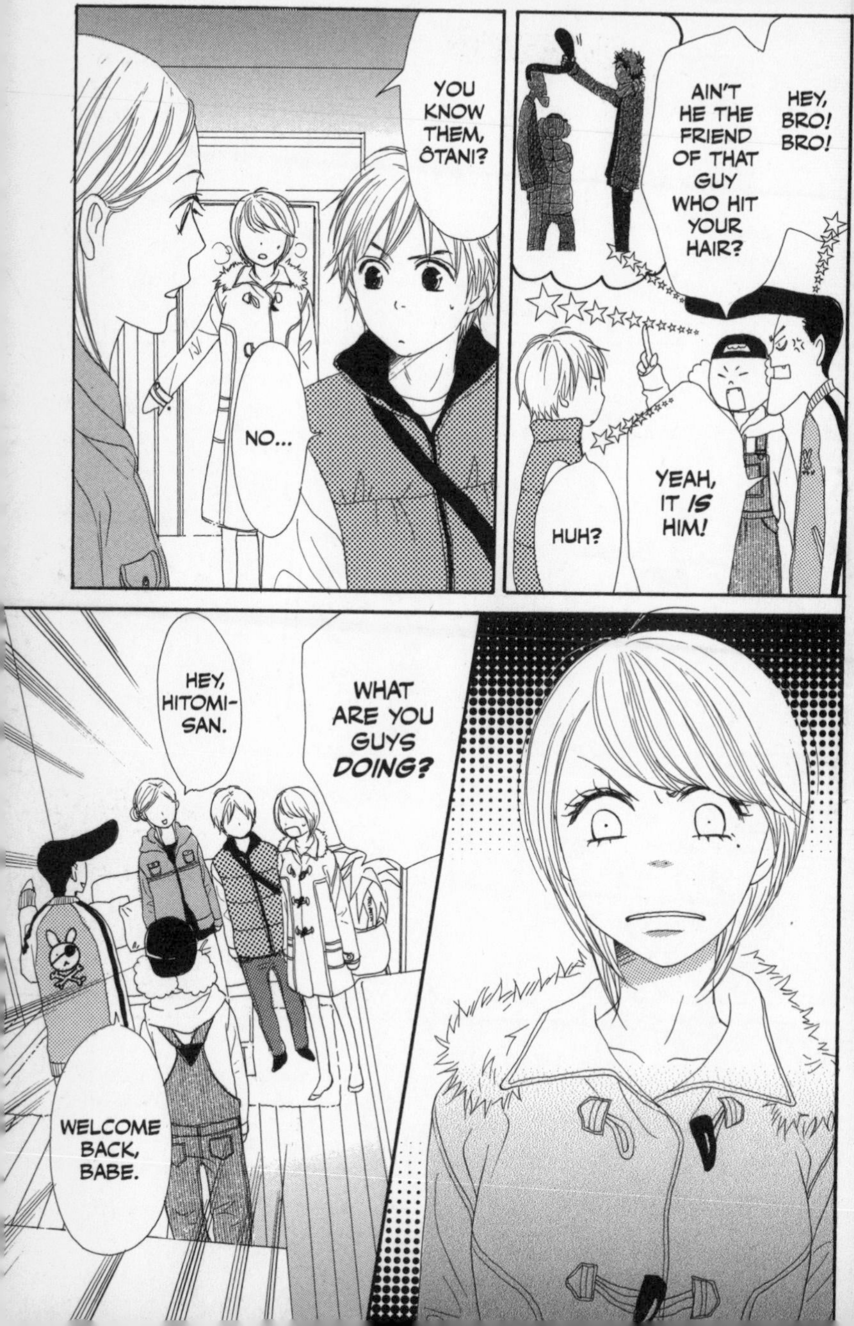

HEY, BRO! BRO!
AIN'T HE THE FRIEND OF THAT GUY WHO HIT YOUR HAIR?
YEAH, IT *IS* HIM!
HUH?
YOU KNOW THEM, ŌTANI?
NO...
WHAT ARE YOU GUYS *DOING?*
HEY, HITOMI-SAN.
WELCOME BACK, BABE.

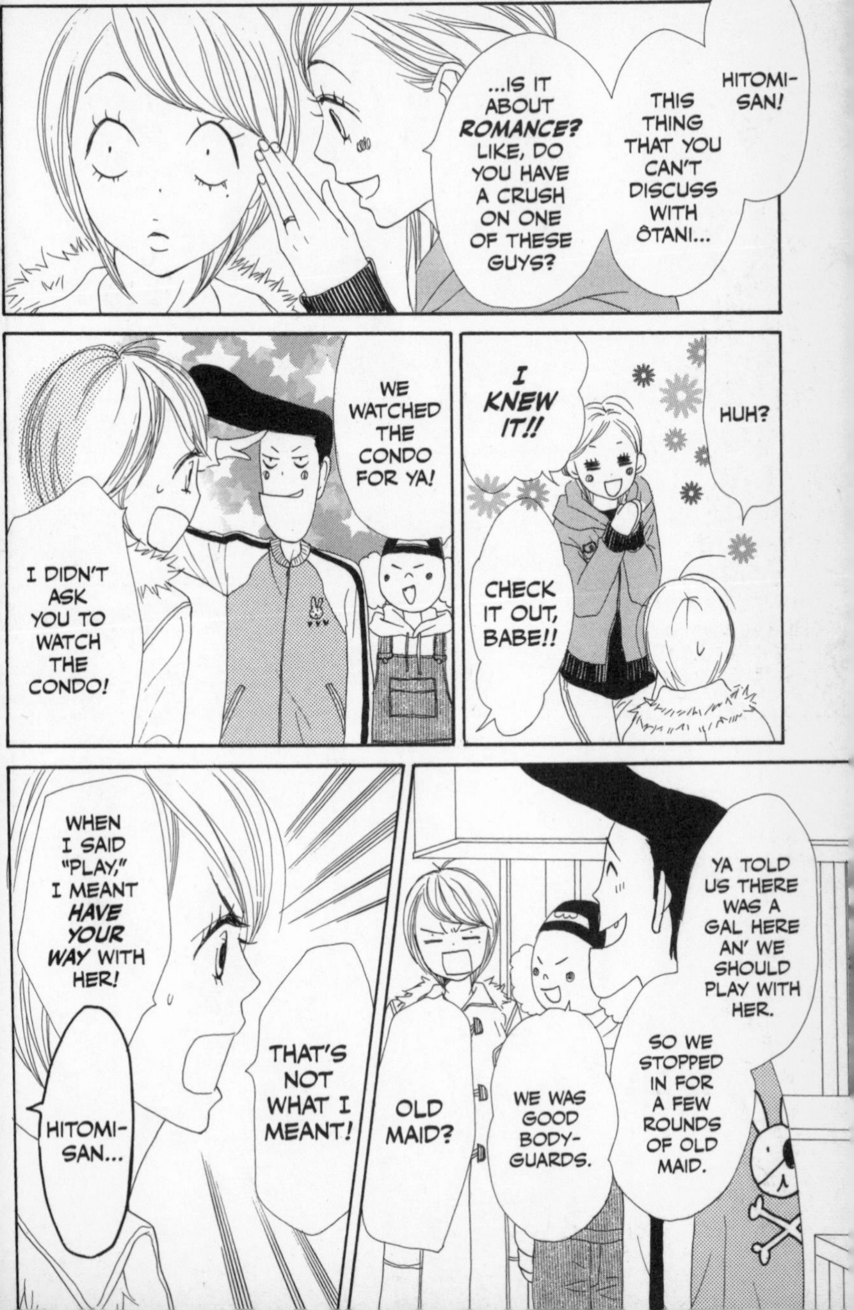
HITOMI-SAN!
THIS THING THAT YOU CAN'T DISCUSS WITH ŌTANI...
...IS IT ABOUT *ROMANCE?* LIKE, DO YOU HAVE A CRUSH ON ONE OF THESE GUYS?
HUH?
I KNEW IT!!
CHECK IT OUT, BABE!!
WE WATCHED THE CONDO FOR YA!
I DIDN'T ASK YOU TO WATCH THE CONDO!
YA TOLD US THERE WAS A GAL HERE AN' WE SHOULD PLAY WITH HER.
SO WE STOPPED IN FOR A FEW ROUNDS OF OLD MAID.
WE WAS GOOD BODY-GUARDS.
OLD MAID?
THAT'S NOT WHAT I MEANT!
WHEN I SAID "PLAY," I MEANT *HAVE YOUR WAY* WITH HER!
HITOMI-SAN...

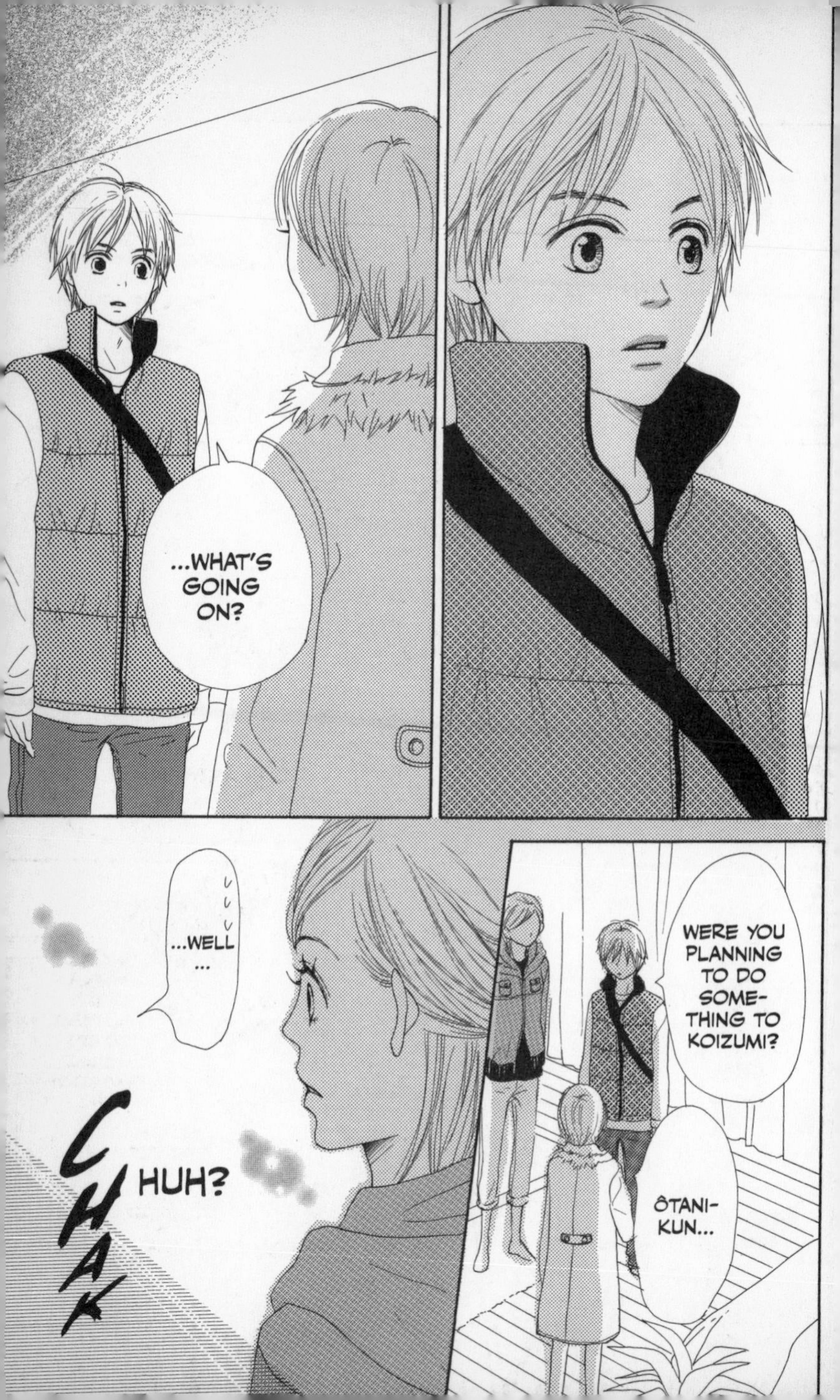
...WHAT'S GOING ON?
WERE YOU PLANNING TO DO SOME-THING TO KOIZUMI?
ŌTANI-KUN...
...WELL ...
HUH?
CHAK

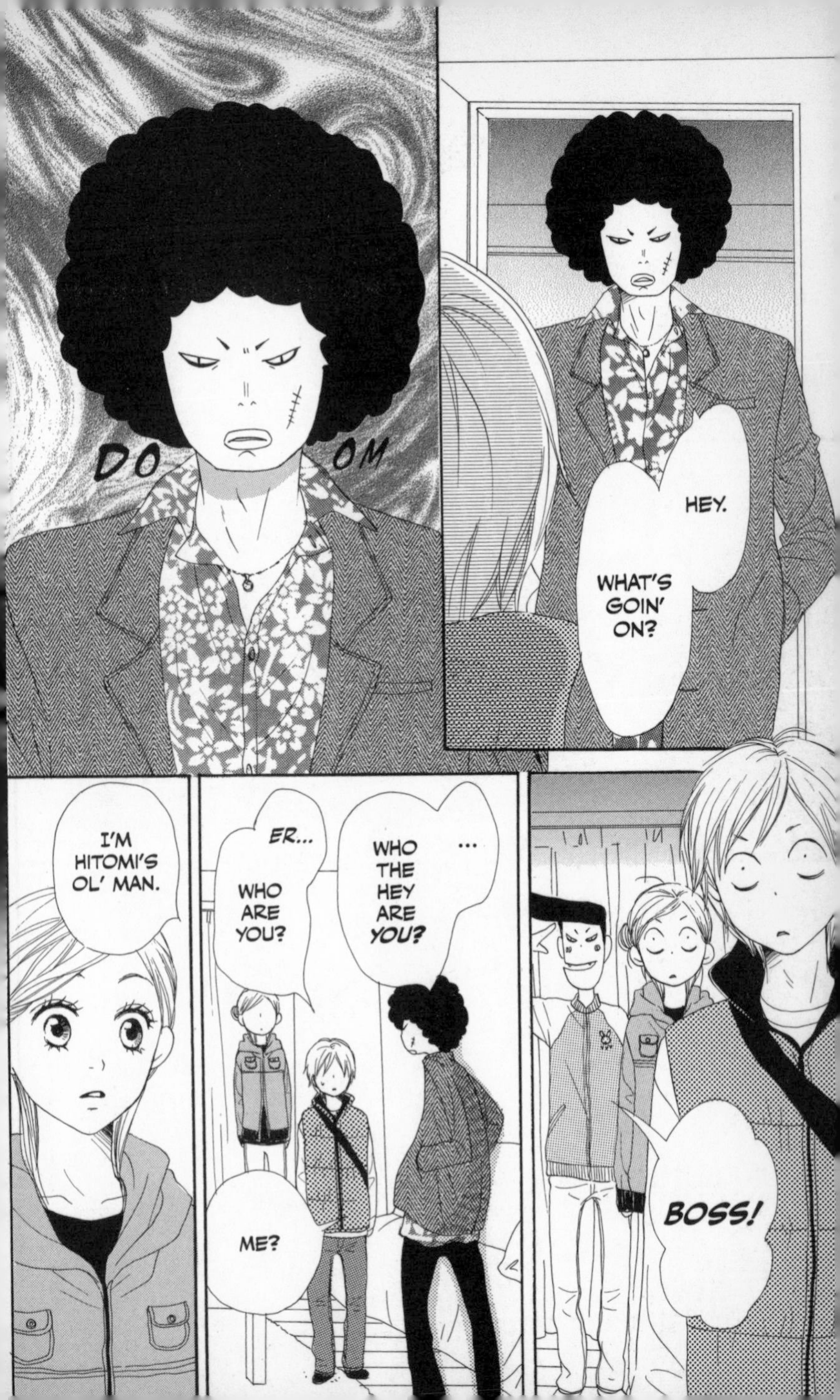
HEY.
WHAT'S GOIN' ON?
DO OM
BOSS!
...
WHO THE HEY ARE YOU?
ER... WHO ARE YOU?
ME?
I'M HITOMI'S OL' MAN.

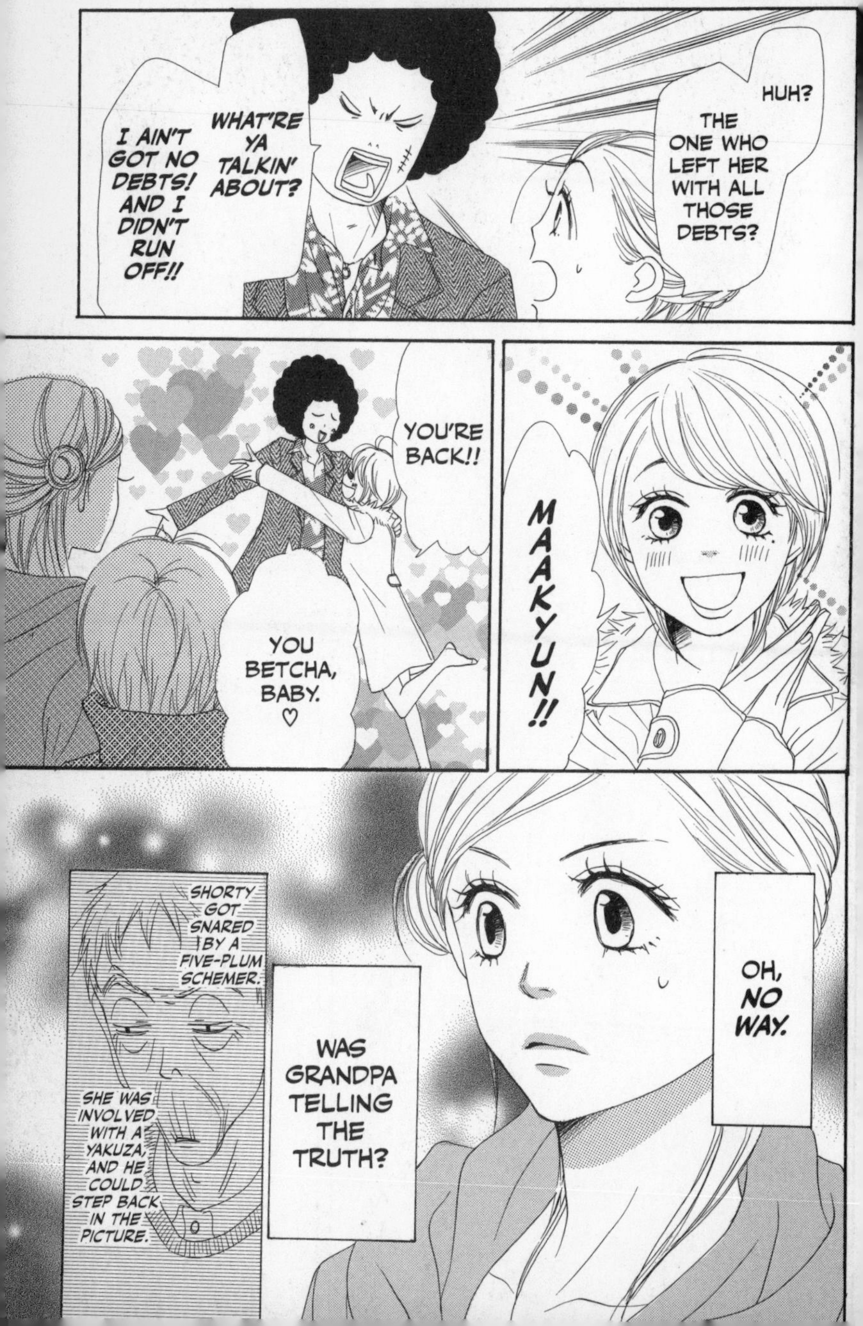
HUH?
THE ONE WHO LEFT HER WITH ALL THOSE DEBTS?
WHAT'RE YA TALKIN' ABOUT?
I AIN'T GOT NO DEBTS! AND I DIDN'T RUN OFF!!
MAAKYUN!!
YOU'RE BACK!!
YOU BETCHA, BABY. ♡
OH, NO WAY.
WAS GRANDPA TELLING THE TRUTH?
SHORTY GOT SNARED BY A FIVE-PLUM SCHEMER.
SHE WAS INVOLVED WITH A YAKUZA, AND HE COULD STEP BACK IN THE PICTURE.

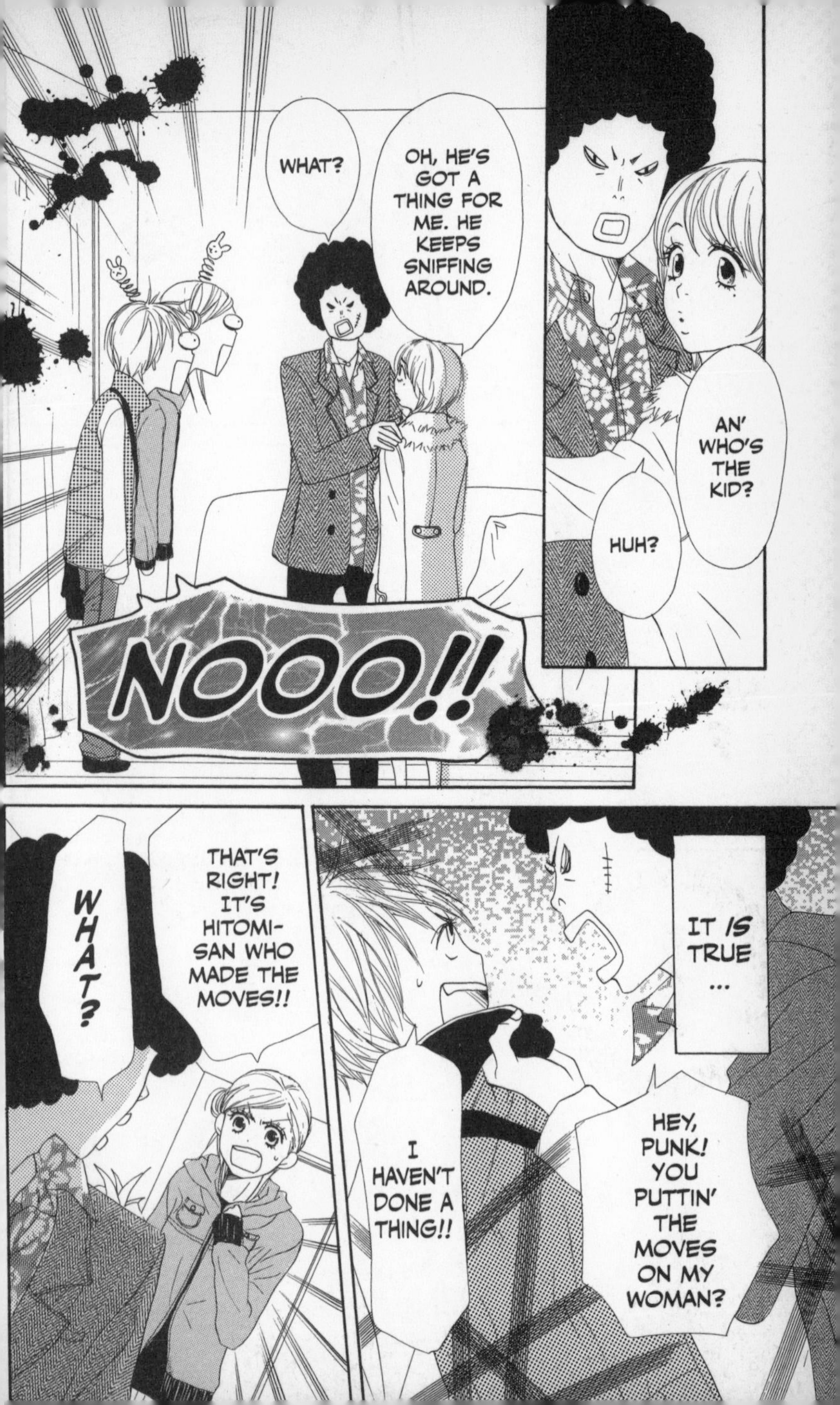
AN' WHO'S THE KID?
HUH?
OH, HE'S GOT A THING FOR ME. HE KEEPS SNIFFING AROUND.
WHAT?
NOOO!!
IT *IS* TRUE ...
HEY, PUNK! YOU PUTTIN' THE MOVES ON MY WOMAN?
I HAVEN'T DONE A THING!!
THAT'S RIGHT! IT'S HITOMI-SAN WHO MADE THE MOVES!!
WHAT?

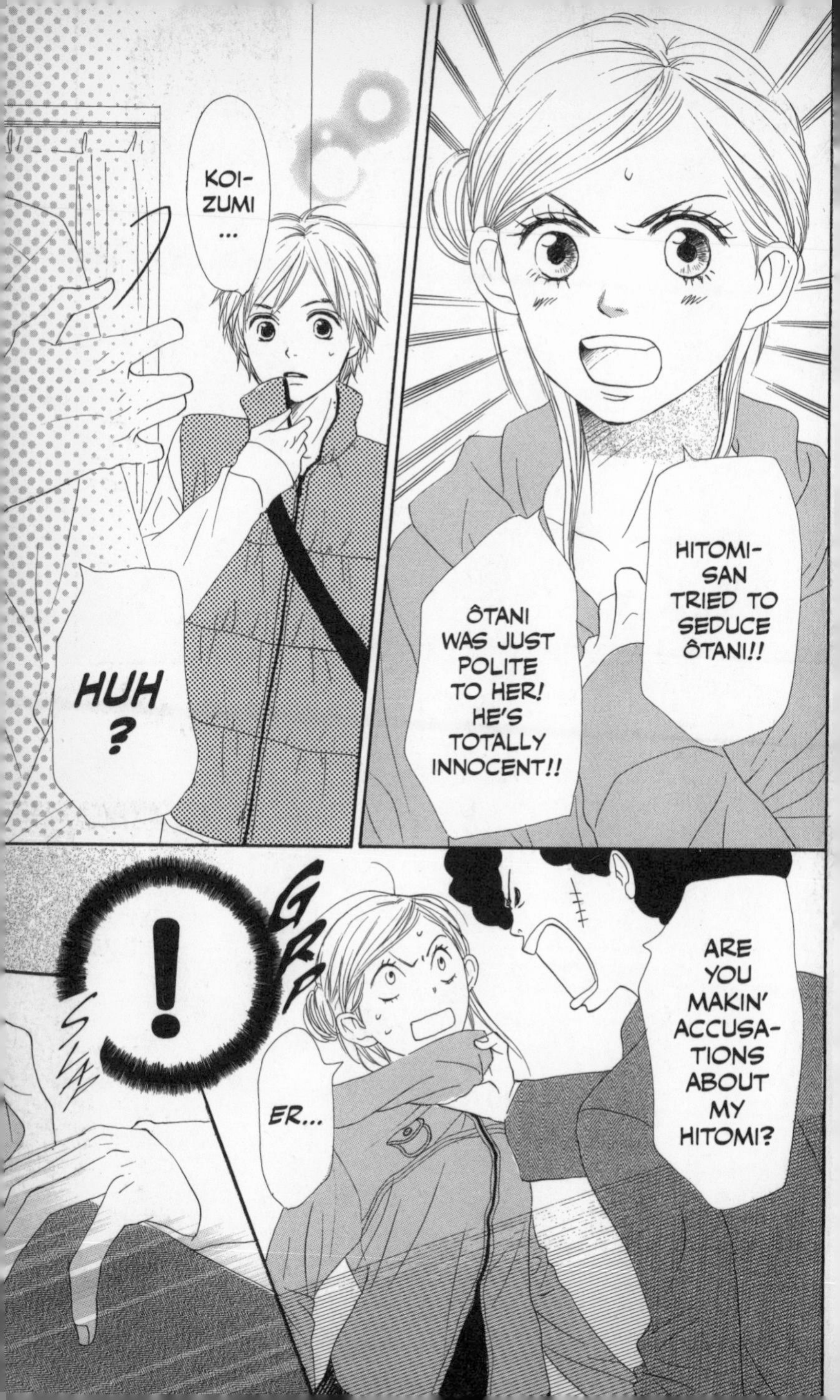
HITOMI-SAN TRIED TO SEDUCE ÔTANI!!
ÔTANI WAS JUST POLITE TO HER! HE'S TOTALLY INNOCENT!!
KOI-ZUMI ...
HUH?
ARE YOU MAKIN' ACCUSATIONS ABOUT MY HITOMI?
GRP
!
ER...

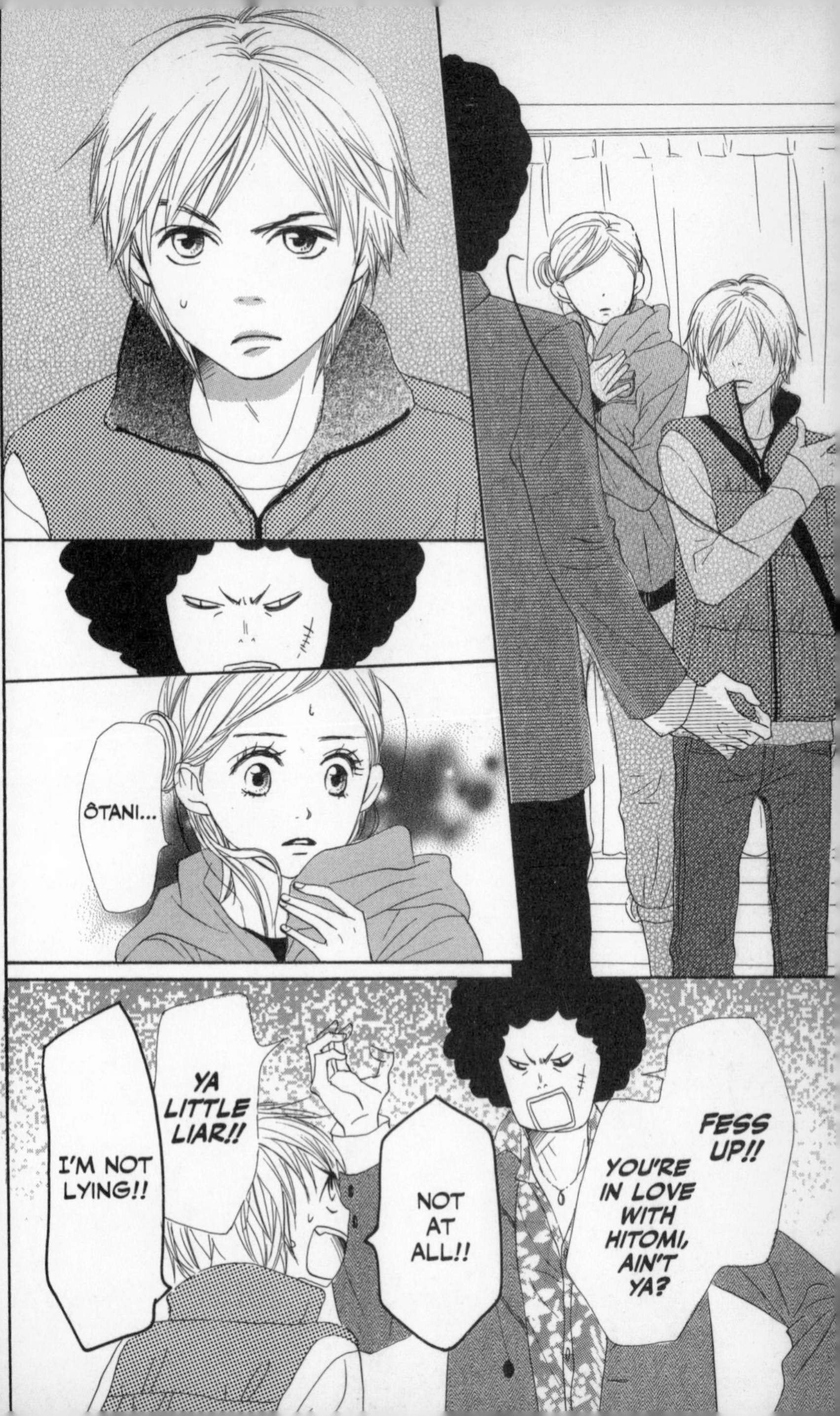
ŌTANI...
FESS UP!!
YOU'RE IN LOVE WITH HITOMI, AIN'T YA?
NOT AT ALL!!
YA LITTLE LIAR!!
I'M NOT LYING!!

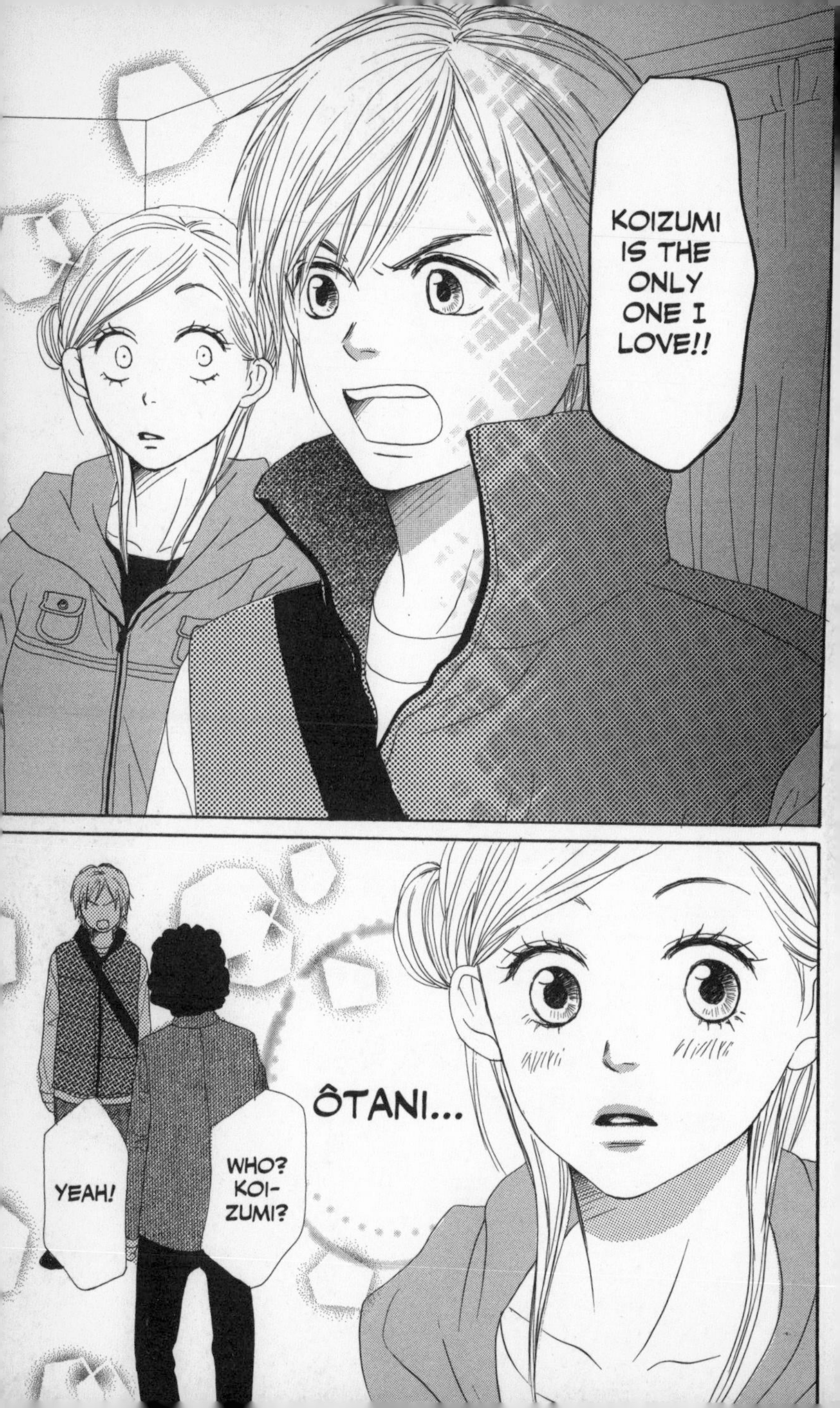
KOIZUMI IS THE ONLY ONE I LOVE!!
ÔTANI...
WHO? KOI-ZUMI?
YEAH!

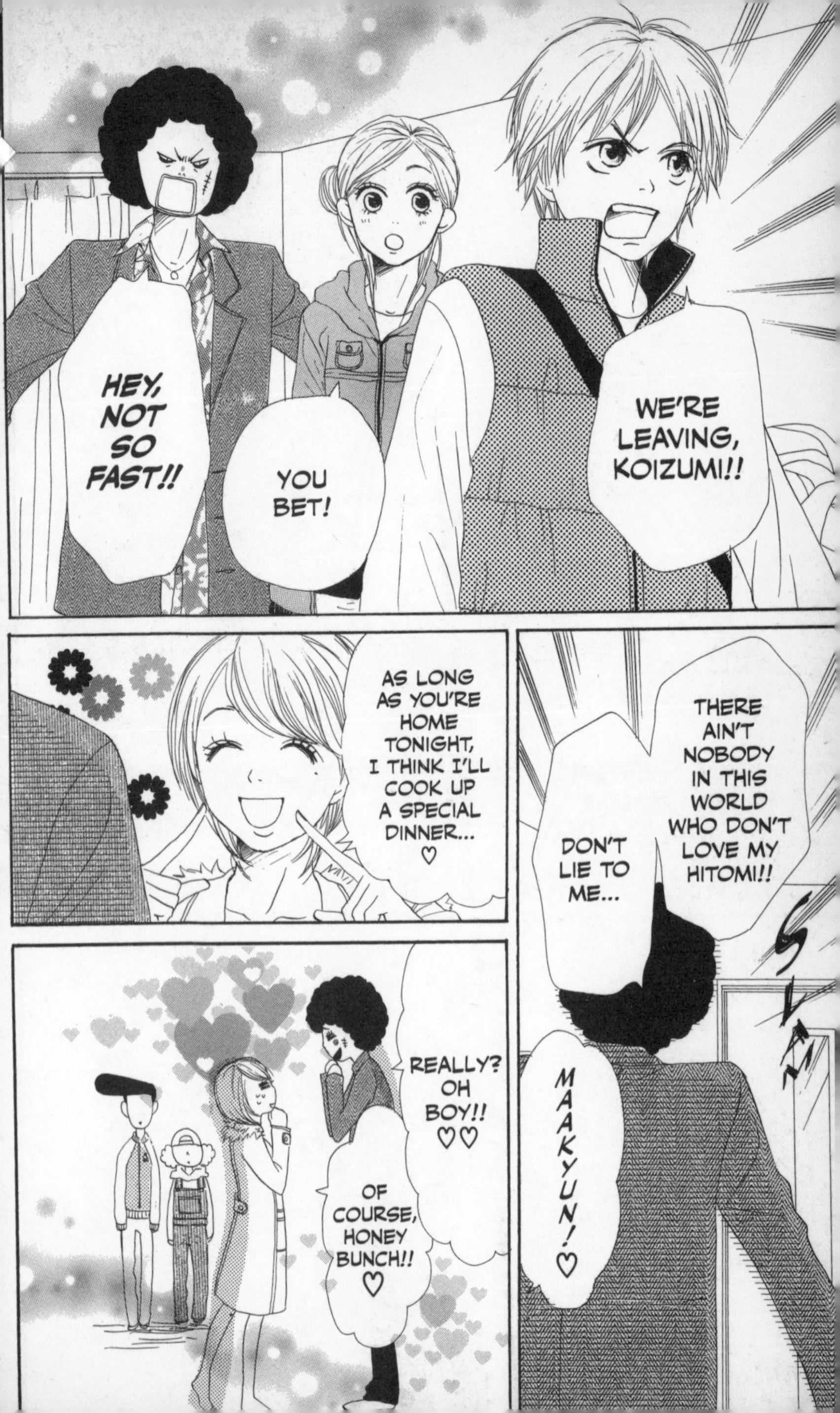
WE'RE LEAVING, KOIZUMI!!
YOU BET!
HEY, NOT SO FAST!!
THERE AIN'T NOBODY IN THIS WORLD WHO DON'T LOVE MY HITOMI!!
DON'T LIE TO ME...
MAAKYUN! ♡
AS LONG AS YOU'RE HOME TONIGHT, I THINK I'LL COOK UP A SPECIAL DINNER... ♡
REALLY? OH BOY!! ♡♡
OF COURSE, HONEY BUNCH!! ♡

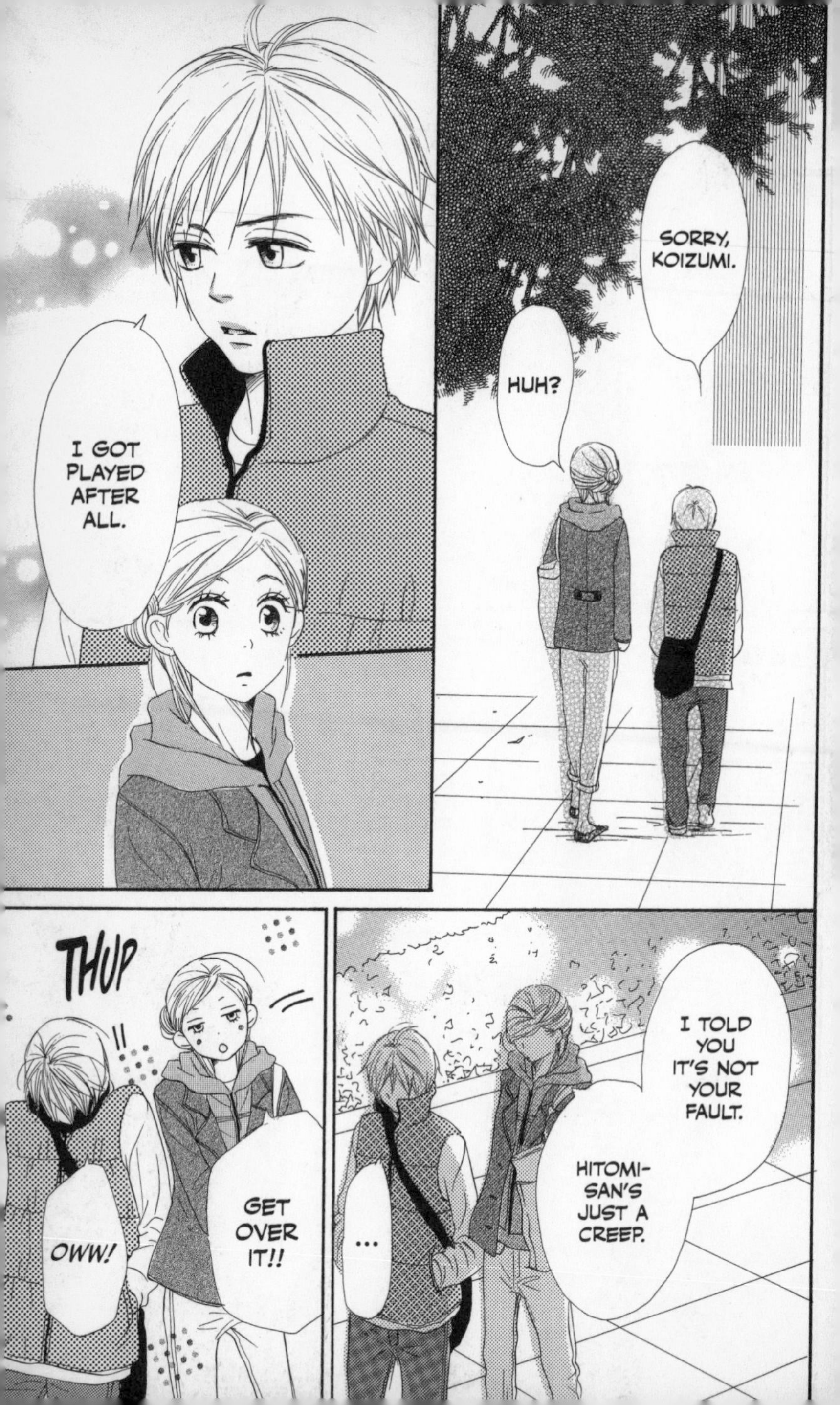
SORRY, KOIZUMI.
HUH?
I GOT PLAYED AFTER ALL.
I TOLD YOU IT'S NOT YOUR FAULT.
HITOMI-SAN'S JUST A CREEP.
...
THUP
!!
GET OVER IT!!
OWW!

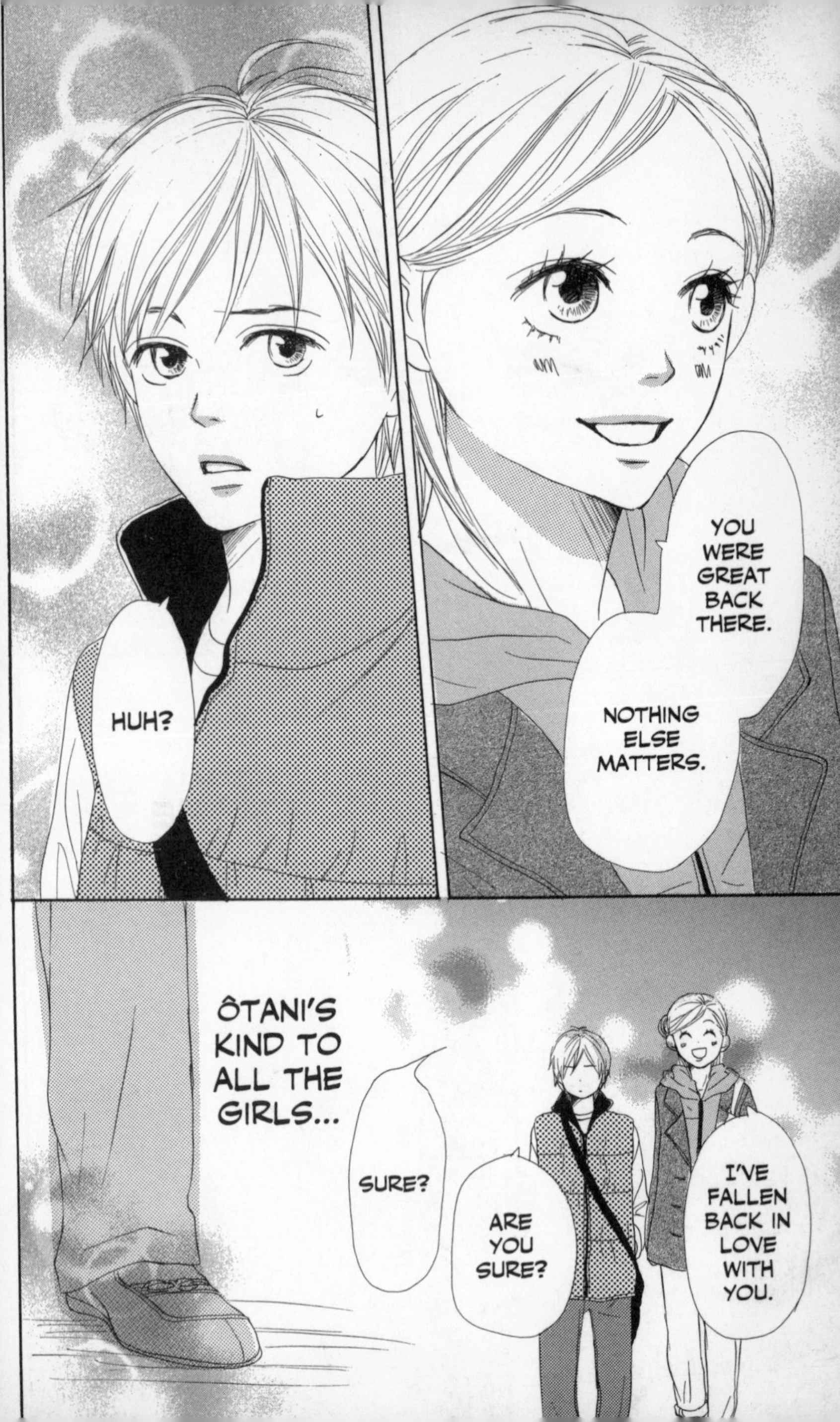
YOU WERE GREAT BACK THERE.
NOTHING ELSE MATTERS.
HUH?
I'VE FALLEN BACK IN LOVE WITH YOU.
ARE YOU SURE?
SURE?
ÔTANI'S KIND TO ALL THE GIRLS...

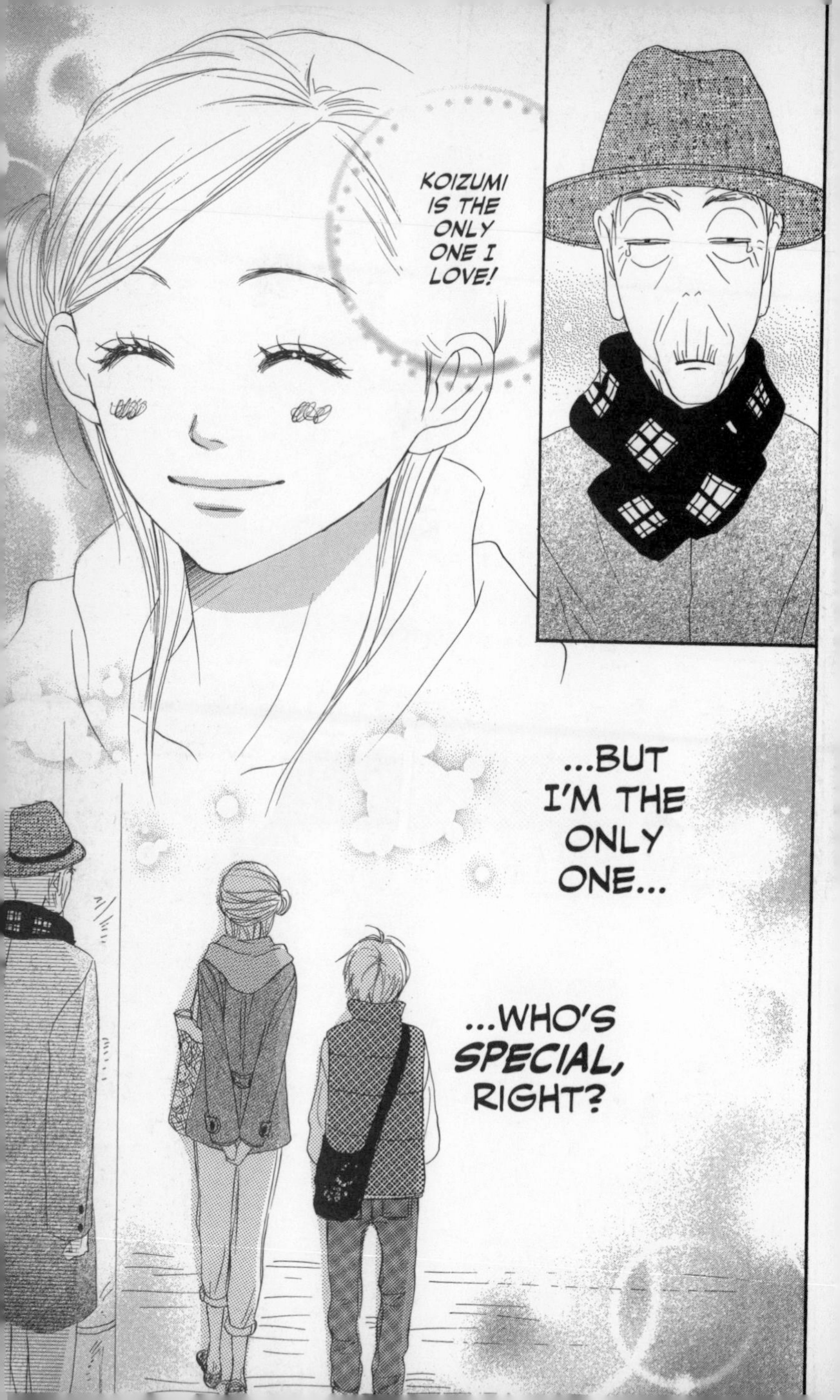
KOIZUMI IS THE ONLY ONE I LOVE!
...BUT I'M THE ONLY ONE...
...WHO'S SPECIAL, RIGHT?

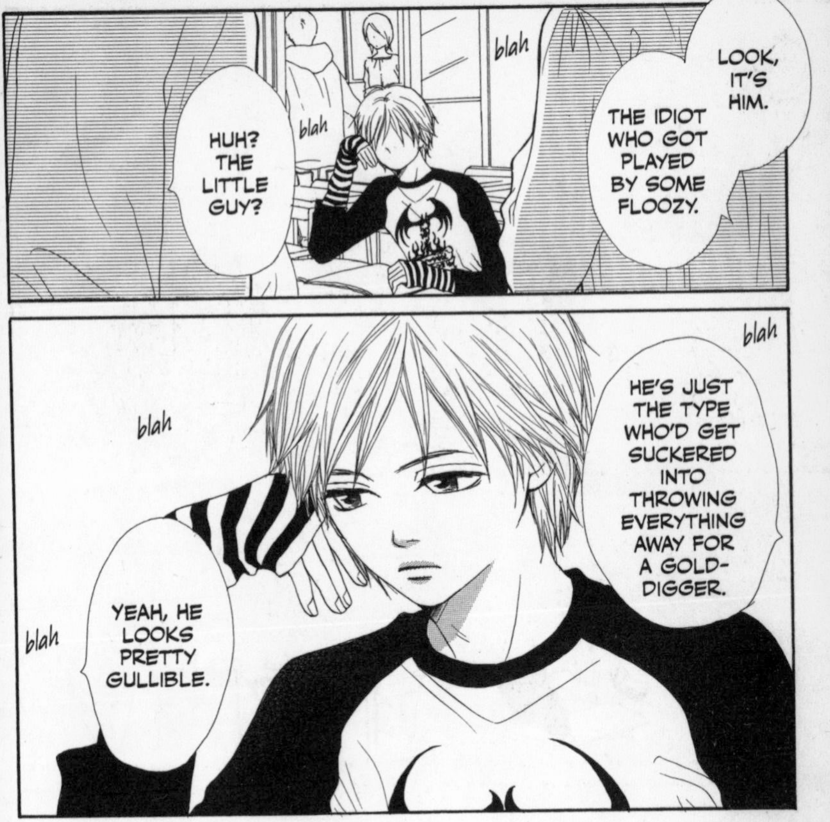
LOOK, IT'S HIM.
THE IDIOT WHO GOT PLAYED BY SOME FLOOZY.
blah
blah
HUH? THE LITTLE GUY?
blah
HE'S JUST THE TYPE WHO'D GET SUCKERED INTO THROWING EVERYTHING AWAY FOR A GOLD-DIGGER.
blah
YEAH, HE LOOKS PRETTY GULLIBLE.
blah

CHAPTER 54

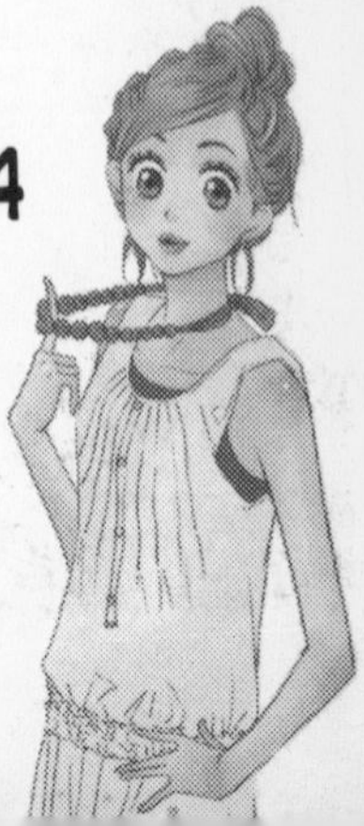

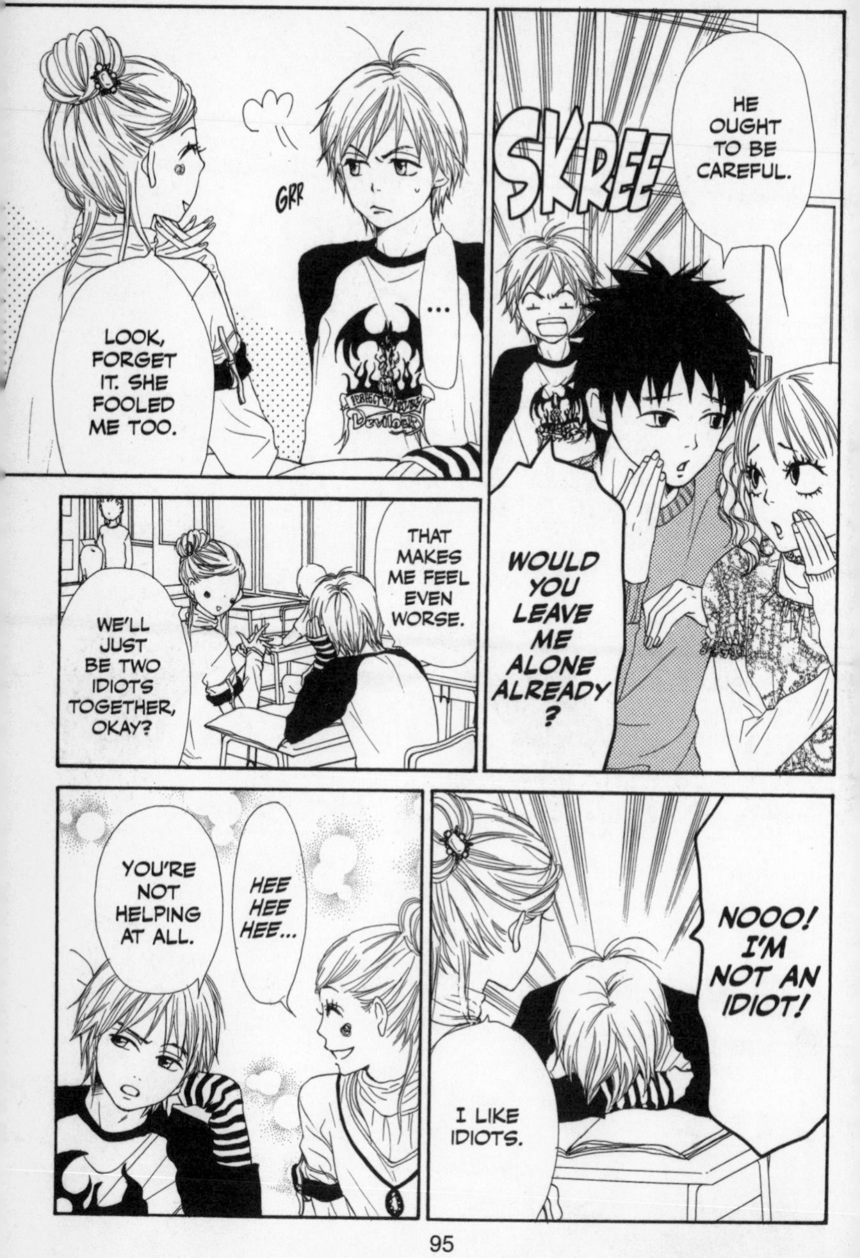
SKREE
HE OUGHT TO BE CAREFUL.
WOULD YOU LEAVE ME ALONE ALREADY?
GRR
...
LOOK, FORGET IT. SHE FOOLED ME TOO.
THAT MAKES ME FEEL EVEN WORSE.
WE'LL JUST BE TWO IDIOTS TOGETHER, OKAY?
NOOO! I'M NOT AN IDIOT!
I LIKE IDIOTS.
HEE HEE HEE...
YOU'RE NOT HELPING AT ALL.

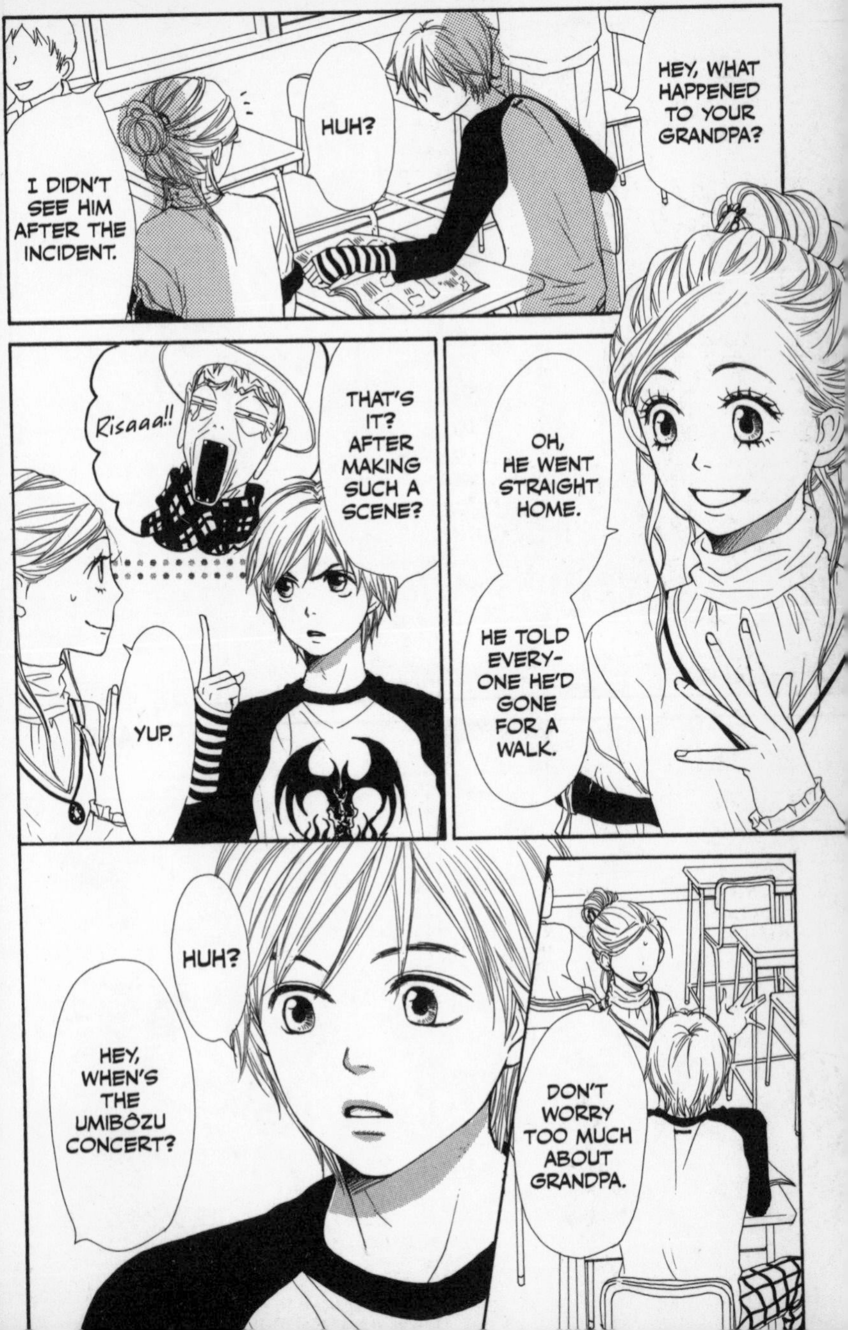
HEY, WHAT HAPPENED TO YOUR GRANDPA?
HUH?
I DIDN'T SEE HIM AFTER THE INCIDENT.
OH, HE WENT STRAIGHT HOME.
HE TOLD EVERY-ONE HE'D GONE FOR A WALK.
THAT'S IT? AFTER MAKING SUCH A SCENE?
Risaaa!!
YUP.
DON'T WORRY TOO MUCH ABOUT GRANDPA.
HUH?
HEY, WHEN'S THE UMIBÔZU CONCERT?

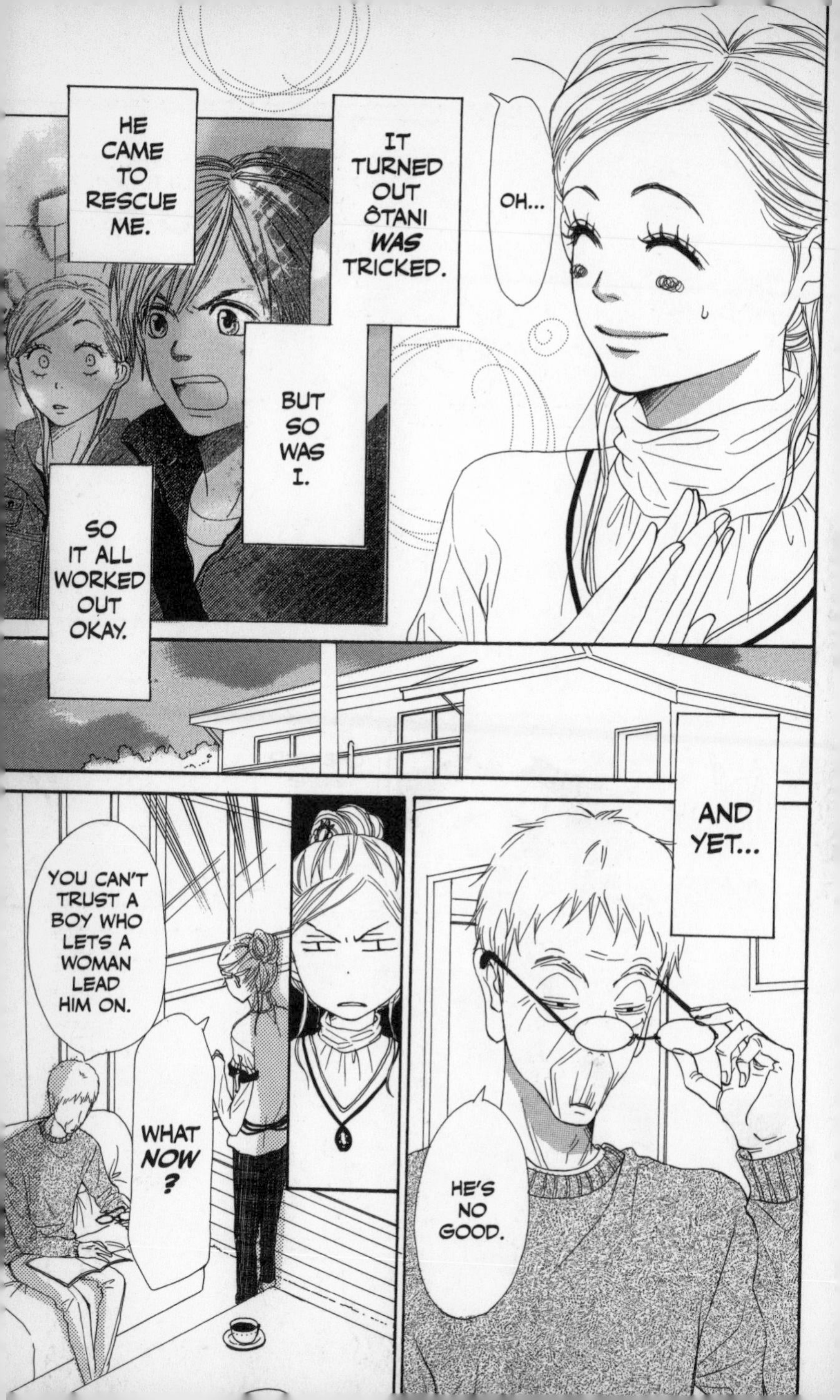
OH...
IT TURNED OUT ŌTANI *WAS* TRICKED.
HE CAME TO RESCUE ME.
BUT SO WAS I.
SO IT ALL WORKED OUT OKAY.
AND YET...
HE'S NO GOOD.
WHAT *NOW*?
YOU CAN'T TRUST A BOY WHO LETS A WOMAN LEAD HIM ON.

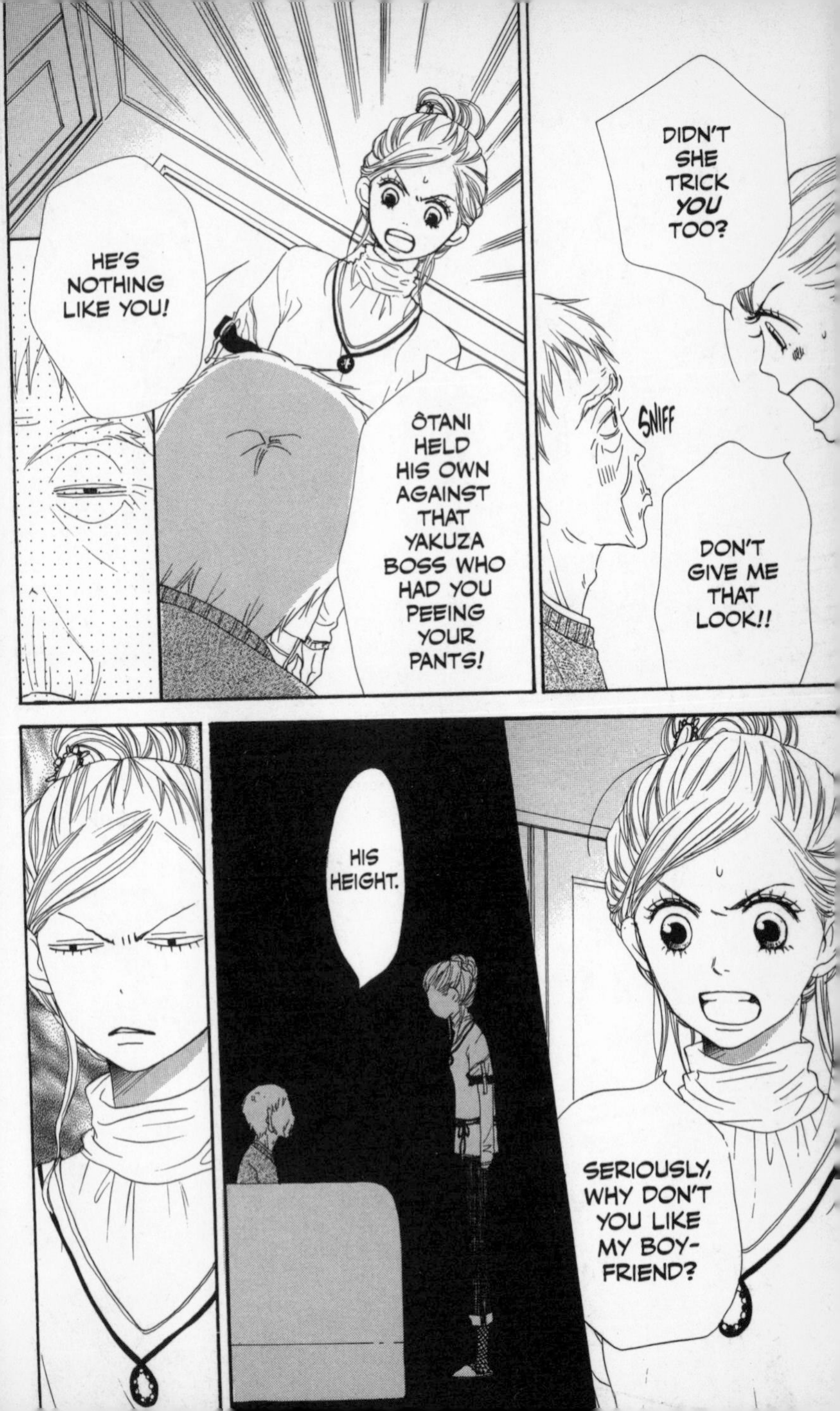

DIDN'T SHE TRICK *YOU* TOO?
SNIFF
DON'T GIVE ME THAT LOOK!!
HE'S NOTHING LIKE YOU!
ÔTANI HELD HIS OWN AGAINST THAT YAKUZA BOSS WHO HAD YOU PEEING YOUR PANTS!
SERIOUSLY, WHY DON'T YOU LIKE MY BOY-FRIEND?
HIS HEIGHT.

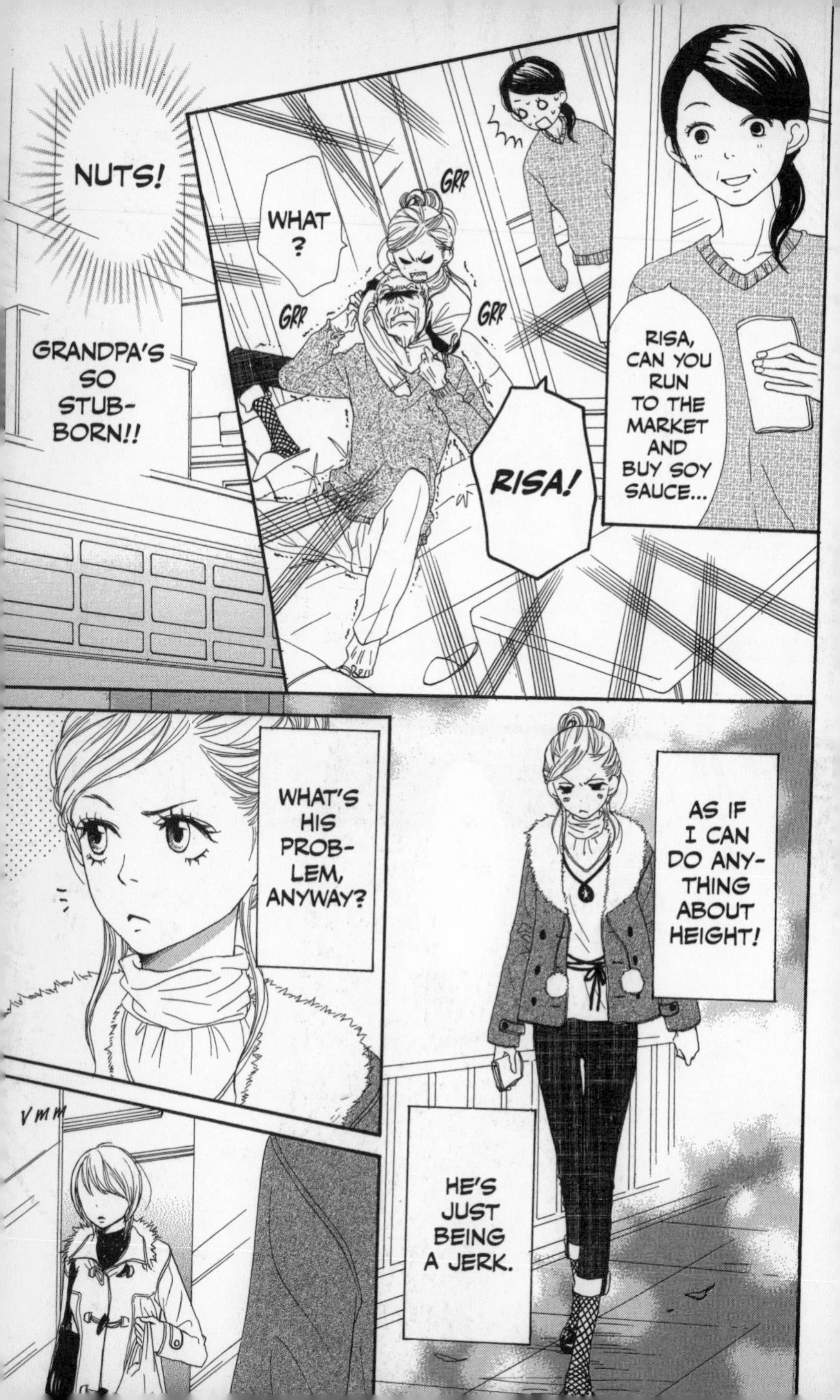

RISA, CAN YOU RUN TO THE MARKET AND BUY SOY SAUCE...
RISA!
GRR
WHAT?
GRR
GRR
NUTS!
GRANDPA'S SO STUB-BORN!!
AS IF I CAN DO ANY-THING ABOUT HEIGHT!
HE'S JUST BEING A JERK.
WHAT'S HIS PROB-LEM, ANYWAY?
VMM

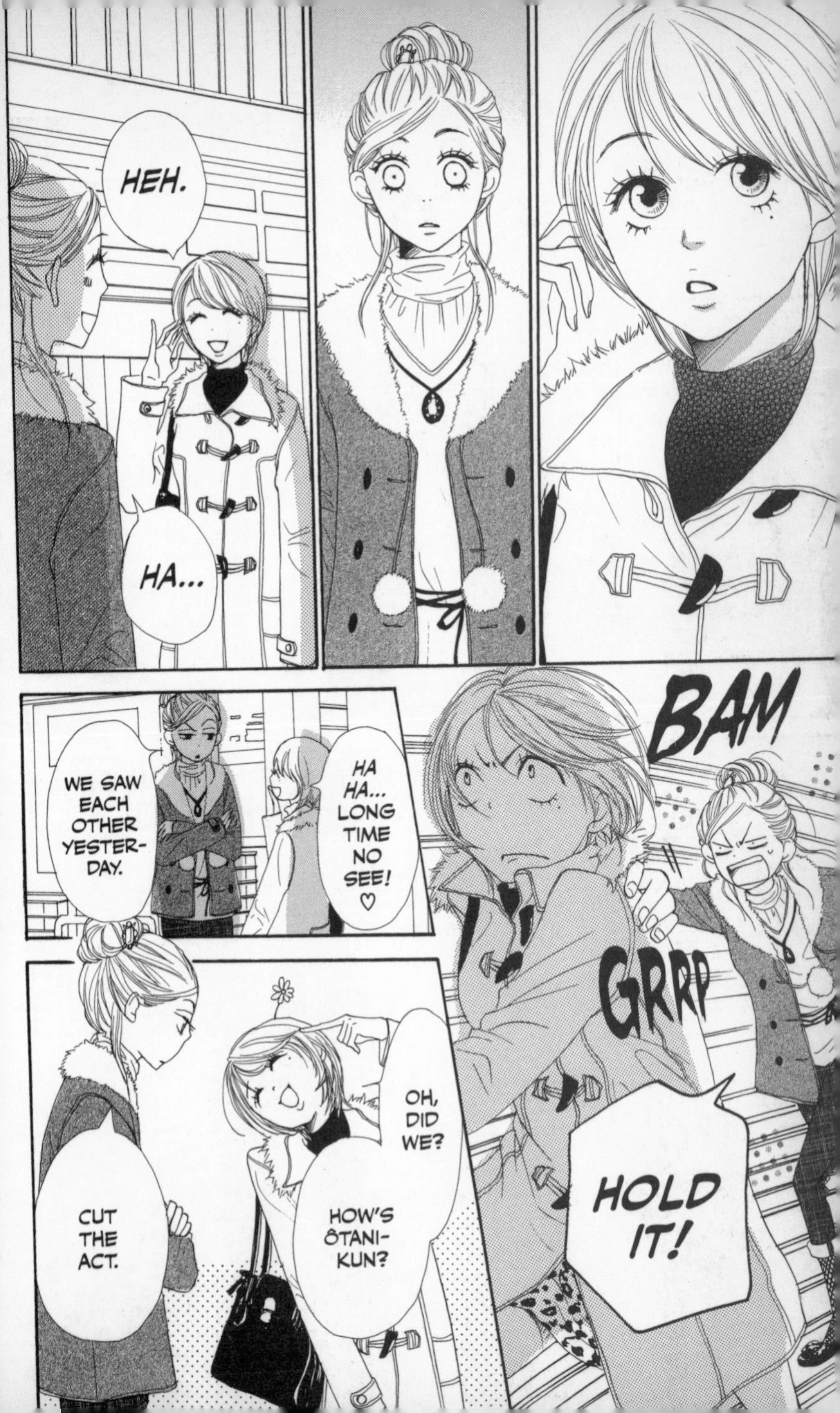
HEH.
HA...
BAM
GRRP
HOLD IT!
HA HA... LONG TIME NO SEE! ♡
WE SAW EACH OTHER YESTER-DAY.
OH, DID WE?
HOW'S ŌTANI-KUN?
CUT THE ACT.

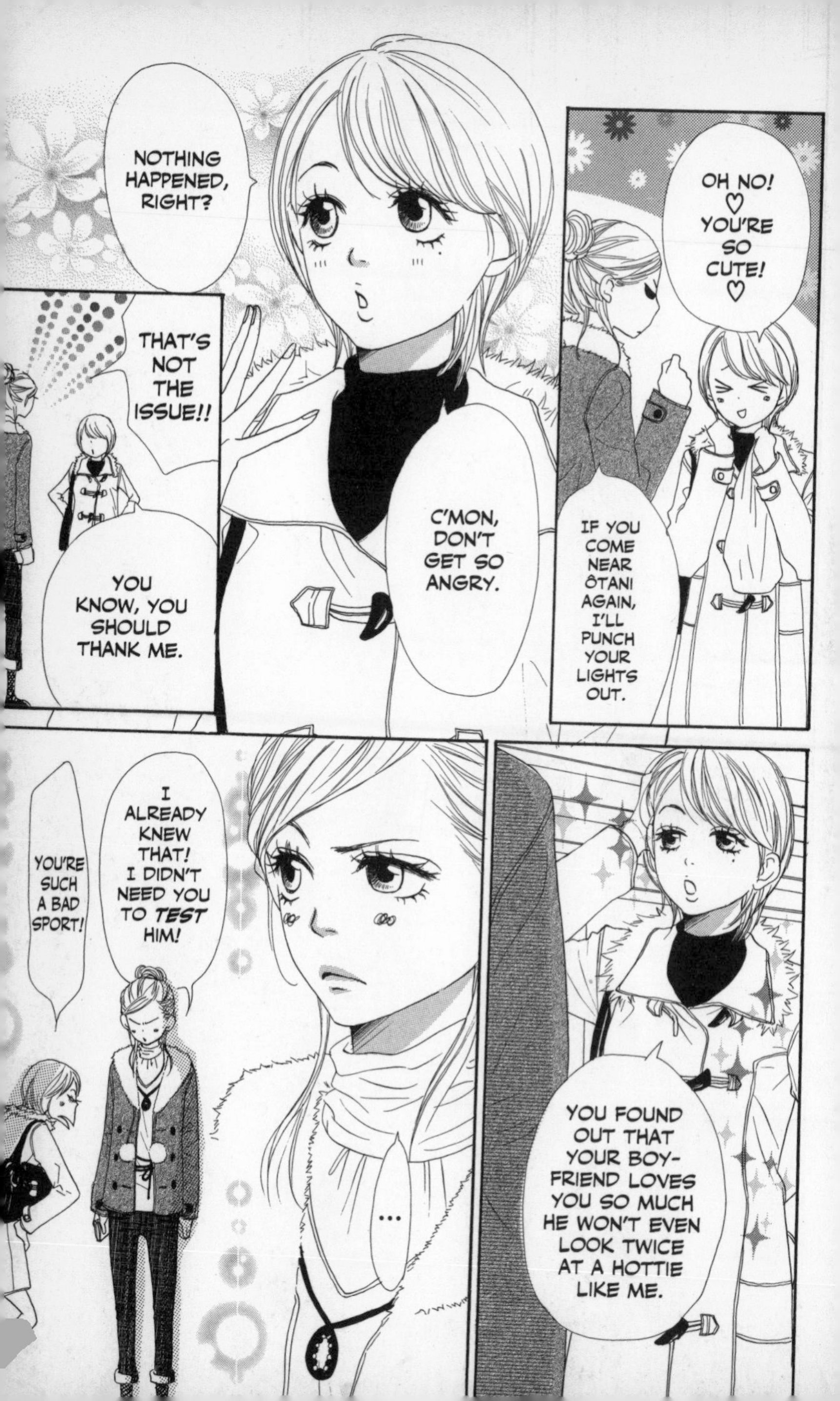
OH NO! ♡ YOU'RE SO CUTE! ♡
IF YOU COME NEAR ÔTANI AGAIN, I'LL PUNCH YOUR LIGHTS OUT.
C'MON, DON'T GET SO ANGRY.
NOTHING HAPPENED, RIGHT?
THAT'S NOT THE ISSUE!!
YOU KNOW, YOU SHOULD THANK ME.
YOU FOUND OUT THAT YOUR BOY-FRIEND LOVES YOU SO MUCH HE WON'T EVEN LOOK TWICE AT A HOTTIE LIKE ME.
...
I ALREADY KNEW THAT! I DIDN'T NEED YOU TO *TEST* HIM!
YOU'RE SUCH A BAD SPORT!

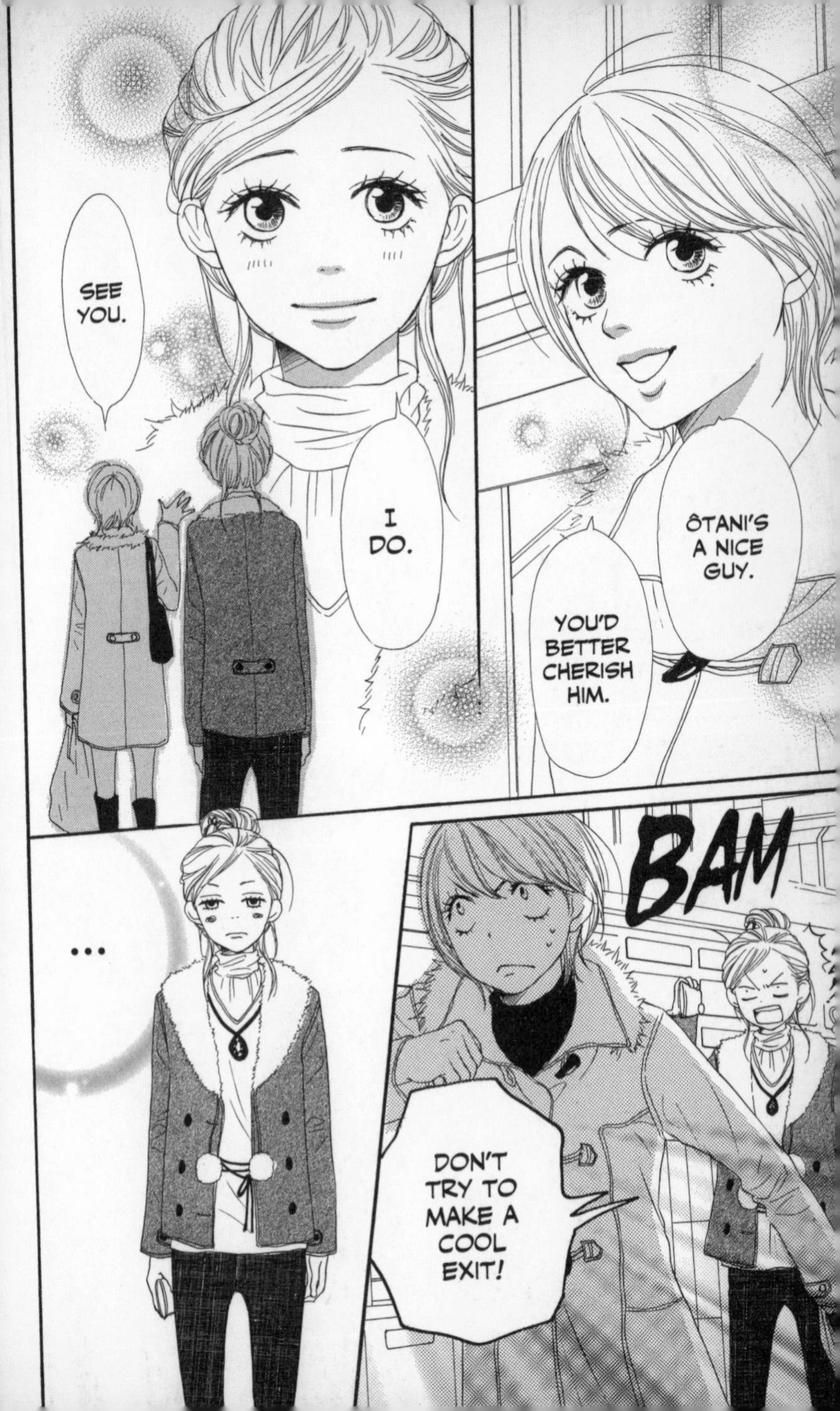
ÔTANI'S A NICE GUY.
YOU'D BETTER CHERISH HIM.
I DO.
SEE YOU.
BAM
DON'T TRY TO MAKE A COOL EXIT!
...

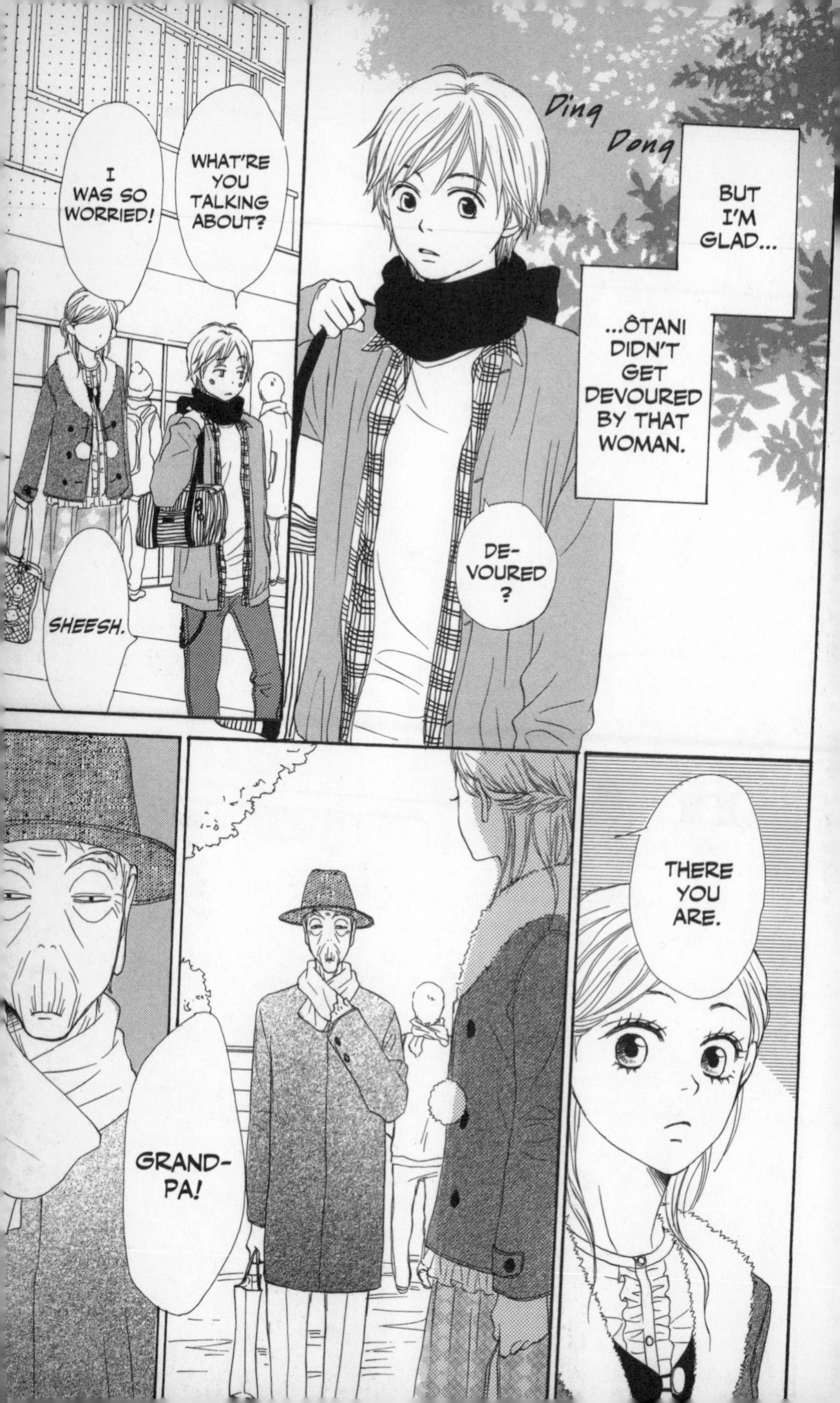
Ding Dong
BUT I'M GLAD...
...ÔTANI DIDN'T GET DEVOURED BY THAT WOMAN.
DE-VOURED?
WHAT'RE YOU TALKING ABOUT?
I WAS SO WORRIED!
SHEESH.
THERE YOU ARE.
GRAND-PA!

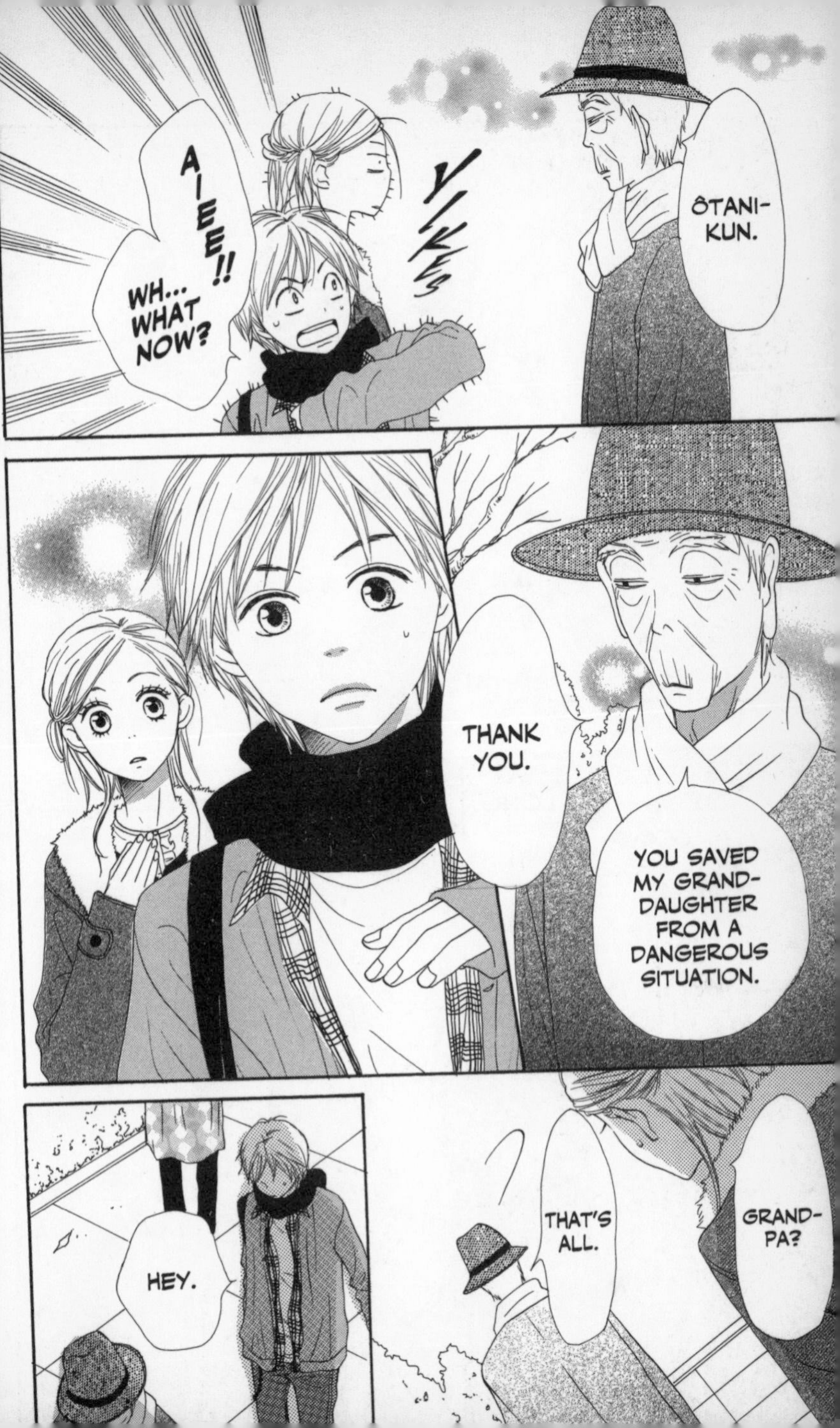
ÔTANI-KUN.
YIKES
AIEE!!
WH... WHAT NOW?
YOU SAVED MY GRAND-DAUGHTER FROM A DANGEROUS SITUATION.
THANK YOU.
GRAND-PA?
THAT'S ALL.
HEY.

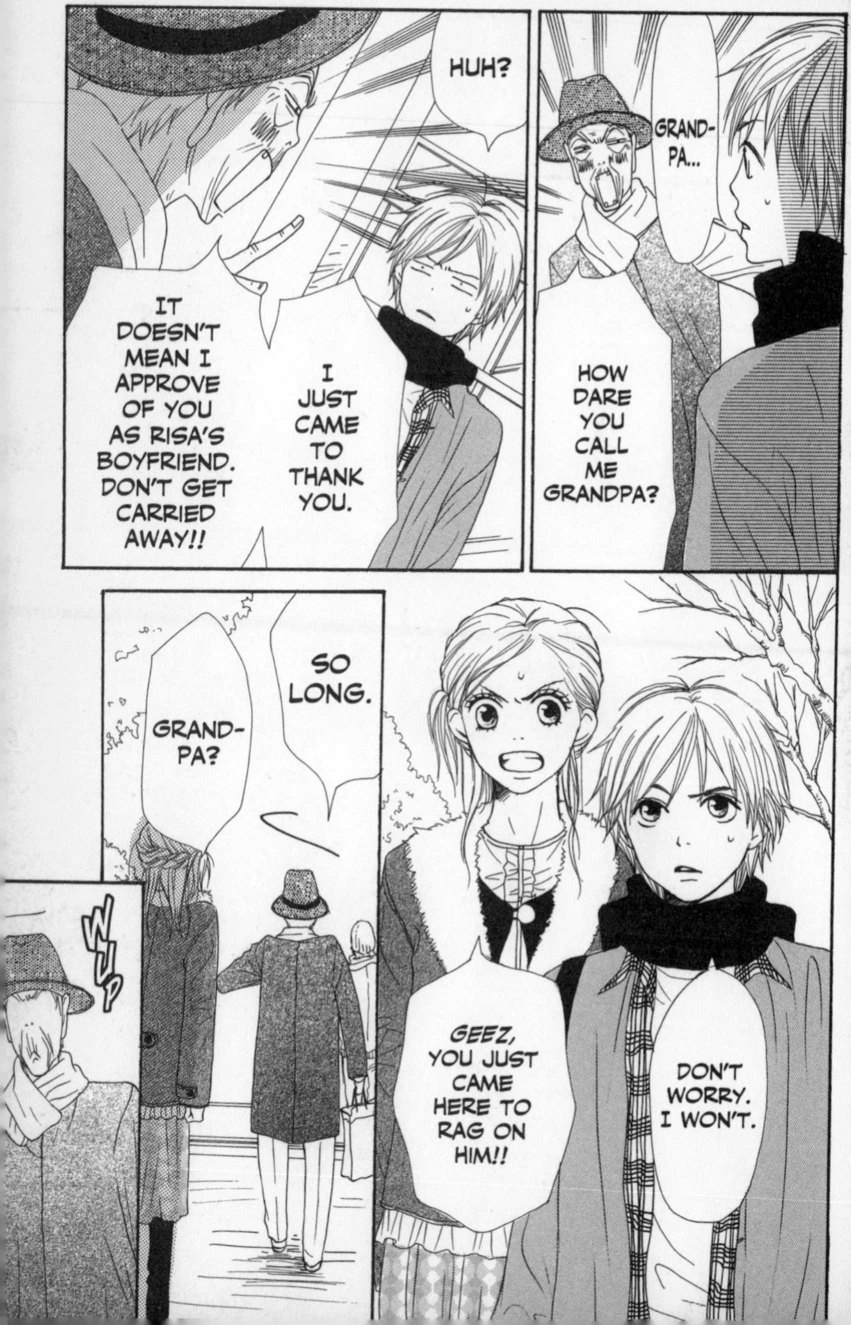
GRAND-PA...
HOW DARE YOU CALL ME GRANDPA?
HUH?
I JUST CAME TO THANK YOU.
IT DOESN'T MEAN I APPROVE OF YOU AS RISA'S BOYFRIEND. DON'T GET CARRIED AWAY!!
GEEZ, YOU JUST CAME HERE TO RAG ON HIM!!
DON'T WORRY. I WON'T.
SO LONG.
GRAND-PA?
WUP

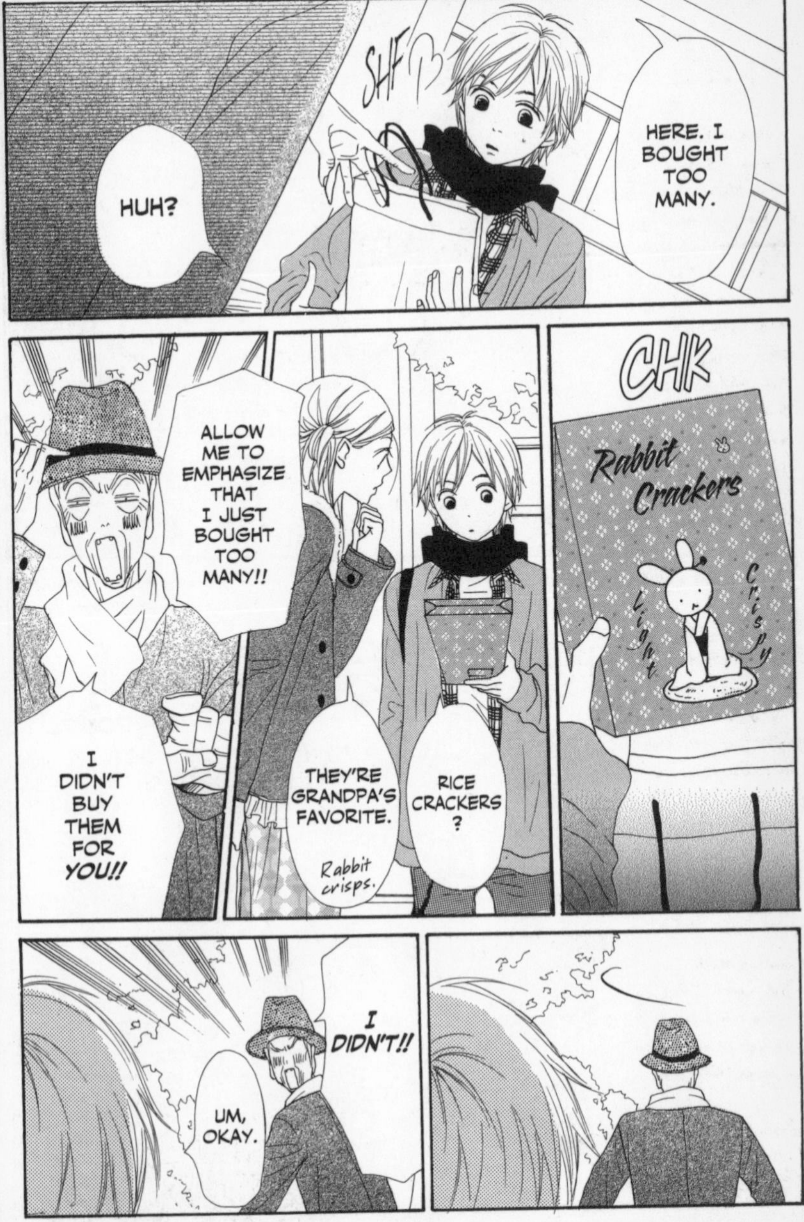
HERE. I BOUGHT TOO MANY.
SHF
HUH?
CHK
Rabbit Crackers
Crispy
Light
RICE CRACKERS ?
THEY'RE GRANDPA'S FAVORITE.
Rabbit crisps.
ALLOW ME TO EMPHASIZE THAT I JUST BOUGHT TOO MANY!!
I DIDN'T BUY THEM FOR *YOU!!*
I DIDN'T!!
UM, OKAY.

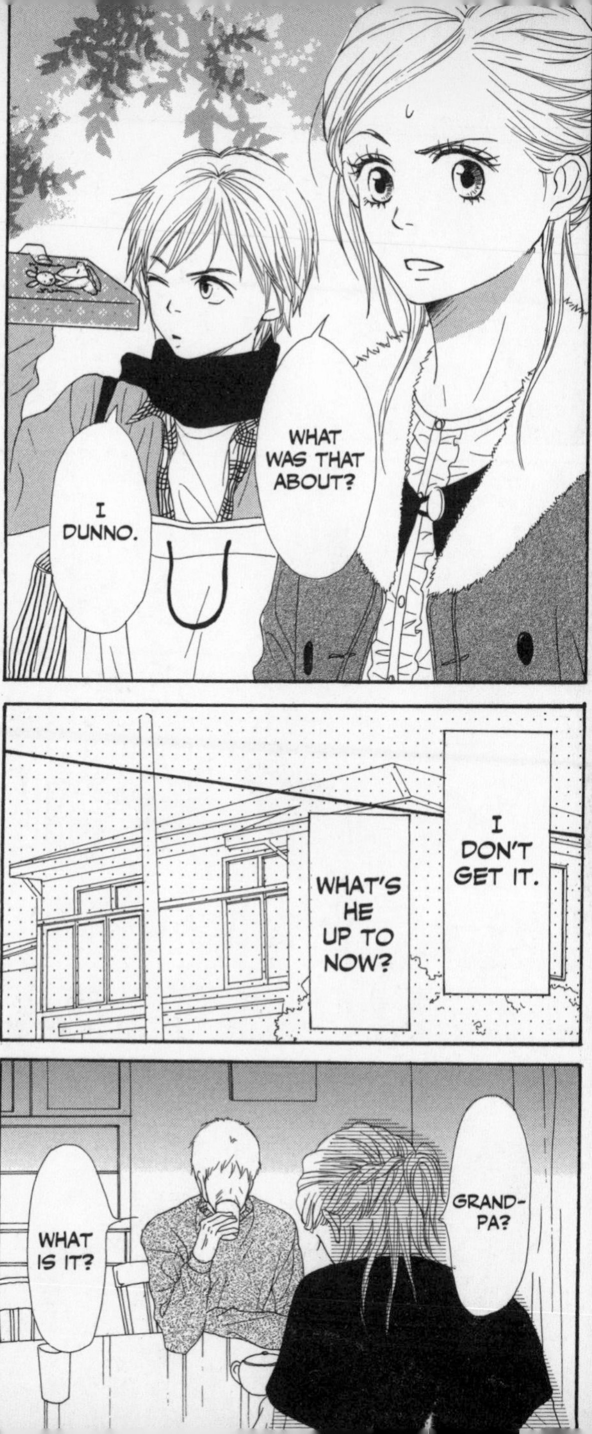
WHAT WAS THAT ABOUT?
I DUNNO.
I DON'T GET IT.
WHAT'S HE UP TO NOW?
GRAND-PA?
WHAT IS IT?

3

Don't mind me.

There are plenty of things I didn't include in the "Making of" report. I mean, so much amazing stuff went on that I didn't have room to describe everything that happened.
But what surprised me the most was the day I went to the set just before they finished shooting. As I was about to go home, the actors who played Risa, Ōtani, Nobu, Nakao, Suzuki and Chiharu—Ema Fujisawa, Teppei Koike, Yusuke Yamazaki, Nami Tamaki, Hiro Mizushima and Risa Kudo—presented me with a card filled with their personal messages. It was full of happy wishes from corner to corner.
For me, this sorry excuse for a manga artist!

I was in heaven.
They were all so great.
During the filming, we had long talks about so many things.

Such angels!!
Thank you.
Thank you so much!!

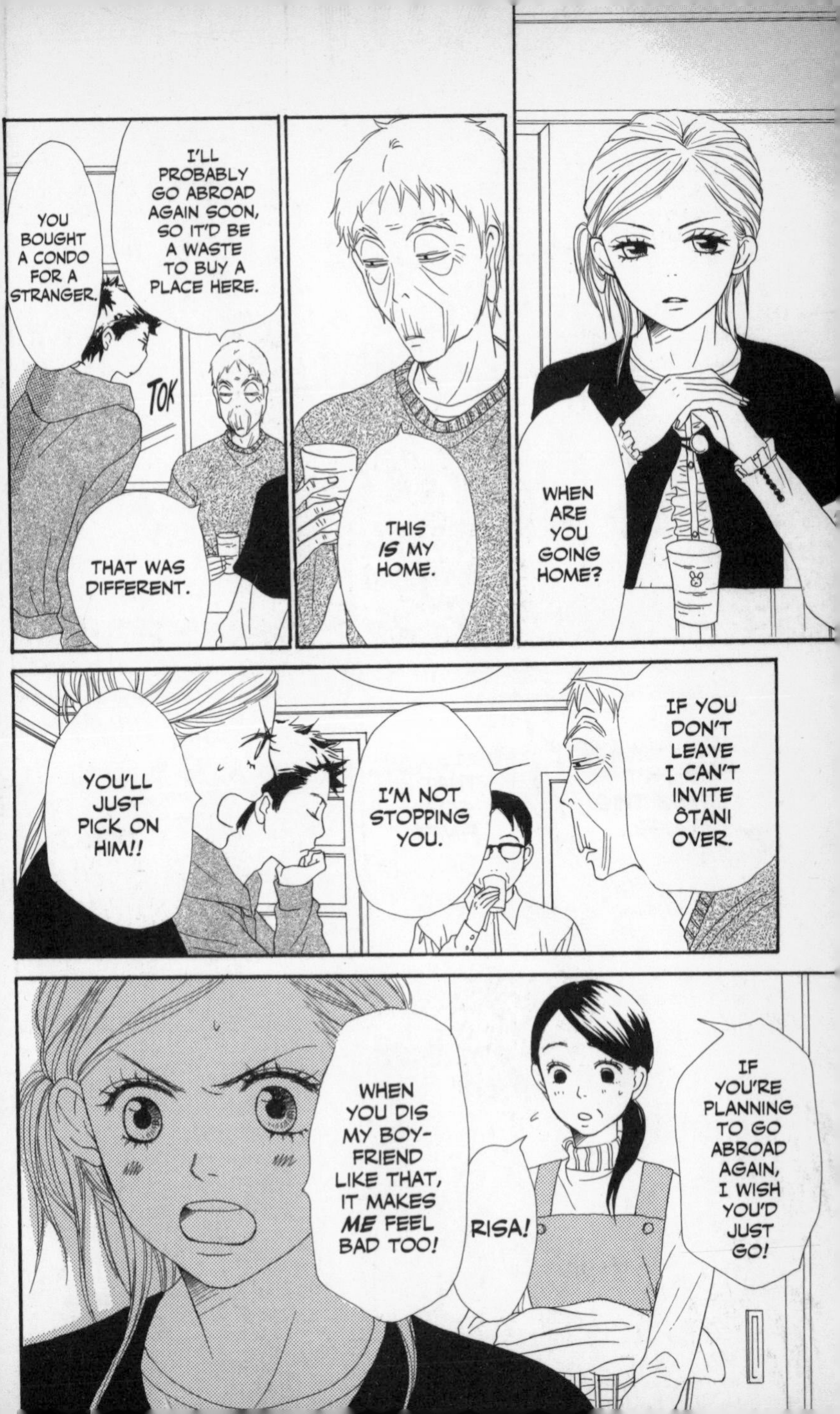
WHEN ARE YOU GOING HOME?
THIS *IS* MY HOME.
I'LL PROBABLY GO ABROAD AGAIN SOON, SO IT'D BE A WASTE TO BUY A PLACE HERE.
YOU BOUGHT A CONDO FOR A STRANGER.
TOK
THAT WAS DIFFERENT.
IF YOU DON'T LEAVE I CAN'T INVITE ŌTANI OVER.
I'M NOT STOPPING YOU.
YOU'LL JUST PICK ON HIM!!
IF YOU'RE PLANNING TO GO ABROAD AGAIN, I WISH YOU'D JUST GO!
RISA!
WHEN YOU DIS MY BOY-FRIEND LIKE THAT, IT MAKES *ME* FEEL BAD TOO!

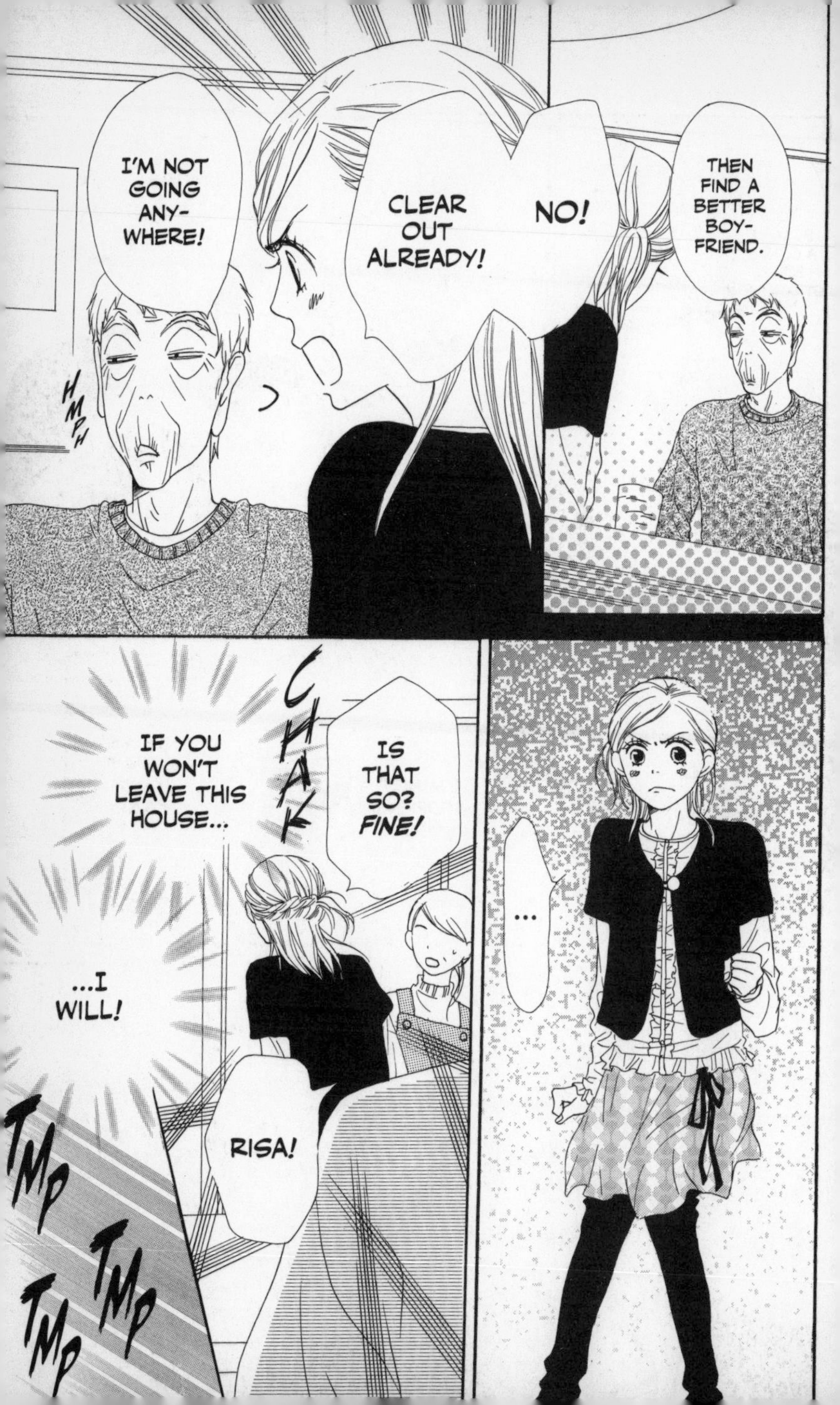
THEN FIND A BETTER BOY-FRIEND.
NO!
CLEAR OUT ALREADY!
I'M NOT GOING ANY-WHERE!
HMPH
...
CHAK
IS THAT SO? FINE!
IF YOU WON'T LEAVE THIS HOUSE...
...I WILL!
RISA!
TMP TMP
TMP TMP

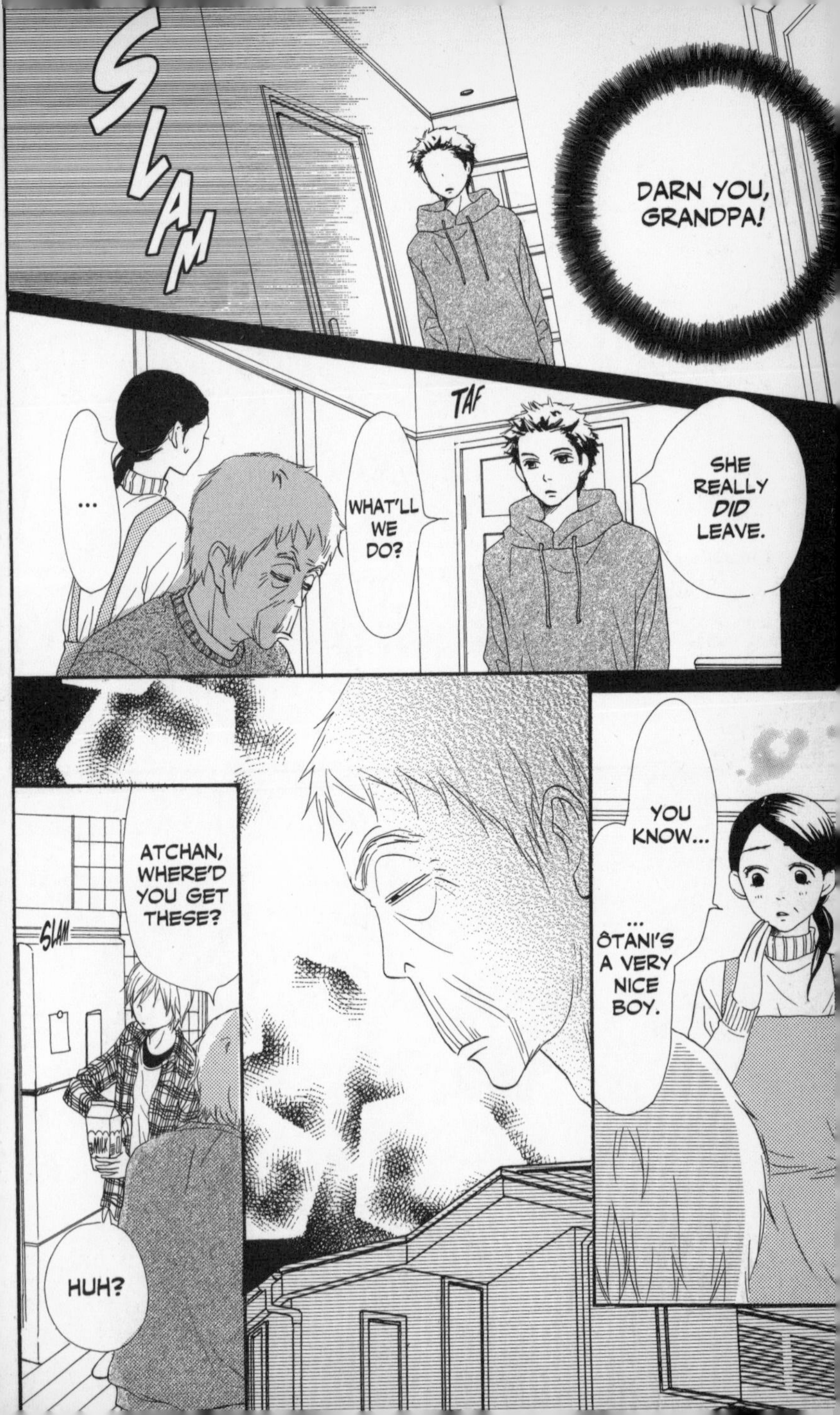
DARN YOU, GRANDPA!
SLAM
SHE REALLY DID LEAVE.
TAF
WHAT'LL WE DO?
...
YOU KNOW...
...ŌTANI'S A VERY NICE BOY.
ATCHAN, WHERE'D YOU GET THESE?
SLAM
MILK
HUH?

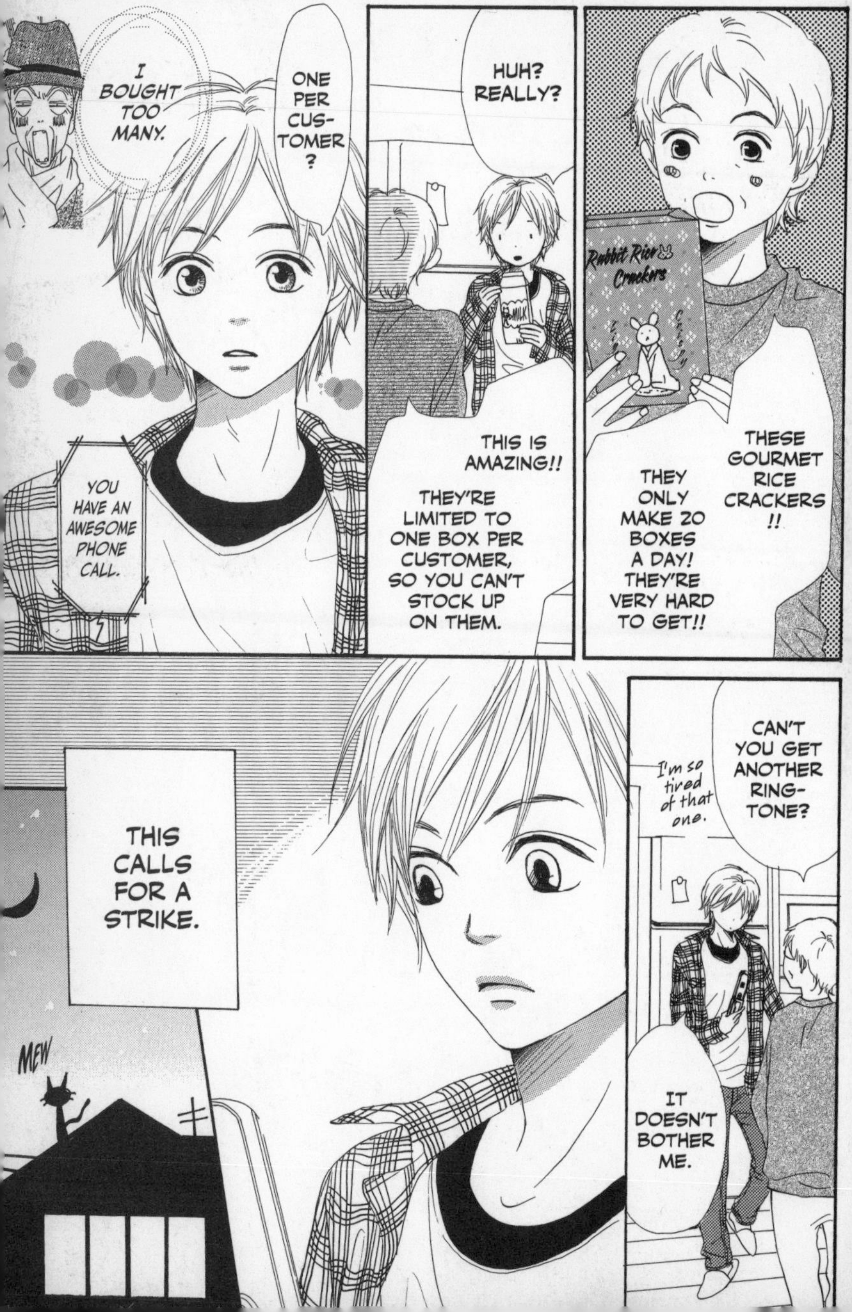
THESE GOURMET RICE CRACKERS!!
Rabbit Rice Crackers
THEY ONLY MAKE 20 BOXES A DAY! THEY'RE VERY HARD TO GET!!
HUH? REALLY?
THIS IS AMAZING!!
THEY'RE LIMITED TO ONE BOX PER CUSTOMER, SO YOU CAN'T STOCK UP ON THEM.
ONE PER CUS-TOMER?
I BOUGHT TOO MANY.
YOU HAVE AN AWESOME PHONE CALL.
CAN'T YOU GET ANOTHER RING-TONE?
I'm so tired of that one.
IT DOESN'T BOTHER ME.
THIS CALLS FOR A STRIKE.
MEW

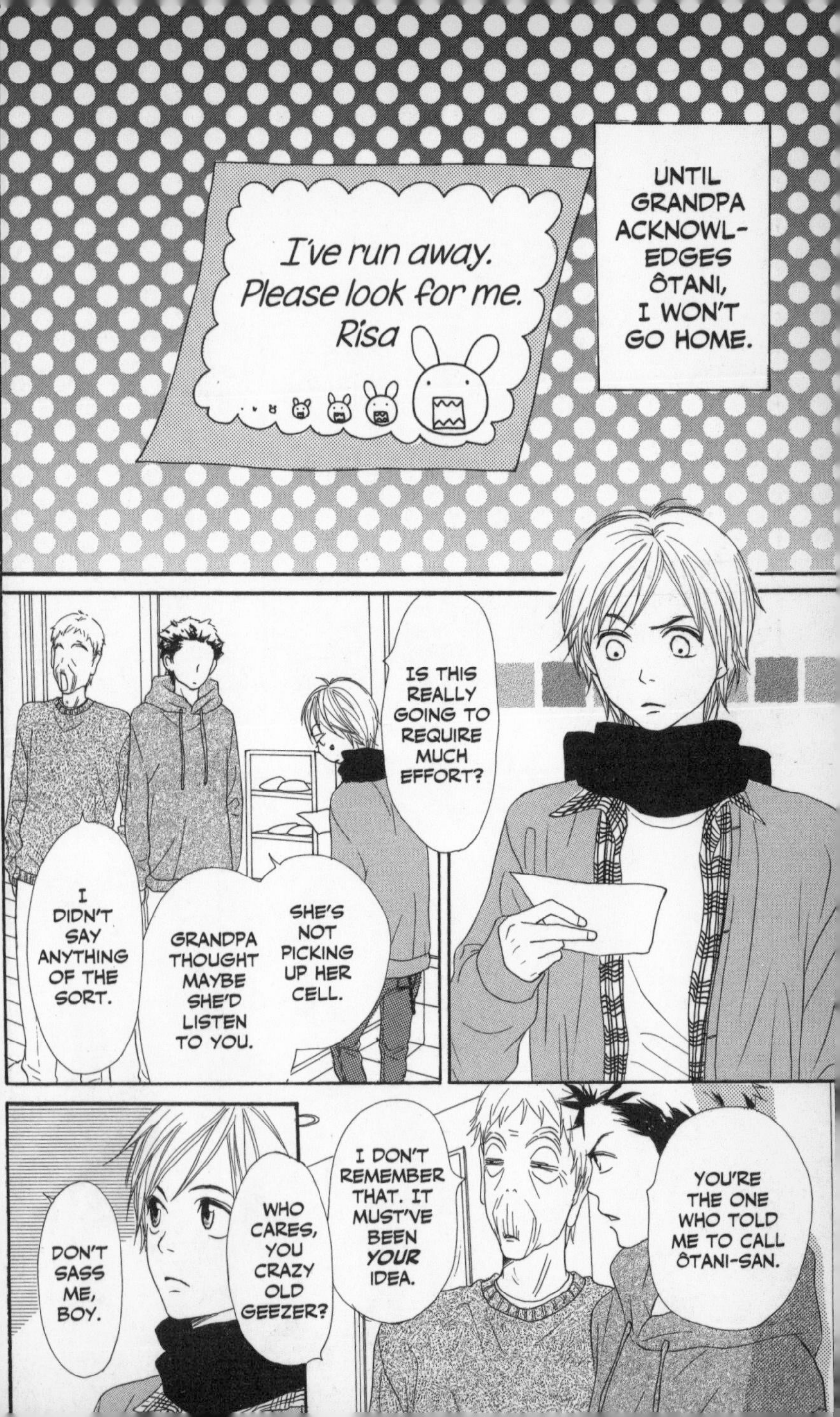
UNTIL GRANDPA ACKNOWL-EDGES ÔTANI, I WON'T GO HOME.
I've run away. Please look for me. Risa
IS THIS REALLY GOING TO REQUIRE MUCH EFFORT?
SHE'S NOT PICKING UP HER CELL.
GRANDPA THOUGHT MAYBE SHE'D LISTEN TO YOU.
I DIDN'T SAY ANYTHING OF THE SORT.
YOU'RE THE ONE WHO TOLD ME TO CALL ÔTANI-SAN.
I DON'T REMEMBER THAT. IT MUST'VE BEEN *YOUR* IDEA.
WHO CARES, YOU CRAZY OLD GEEZER?
DON'T SASS ME, BOY.

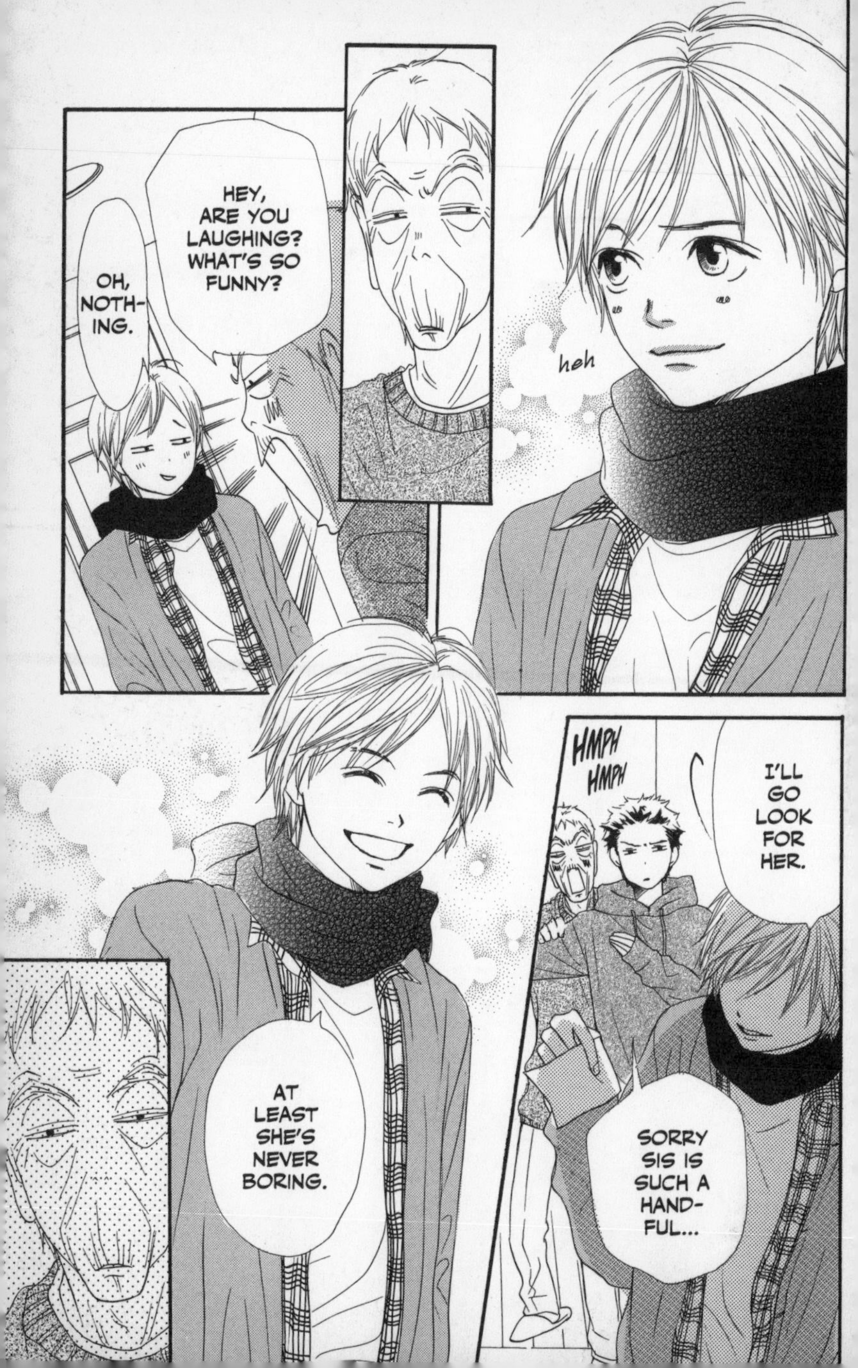
heh
HEY, ARE YOU LAUGHING? WHAT'S SO FUNNY?
OH, NOTHING.
I'LL GO LOOK FOR HER.
HMPH HMPH
SORRY SIS IS SUCH A HANDFUL...
AT LEAST SHE'S NEVER BORING.

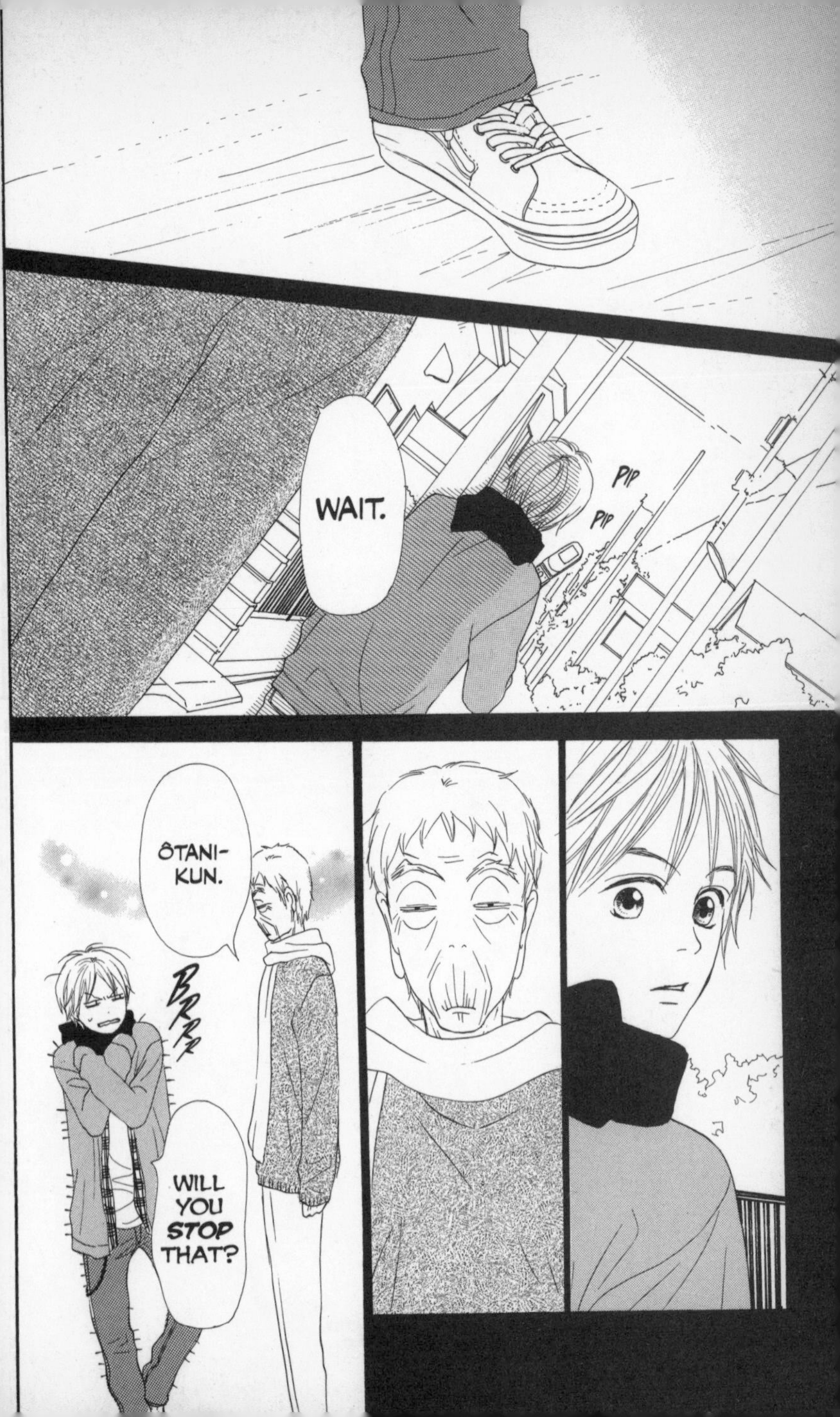
WAIT.
PIP
PIP
ŌTANI-KUN.
BRRR
WILL YOU STOP THAT?

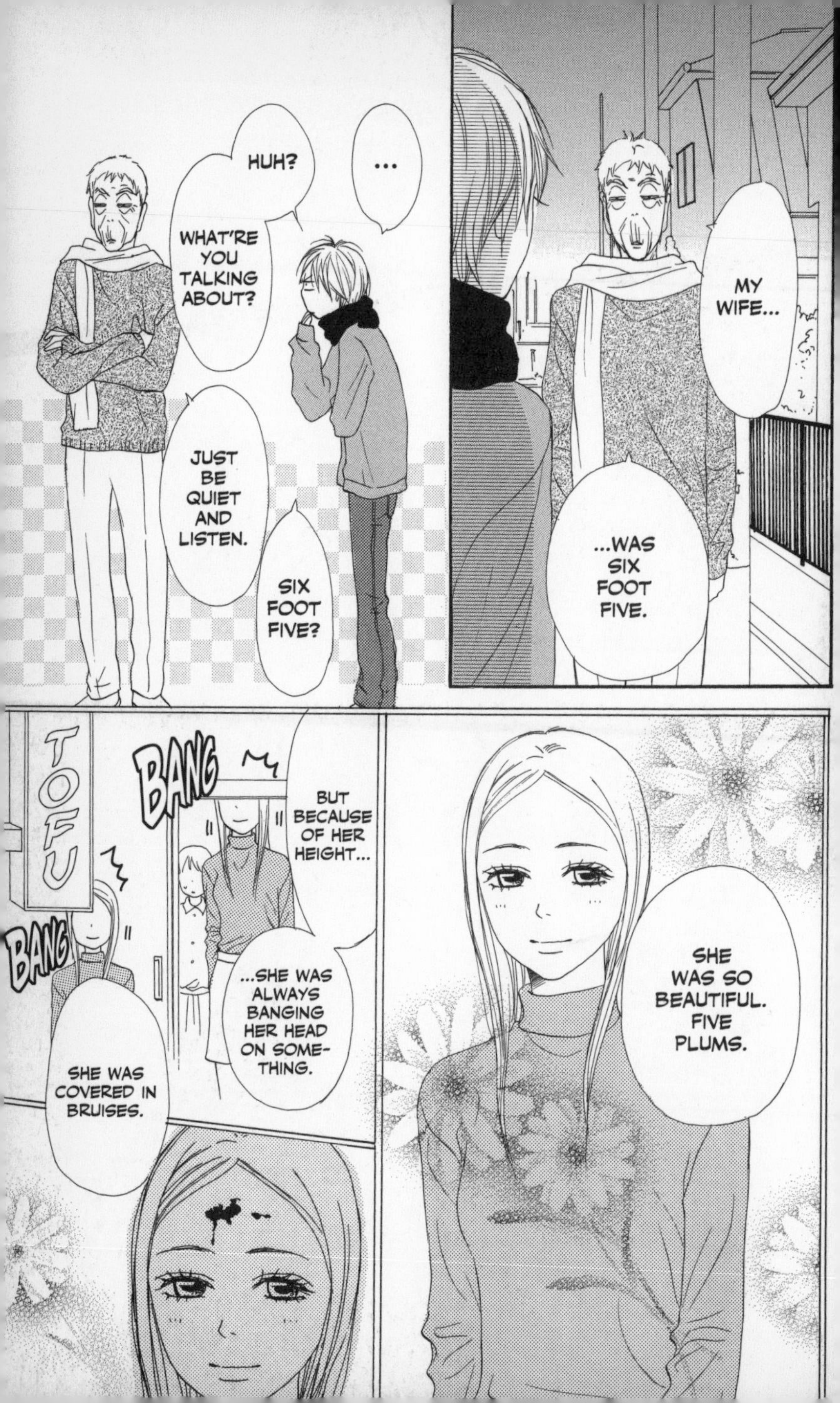
MY WIFE...
...WAS SIX FOOT FIVE.
...
HUH?
WHAT'RE YOU TALKING ABOUT?
JUST BE QUIET AND LISTEN.
SIX FOOT FIVE?
SHE WAS SO BEAUTIFUL. FIVE PLUMS.
BUT BECAUSE OF HER HEIGHT...
BANG
TOFU
...SHE WAS ALWAYS BANGING HER HEAD ON SOME-THING.
BANG
SHE WAS COVERED IN BRUISES.

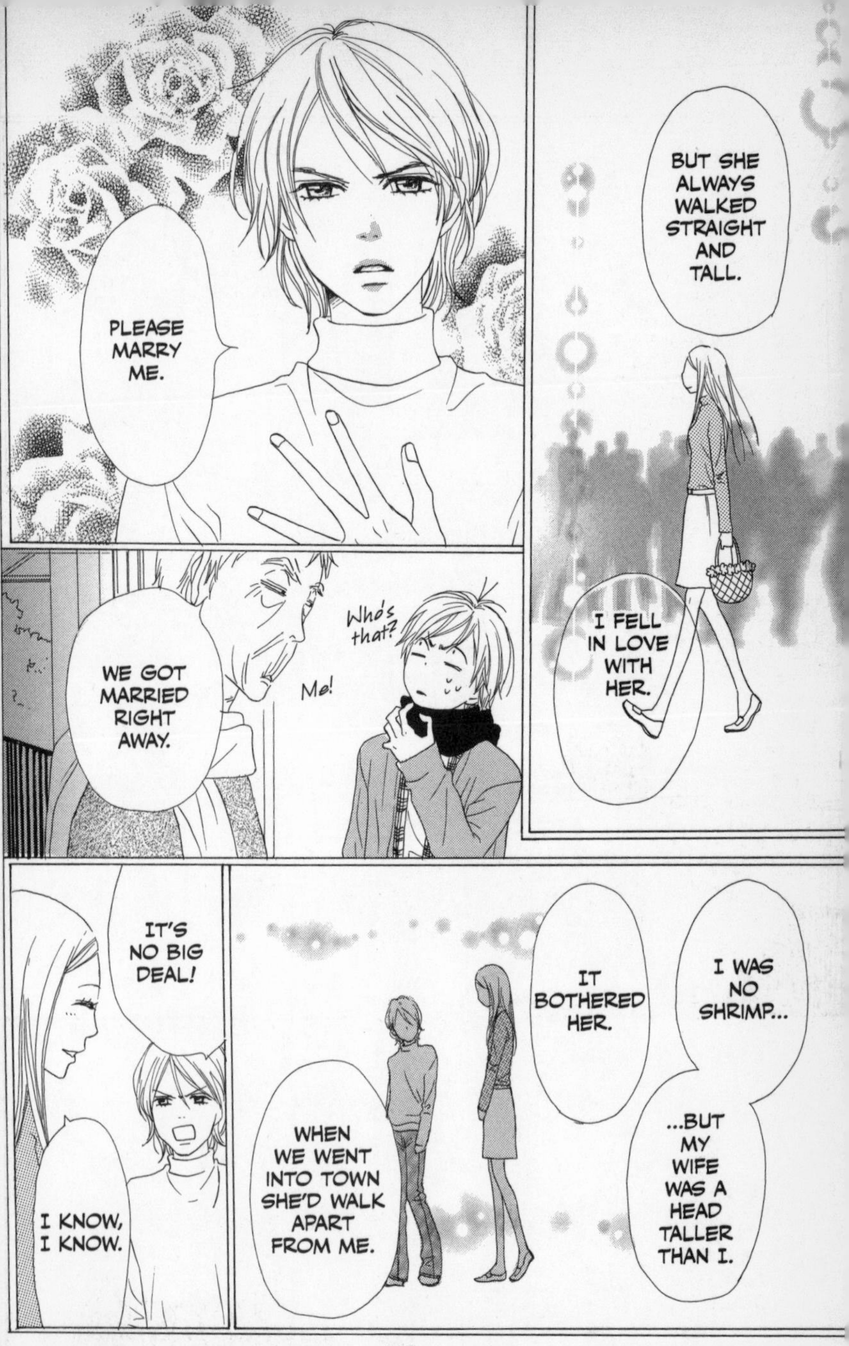
BUT SHE ALWAYS WALKED STRAIGHT AND TALL.
I FELL IN LOVE WITH HER.
PLEASE MARRY ME.
WE GOT MARRIED RIGHT AWAY.
Who's that?
Me!
I WAS NO SHRIMP...
...BUT MY WIFE WAS A HEAD TALLER THAN I.
IT BOTHERED HER.
WHEN WE WENT INTO TOWN SHE'D WALK APART FROM ME.
IT'S NO BIG DEAL!
I KNOW, I KNOW.

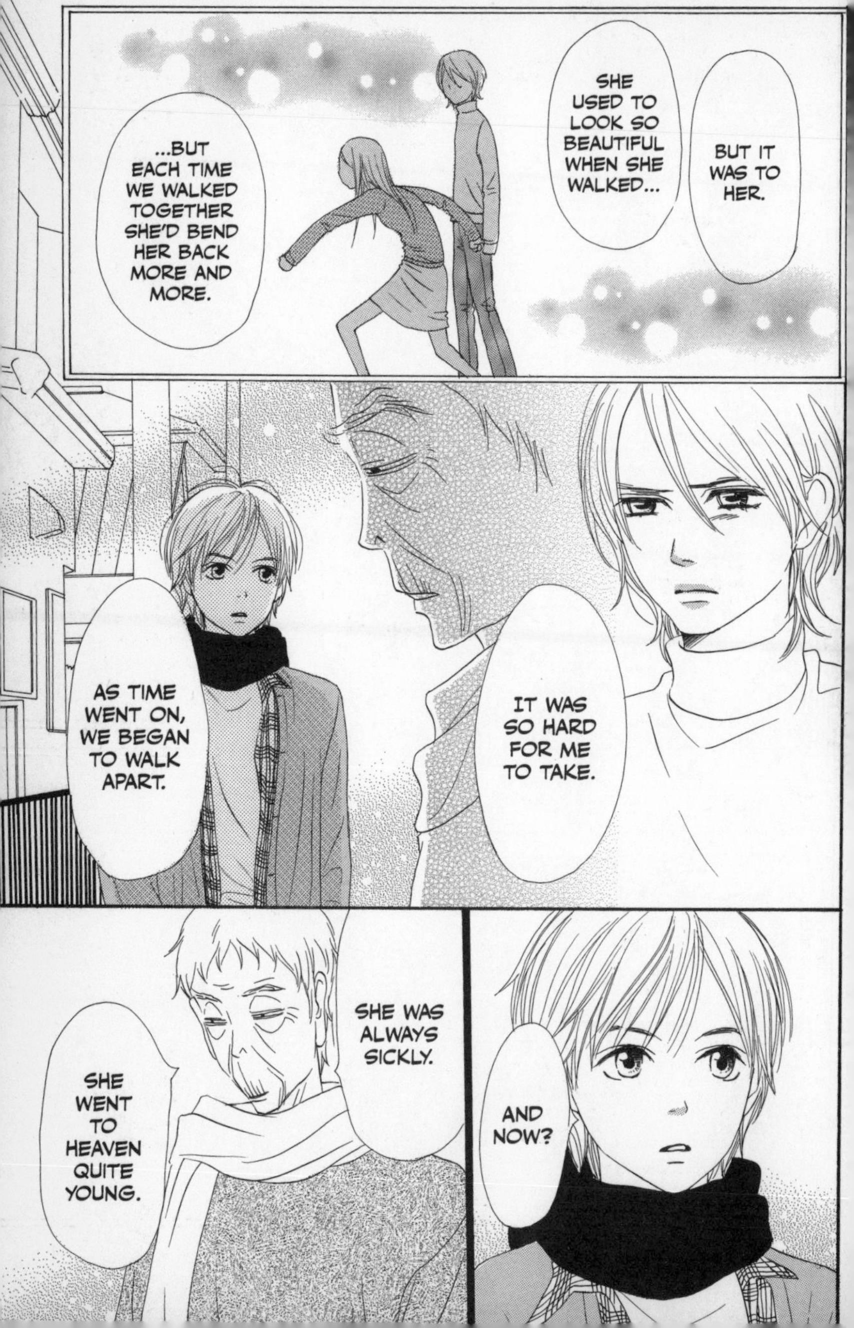
BUT IT WAS TO HER.
SHE USED TO LOOK SO BEAUTIFUL WHEN SHE WALKED...
...BUT EACH TIME WE WALKED TOGETHER SHE'D BEND HER BACK MORE AND MORE.
IT WAS SO HARD FOR ME TO TAKE.
AS TIME WENT ON, WE BEGAN TO WALK APART.
AND NOW?
SHE WAS ALWAYS SICKLY.
SHE WENT TO HEAVEN QUITE YOUNG.

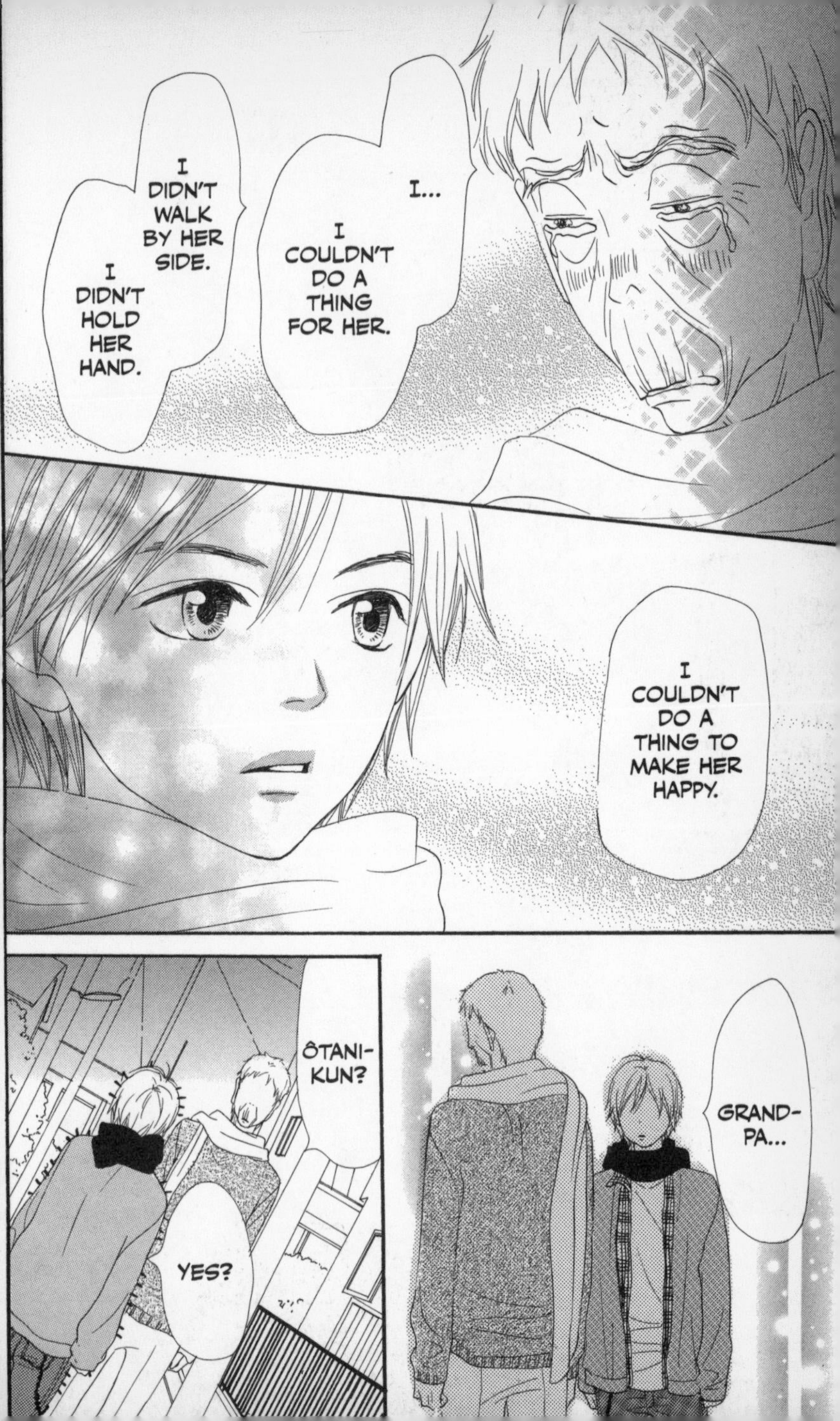
I...
I COULDN'T DO A THING FOR HER.
I DIDN'T WALK BY HER SIDE.
I DIDN'T HOLD HER HAND.
I COULDN'T DO A THING TO MAKE HER HAPPY.
GRAND-PA...
ŌTANI-KUN?
YES?

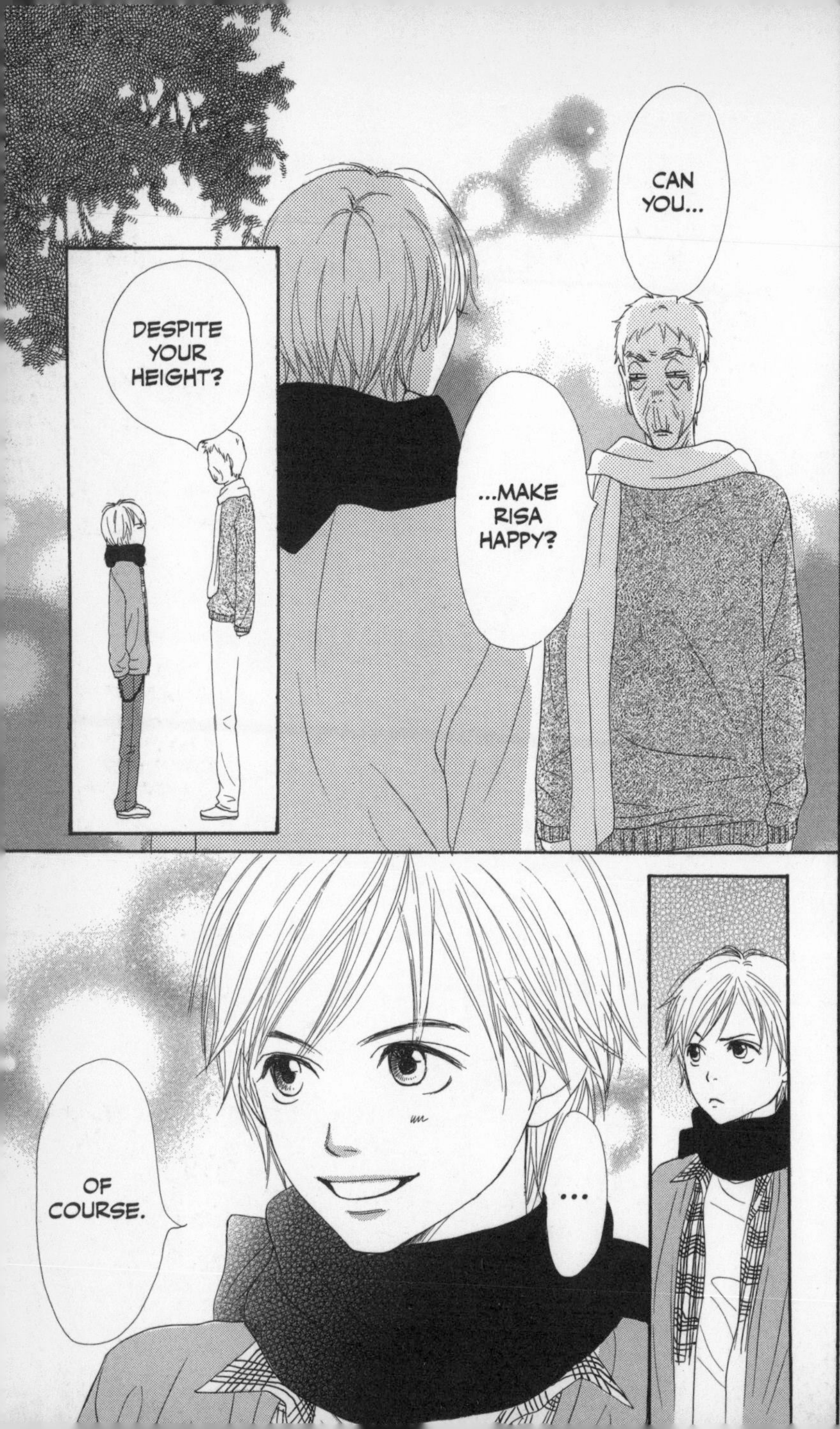
CAN YOU...
...MAKE RISA HAPPY?
DESPITE YOUR HEIGHT?
...
OF COURSE.

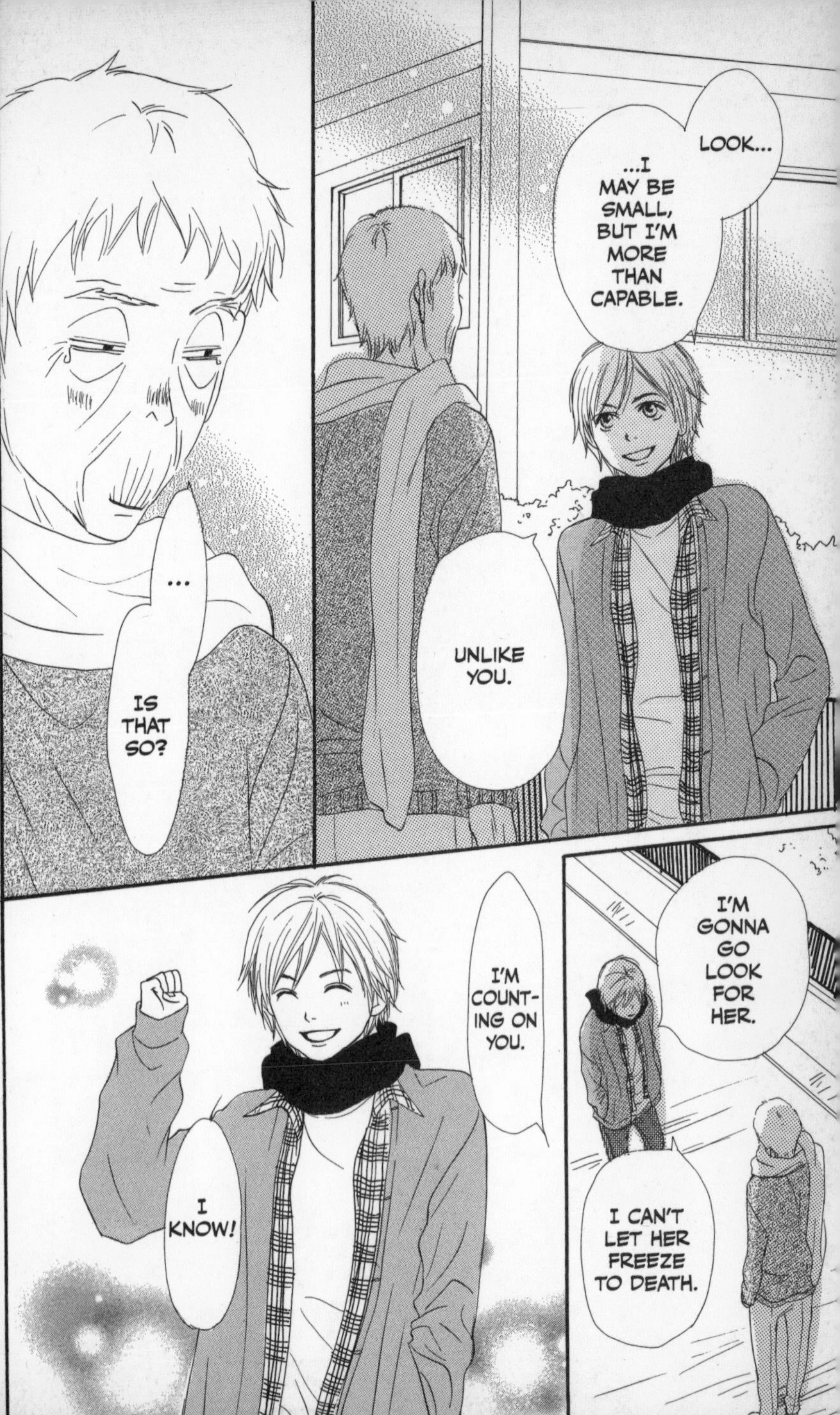
LOOK...
...I MAY BE SMALL, BUT I'M MORE THAN CAPABLE.
UNLIKE YOU.
...
IS THAT SO?
I'M GONNA GO LOOK FOR HER.
I CAN'T LET HER FREEZE TO DEATH.
I'M COUNT-ING ON YOU.
I KNOW!

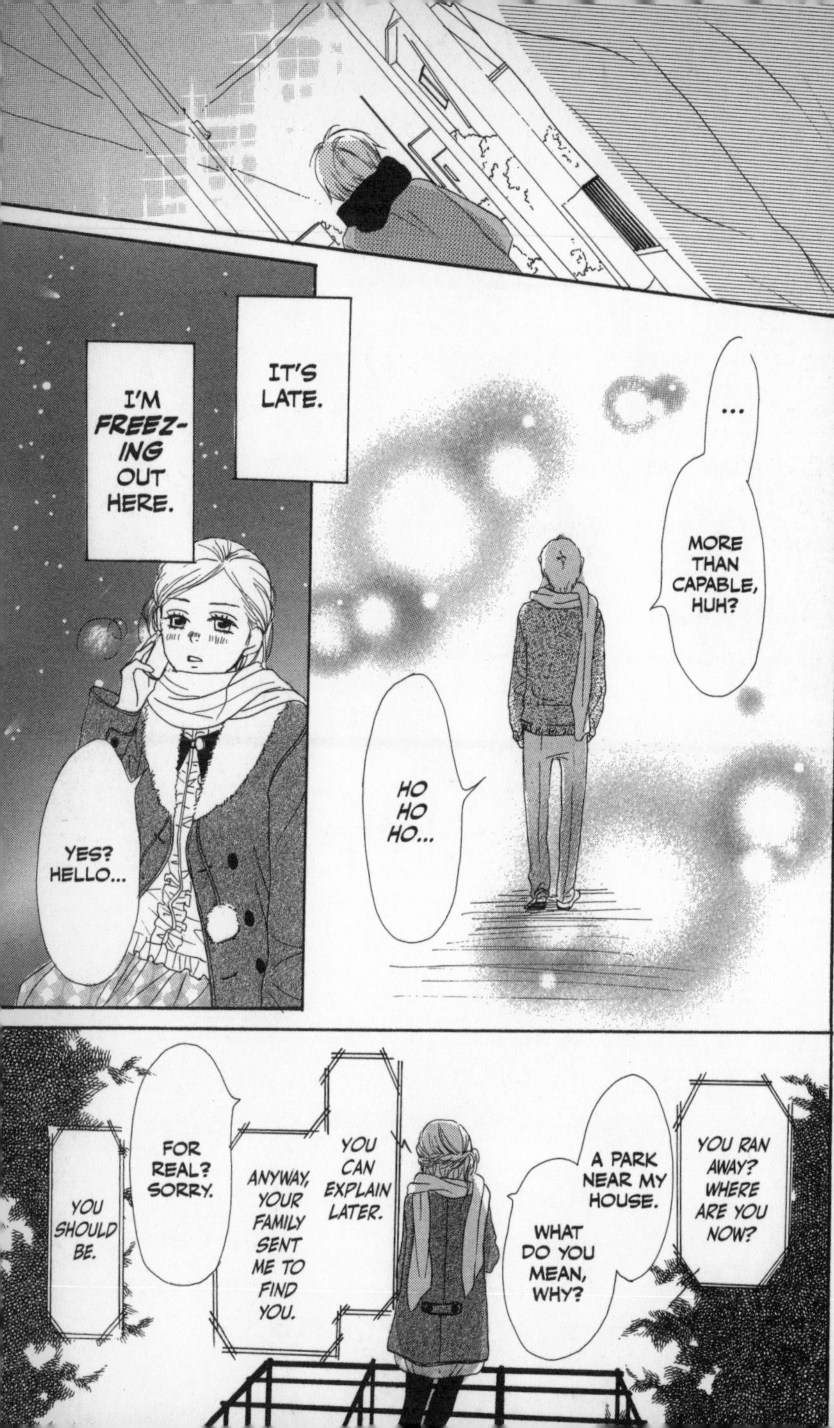
...
MORE THAN CAPABLE, HUH?
HO HO HO...
IT'S LATE.
I'M FREEZING OUT HERE.
YES? HELLO...
YOU RAN AWAY? WHERE ARE YOU NOW?
A PARK NEAR MY HOUSE.
WHAT DO YOU MEAN, WHY?
YOU CAN EXPLAIN LATER.
ANYWAY, YOUR FAMILY SENT ME TO FIND YOU.
FOR REAL? SORRY.
YOU SHOULD BE.

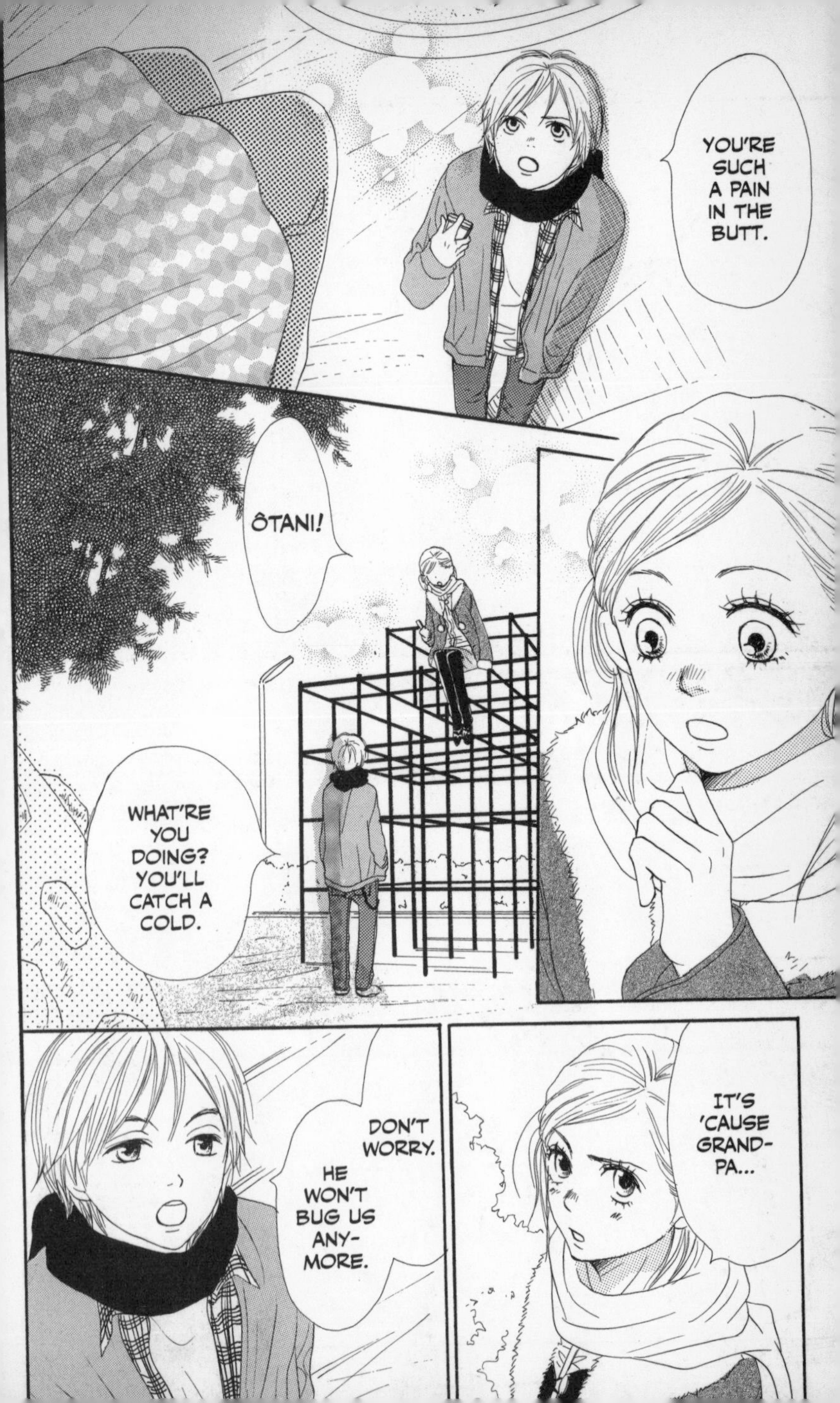
YOU'RE SUCH A PAIN IN THE BUTT.
ÔTANI!
WHAT'RE YOU DOING? YOU'LL CATCH A COLD.
IT'S 'CAUSE GRAND-PA...
DON'T WORRY.
HE WON'T BUG US ANY-MORE.

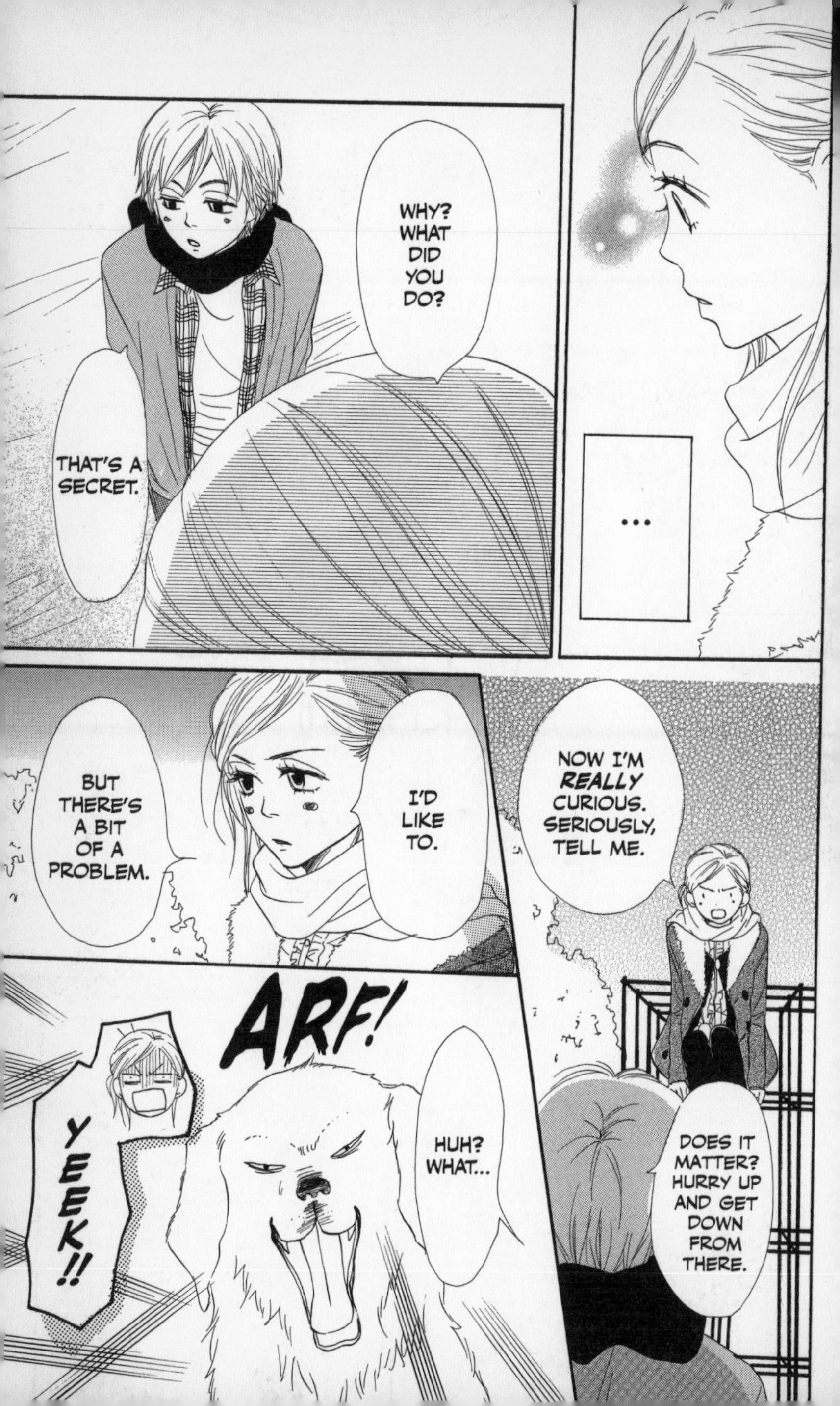
...
WHY? WHAT DID YOU DO?
THAT'S A SECRET.
NOW I'M *REALLY* CURIOUS. SERIOUSLY, TELL ME.
I'D LIKE TO.
BUT THERE'S A BIT OF A PROBLEM.
DOES IT MATTER? HURRY UP AND GET DOWN FROM THERE.
HUH? WHAT...
ARF!
YEEK!!

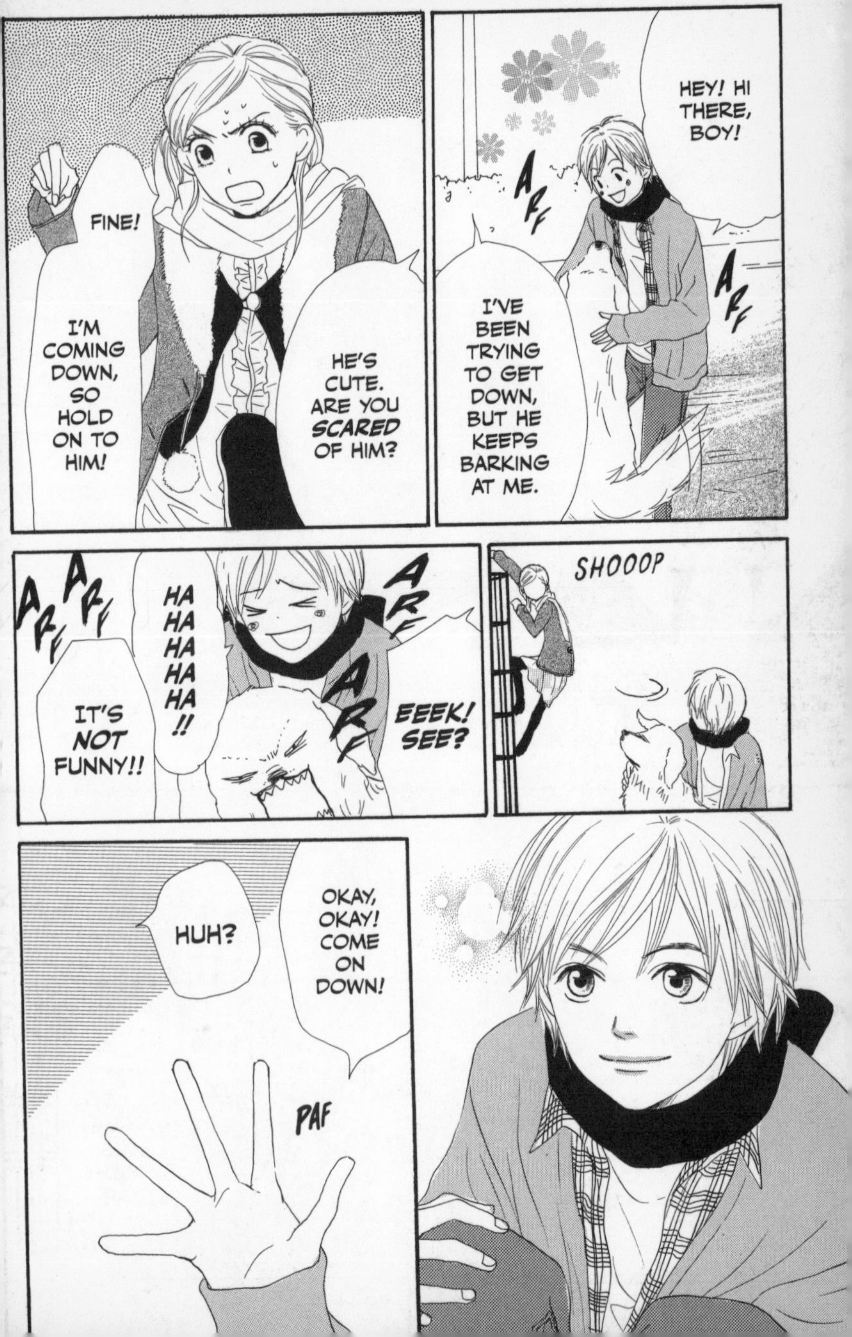
HEY! HI THERE, BOY!
ARF
ARF
I'VE BEEN TRYING TO GET DOWN, BUT HE KEEPS BARKING AT ME.
HE'S CUTE. ARE YOU SCARED OF HIM?
FINE!
I'M COMING DOWN, SO HOLD ON TO HIM!
SHOOOP
ARF
EEEK! SEE?
ARF
HA HA HA HA HA!!
IT'S NOT FUNNY!!
ARF
ARF
OKAY, OKAY! COME ON DOWN!
HUH?
PAF

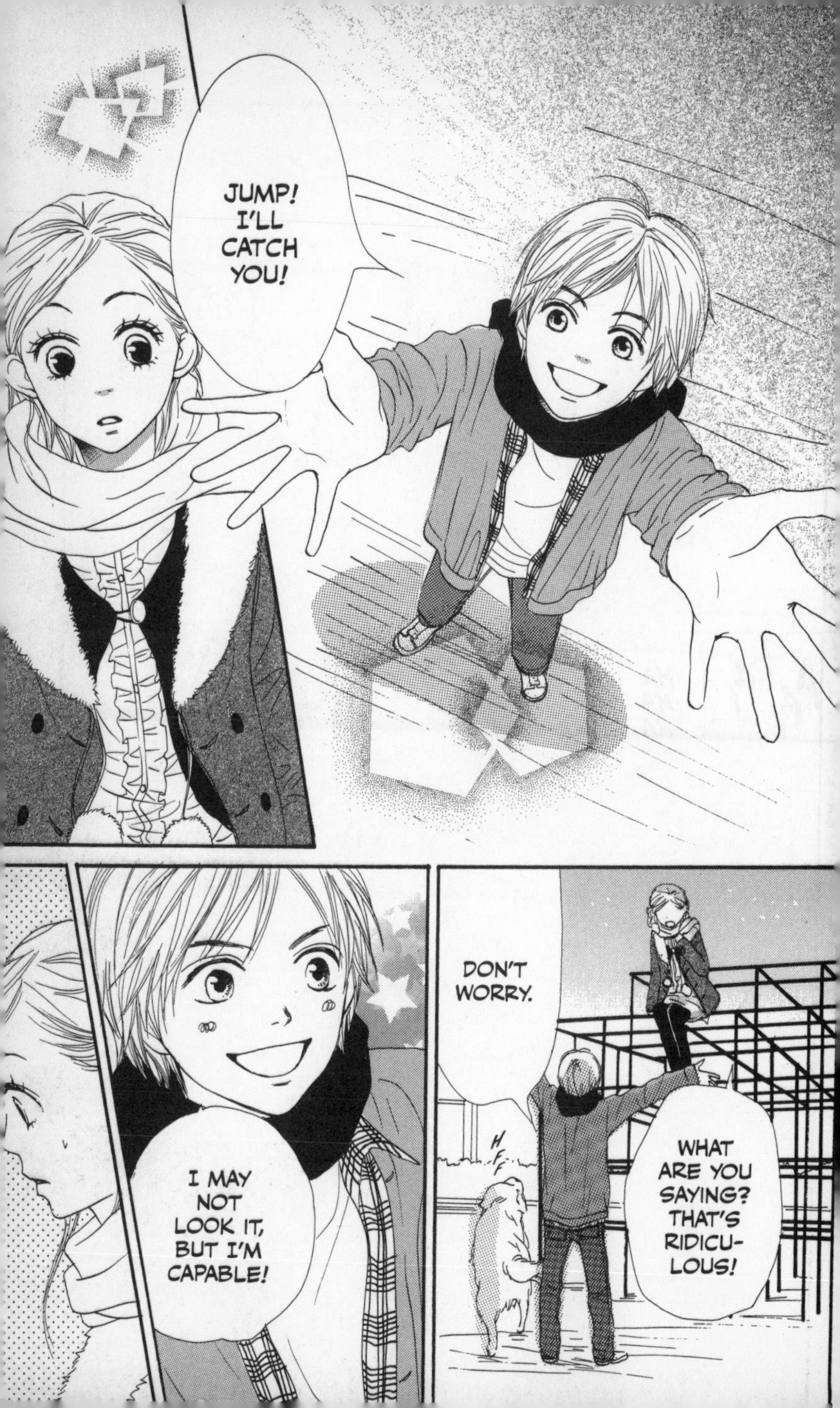
JUMP! I'LL CATCH YOU!
DON'T WORRY.
WHAT ARE YOU SAYING? THAT'S RIDICU-LOUS!
HFF
I MAY NOT LOOK IT, BUT I'M CAPABLE!

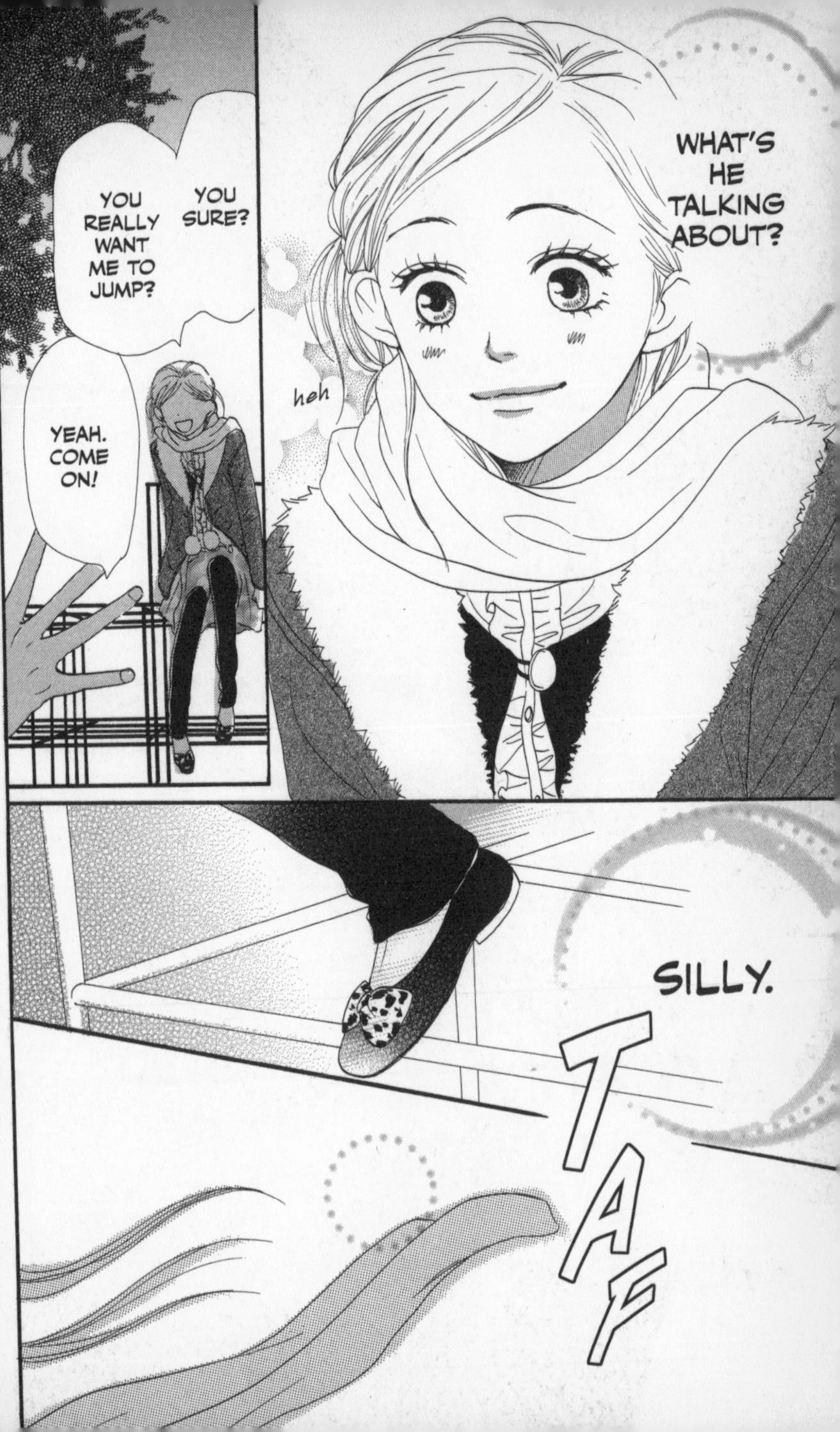

WHAT'S HE TALKING ABOUT?
heh
YOU SURE?
YOU REALLY WANT ME TO JUMP?
YEAH. COME ON!
SILLY.
TAF

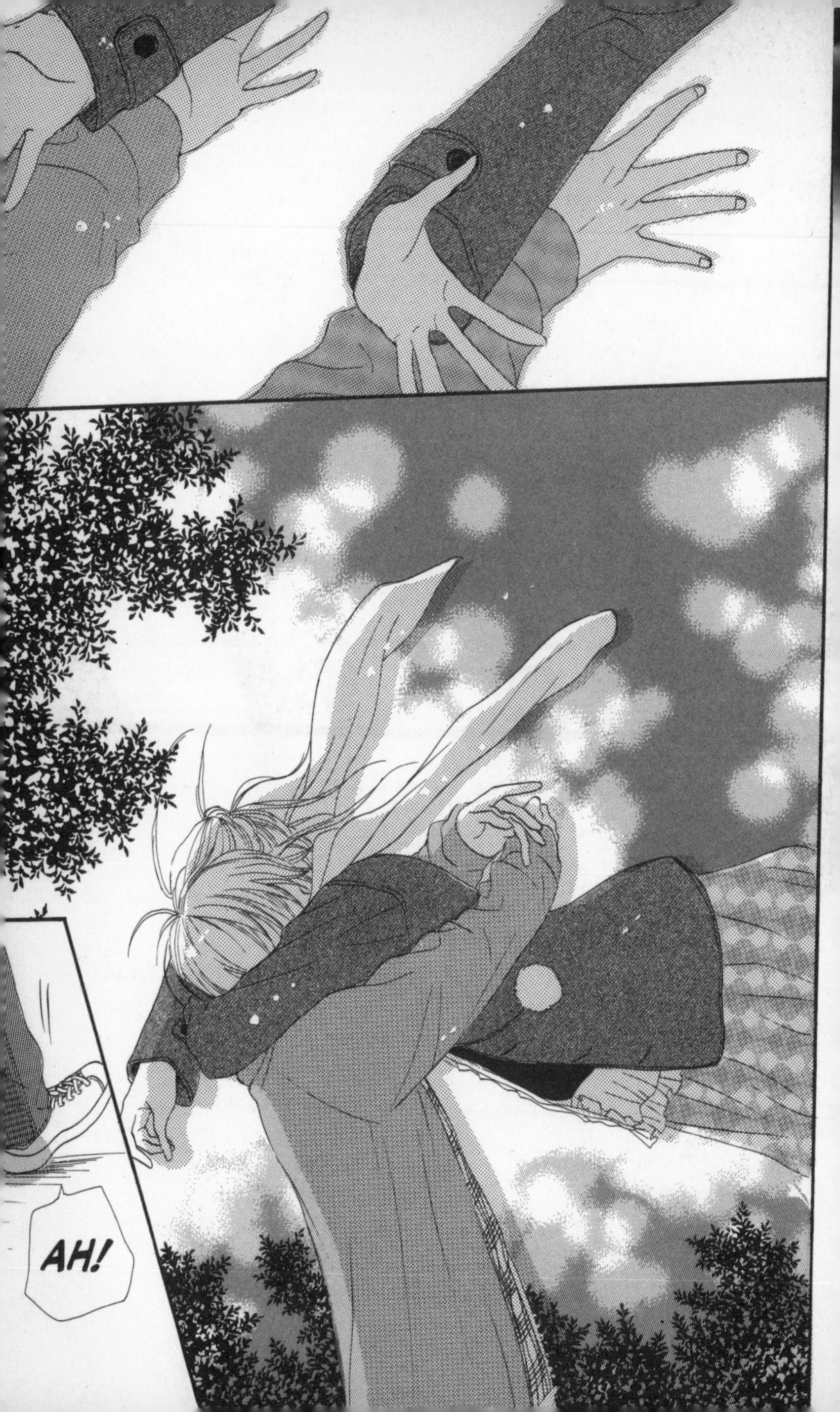
AH!

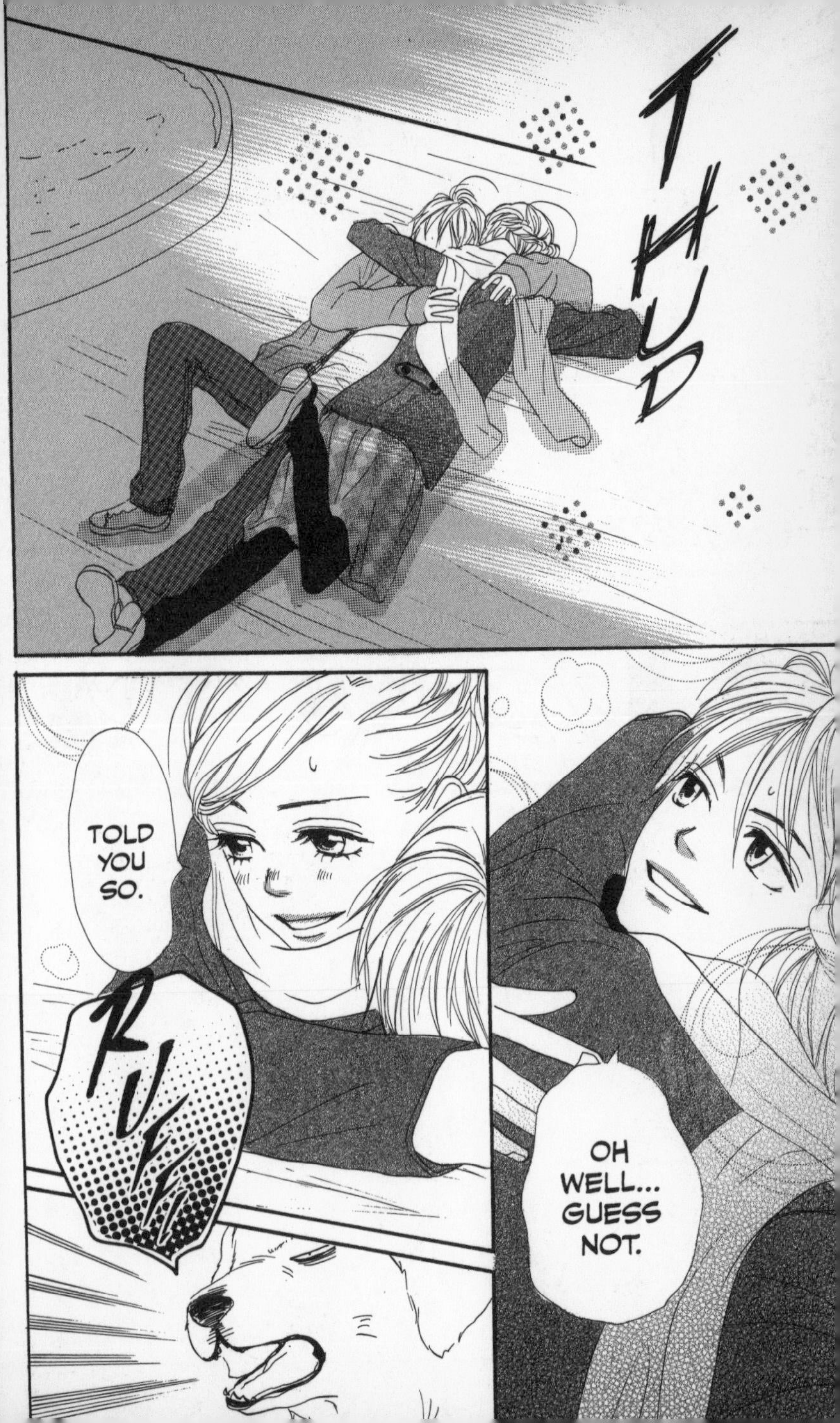
THUD
OH WELL... GUESS NOT.
TOLD YOU SO.

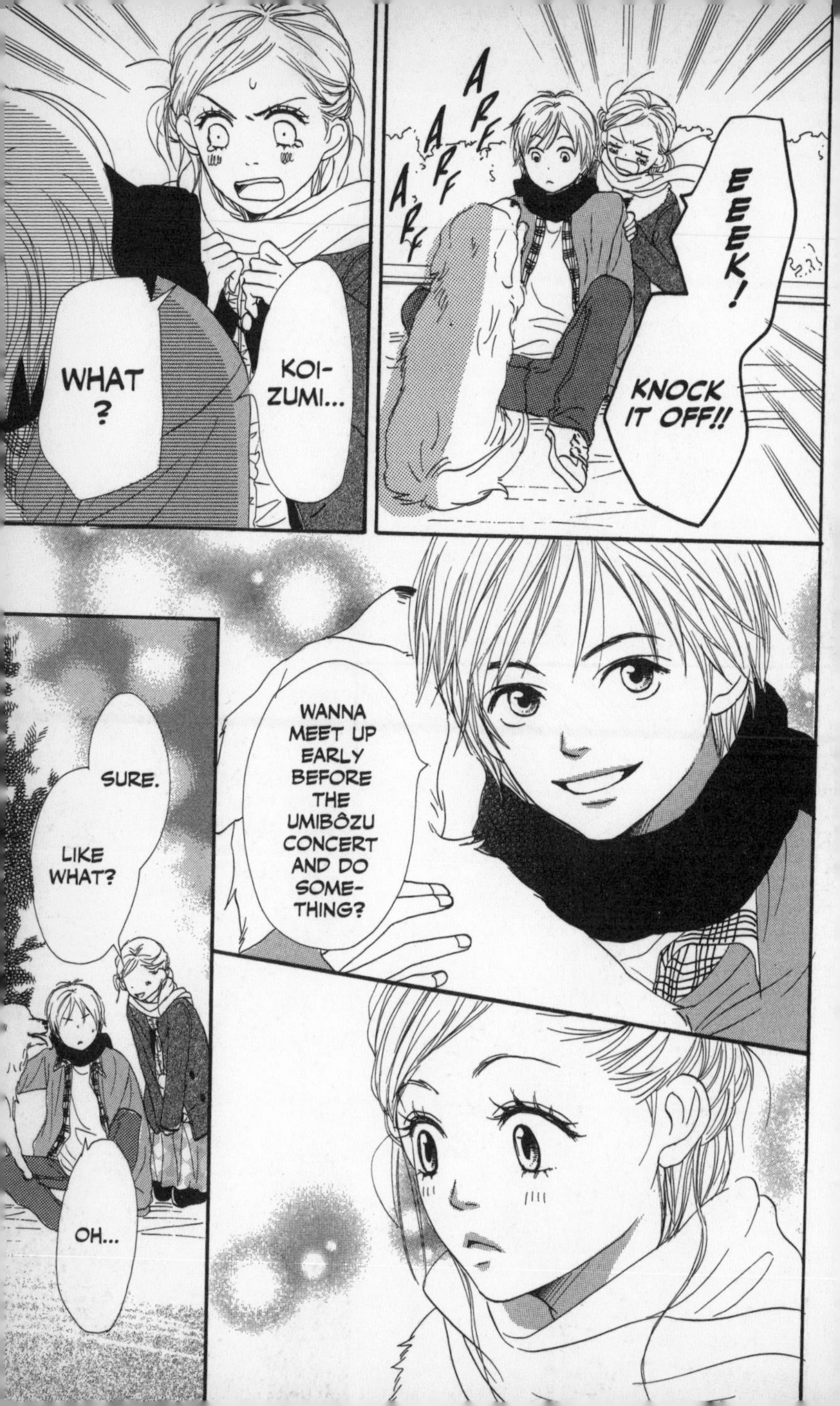
EEEK!
ARF ARF ARF
KNOCK IT OFF!!
KOI-ZUMI...
WHAT?
WANNA MEET UP EARLY BEFORE THE UMIBÔZU CONCERT AND DO SOME-THING?
SURE.
LIKE WHAT?
OH...

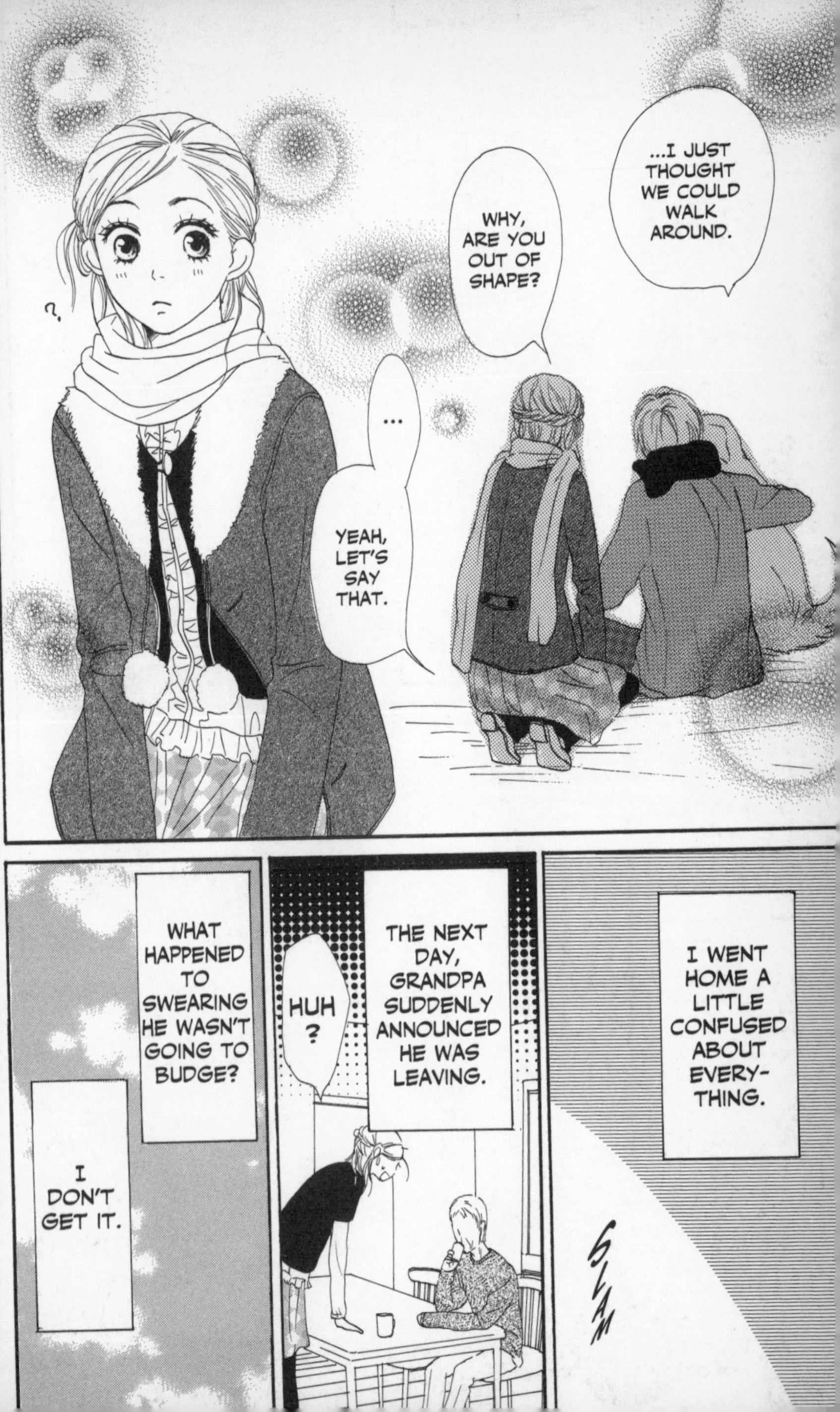
...I JUST THOUGHT WE COULD WALK AROUND.
WHY, ARE YOU OUT OF SHAPE?
...
YEAH, LET'S SAY THAT.
I WENT HOME A LITTLE CONFUSED ABOUT EVERY-THING.
SLAM
THE NEXT DAY, GRANDPA SUDDENLY ANNOUNCED HE WAS LEAVING.
HUH?
WHAT HAPPENED TO SWEARING HE WASN'T GOING TO BUDGE?
I DON'T GET IT.

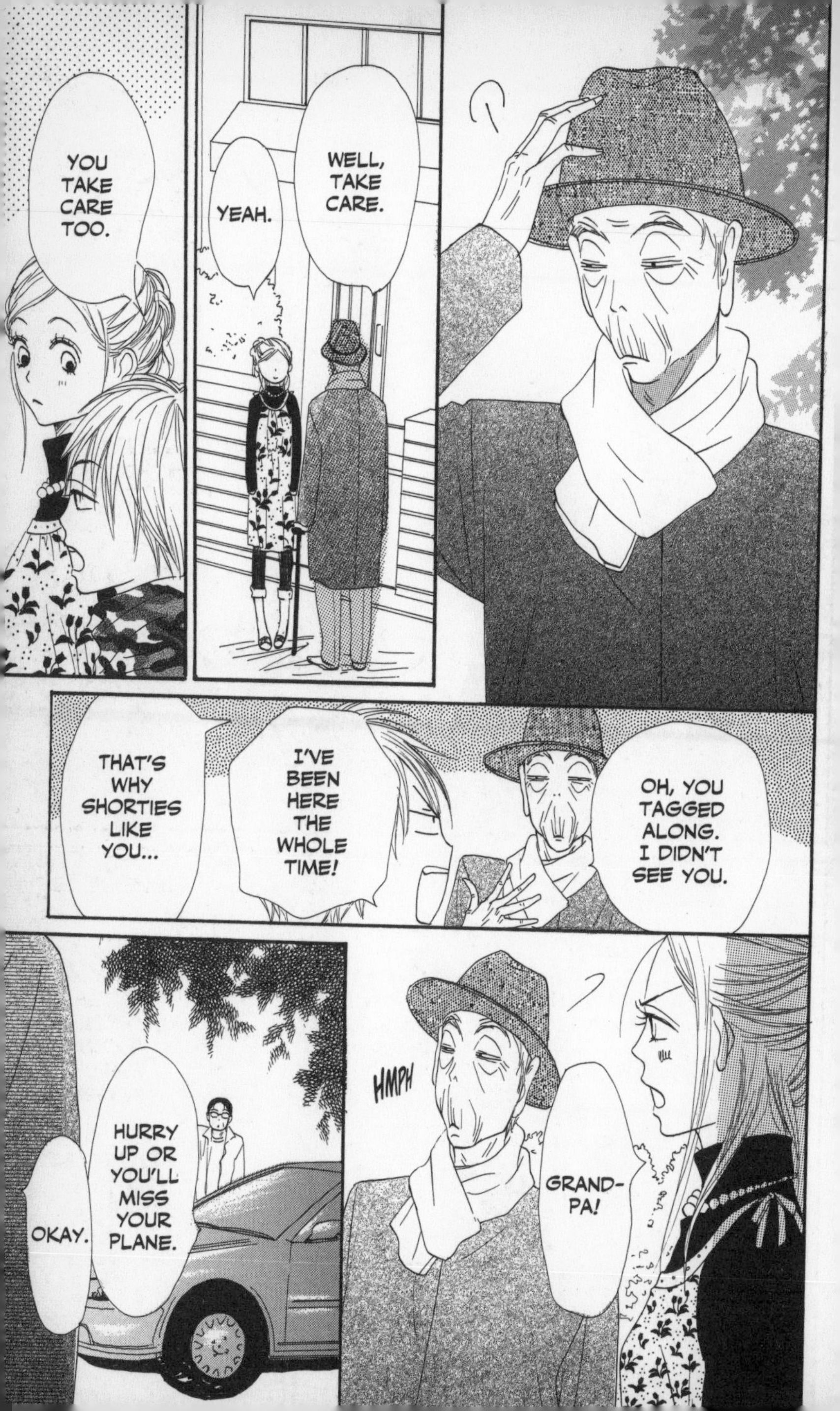
WELL, TAKE CARE.
YEAH.
YOU TAKE CARE TOO.
OH, YOU TAGGED ALONG. I DIDN'T SEE YOU.
I'VE BEEN HERE THE WHOLE TIME!
THAT'S WHY SHORTIES LIKE YOU...
GRAND-PA!
HMPH
HURRY UP OR YOU'LL MISS YOUR PLANE.
OKAY.

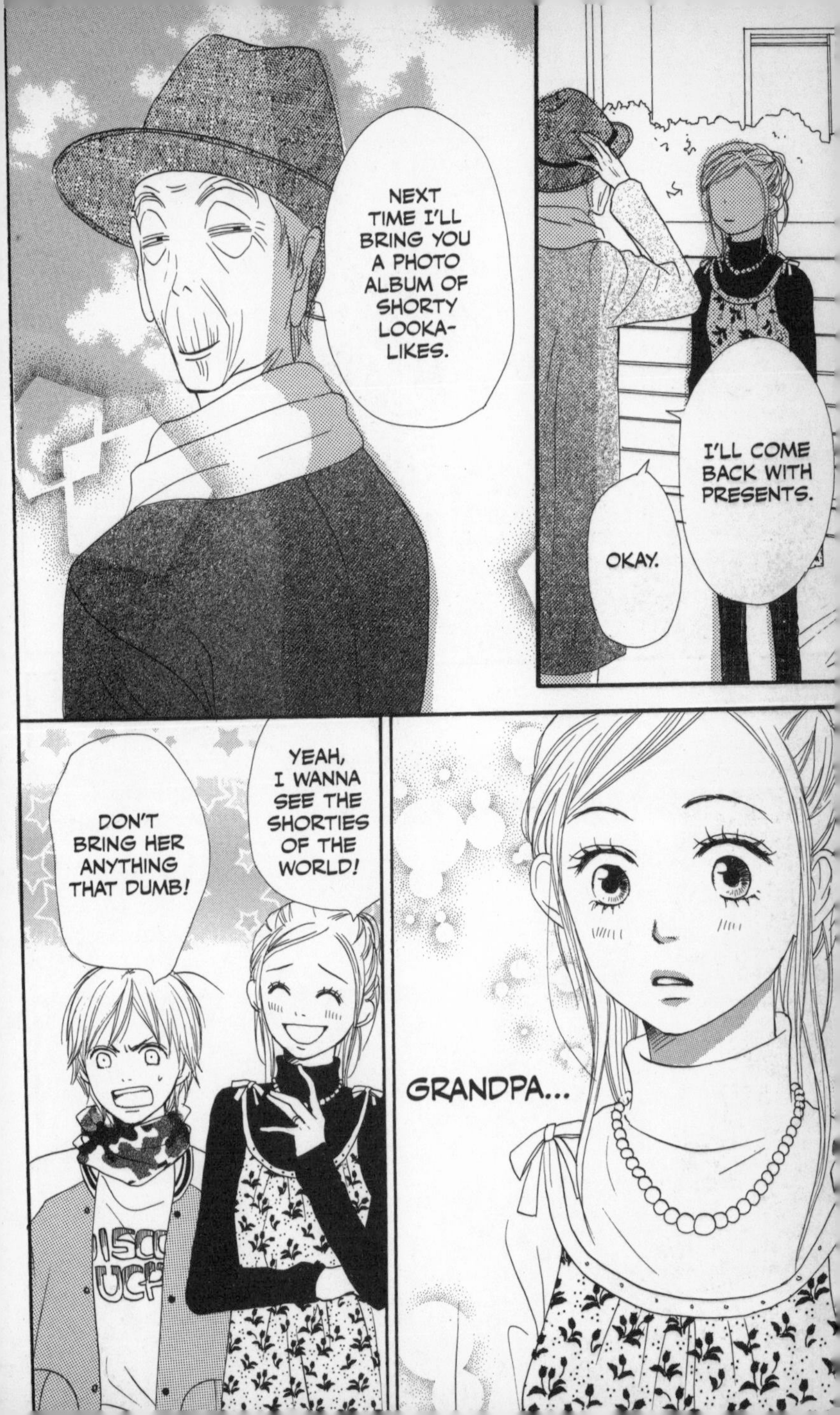
I'LL COME BACK WITH PRESENTS.
OKAY.
NEXT TIME I'LL BRING YOU A PHOTO ALBUM OF SHORTY LOOKA-LIKES.
GRANDPA...
YEAH, I WANNA SEE THE SHORTIES OF THE WORLD!
DON'T BRING HER ANYTHING THAT DUMB!

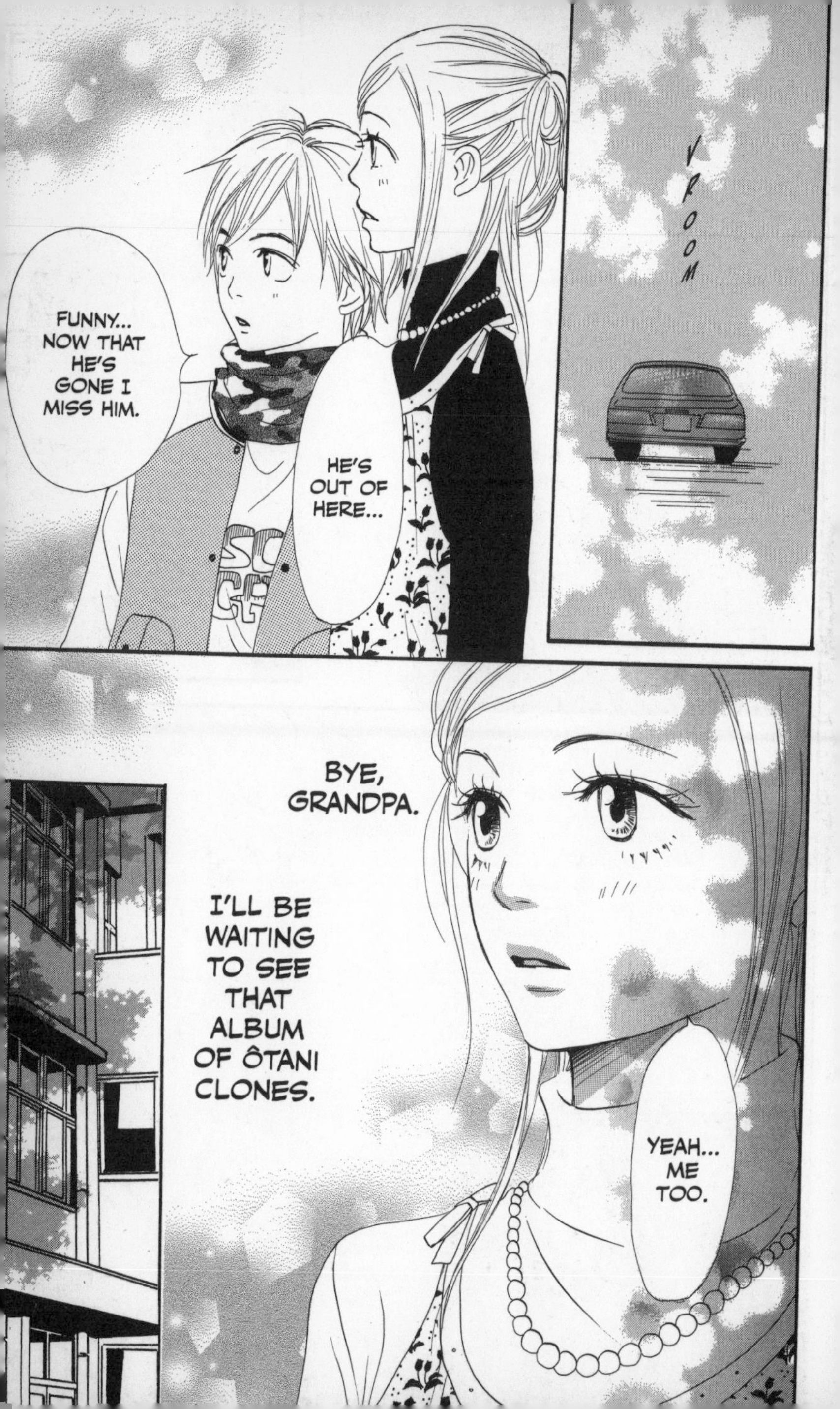
VROOM
HE'S OUT OF HERE...
FUNNY... NOW THAT HE'S GONE I MISS HIM.
BYE, GRANDPA.
I'LL BE WAITING TO SEE THAT ALBUM OF ÔTANI CLONES.
YEAH... ME TOO.

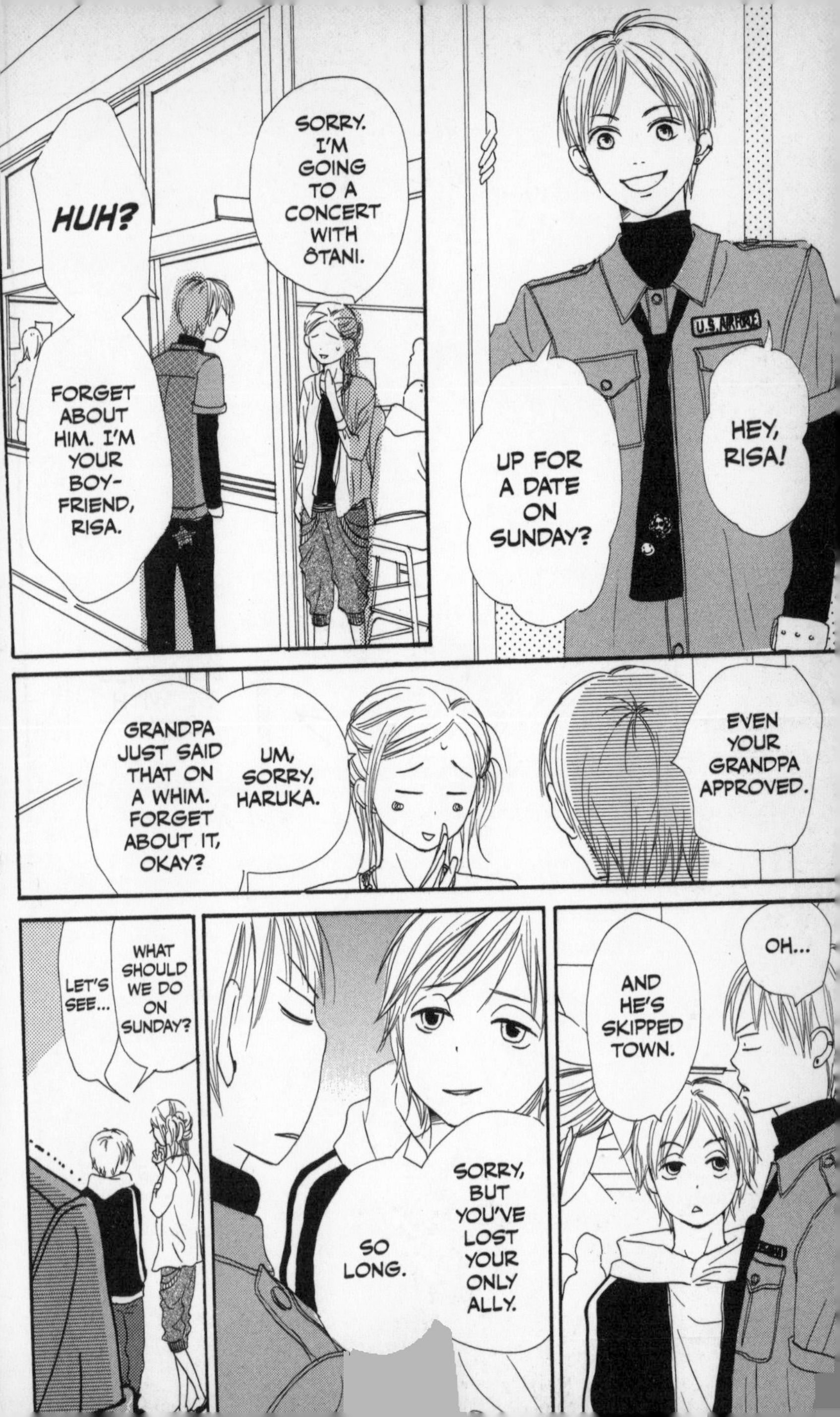
U.S. AIRFORCE
HEY, RISA!
UP FOR A DATE ON SUNDAY?
SORRY. I'M GOING TO A CONCERT WITH ŌTANI.
HUH?
FORGET ABOUT HIM. I'M YOUR BOY-FRIEND, RISA.
EVEN YOUR GRANDPA APPROVED.
UM, SORRY, HARUKA.
GRANDPA JUST SAID THAT ON A WHIM. FORGET ABOUT IT, OKAY?
OH...
AND HE'S SKIPPED TOWN.
SORRY, BUT YOU'VE LOST YOUR ONLY ALLY.
SO LONG.
WHAT SHOULD WE DO ON SUNDAY?
LET'S SEE...

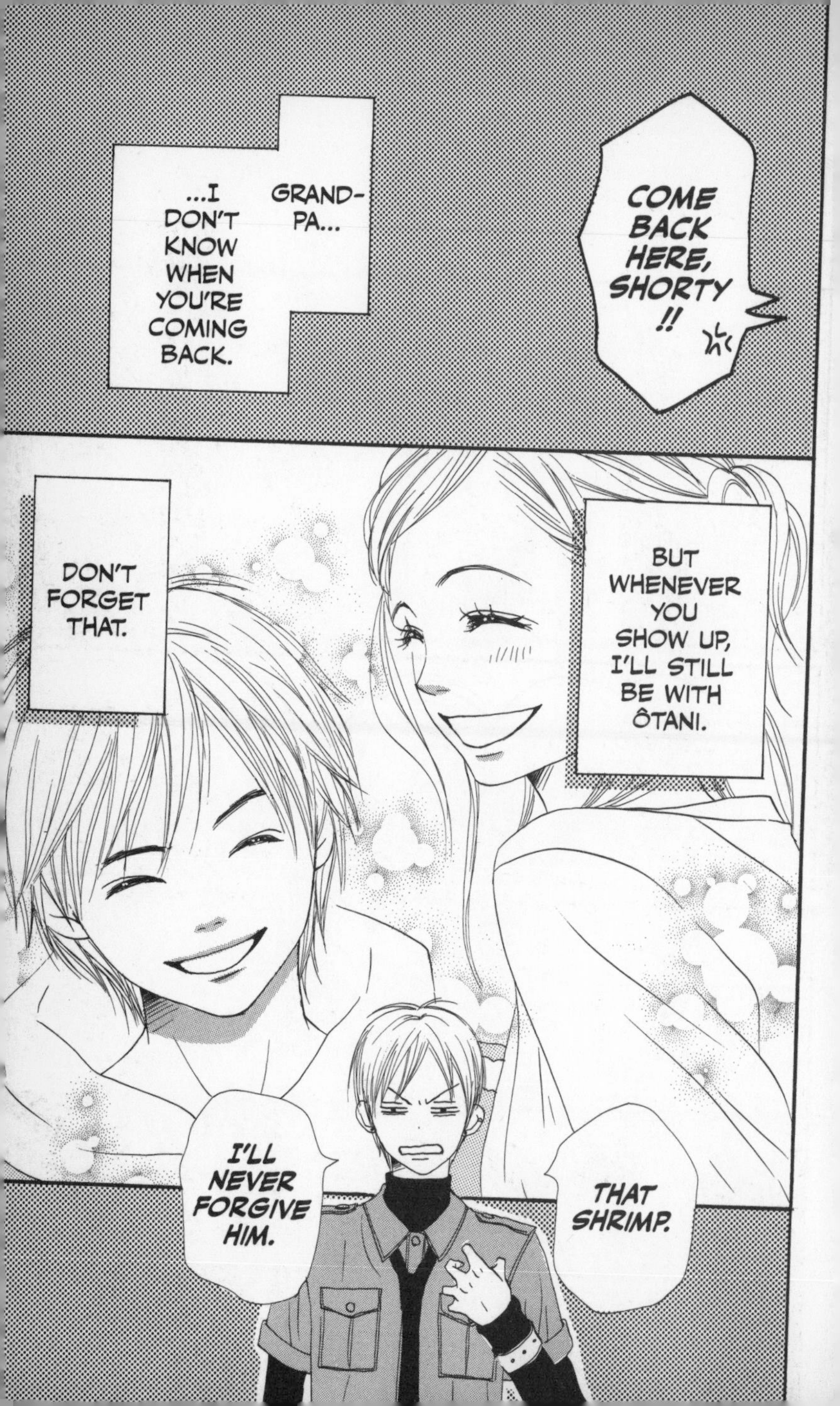
COME BACK HERE, SHORTY!!
GRAND-PA...
...I DON'T KNOW WHEN YOU'RE COMING BACK.
BUT WHENEVER YOU SHOW UP, I'LL STILL BE WITH ÔTANI.
DON'T FORGET THAT.
THAT SHRIMP.
I'LL NEVER FORGIVE HIM.

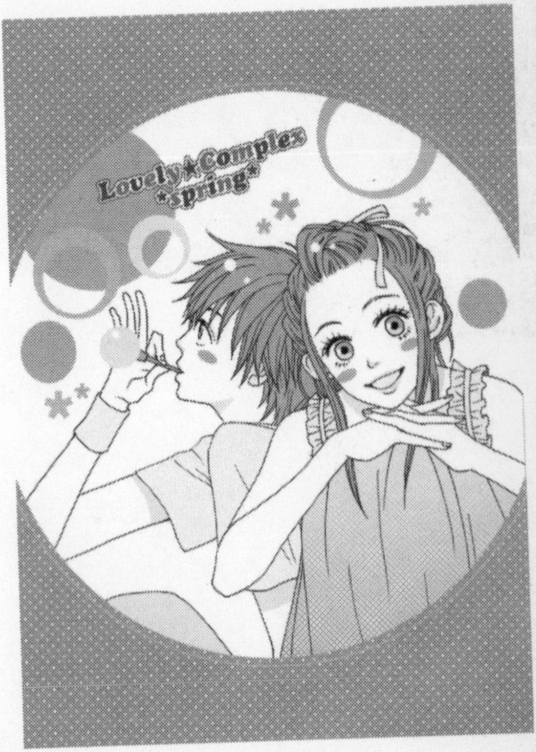
Lovely★Complex
spring

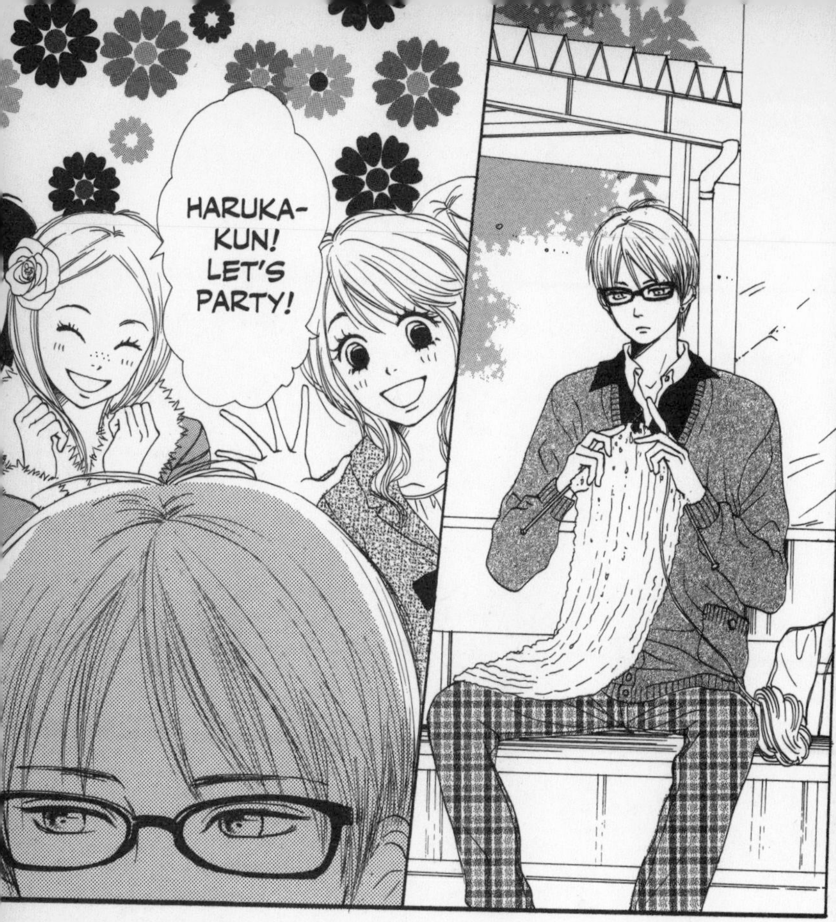
HARUKA-KUN! LET'S PARTY!

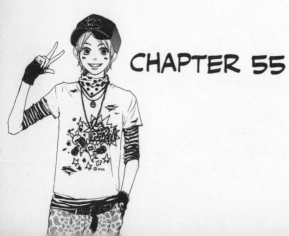

CHAPTER 55

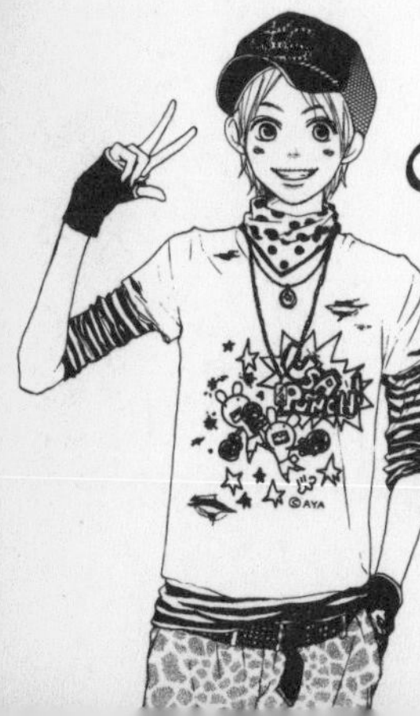

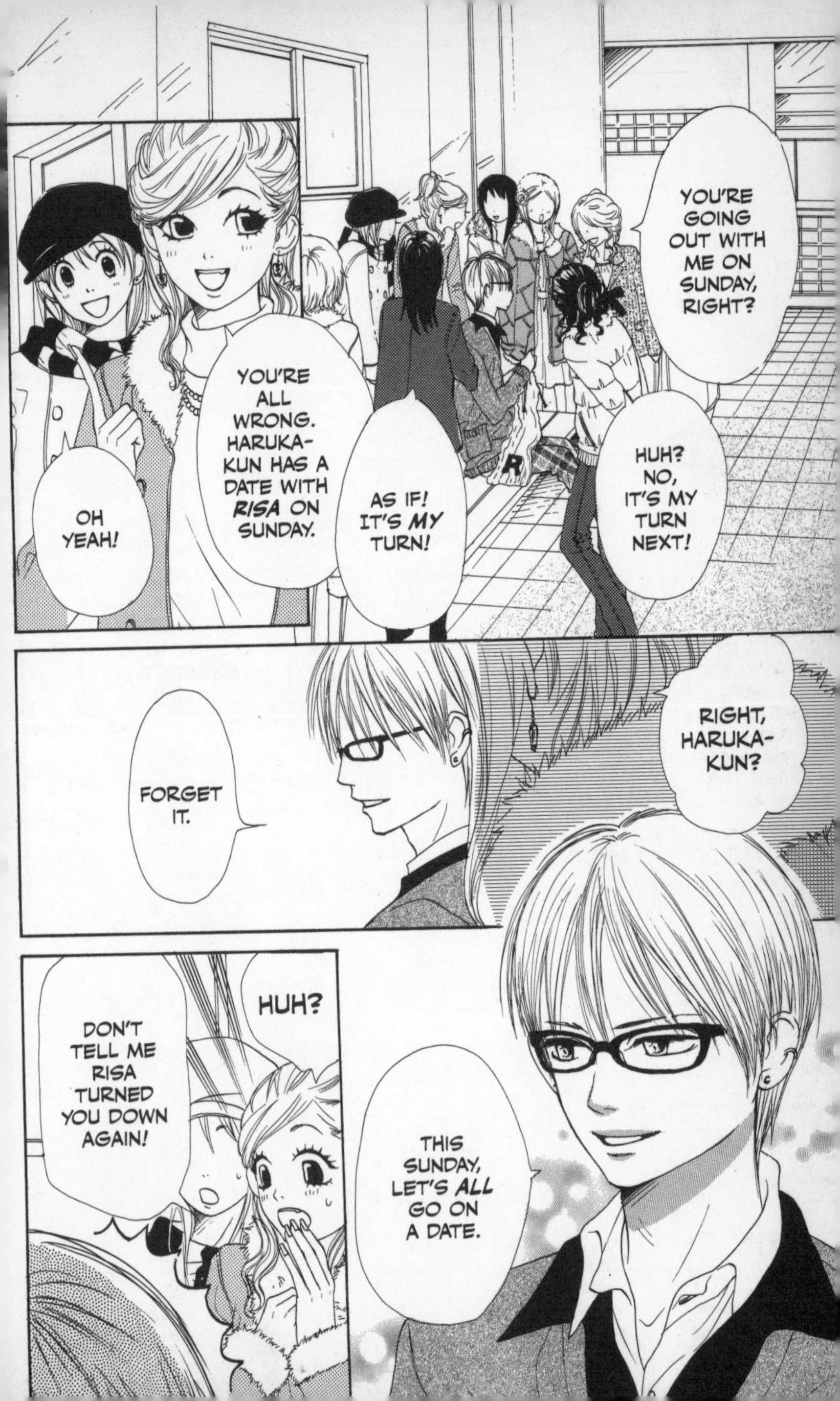

YOU'RE GOING OUT WITH ME ON SUNDAY, RIGHT?
HUH? NO, IT'S MY TURN NEXT!
AS IF! IT'S *MY* TURN!
YOU'RE ALL WRONG. HARUKA-KUN HAS A DATE WITH *RISA* ON SUNDAY.
OH YEAH!
RIGHT, HARUKA-KUN?
FORGET IT.
THIS SUNDAY, LET'S *ALL* GO ON A DATE.
HUH?
DON'T TELL ME RISA TURNED YOU DOWN AGAIN!

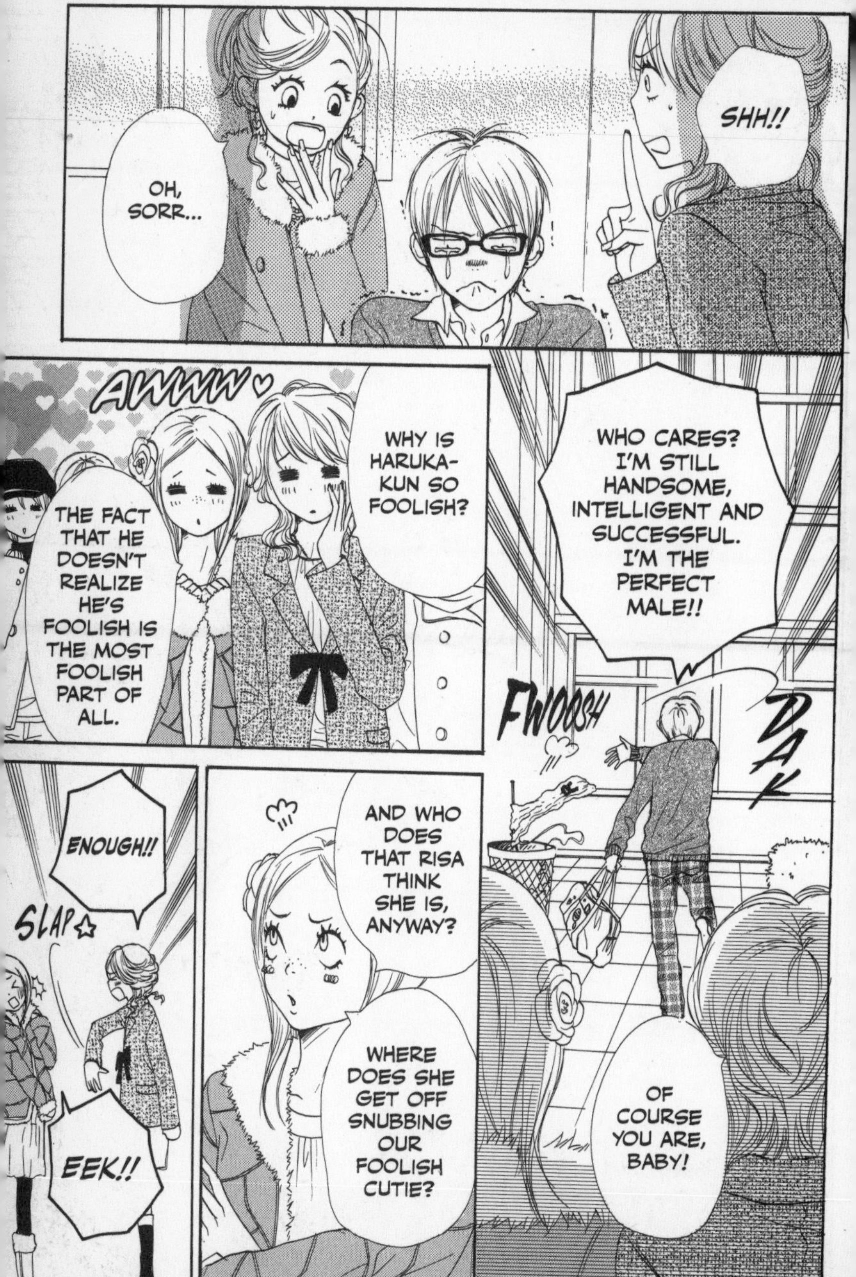
SHH!!
OH, SORR...
WHO CARES? I'M STILL HANDSOME, INTELLIGENT AND SUCCESSFUL. I'M THE PERFECT MALE!!
FWOOSH
DAK
OF COURSE YOU ARE, BABY!
WHY IS HARUKA-KUN SO FOOLISH?
AWWW♡
THE FACT THAT HE DOESN'T REALIZE HE'S FOOLISH IS THE MOST FOOLISH PART OF ALL.
AND WHO DOES THAT RISA THINK SHE IS, ANYWAY?
WHERE DOES SHE GET OFF SNUBBING OUR FOOLISH CUTIE?
ENOUGH!!
SLAP☆
EEK!!

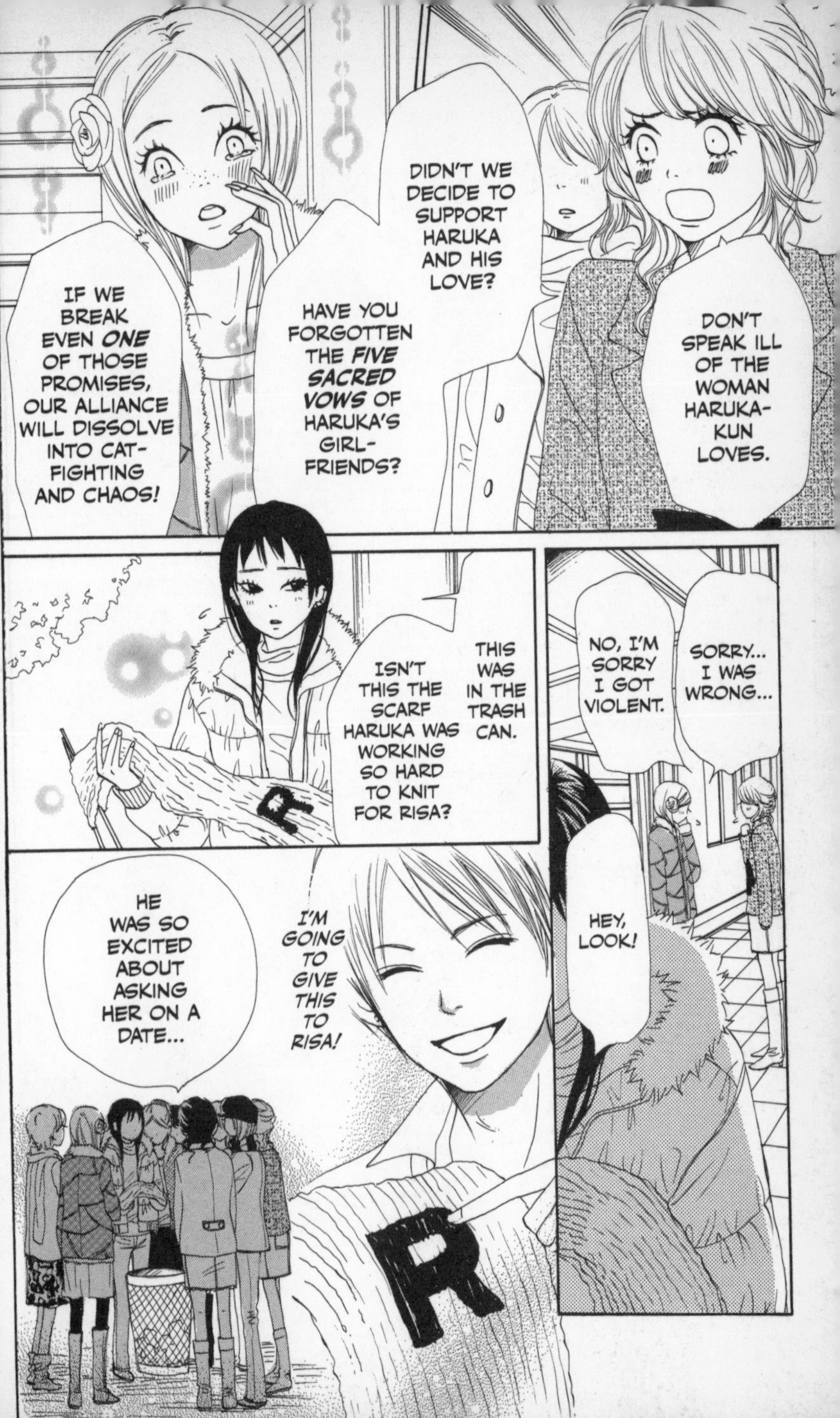
DON'T SPEAK ILL OF THE WOMAN HARUKA-KUN LOVES.
DIDN'T WE DECIDE TO SUPPORT HARUKA AND HIS LOVE?
HAVE YOU FORGOTTEN THE *FIVE SACRED VOWS* OF HARUKA'S GIRLFRIENDS?
IF WE BREAK EVEN *ONE* OF THOSE PROMISES, OUR ALLIANCE WILL DISSOLVE INTO CAT-FIGHTING AND CHAOS!
SORRY... I WAS WRONG...
NO, I'M SORRY I GOT VIOLENT.
HEY, LOOK!
THIS WAS IN THE TRASH CAN.
ISN'T THIS THE SCARF HARUKA WAS WORKING SO HARD TO KNIT FOR RISA?
I'M GOING TO GIVE THIS TO RISA!
HE WAS SO EXCITED ABOUT ASKING HER ON A DATE...

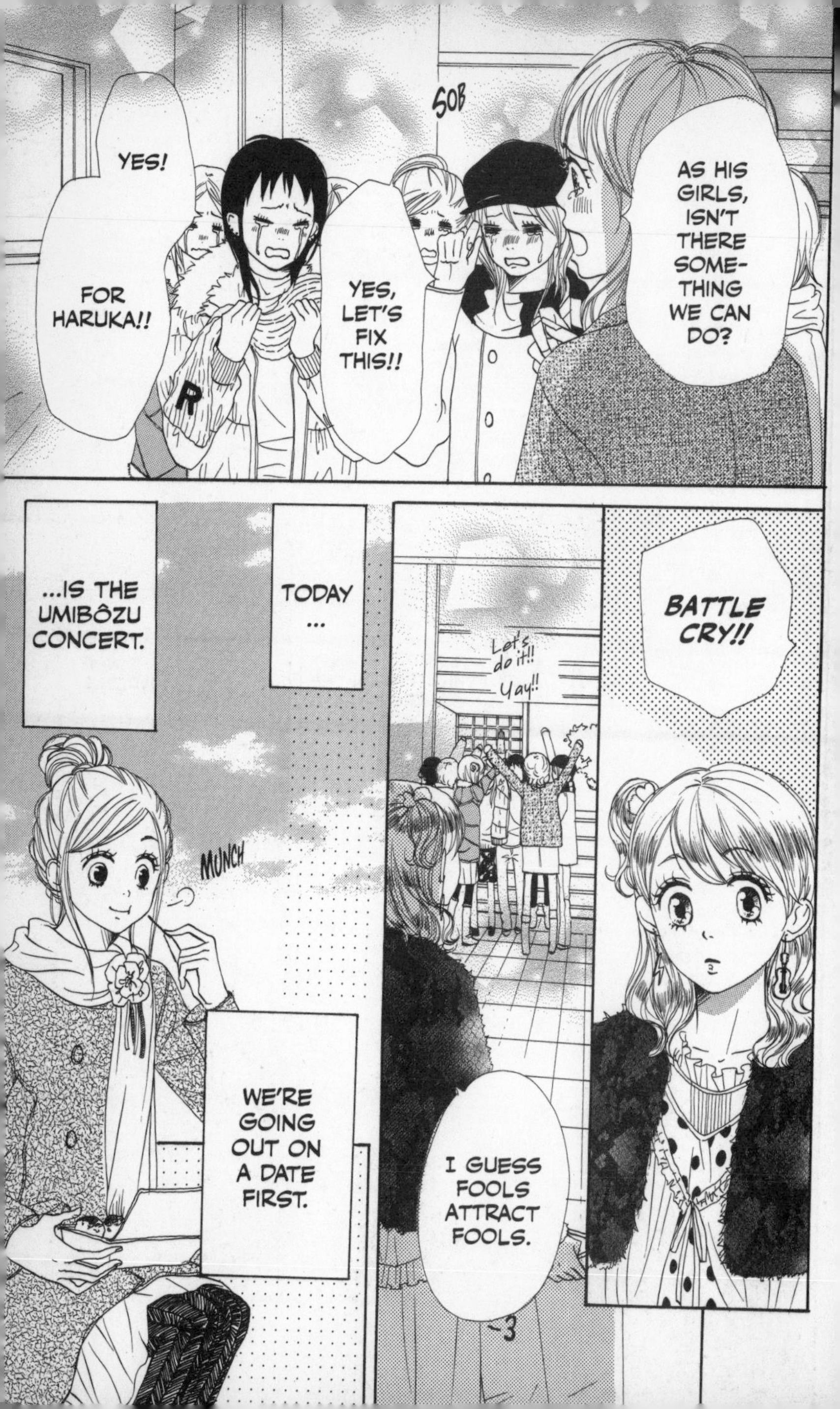

AS HIS GIRLS, ISN'T THERE SOME-THING WE CAN DO?
SOB
YES, LET'S FIX THIS!!
YES!
FOR HARUKA!!
BATTLE CRY!!
Let's do it!!
Yay!!
I GUESS FOOLS ATTRACT FOOLS.
TODAY ...
...IS THE UMIBÔZU CONCERT.
MUNCH
WE'RE GOING OUT ON A DATE FIRST.

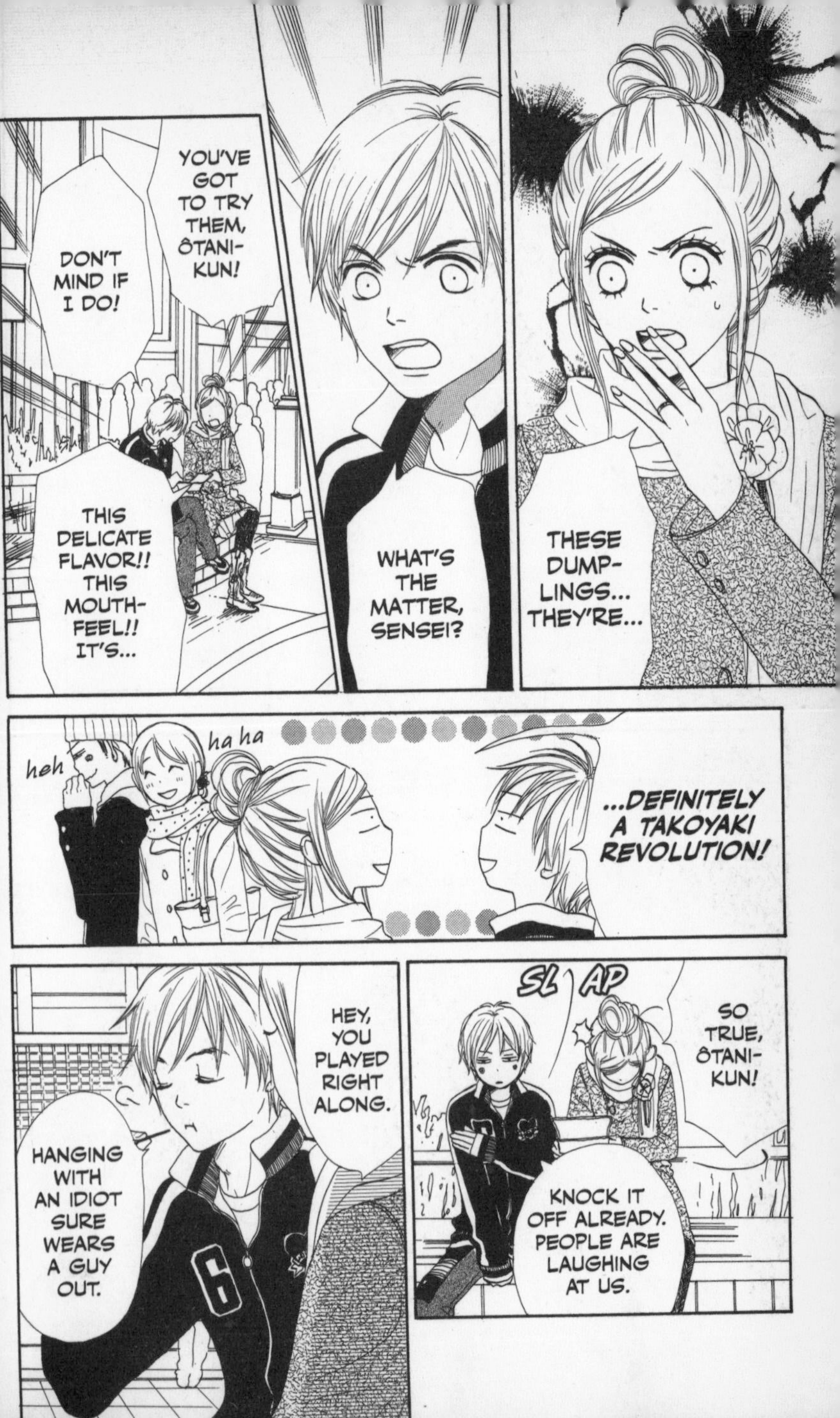

THESE DUMP-LINGS... THEY'RE...
WHAT'S THE MATTER, SENSEI?
YOU'VE GOT TO TRY THEM, ÔTANI-KUN!
DON'T MIND IF I DO!
THIS DELICATE FLAVOR!! THIS MOUTH-FEEL!! IT'S...
...DEFINITELY A TAKOYAKI REVOLUTION!
ha ha
heh
SLAP
SO TRUE, ŌTANI-KUN!
KNOCK IT OFF ALREADY. PEOPLE ARE LAUGHING AT US.
HEY, YOU PLAYED RIGHT ALONG.
HANGING WITH AN IDIOT SURE WEARS A GUY OUT.

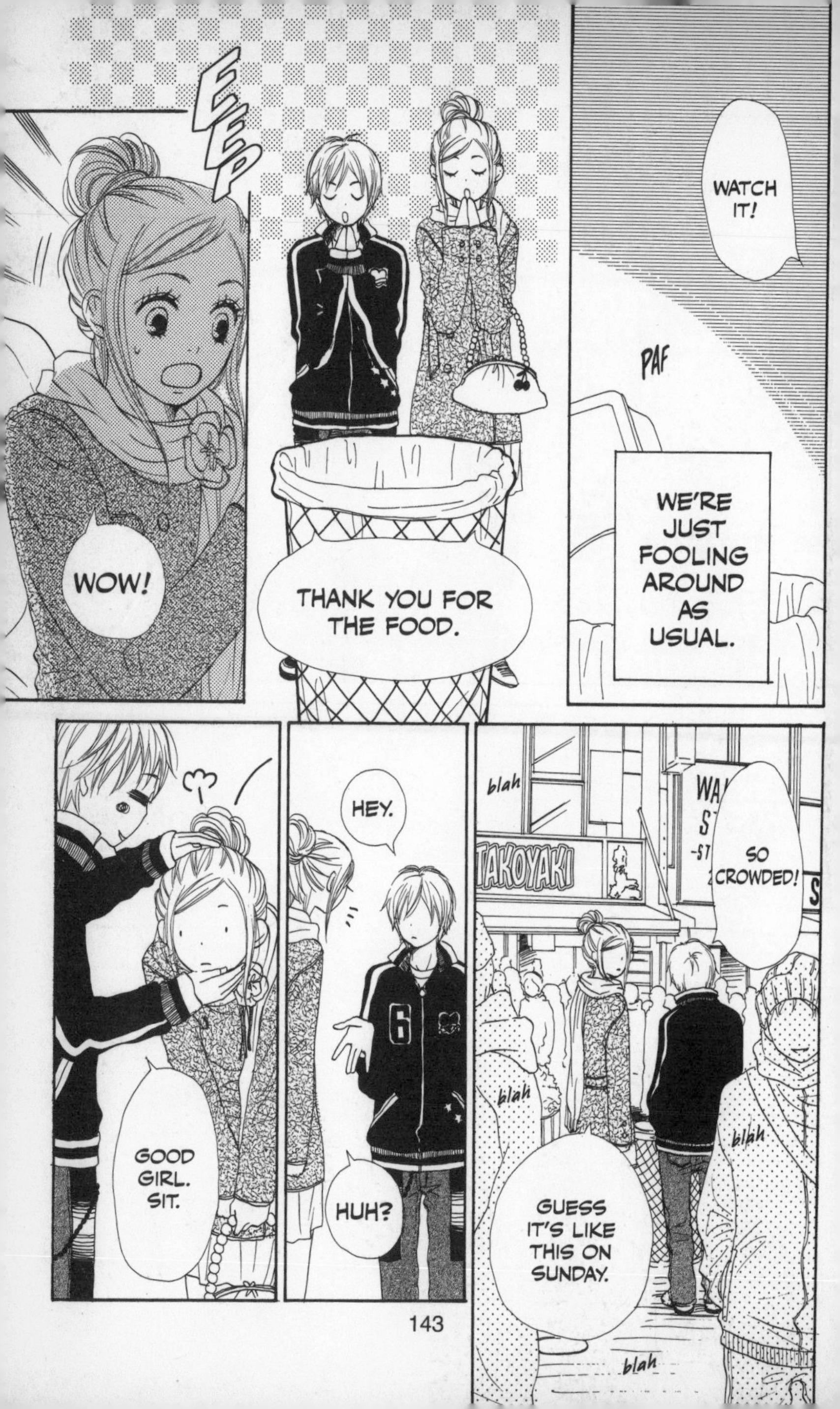
WATCH IT!
PAF
WE'RE JUST FOOLING AROUND AS USUAL.
THANK YOU FOR THE FOOD.
EEP
WOW!
blah
SO CROWDED!
TAKOYAKI
blah
blah
GUESS IT'S LIKE THIS ON SUNDAY.
blah
HEY.
HUH?
GOOD GIRL. SIT.

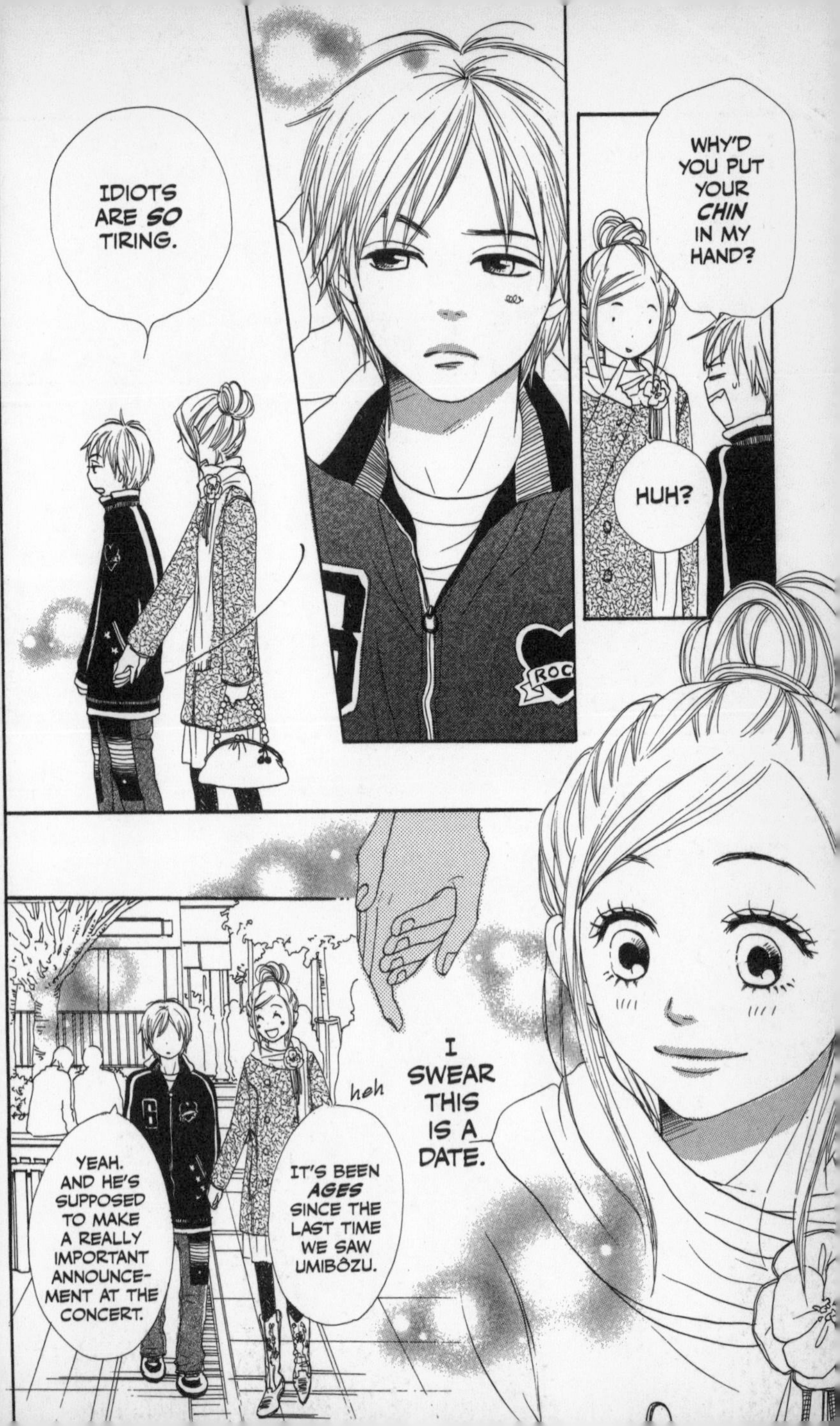

WHY'D YOU PUT YOUR *CHIN* IN MY HAND?
HUH?
IDIOTS ARE *SO* TIRING.
I SWEAR THIS IS A DATE.
heh
IT'S BEEN *AGES* SINCE THE LAST TIME WE SAW UMIBÔZU.
YEAH. AND HE'S SUPPOSED TO MAKE A REALLY IMPORTANT ANNOUNCE-MENT AT THE CONCERT.

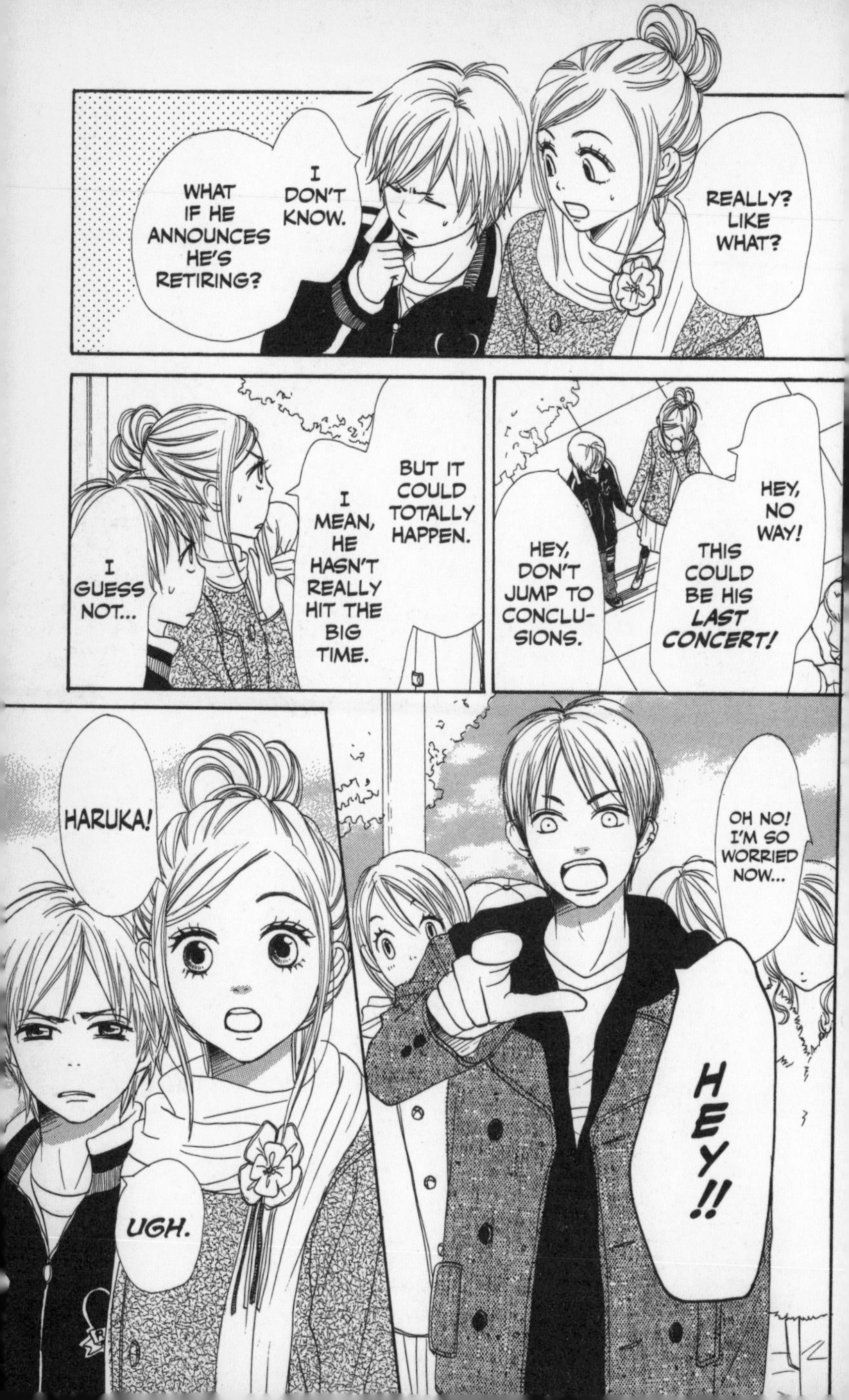
REALLY? LIKE WHAT?
I DON'T KNOW.
WHAT IF HE ANNOUNCES HE'S RETIRING?
HEY, NO WAY! THIS COULD BE HIS *LAST CONCERT!*
HEY, DON'T JUMP TO CONCLU-SIONS.
BUT IT COULD TOTALLY HAPPEN.
I MEAN, HE HASN'T REALLY HIT THE BIG TIME.
I GUESS NOT...
OH NO! I'M SO WORRIED NOW...
HEY!!
HARUKA!
UGH.

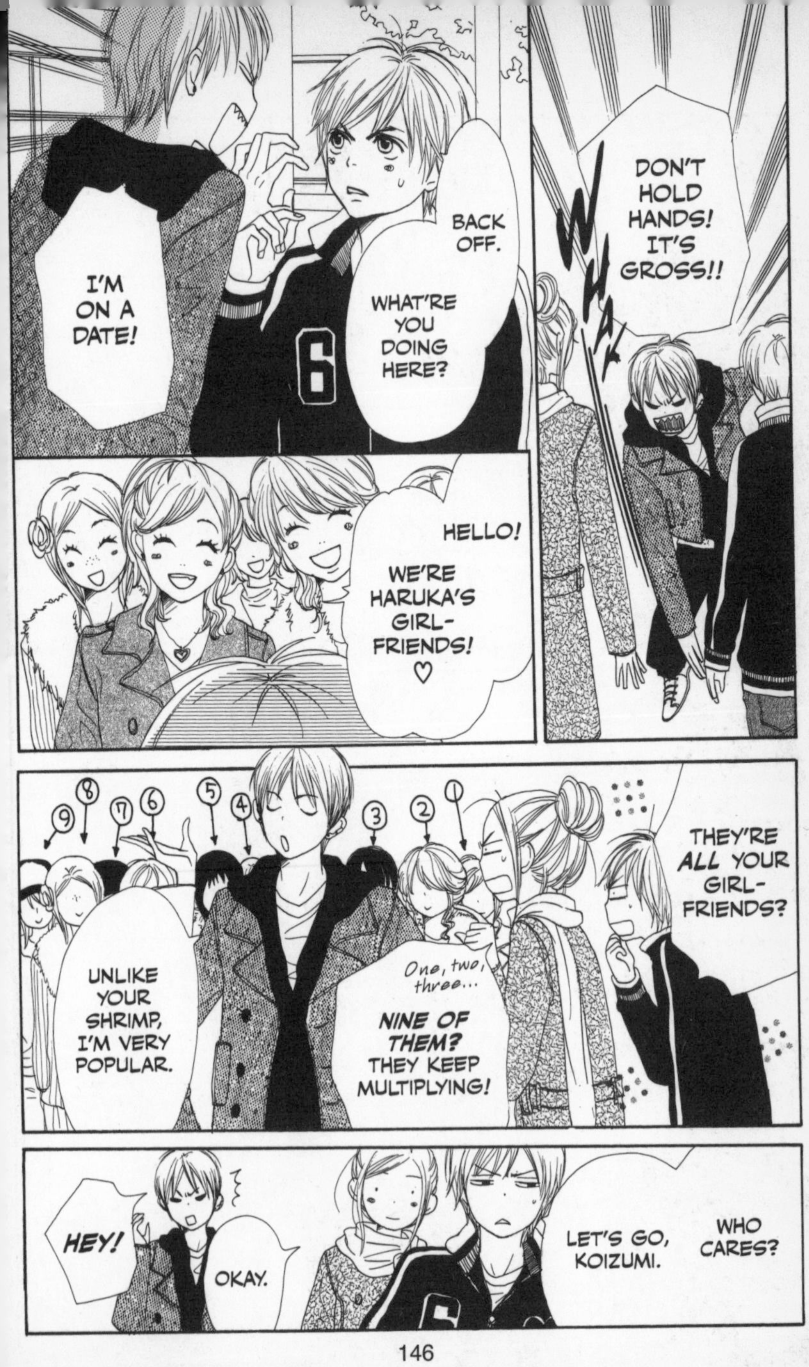
WHAP
DON'T HOLD HANDS! IT'S GROSS!!
BACK OFF.
WHAT'RE YOU DOING HERE?
I'M ON A DATE!
HELLO!
WE'RE HARUKA'S GIRL-FRIENDS! ♡
THEY'RE *ALL* YOUR GIRL-FRIENDS?
1 2 3 4 5 6 7 8 9
One, two, three...
NINE OF THEM? THEY KEEP MULTIPLYING!
UNLIKE YOUR SHRIMP, I'M VERY POPULAR.
WHO CARES?
LET'S GO, KOIZUMI.
OKAY.
HEY!

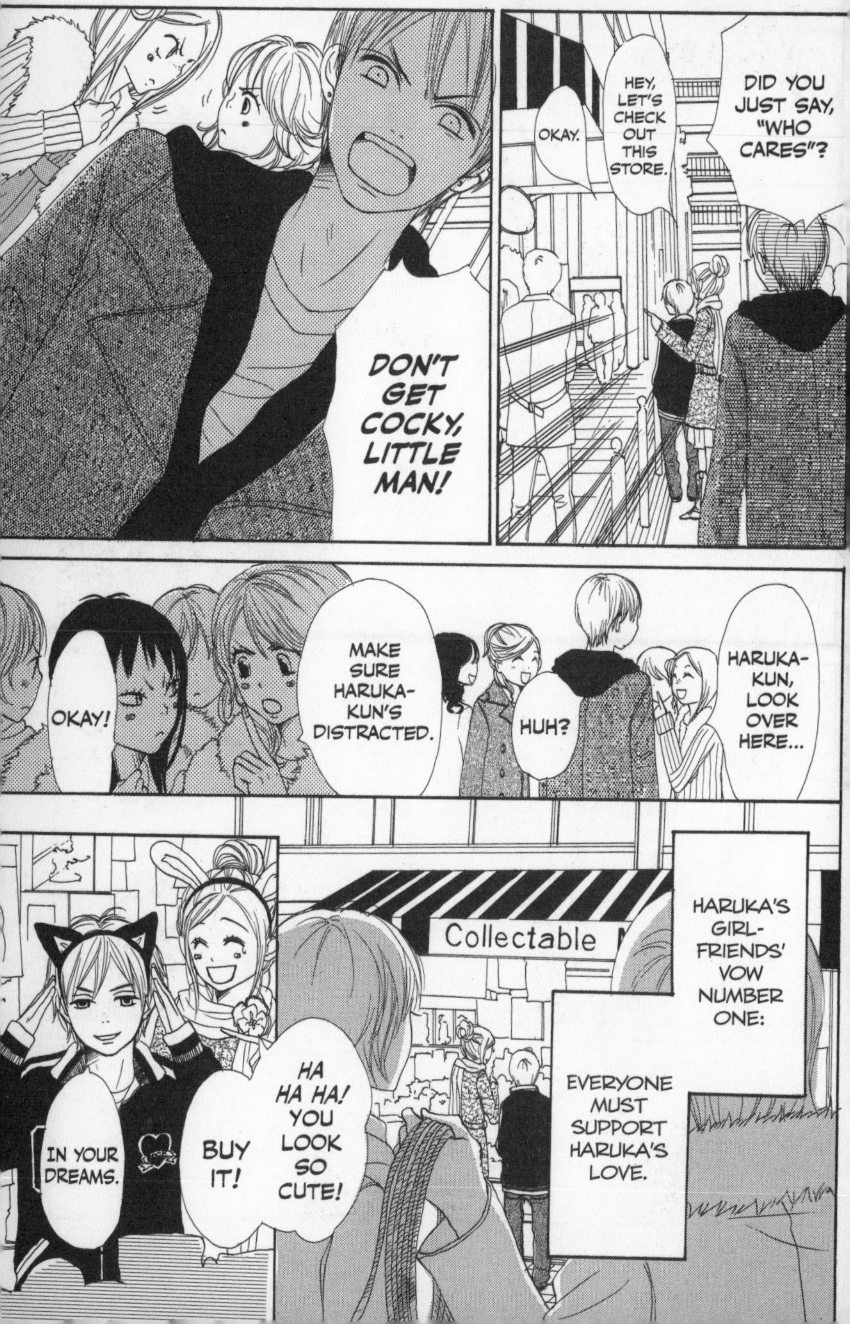
DID YOU JUST SAY, "WHO CARES"?
HEY, LET'S CHECK OUT THIS STORE.
OKAY.
DON'T GET COCKY, LITTLE MAN!
HARUKA-KUN, LOOK OVER HERE...
HUH?
MAKE SURE HARUKA-KUN'S DISTRACTED.
OKAY!
HARUKA'S GIRL-FRIENDS' VOW NUMBER ONE:
Collectable
EVERYONE MUST SUPPORT HARUKA'S LOVE.
HA HA HA! YOU LOOK SO CUTE!
BUY IT!
IN YOUR DREAMS.

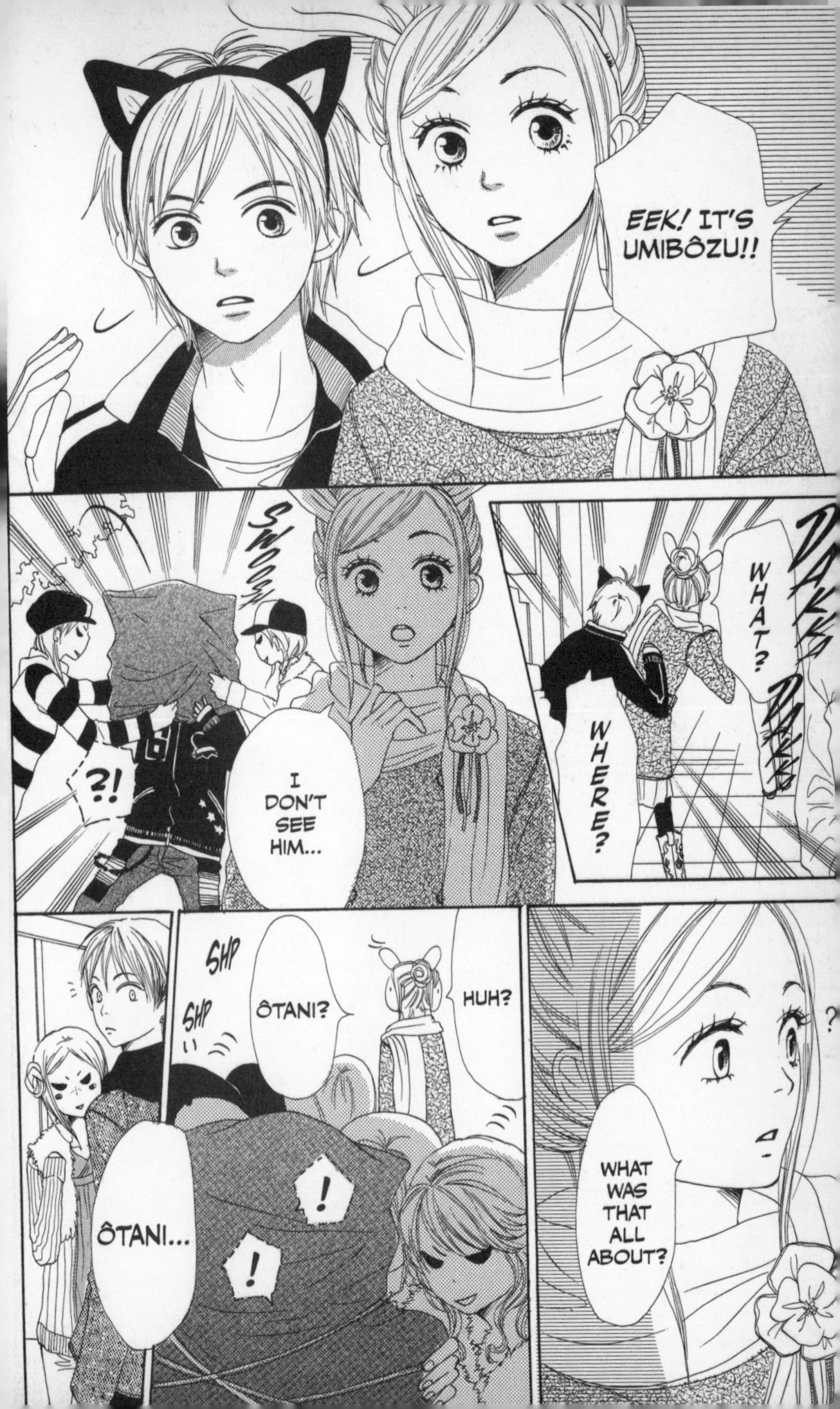
EEK! IT'S UMIBÔZU!!
DAKK DAKK
WHAT?
WHERE?
SWOOSH
I DON'T SEE HIM...
?!
WHAT WAS THAT ALL ABOUT?
?
HUH?
ÔTANI?
SHP
SHP
!
!
ÔTANI...

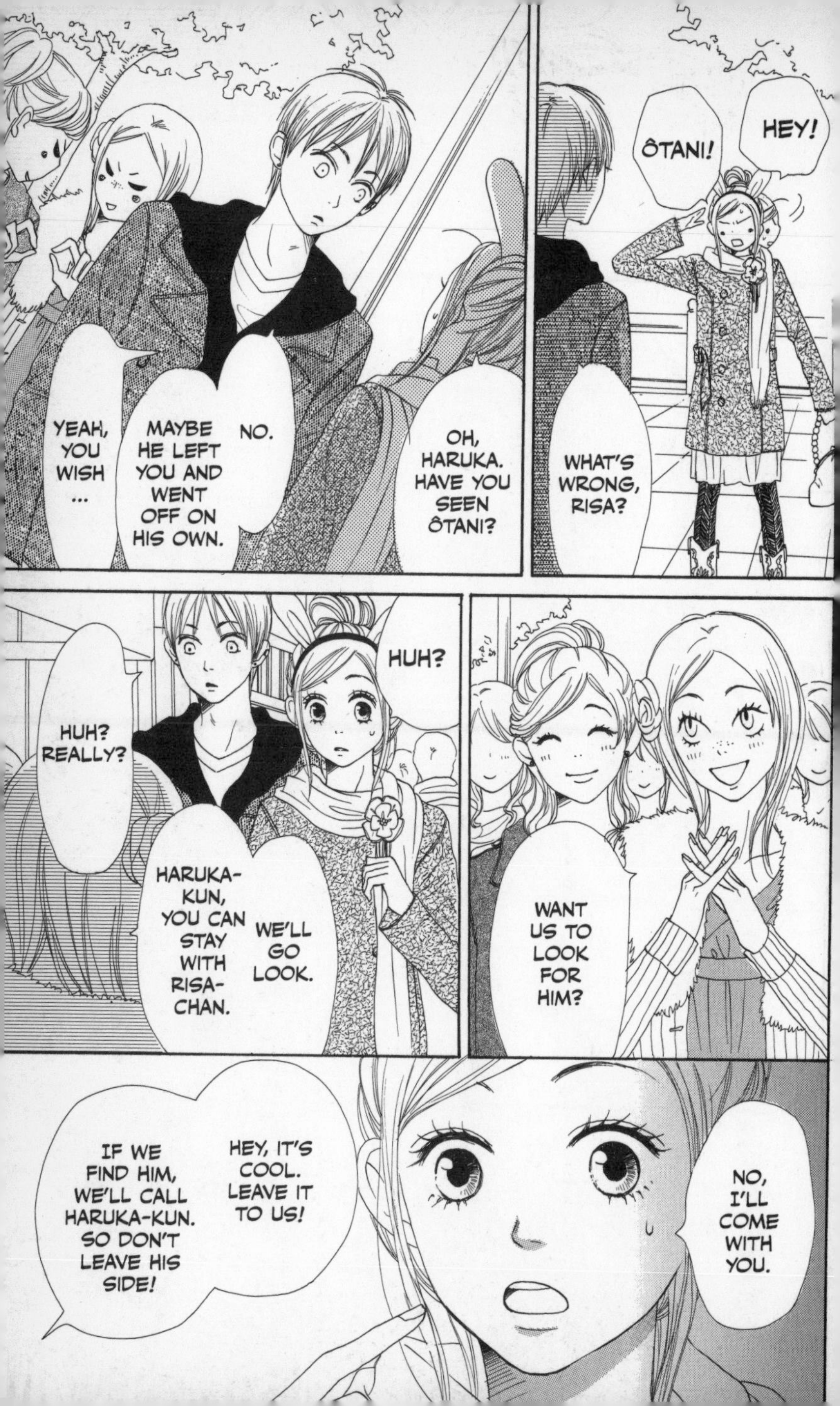
HEY!
ÔTANI!
WHAT'S WRONG, RISA?
OH, HARUKA. HAVE YOU SEEN ÔTANI?
NO.
MAYBE HE LEFT YOU AND WENT OFF ON HIS OWN.
YEAH, YOU WISH ...
WANT US TO LOOK FOR HIM?
HUH?
WE'LL GO LOOK.
HARUKA-KUN, YOU CAN STAY WITH RISA-CHAN.
HUH? REALLY?
NO, I'LL COME WITH YOU.
HEY, IT'S COOL. LEAVE IT TO US!
IF WE FIND HIM, WE'LL CALL HARUKA-KUN. SO DON'T LEAVE HIS SIDE!

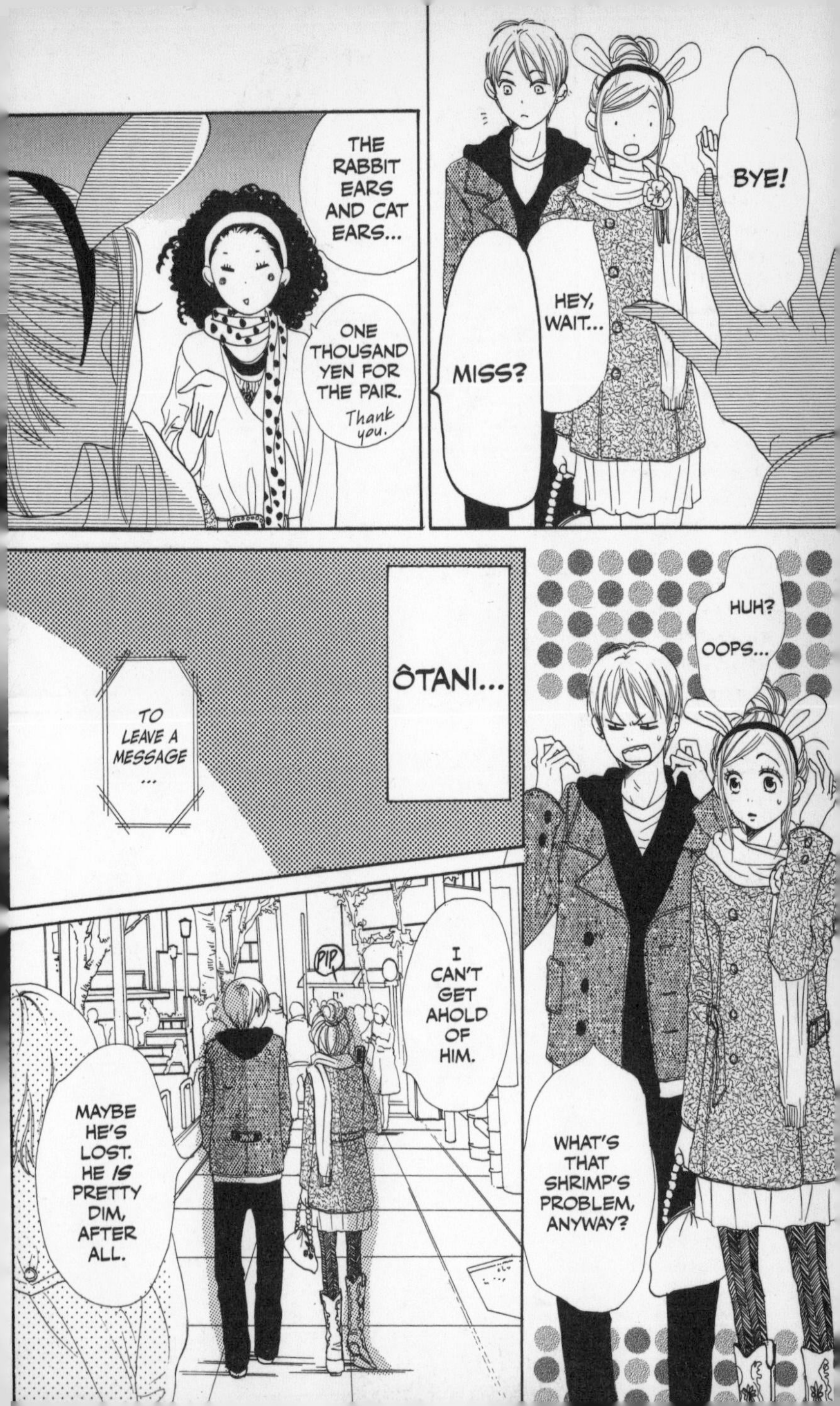
BYE!
HEY, WAIT...
MISS?
THE RABBIT EARS AND CAT EARS...
ONE THOUSAND YEN FOR THE PAIR.
Thank you.
HUH?
OOPS...
WHAT'S THAT SHRIMP'S PROBLEM, ANYWAY?
ÔTANI...
TO LEAVE A MESSAGE ...
PIP
I CAN'T GET AHOLD OF HIM.
MAYBE HE'S LOST. HE *IS* PRETTY DIM, AFTER ALL.

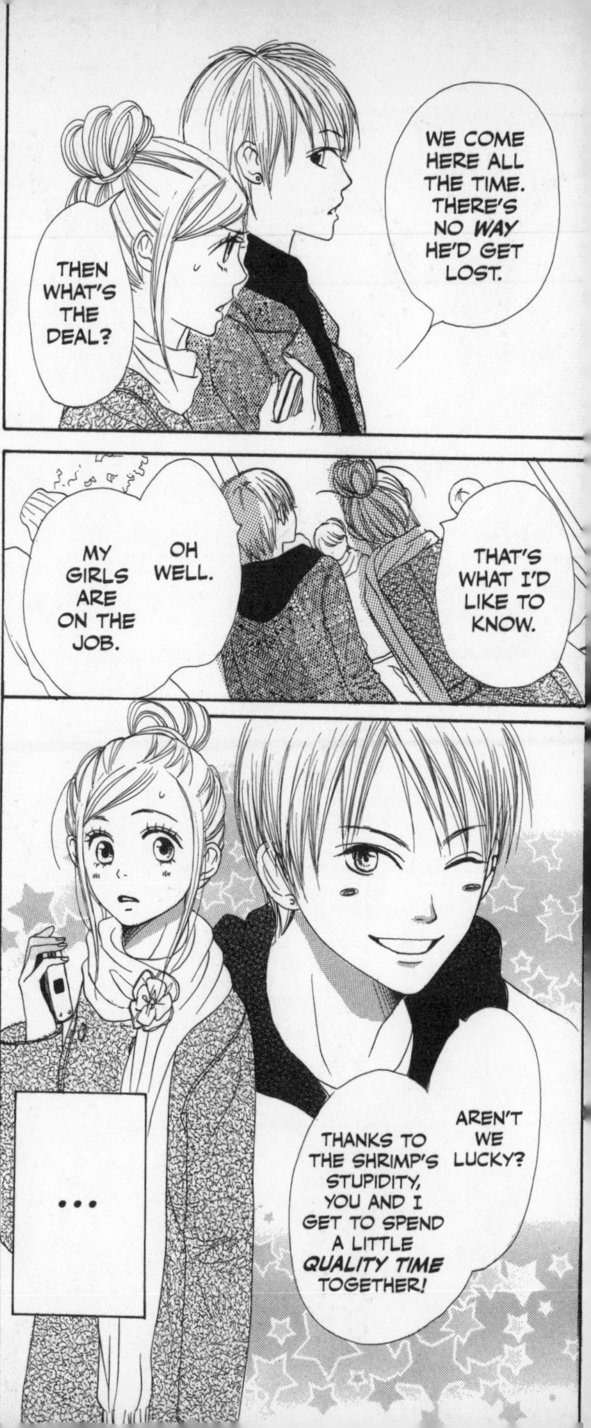
WE COME HERE ALL THE TIME. THERE'S NO *WAY* HE'D GET LOST.
THEN WHAT'S THE DEAL?
THAT'S WHAT I'D LIKE TO KNOW.
OH WELL.
MY GIRLS ARE ON THE JOB.
AREN'T WE LUCKY?
THANKS TO THE SHRIMP'S STUPIDITY, YOU AND I GET TO SPEND A LITTLE *QUALITY TIME* TOGETHER!
...

④

Another P.S.
The Love★Com video game is now on sale!! Isn't that awesome? A game!! Thanks so much to the game designers. My shaky drawings have been perfectly reproduced and I'm delighted. I'm going to play it too. Please try it, everyone! Also, Love★Com merchandise is now on sale nationwide. Thank you.
And it's been adapted into a novel by Nao Kokoro. Imagine: this action-packed manga is now a novel! Thank you! Oh, and the theme song for the movie, written and performed by the singer Misono-san, matches the Love★Com style perfectly. "Speed Love" is a really cute song, so please listen to it! Yes! Oh dear, I'm already running out of space. This has been a report from marketing director Nakahara. Let's meet again in volume 15! I hope I make it...

Aya
June 2006

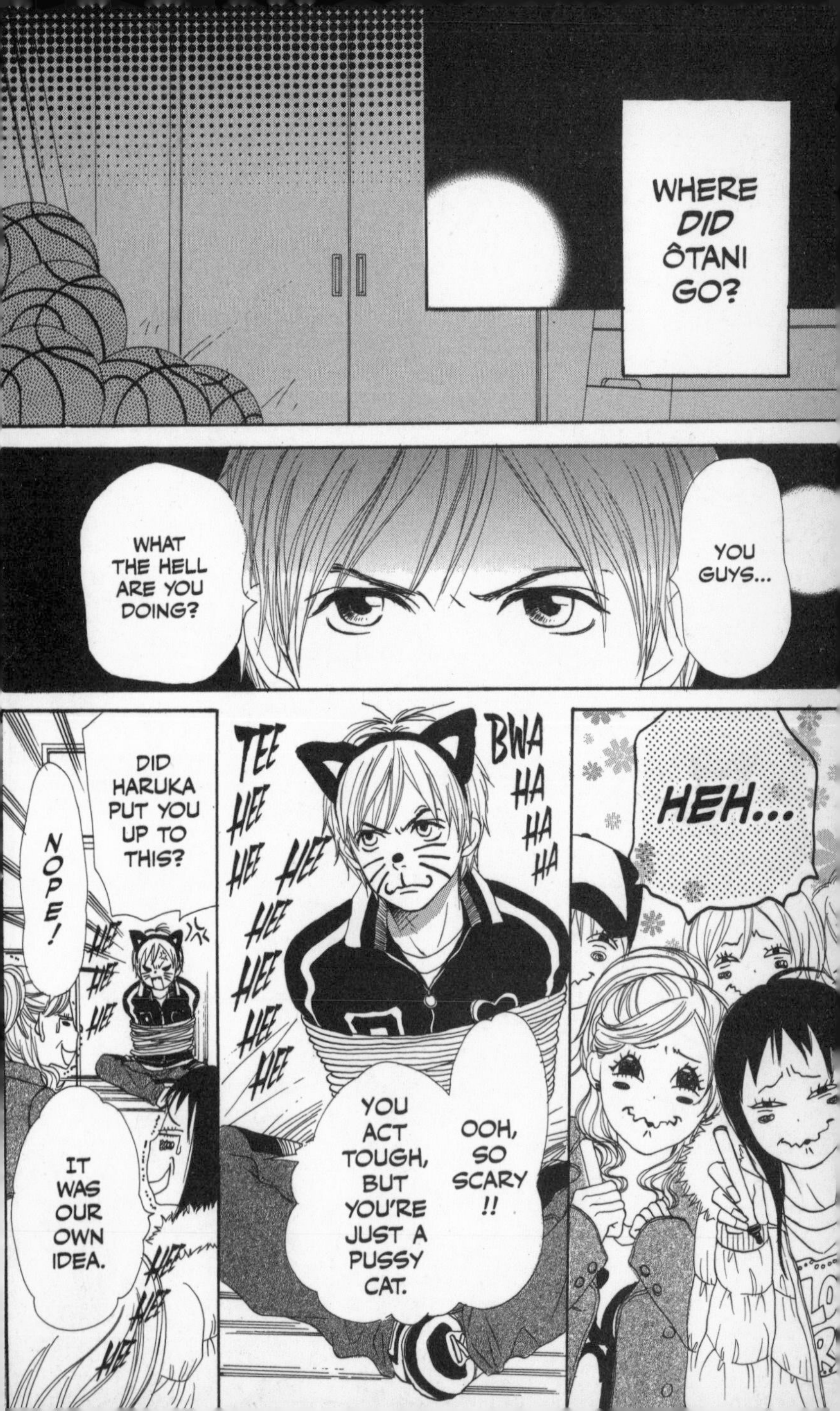
WHERE DID ÔTANI GO?
YOU GUYS...
WHAT THE HELL ARE YOU DOING?
HEH...
BWA HA HA HA
TEE HEE HEE HEE HEE HEE HEE HEE HEE
OOH, SO SCARY!!
YOU ACT TOUGH, BUT YOU'RE JUST A PUSSY CAT.
DID HARUKA PUT YOU UP TO THIS?
NOPE!
HEE HEE HEE
IT WAS OUR OWN IDEA.
HEE HEE HEE

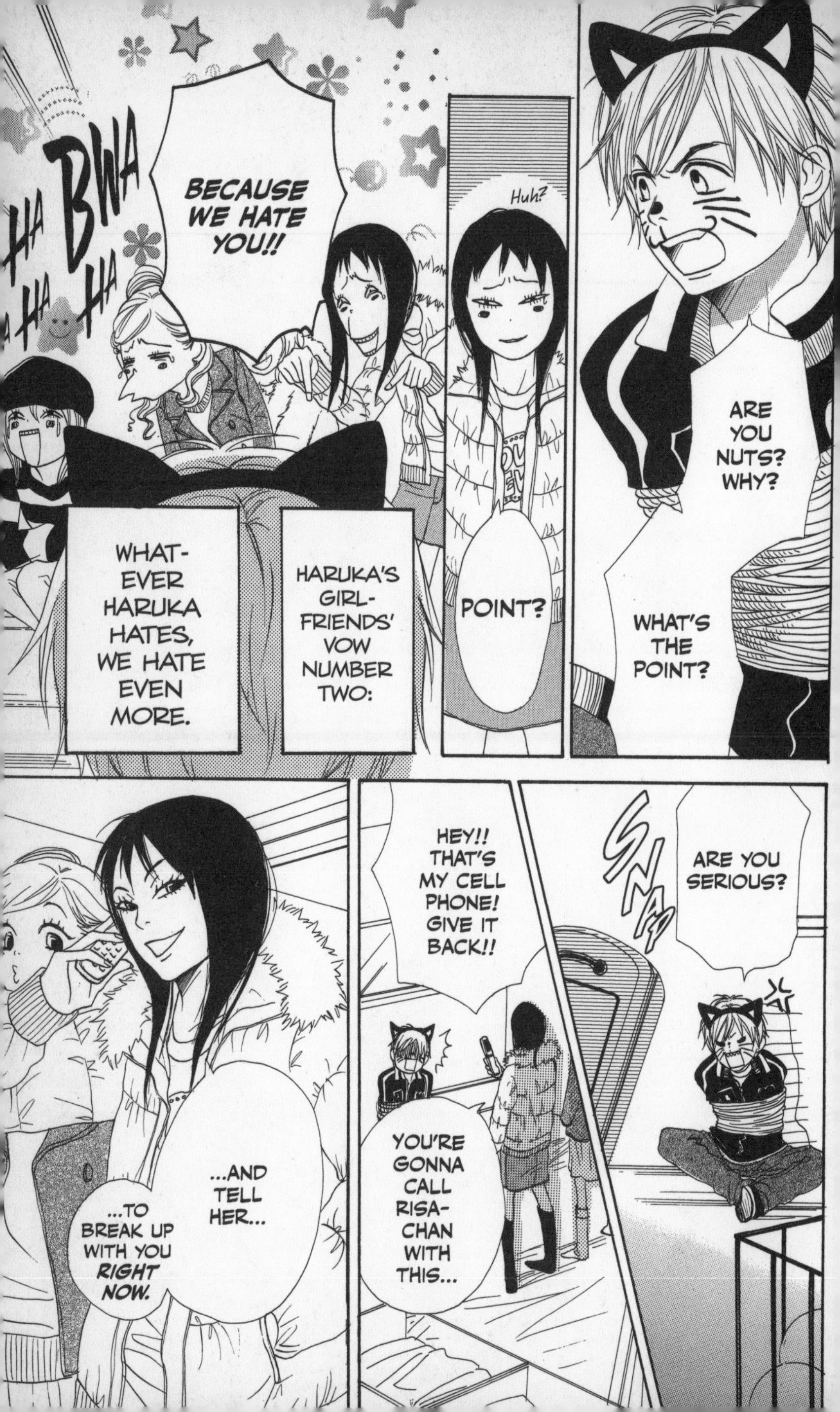

ARE YOU NUTS? WHY?
WHAT'S THE POINT?
Huh?
POINT?
HARUKA'S GIRL-FRIENDS' VOW NUMBER TWO:
WHAT-EVER HARUKA HATES, WE HATE EVEN MORE.
BECAUSE WE HATE YOU!!
BWA HA HA HA HA HA
ARE YOU SERIOUS?
SNAP
HEY!! THAT'S MY CELL PHONE! GIVE IT BACK!!
YOU'RE GONNA CALL RISA-CHAN WITH THIS...
...AND TELL HER...
...TO BREAK UP WITH YOU *RIGHT NOW.*

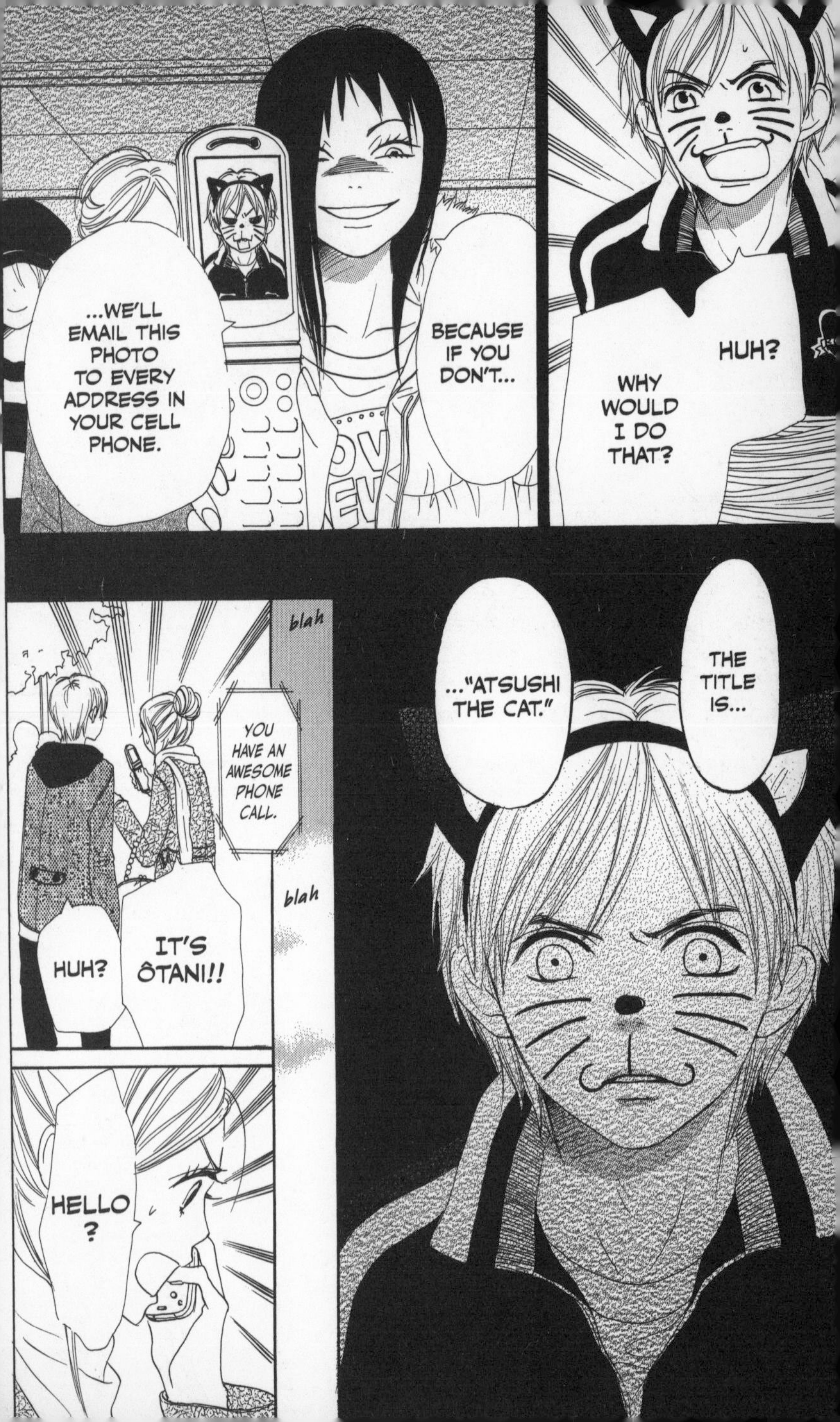
HUH?
WHY WOULD I DO THAT?
BECAUSE IF YOU DON'T...
...WE'LL EMAIL THIS PHOTO TO EVERY ADDRESS IN YOUR CELL PHONE.
THE TITLE IS...
..."ATSUSHI THE CAT."
blah
YOU HAVE AN AWESOME PHONE CALL.
blah
IT'S ÔTANI!!
HUH?
HELLO?

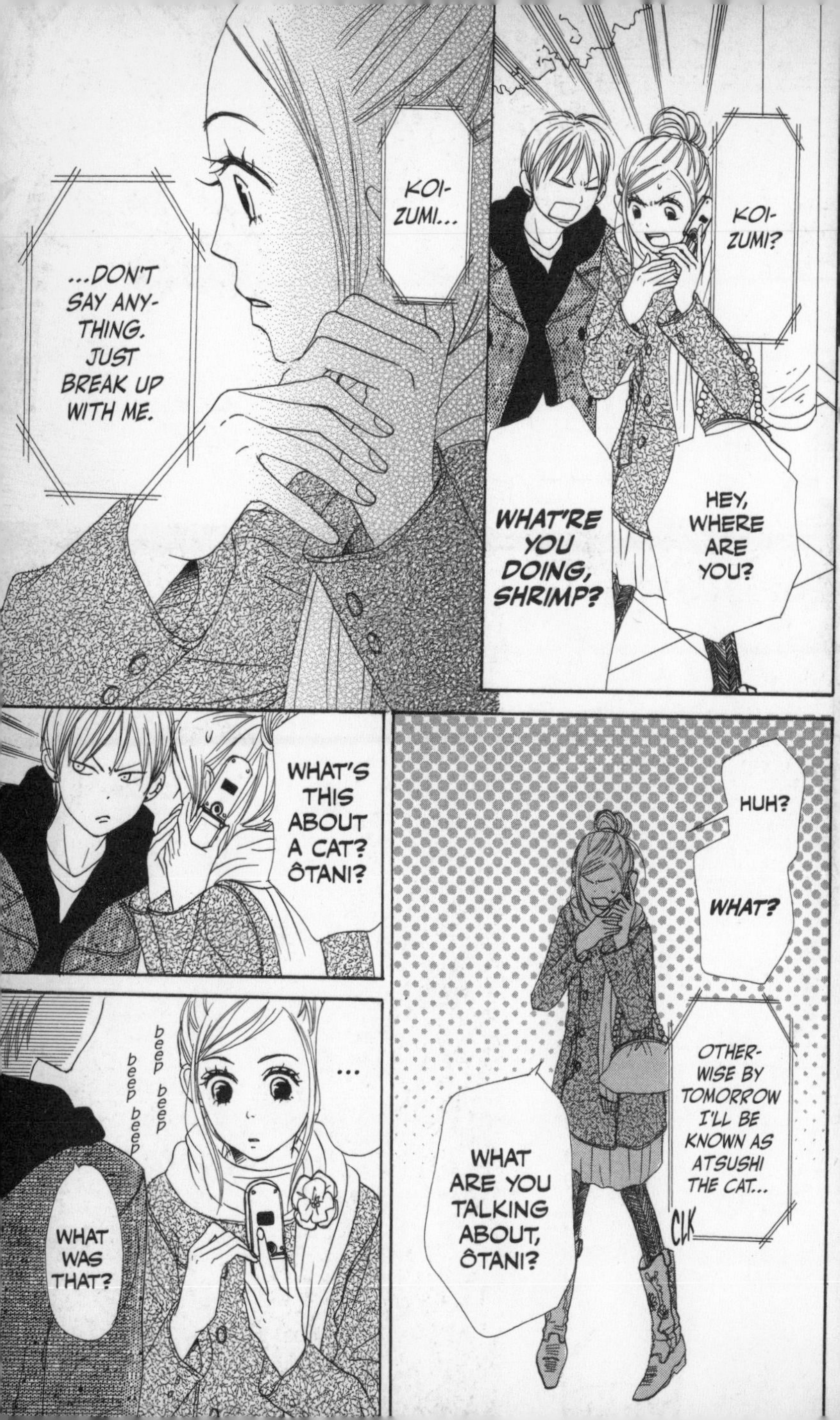
KOI-ZUMI?
HEY, WHERE ARE YOU?
WHAT'RE YOU DOING, SHRIMP?
KOI-ZUMI...
...DON'T SAY ANY-THING. JUST BREAK UP WITH ME.
HUH?
WHAT?
OTHER-WISE BY TOMORROW I'LL BE KNOWN AS ATSUSHI THE CAT...
CLK
WHAT ARE YOU TALKING ABOUT, ÔTANI?
WHAT'S THIS ABOUT A CAT? ÔTANI?
...
beep beep
beep beep
WHAT WAS THAT?

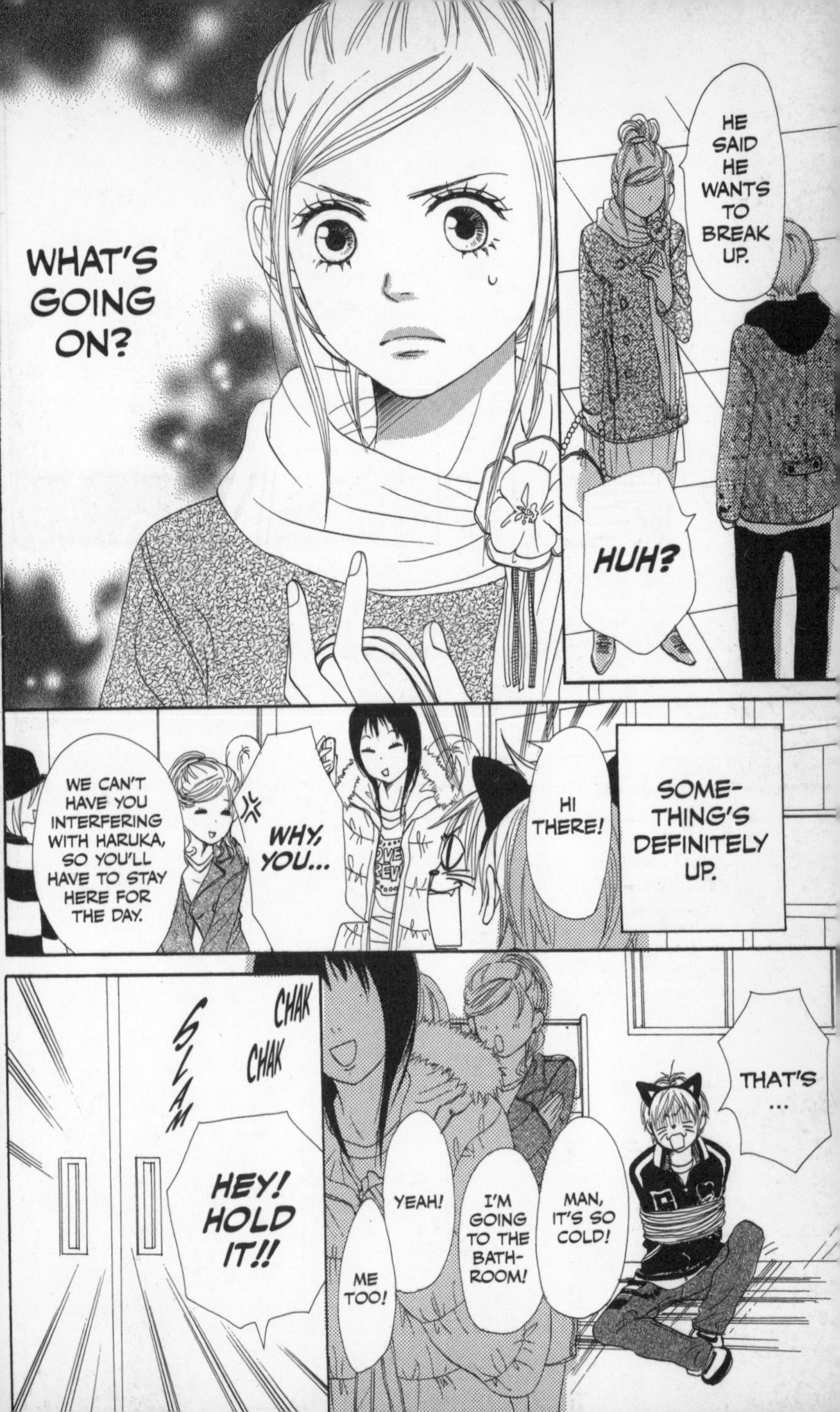
HE SAID HE WANTS TO BREAK UP.
HUH?
WHAT'S GOING ON?
SOME-THING'S DEFINITELY UP.
HI THERE!
WHY, YOU...
WE CAN'T HAVE YOU INTERFERING WITH HARUKA, SO YOU'LL HAVE TO STAY HERE FOR THE DAY.
THAT'S ...
MAN, IT'S SO COLD!
I'M GOING TO THE BATH-ROOM!
YEAH!
ME TOO!
CHAK CHAK
SLAM
HEY! HOLD IT!!

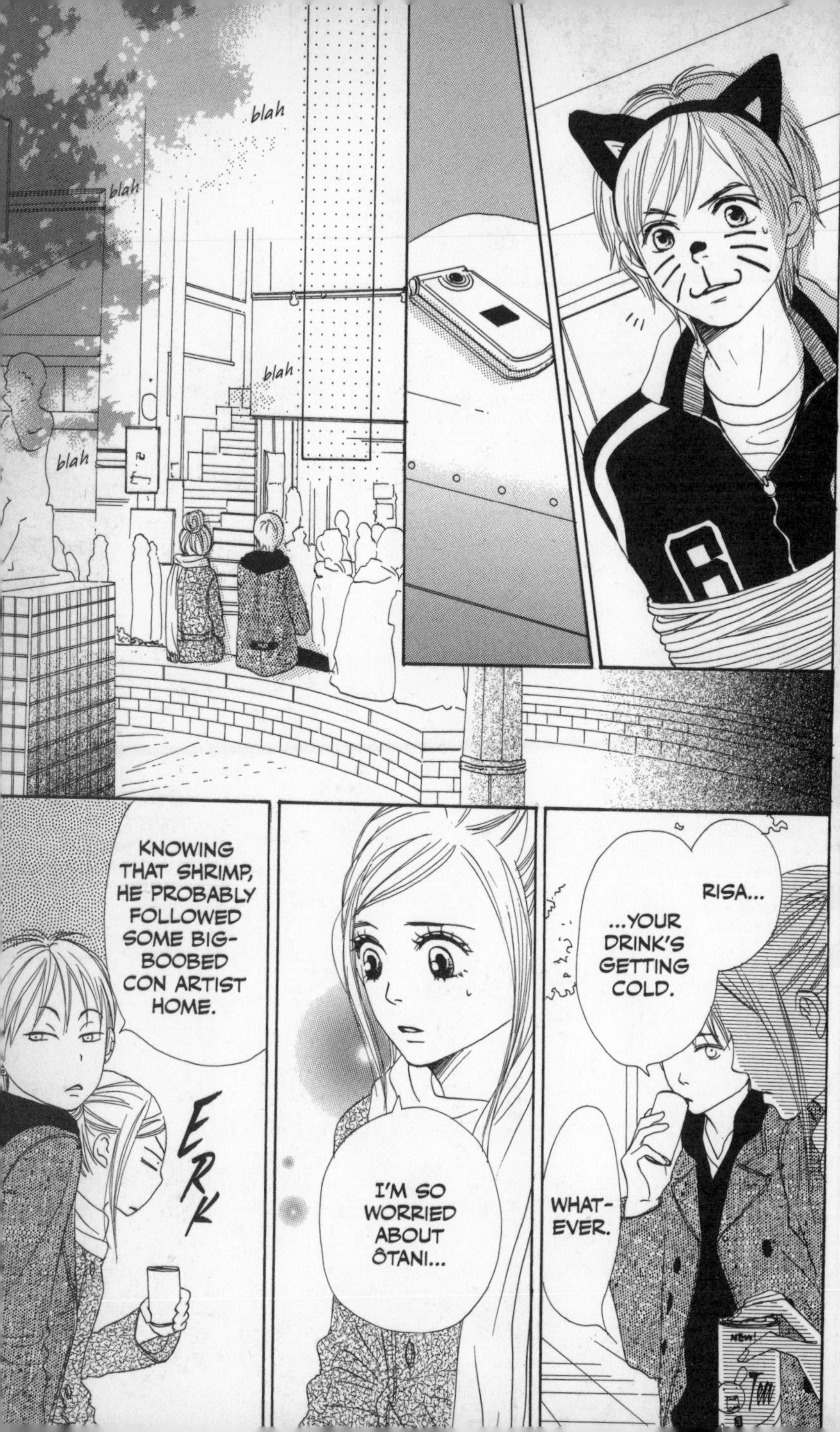
blah
blah
blah
blah
RISA...
...YOUR DRINK'S GETTING COLD.
WHAT-EVER.
I'M SO WORRIED ABOUT ŌTANI...
KNOWING THAT SHRIMP, HE PROBABLY FOLLOWED SOME BIG-BOOBED CON ARTIST HOME.
ERK

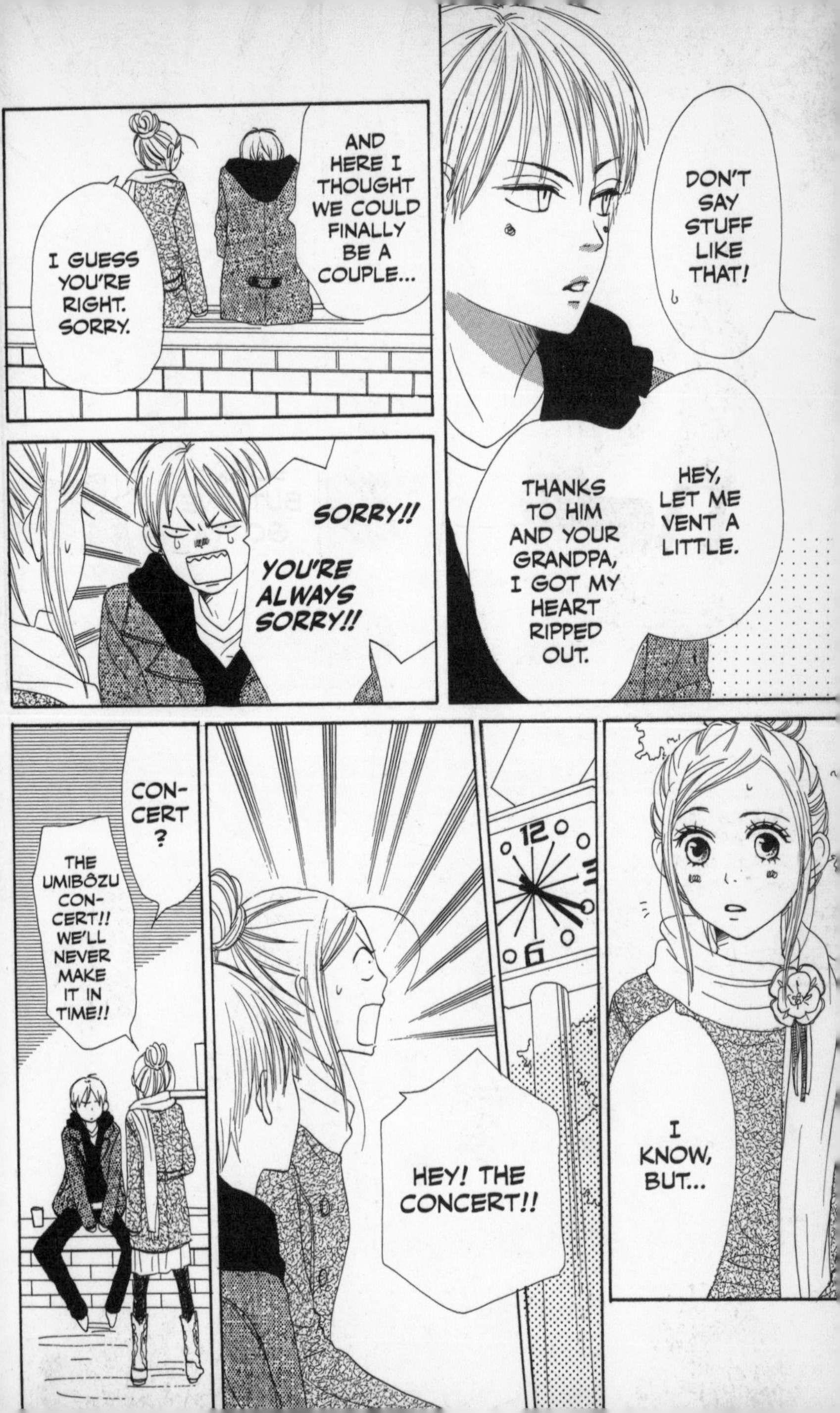
DON'T SAY STUFF LIKE THAT!
HEY, LET ME VENT A LITTLE.
THANKS TO HIM AND YOUR GRANDPA, I GOT MY HEART RIPPED OUT.
AND HERE I THOUGHT WE COULD FINALLY BE A COUPLE...
I GUESS YOU'RE RIGHT. SORRY.
SORRY!!
YOU'RE ALWAYS SORRY!!
I KNOW, BUT...
12
3
6
HEY! THE CONCERT!!
CON-CERT?
THE UMIBÔZU CON-CERT!! WE'LL NEVER MAKE IT IN TIME!!

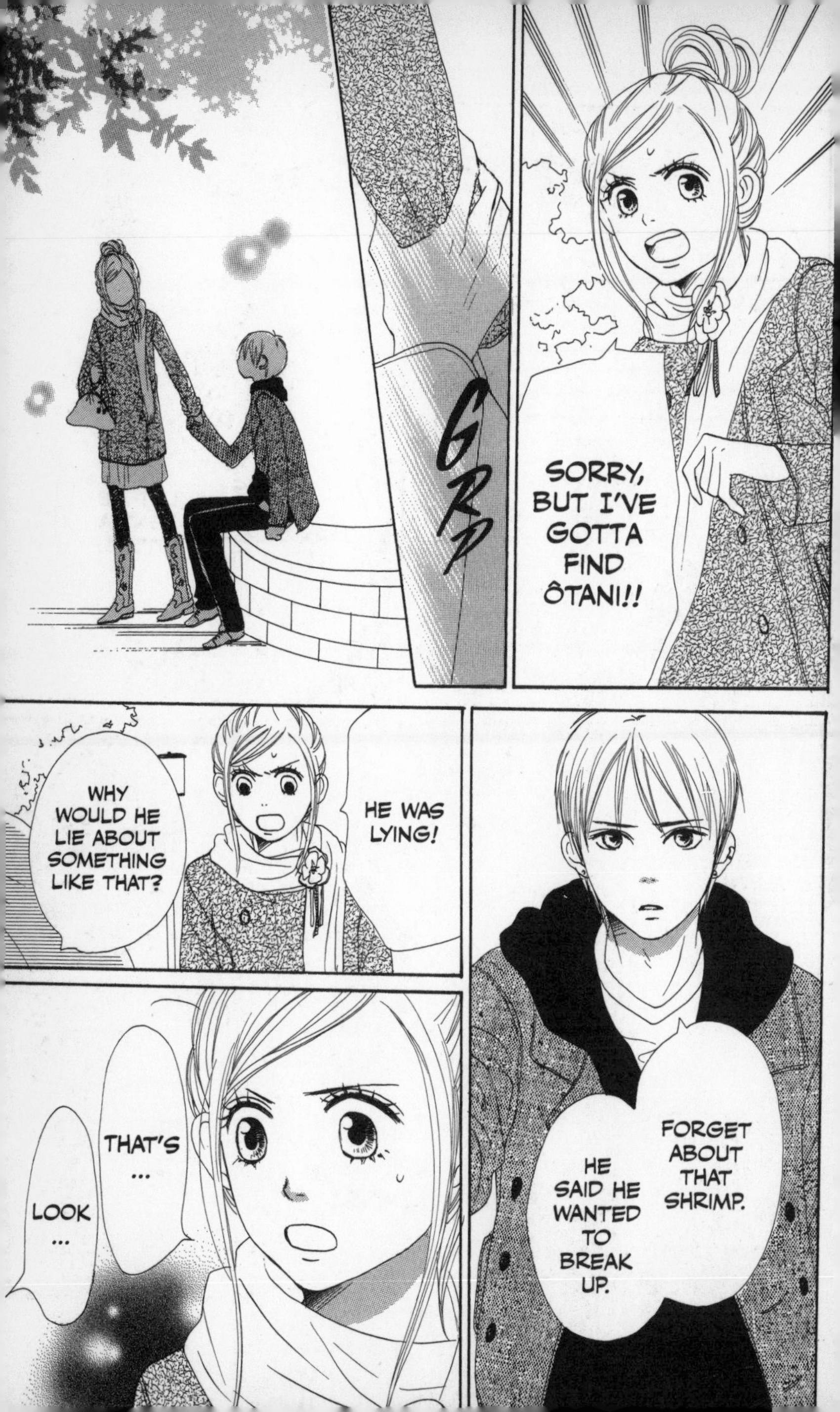
SORRY, BUT I'VE GOTTA FIND ÔTANI!!
GRR
FORGET ABOUT THAT SHRIMP.
HE SAID HE WANTED TO BREAK UP.
HE WAS LYING!
WHY WOULD HE LIE ABOUT SOMETHING LIKE THAT?
THAT'S ...
LOOK ...

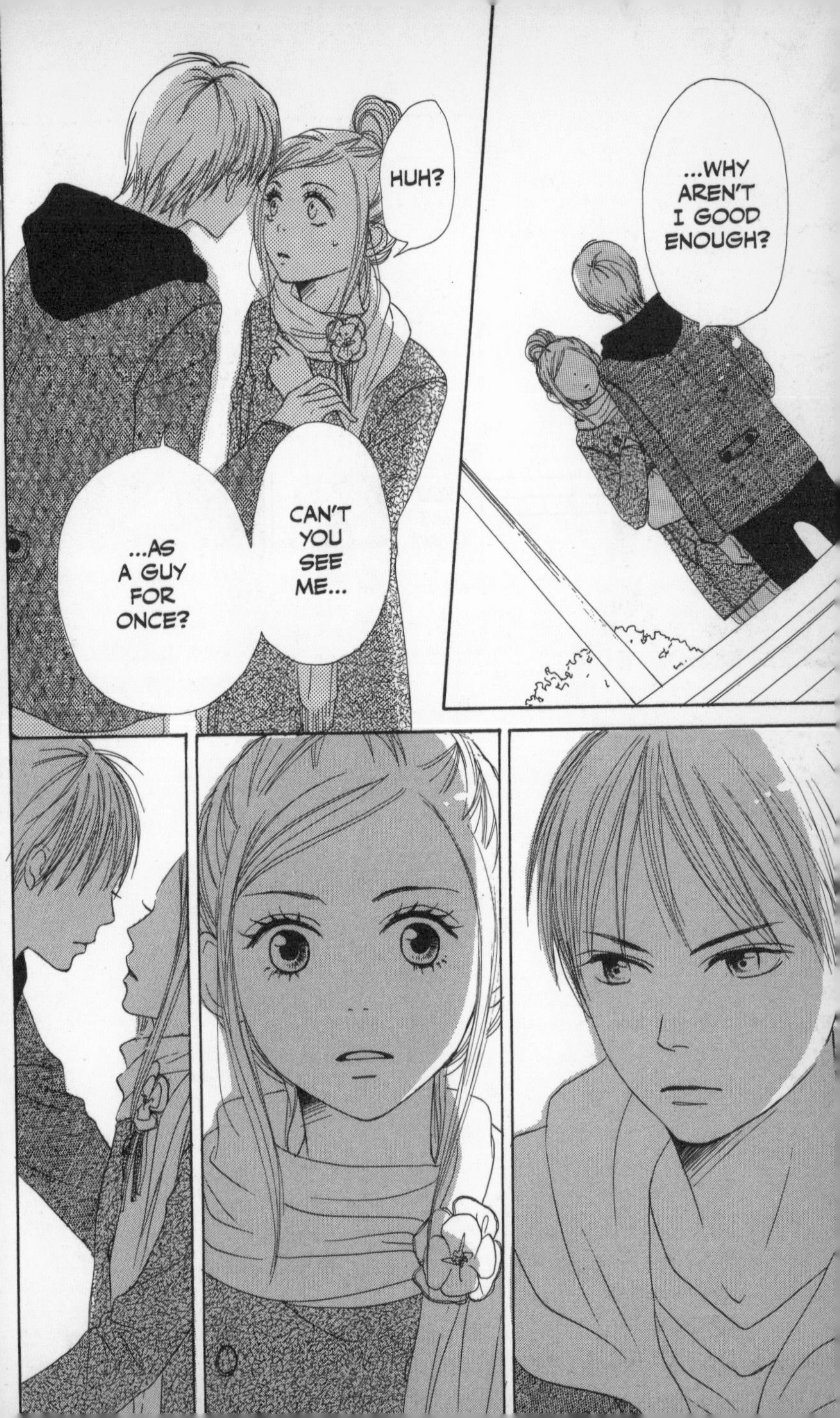
...WHY AREN'T I GOOD ENOUGH?
HUH?
CAN'T YOU SEE ME...
...AS A GUY FOR ONCE?

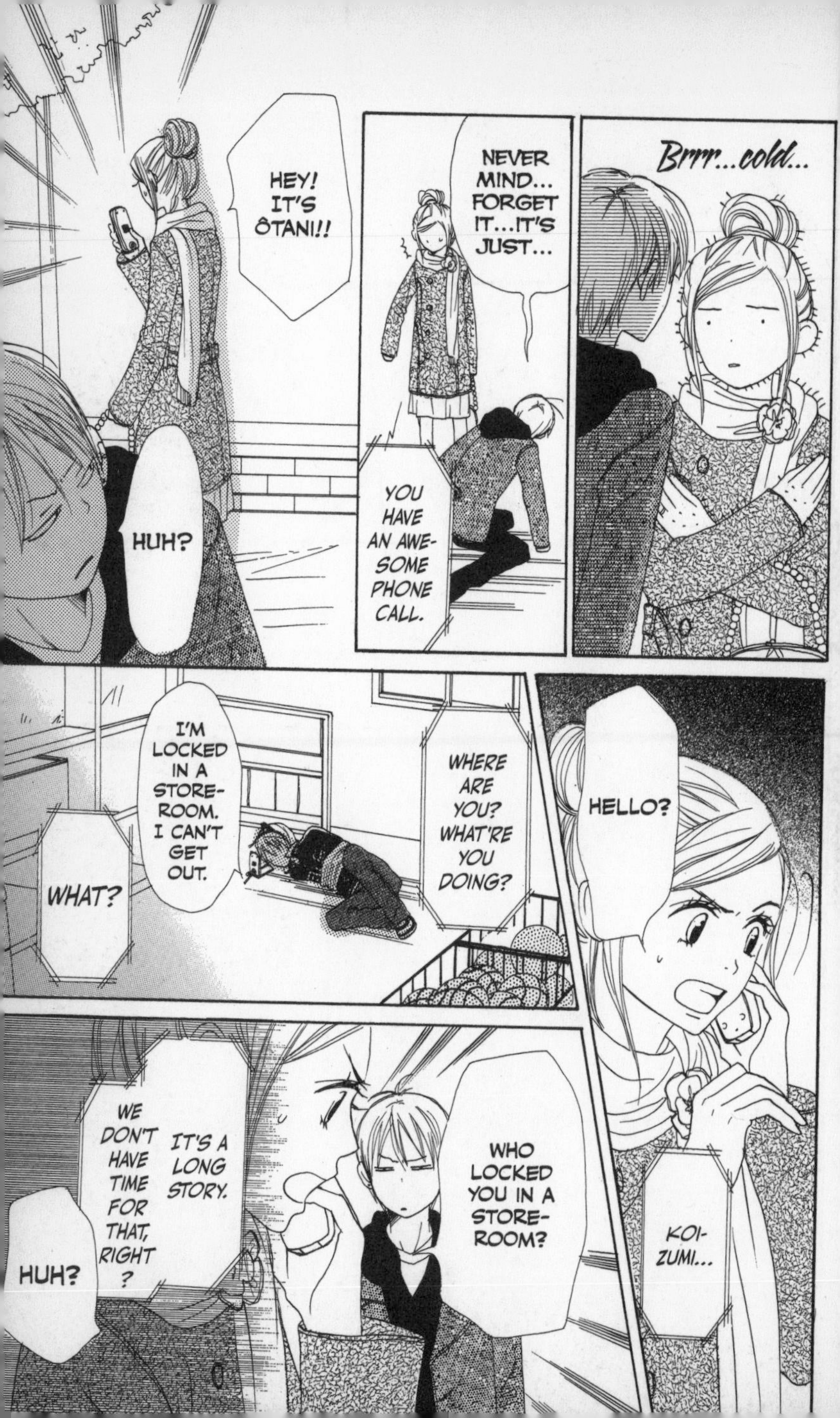

Brrr...cold...
NEVER MIND... FORGET IT...IT'S JUST...
YOU HAVE AN AWE-SOME PHONE CALL.
HEY! IT'S ŌTANI!!
HUH?
HELLO?
KOI-ZUMI...
WHERE ARE YOU? WHAT'RE YOU DOING?
I'M LOCKED IN A STORE-ROOM. I CAN'T GET OUT.
WHAT?
WHO LOCKED YOU IN A STORE-ROOM?
IT'S A LONG STORY.
WE DON'T HAVE TIME FOR THAT, RIGHT?
HUH?

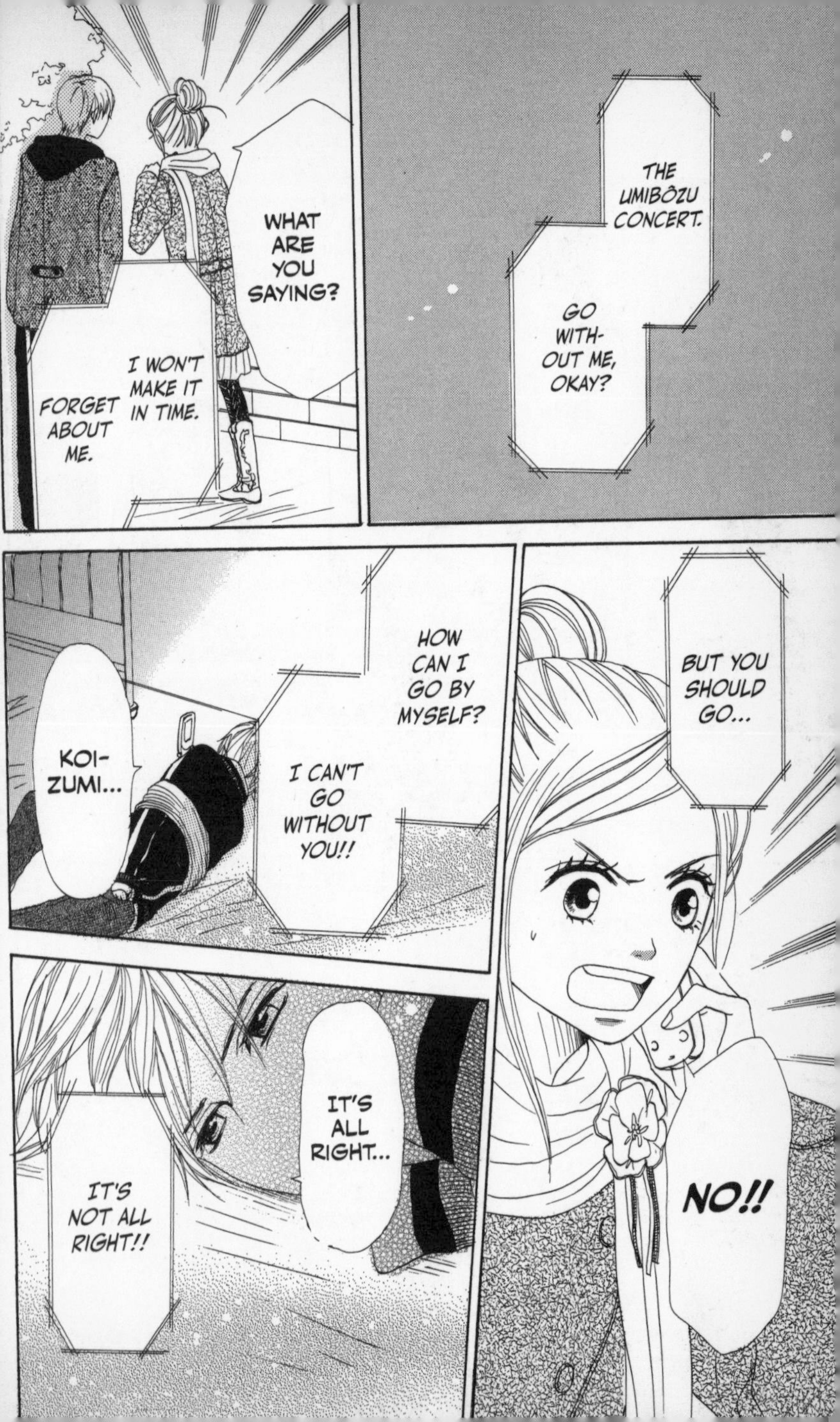
THE UMIBÔZU CONCERT.
GO WITH-OUT ME, OKAY?
WHAT ARE YOU SAYING?
I WON'T MAKE IT IN TIME.
FORGET ABOUT ME.
BUT YOU SHOULD GO...
NO!!
HOW CAN I GO BY MYSELF?
I CAN'T GO WITHOUT YOU!!
KOI-ZUMI...
IT'S ALL RIGHT...
IT'S NOT ALL RIGHT!!

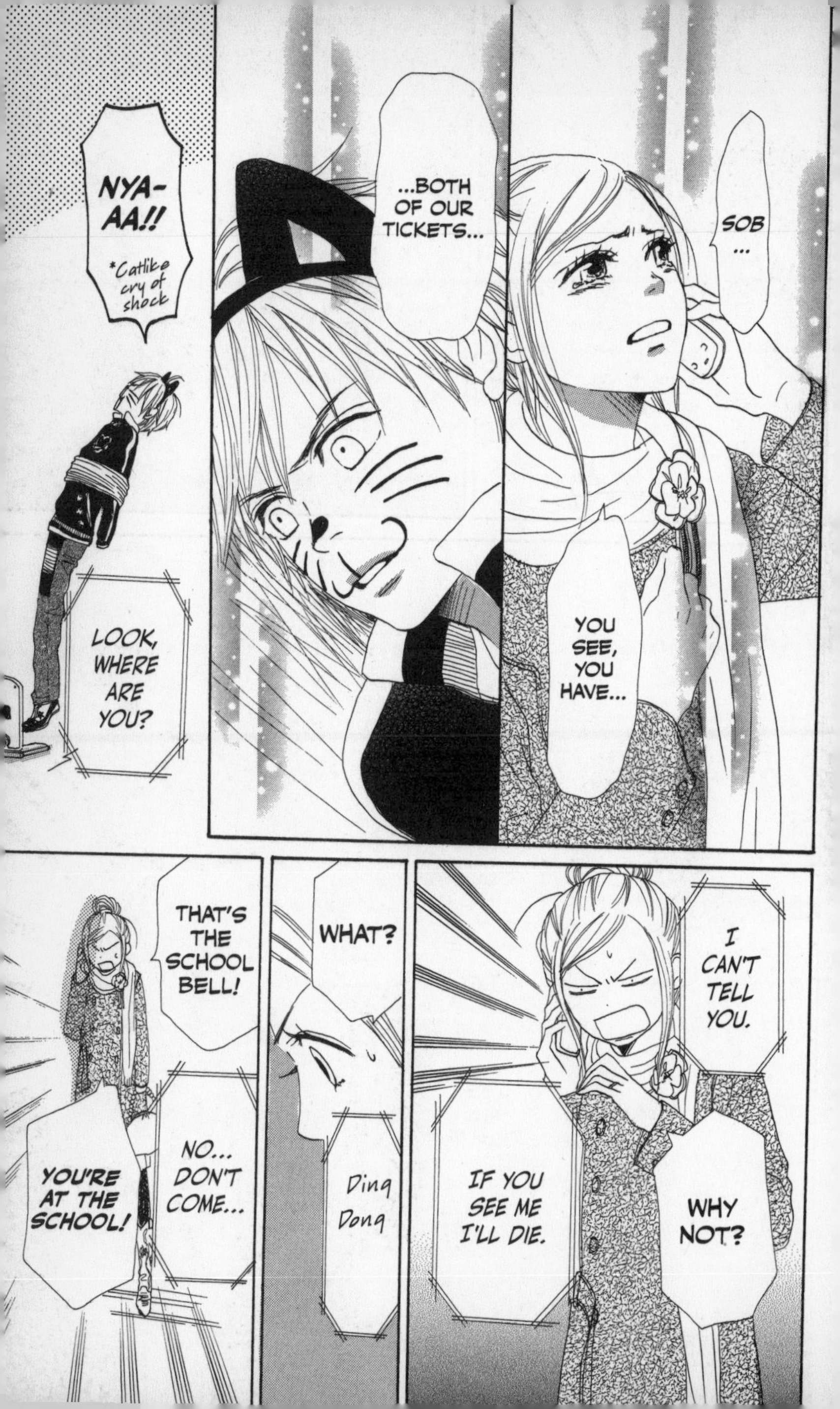
SOB ...
YOU SEE, YOU HAVE...
...BOTH OF OUR TICKETS...
NYA-AA!!
*Catlike cry of shock
LOOK, WHERE ARE YOU?
I CAN'T TELL YOU.
WHY NOT?
IF YOU SEE ME I'LL DIE.
WHAT?
Ding Dong
THAT'S THE SCHOOL BELL!
NO... DON'T COME...
YOU'RE AT THE SCHOOL!

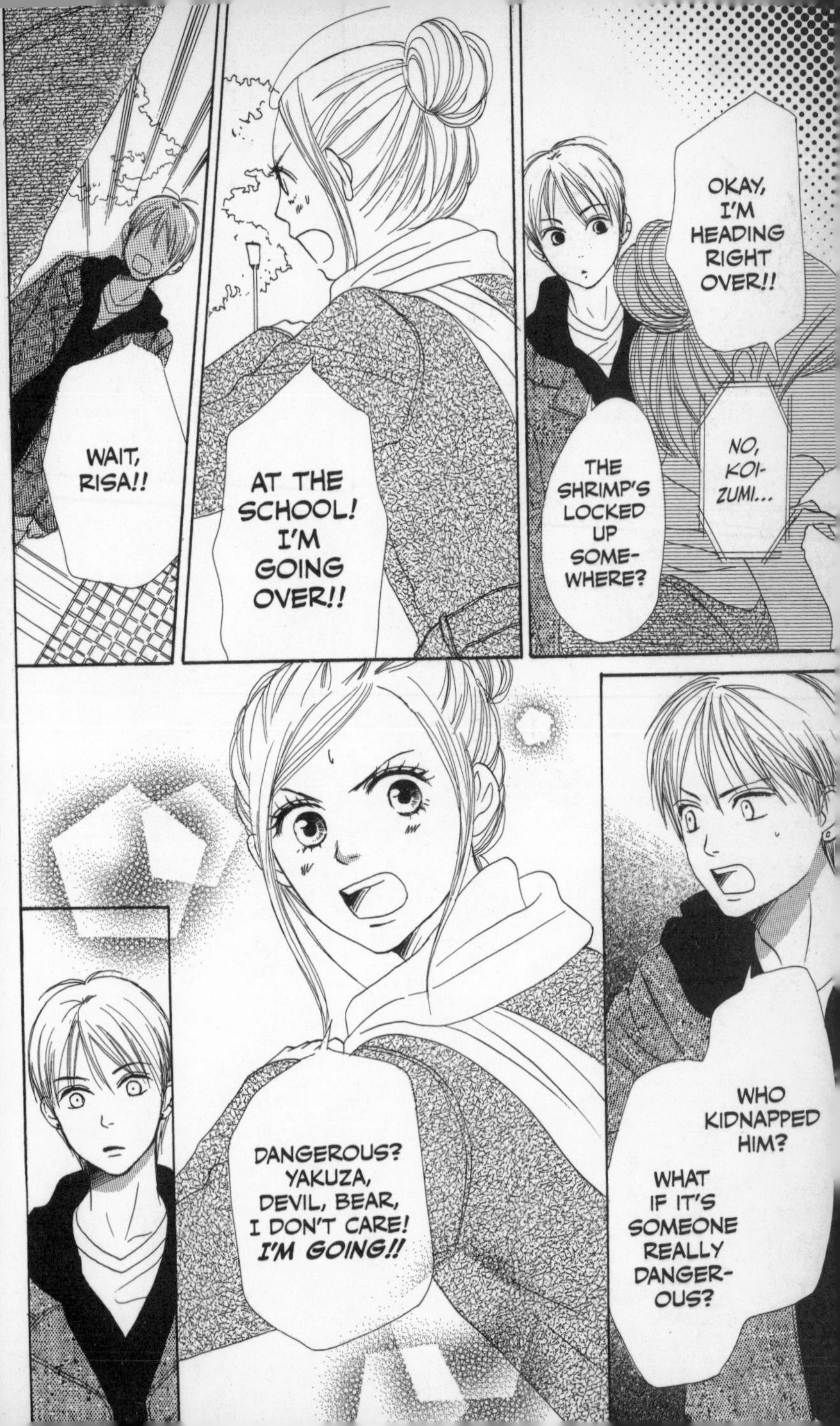
OKAY, I'M HEADING RIGHT OVER!!
NO, KOIZUMI...
THE SHRIMP'S LOCKED UP SOMEWHERE?
AT THE SCHOOL! I'M GOING OVER!!
WAIT, RISA!!
WHO KIDNAPPED HIM?
WHAT IF IT'S SOMEONE REALLY DANGEROUS?
DANGEROUS? YAKUZA, DEVIL, BEAR, I DON'T CARE! *I'M GOING!!*

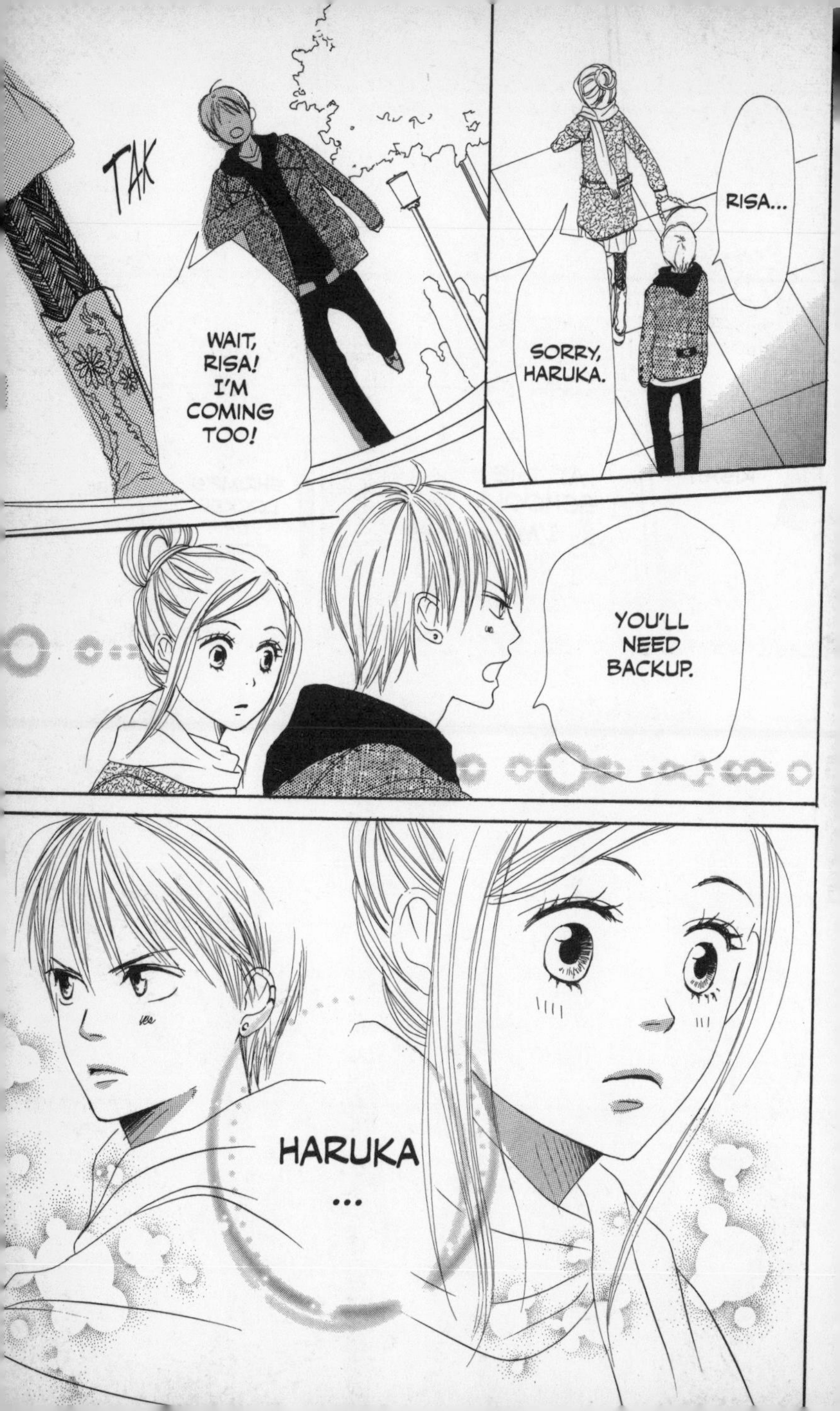
RISA...
SORRY, HARUKA.
TAK
WAIT, RISA! I'M COMING TOO!
YOU'LL NEED BACKUP.
HARUKA ...

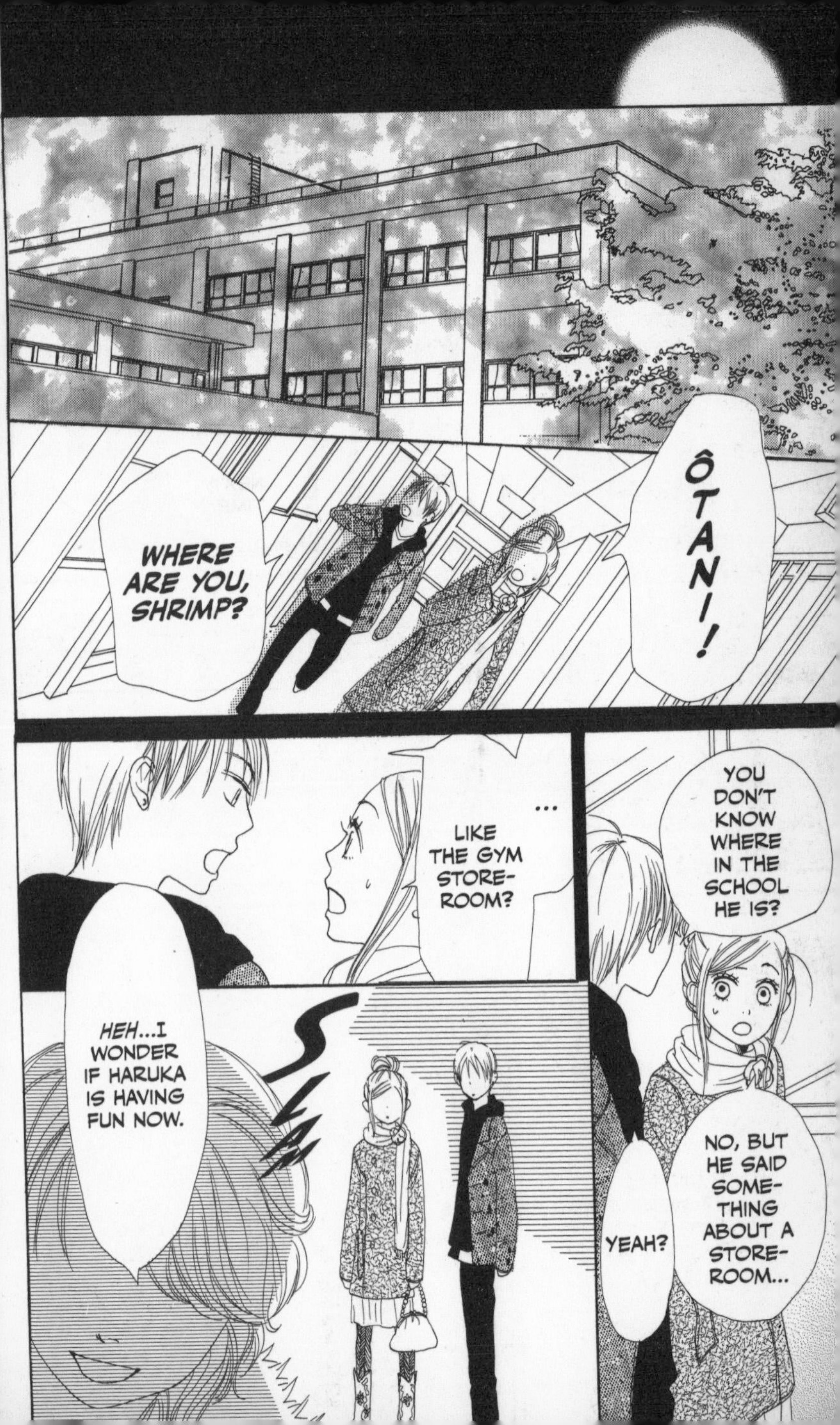
ÔTANI!
WHERE ARE YOU, SHRIMP?
YOU DON'T KNOW WHERE IN THE SCHOOL HE IS?
NO, BUT HE SAID SOME-THING ABOUT A STORE-ROOM...
YEAH?
...
LIKE THE GYM STORE-ROOM?
HEH...I WONDER IF HARUKA IS HAVING FUN NOW.

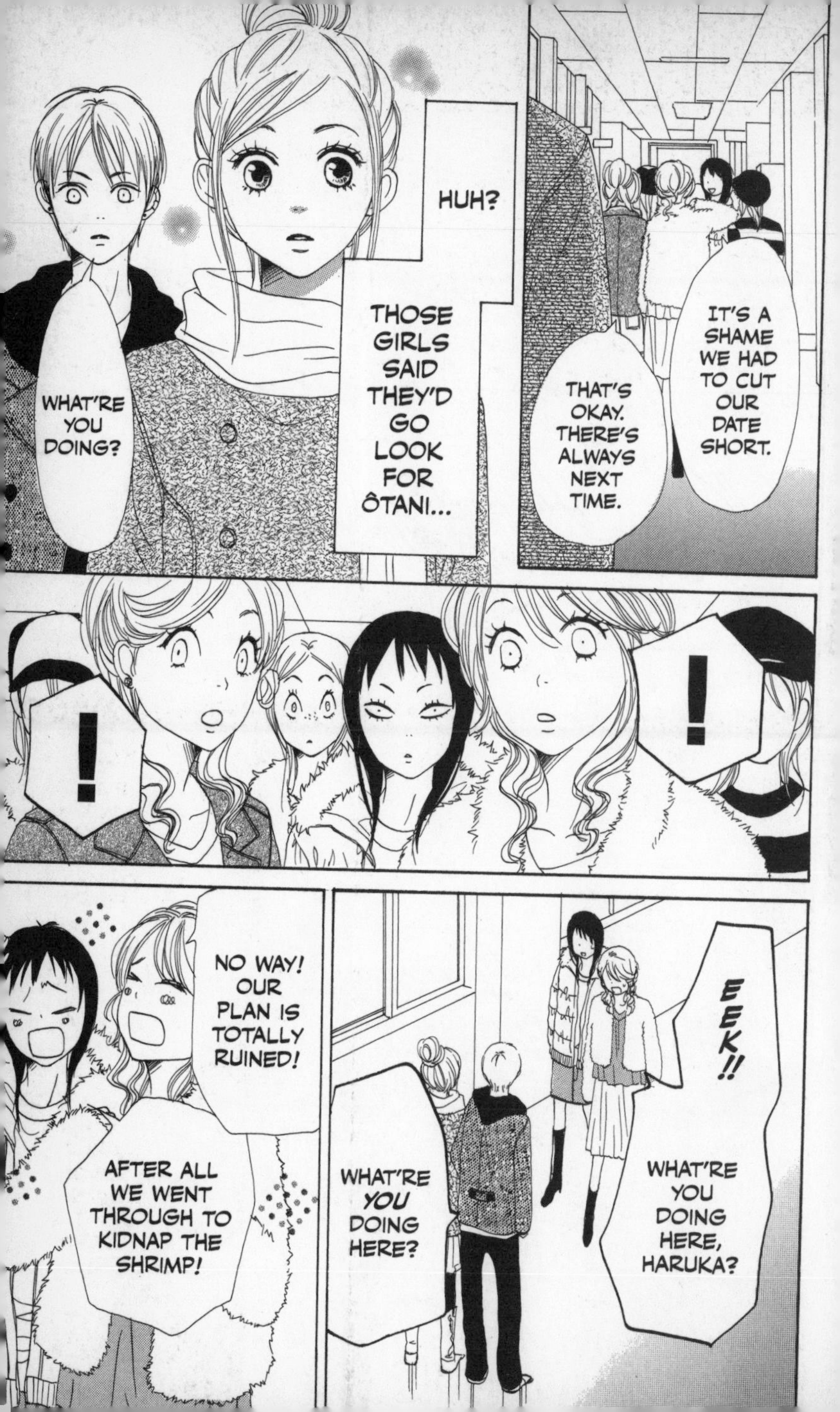
IT'S A SHAME WE HAD TO CUT OUR DATE SHORT.
THAT'S OKAY. THERE'S ALWAYS NEXT TIME.
HUH?
THOSE GIRLS SAID THEY'D GO LOOK FOR ÔTANI...
WHAT'RE YOU DOING?
!
!
EEK!!
WHAT'RE YOU DOING HERE, HARUKA?
WHAT'RE *YOU* DOING HERE?
NO WAY! OUR PLAN IS TOTALLY RUINED!
AFTER ALL WE WENT THROUGH TO KIDNAP THE SHRIMP!

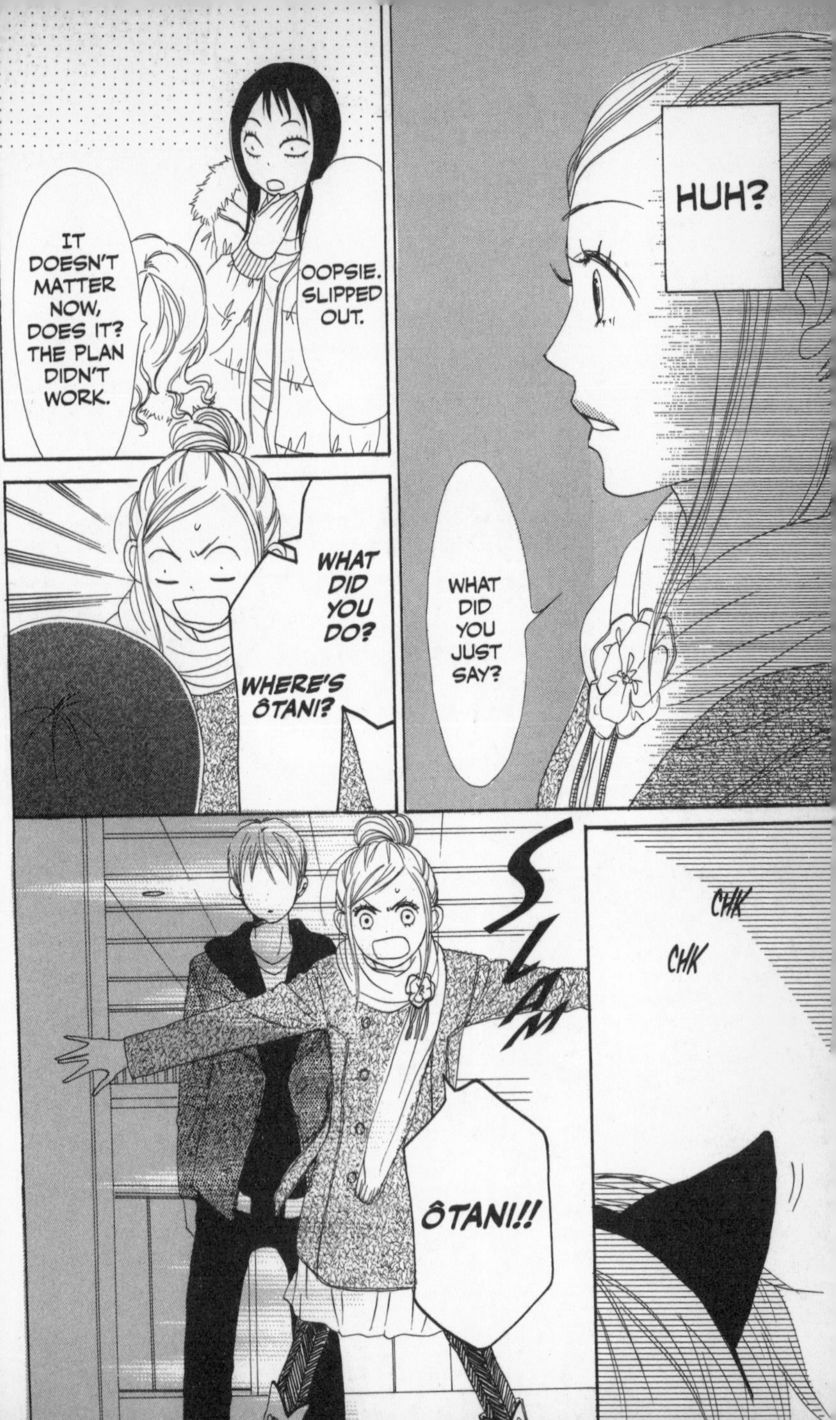
HUH?
WHAT DID YOU JUST SAY?
OOPSIE. SLIPPED OUT.
IT DOESN'T MATTER NOW, DOES IT? THE PLAN DIDN'T WORK.
WHAT DID YOU DO?
WHERE'S ÔTANI?
CHK
CHK
SLAM
ÔTANI!!

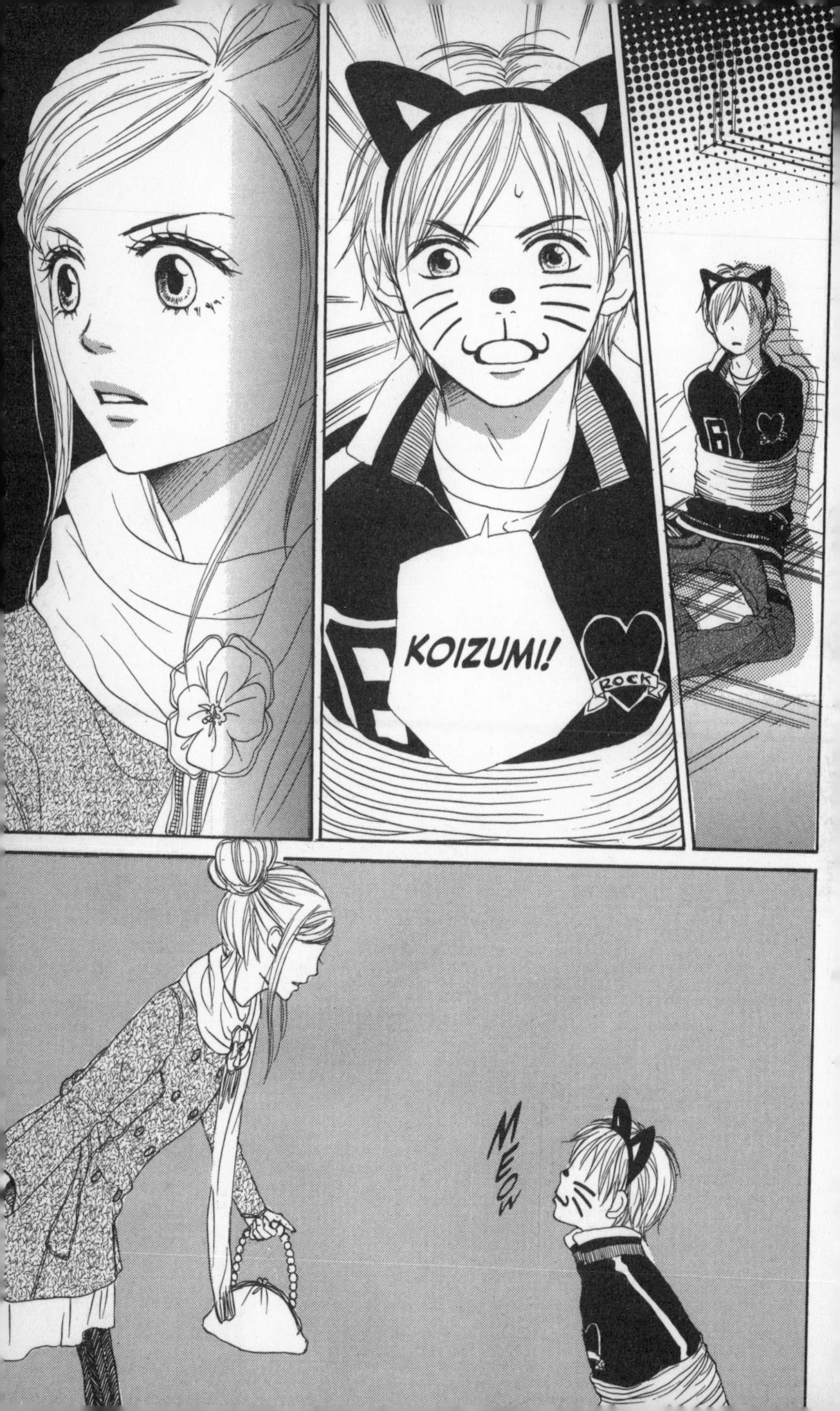
KOIZUMI!
MEOW

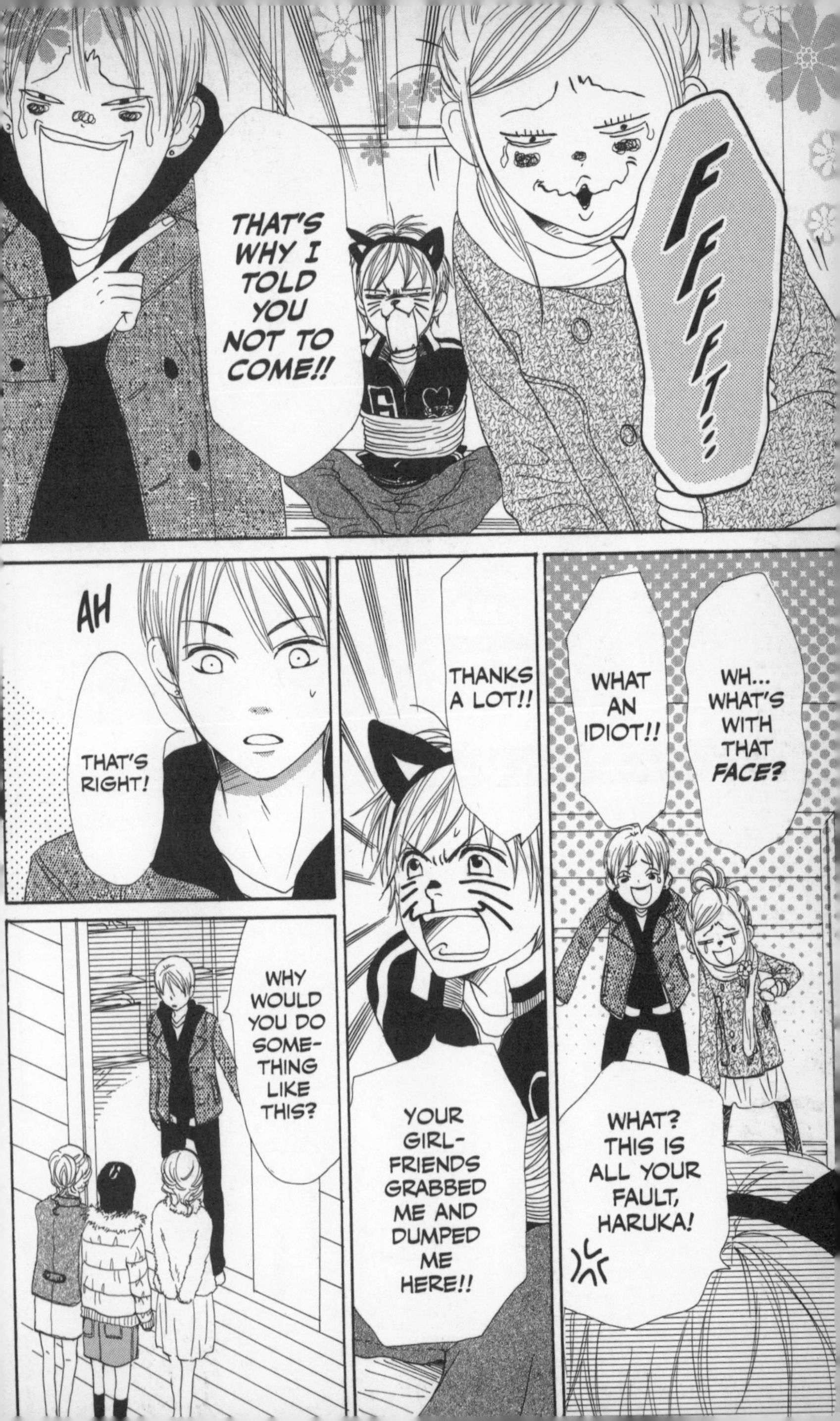
FFFT...
THAT'S WHY I TOLD YOU NOT TO COME!!
WH... WHAT'S WITH THAT FACE?
WHAT AN IDIOT!!
WHAT? THIS IS ALL YOUR FAULT, HARUKA!
THANKS A LOT!!
YOUR GIRL-FRIENDS GRABBED ME AND DUMPED ME HERE!!
AH
THAT'S RIGHT!
WHY WOULD YOU DO SOME-THING LIKE THIS?

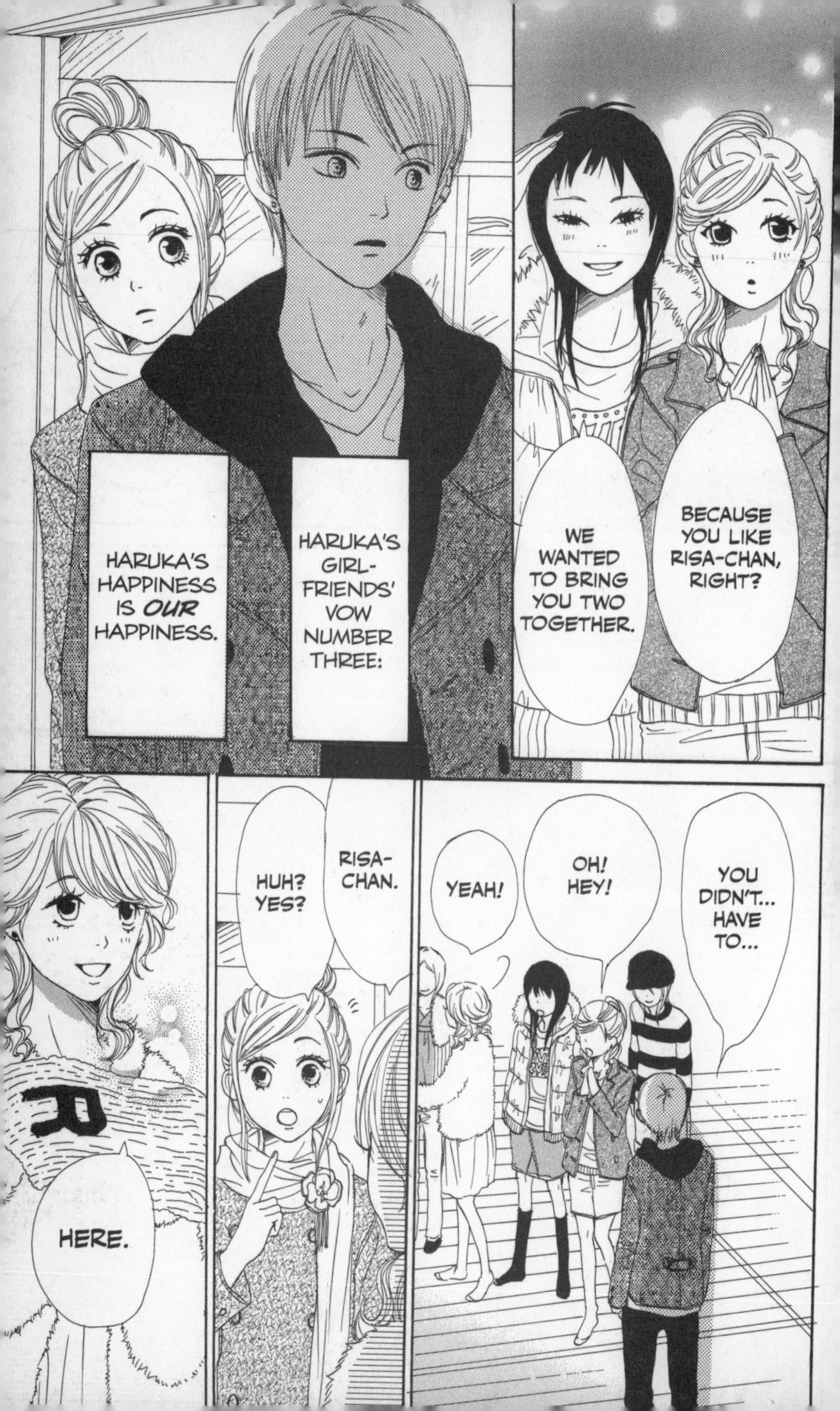

BECAUSE YOU LIKE RISA-CHAN, RIGHT?
WE WANTED TO BRING YOU TWO TOGETHER.
HARUKA'S GIRL-FRIENDS' VOW NUMBER THREE:
HARUKA'S HAPPINESS IS *OUR* HAPPINESS.
YOU DIDN'T... HAVE TO...
OH! HEY!
YEAH!
RISA-CHAN.
HUH? YES?
HERE.

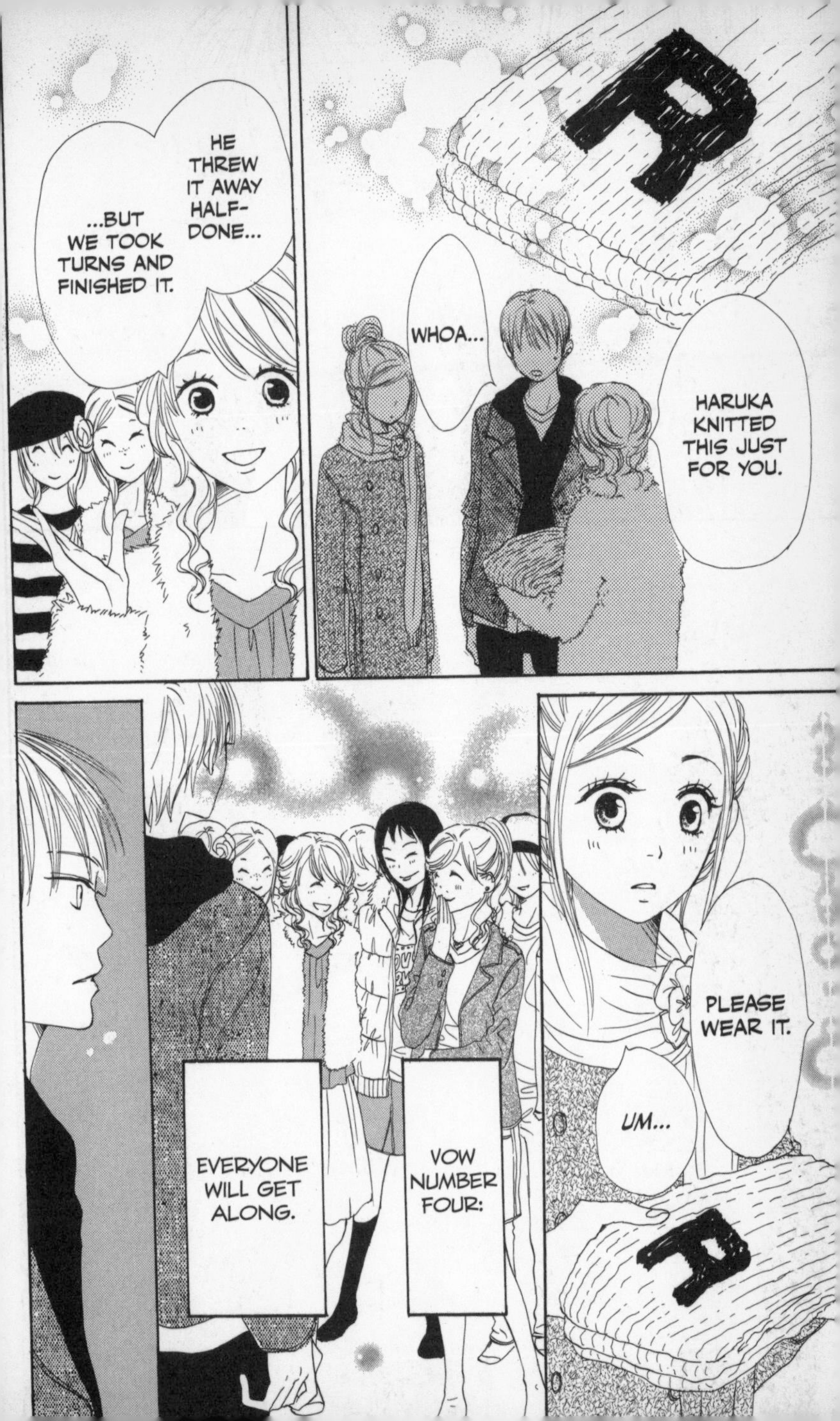
HARUKA KNITTED THIS JUST FOR YOU.
WHOA...
HE THREW IT AWAY HALF-DONE...
...BUT WE TOOK TURNS AND FINISHED IT.
PLEASE WEAR IT.
UM...
VOW NUMBER FOUR:
EVERYONE WILL GET ALONG.

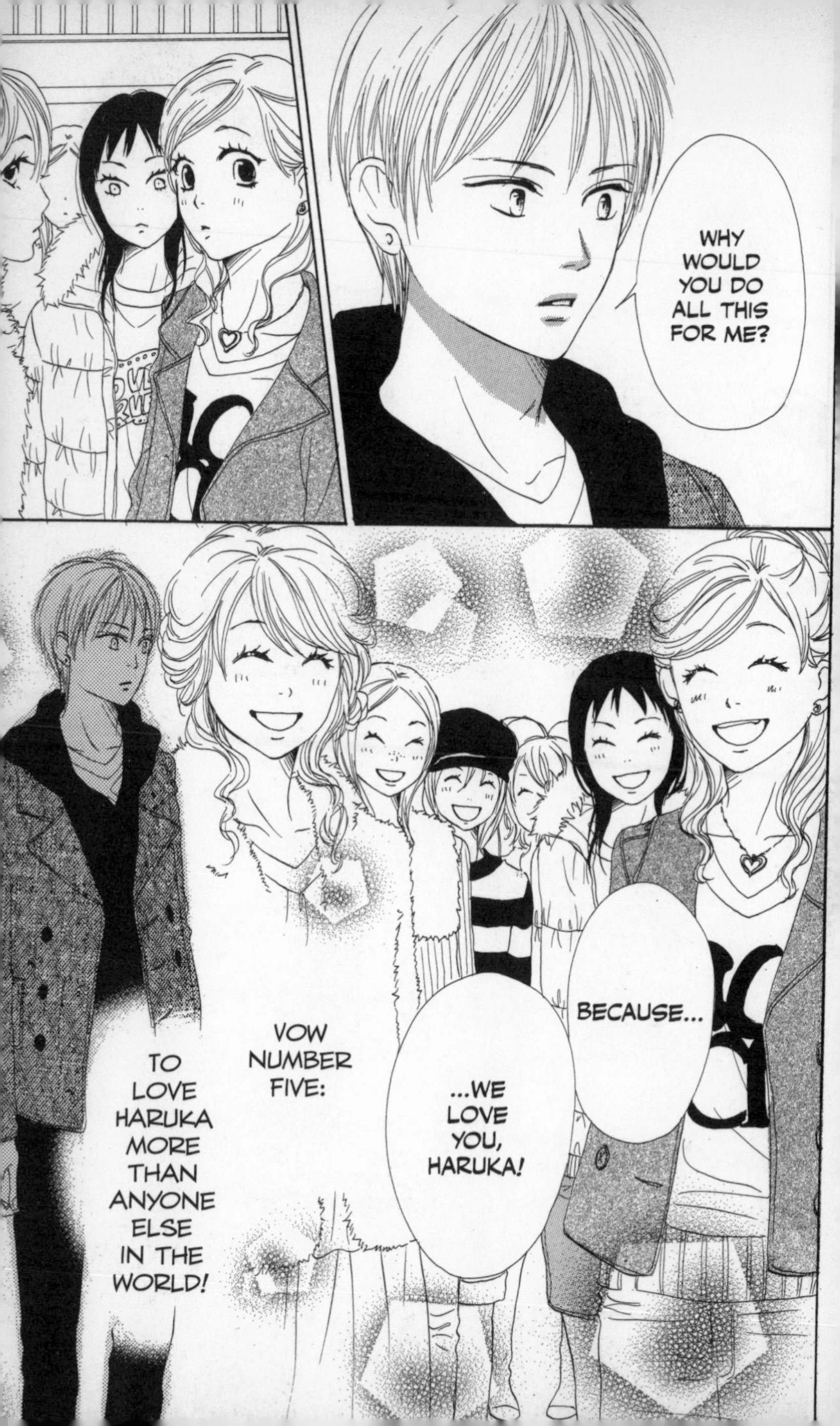
WHY WOULD YOU DO ALL THIS FOR ME?
BECAUSE...
...WE LOVE YOU, HARUKA!
VOW NUMBER FIVE:
TO LOVE HARUKA MORE THAN ANYONE ELSE IN THE WORLD!

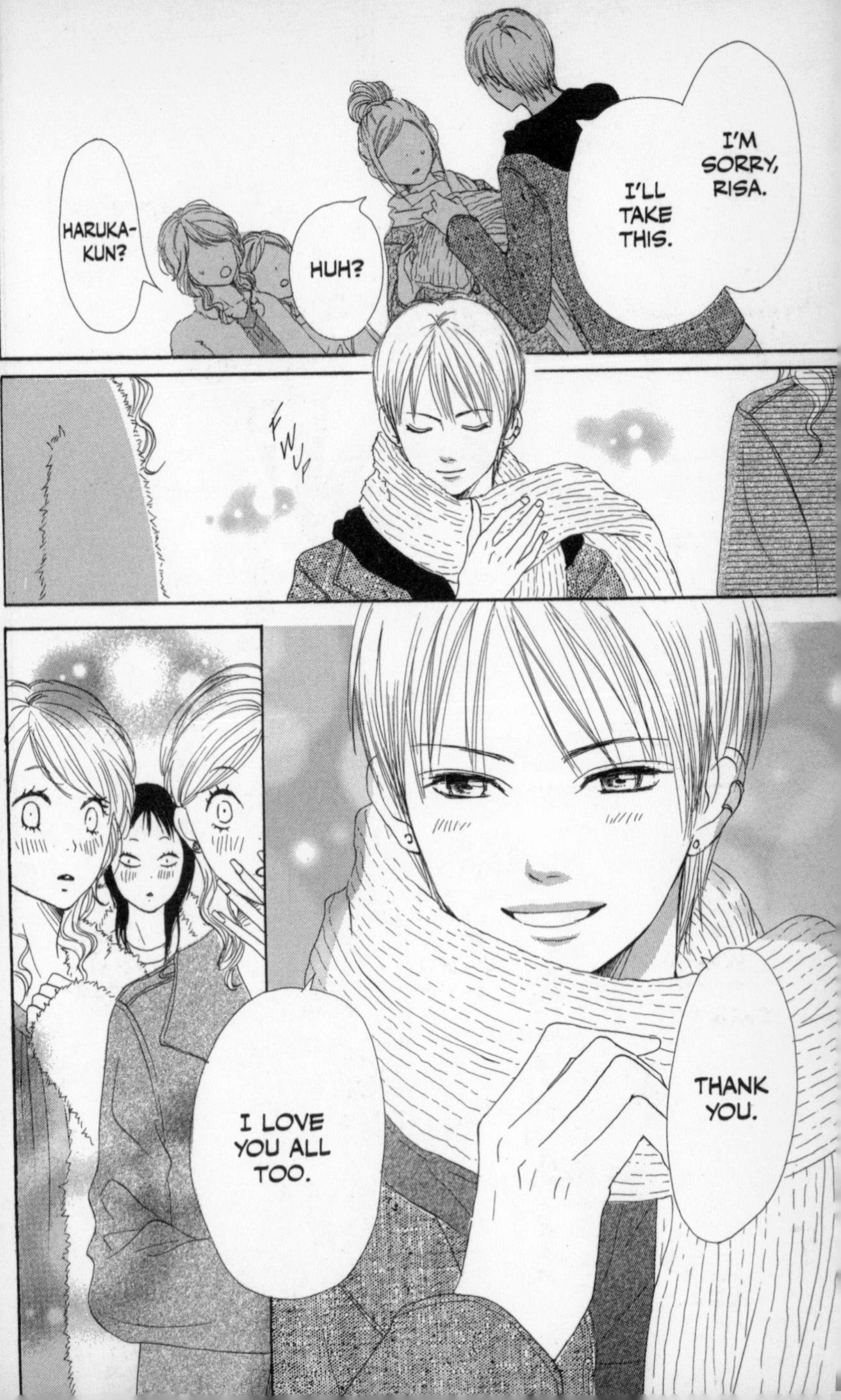
I'M SORRY, RISA.
I'LL TAKE THIS.
HUH?
HARUKA-KUN?
FWUP
THANK YOU.
I LOVE YOU ALL TOO.

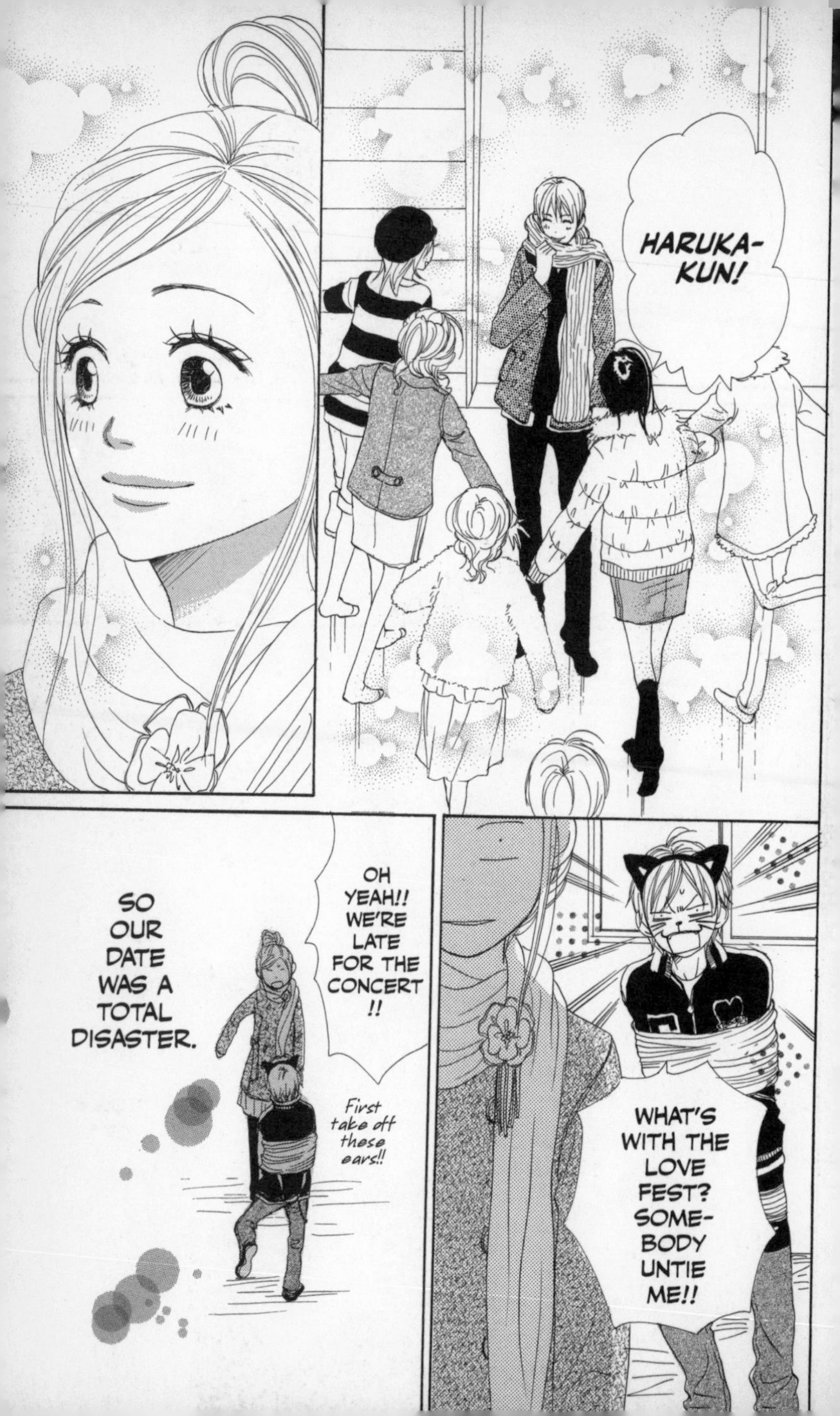
HARUKA-KUN!
WHAT'S WITH THE LOVE FEST? SOMEBODY UNTIE ME!!
OH YEAH!! WE'RE LATE FOR THE CONCERT!!
First take off these ears!!
SO OUR DATE WAS A TOTAL DISASTER.

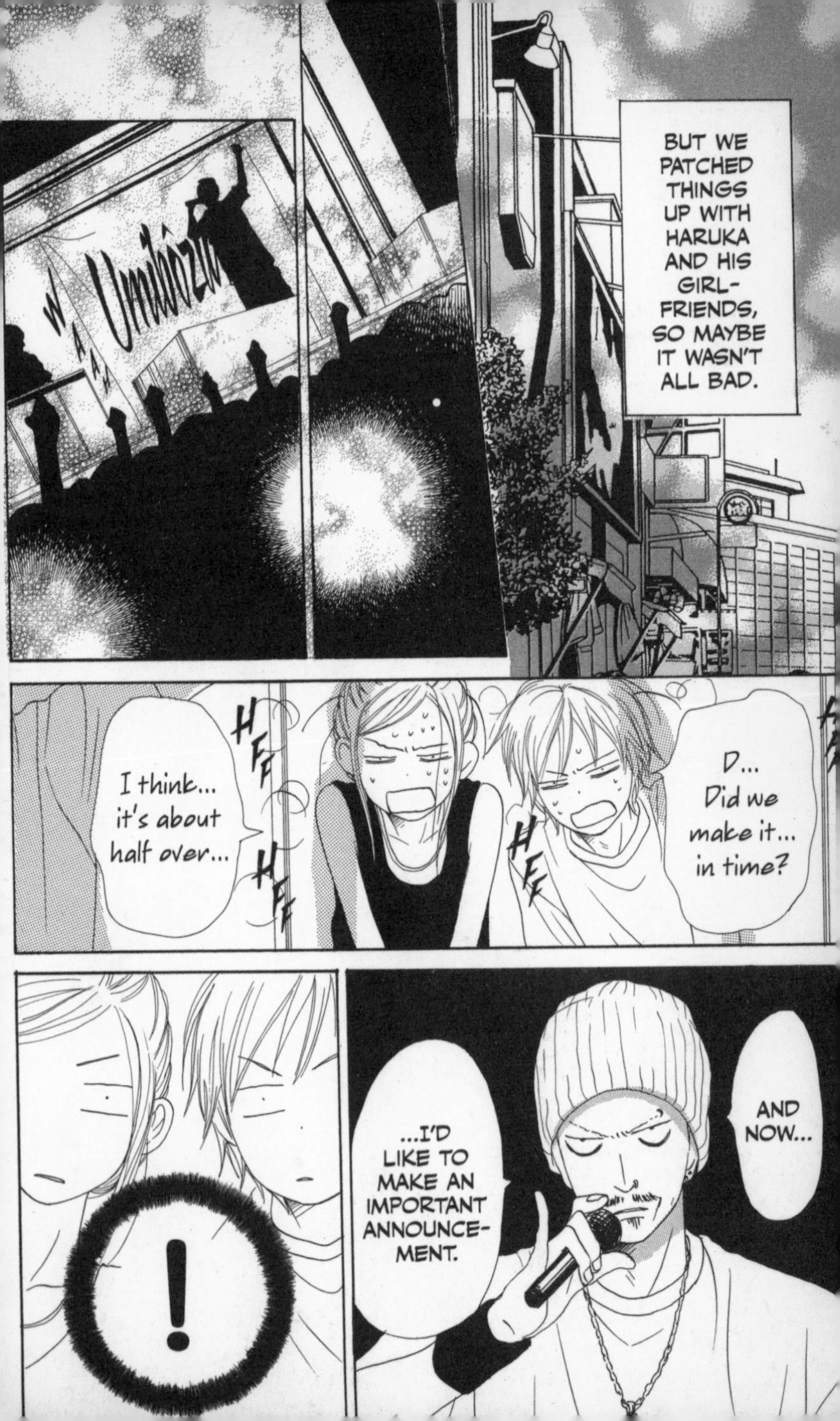
BUT WE PATCHED THINGS UP WITH HARUKA AND HIS GIRL-FRIENDS, SO MAYBE IT WASN'T ALL BAD.
Umibôzu
WAAA
HFF
D... Did we make it... in time?
HFF
HFF
I think... it's about half over...
AND NOW...
...I'D LIKE TO MAKE AN IMPORTANT ANNOUNCE-MENT.
!

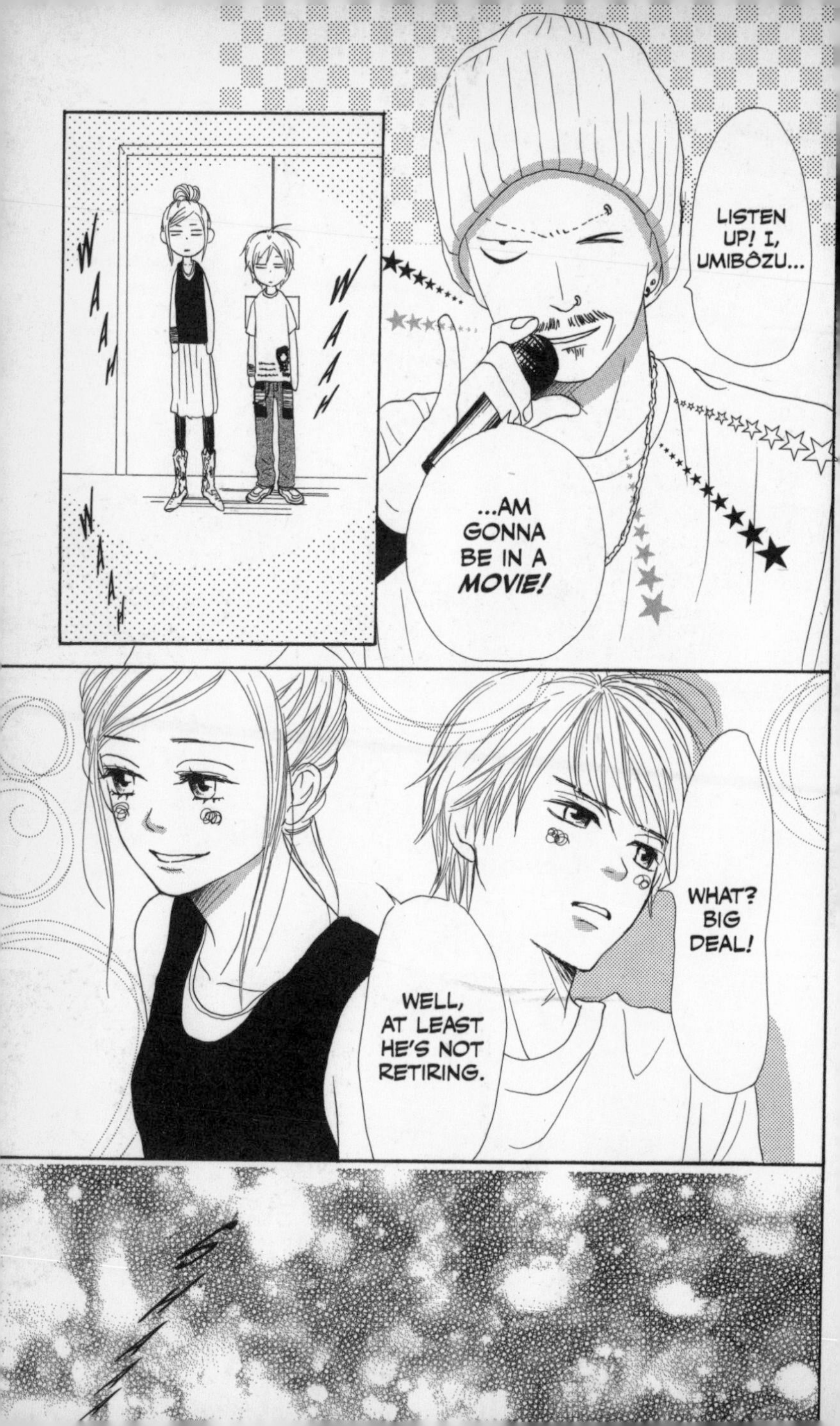
LISTEN UP! I, UMIBÔZU...
...AM GONNA BE IN A *MOVIE!*
WAAAH
WAAAH
WAAAH
WHAT? BIG DEAL!
WELL, AT LEAST HE'S NOT RETIRING.

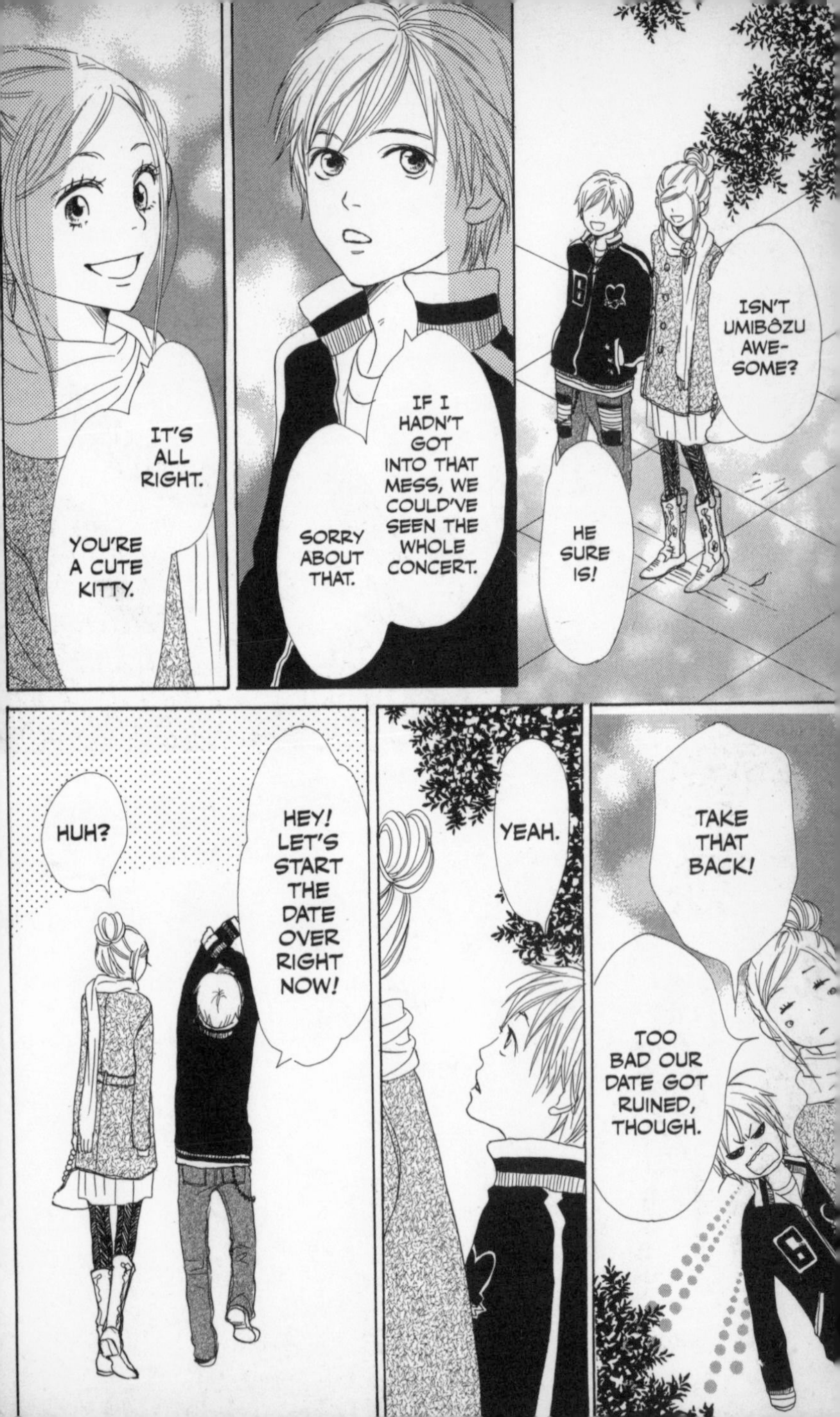
ISN'T UMIBÔZU AWE-SOME?
HE SURE IS!
IF I HADN'T GOT INTO THAT MESS, WE COULD'VE SEEN THE WHOLE CONCERT.
SORRY ABOUT THAT.
IT'S ALL RIGHT.
YOU'RE A CUTE KITTY.
TAKE THAT BACK!
TOO BAD OUR DATE GOT RUINED, THOUGH.
YEAH.
HEY! LET'S START THE DATE OVER RIGHT NOW!
HUH?

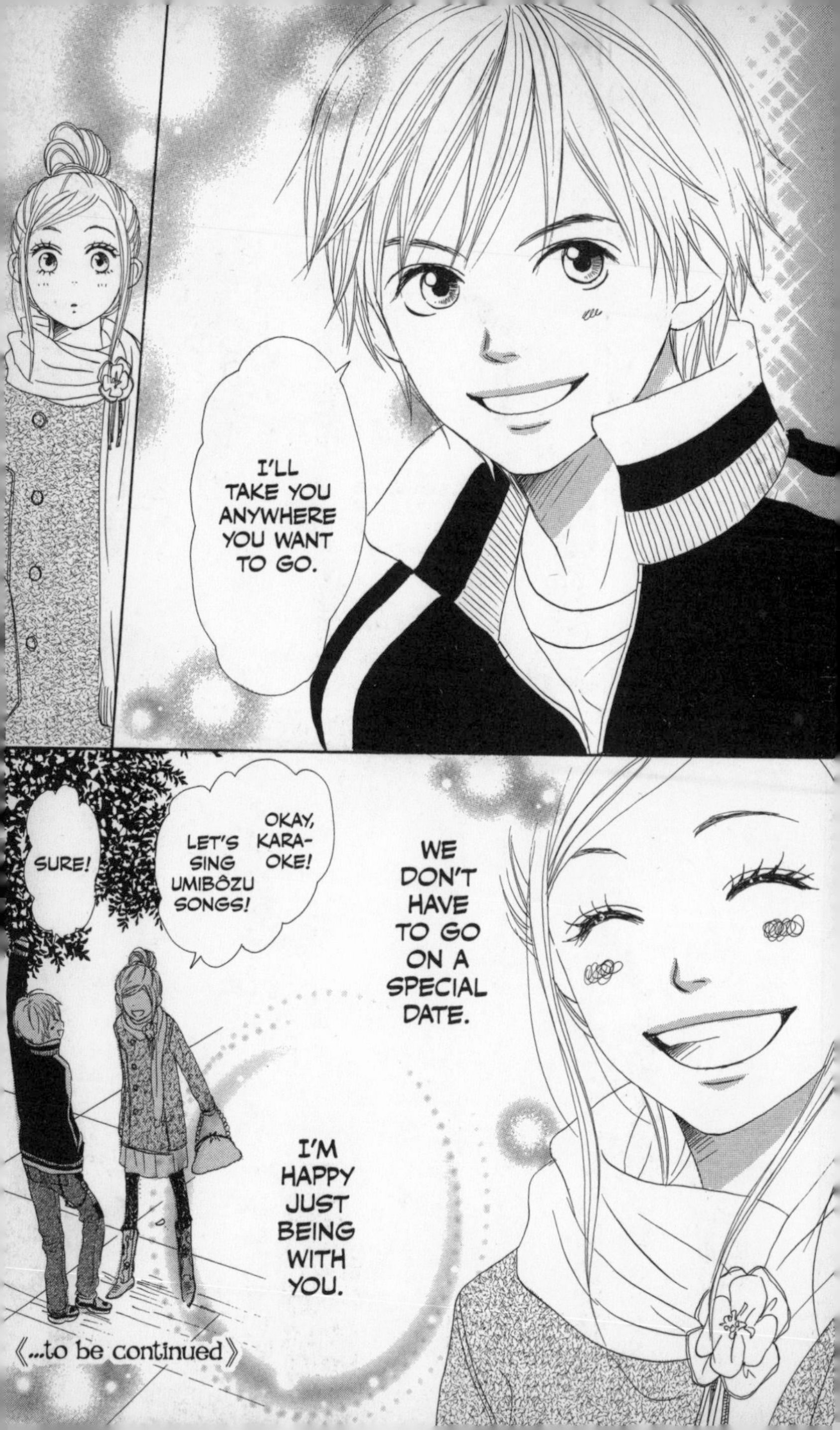
I'LL TAKE YOU ANYWHERE YOU WANT TO GO.
WE DON'T HAVE TO GO ON A SPECIAL DATE.
I'M HAPPY JUST BEING WITH YOU.
OKAY, KARAOKE!
LET'S SING UMIBÔZU SONGS!
SURE!
《...to be continued》

I bought an acoustic guitar. Years ago, in my zeal, I played guitar in a band, but I was terrible. So what am I doing buying a guitar now? It would be nice if I could play something...this time.

Aya Nakahara won the 2003 Shogakukan Manga Award for her breakthrough hit *Love★Com*, which was made into a major motion picture and a PS2 game in 2006. She debuted with *Haru to Kuuki Nichiyou-bi* in 1995, and her other works include *HANADA* and *Himitsu Kichi*.

LOVE★COM VOL 14
The Shojo Beat Manga Edition

STORY AND ART BY
AYA NAKAHARA

Translation/JN Productions
English Adaptation/Shaenon K. Garrity
Touch-up Art & Lettering/Gia Cam Luc
Design/Yuki Ameda
Editor/Carrie Shepherd

VP, Production/Alvin Lu
VP, Publishing Licensing/Rika Inouye
VP, Sales & Product Marketing/Gonzalo Ferreyra
VP, Creative/Linda Espinosa
Publisher/Hyoe Narita

Printed in Canada

Published by VIZ Media, LLC
P.O. Box 77010
San Francisco, CA 94107

Shojo Beat Manga Edition
10 9 8 7 6 5 4 3 2 1
First printing, September 2009

store.viz.com

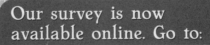